THE FEDERATED STATES OF MICRONESIA'S ENGAGEMENT WITH THE OUTSIDE WORLD

CONTROL, SELF-PRESERVATION AND CONTINUITY

THE FEDERATED STATES OF MICRONESIA'S ENGAGEMENT WITH THE OUTSIDE WORLD

CONTROL, SELF-PRESERVATION AND CONTINUITY

GONZAGA PUAS

Australian
National
University

PRESS

PACIFIC SERIES

ANU PRESS

Published by ANU Press
The Australian National University
Acton ACT 2601, Australia
Email: anupress@anu.edu.au

Available to download for free at press.anu.edu.au

ISBN (print): 9781760464646
ISBN (online): 9781760464653

WorldCat (print): 1268008046
WorldCat (online): 1267996911

DOI: 10.22459/FSMEOW.2021

Cover design and layout by ANU Press

This book is published under the aegis of the Pacific Editorial Committee of the ANU Press.

Contents

List of Figures

List of acronyms

ABCFM	American Board of Commissioners for Foreign Missions
ADB	Asian Development Bank
ANU	The Australian National University
CNMI	Commonwealth of the Northern Marianas Islands
COM	College of Micronesia
ConCon	Constitutional Convention
CR	Congress Resolution
DAS	diasporic *ainang* system
DOI	Department of the Interior
EEZ	exclusive economic zone
ETG	Exhibition Travel Group
FSM	Federated States of Micronesia
GDP	gross domestic product
IMF	International Monetary Fund
JEMCO	Joint Economic Management Committee Office
MIRAB	migration, remittance, aid and bureaucracy
PRC	People's Republic of China
PROFIT	people considerations, resource management, overseas engagement, finance, insurance and taxation, and transportation
SBOC	Office of Statistics, Budget and Economic Management, Overseas Development Assistance, and Compact Management
SITE	small islands tourist economies
TTPI	Trust Territory of the Pacific Islands

UN	United Nations
UNFCC	United Nations Framework Convention on Climate Change
USDA	United States Department of Agriculture
USSR	Union of Soviet Socialist Republics
WWII	World War II

Acknowledgements

To my wife, Kerry, and our two daughters, Anelita and Jessica Puas. Thank you for your nurturing love and support during my writing of this book. My deep and sincere thanks to Paul D'Arcy and Greg Fry for their guidance, assistance and patience. Without you this book would never have come to fruition.

This book is dedicated to all the people of the Federated States of Micronesia who have taught me about our history and how we have managed through many centuries of colonial turbulence. In the end, we remain in control of ourselves now and into the distant future.

Glossary of Mortlockese Terms

Afaker	belonging to one's father's clan as secondary to one's mother clan in the Mortlockese–Chuukese matrilineal clanship system
Afeliel	metaphoric speech to hide the real meanings or motives
Aiku	distribution of, especially food provided by the United States Department of Agriculture (USDA) after natural disasters
Ainang	the clanship system
Aipwa	following the foot steps
Alislis fengan	caring for each other
Allik	laws
Amwinimwin	psychological punishment aimed towards relatives who have upset you, particularly teenage/ young adult reaction to scolding by their elders. This could lead to self-inflicted injury or suicide.
Angangen fanou	community work
Anukis	the lesser gods
Anulap	the supreme god
Anun	ghosts of
Apupulu	wedding or getting married
Apwarik	a traditional open community dance where young people came together to establish future relationship

Aterenges	relatives from both sides of the parents
Awosiwos	the art of creating confusion
Eaea fengan	sharing of resources
Eoranei	traditions
Faal	clan meeting house
Failifel	tattoo
Fal	carving something into shape
Fanou	land
Fash	pandanus tree
Fauko	fish trap used for the deep side of the lagoon
Fel	sacred
Inepwinou	the first unity in the family system as in the parents and their children
Ioshol	Mortlockese canoe design
Itang	master orator
Kachaw	an extended clan system in Micronesian history that covered parts of the Marshall Islands, Pohnpei, Kosrae, and Chuuk
Kapas apiliwek	reverse psychology to hide the true meanings of words in conversation. Also known as '*kapasan*' on Satowan Island.
Kapasan uruo	historical narratives
Koap	cooperative store
Kolin fanou	indigenous songs of the land
Lamelamen eoranei	traditional religion
Lang	the sky
Lefang	the windy season, normally from September to April
Lenien maur	sleeping place or quarters
Leoo	ancestors
Lerek	the summer season when food is in abundance, normally associated with the breadfruit season from May to August

Leset	fishing sometimes referred to as the sea depending on the context of the conversation
Lofor	traditional body lotion or perfume
Maisuuk	Sailing canoe known throughout Yap and Chuuk for its elaborate design
Maniman	spiritual power
Melimel	strong storms leading to typhoon
Mongo	eat or food
Mosoro	cooking house
Mwalo	a unit in sub-clan
Mwanmei	first picking of the breadfruit season to honour the ancestors
Mwaremwar	flower leis
Mweishen	meeting of or group of
Ngorongor	chants
Otoul	first picking of the coconut season to honour the ancestors
Oushamw	belonging to a clan meeting house
Palou	navigator
Paut	sorcery
Pawrik	dances
Pei lap	main estate for the extended family
Peshe seset	'salty feet from the different seas' or not indigenous to a place
Pisaken eoranei	cultural materials
Pwau	restriction from
Pwera	brave
Rakish	the sea oak tree
Remataw	term referring to people of the sea. Used in the outer islands of Yap and the northwest part of Chuuk.
Roong	life science
Saat	the sea

Safei	medicines
Salei	protein
Shell	display of coconut fronds or a big branch indicating complete restriction of public access to a given area on the land or the reef
Shia	the mangrove tree
Shon ainang	members of a clan
Shon fanuash	people of our island
Shon liken	outsiders
Shon Maikronesia	people of the Federated States of Micronesia
Shon mataw	people of the sea, in reference to the people of the Mortlocks
Shoon wok	rewards given to the great spear after war
Shullapan allik	the supreme law or the Constitution
Sofa	my father's clan in Chuuk
Sor	my mother's clan in Chuuk
Sou	an expert in a given traditional profession
Sou uro	expert historian
Souariras	a legendary figure in the Chuuk lagoon
Taek	turmeric used for body decoration, especially during traditional dances to enhance one's beauty to attract the opposite sex
Titilap	stories and legends
Tokkie	traditional war stick dances
Toor	traditional dress wrapped around the waist
Tukumaun	magic potion
Unupwel	first harvest of the taro season to honour the ancestors
Uruo	history
Uruon ainang	a clan's history
Uruon fanou	history of the land
Urupow	elaborate feathers worn during community dances to attract the opposite sex

Waa	canoe
Waa serek	sailing canoe
Waitawa	communication between the ancestors and the living through channelling
Wiieo	celebration after the completion of a canoe

Introduction

The history of the people of the Federated States of Micronesia's engagement with the outside world has been a neglected area of academic scholarship. Historians have often treated the topic as a footnote, with Micronesians perceived as unseen participants of colonial processes. Consequently, Micronesians' perspectives of their own history have been absent from the main corpus of historical literature. Despite the distorted nature of imperial history, which portrayed Micronesians as primitive savages and unsophisticated people, there is an emerging trend of historical discourse contradicting these images.

In this book, I argue that Micronesians have been dealing successfully with the outside world since the colonisation period. This argument is sustained by examination of oral histories, secondary sources, personal experience, interviews and field research to reconstruct how Micronesian internal processes continued, rather than succumbed to the different waves of colonisation. For example, colonisation did not destroy Micronesian cultures and identities. Instead, Micronesians recontextualised the changing conditions to suit their own circumstances. Their success rested on the indigenous doctrines of adaptation, assimilation and accommodation deeply rooted in the kinship doctrine of *eaea fengen* (sharing) and *alilis fengen* (assisting each other).

Micronesians inhabit an oceanic environment of small islands and big seas. This oceanic world necessitated inter-island contact that crisscrossed the seas following the web of the expansive *ainang* (clanship) system. An oceanic civilisation flourished, rich in maritime activities and infrastructure, knowledge and skills of seafaring, warfare, canoe technology, fishing techniques and conservation practices that perpetuated Micronesian continuity. This oceanic outlook also contained effective mechanisms for dealing with a host of unheralded external influences from beyond the horizon, such as China's emerging influence in the Pacific and the impact of climate change on the Federated States of Micronesia (FSM).

Micronesians perceived such influences as challenges and opportunities to shape and reshape their societies through the processes of accommodation and, later, assimilation for the purposes of adapting to the changing circumstances brought by the four colonial powers that claimed ownership of part or all of what is now the FSM. As colonisation intensified, Micronesians began to organise themselves against outsiders' oppression. Reassertion of independence was the main objective. The opportunity arose post World War II (WWII) with the beginning of decolonisation. The *Constitution of the Federated States of Micronesia* was formally established for the purpose of defining the modern identity of the indigenous people, reasserting and perpetuating Micronesian values and future continuity.

Humble Beginning in Understanding My History

My journey to write this book has been arduous and challenging. It began on my humble island home, Lukunor (also known as Lekinioch),[1] located in the southern region of the state of Chuuk. I learned the *uruo* of my island and its connection to other islands throughout the FSM. The history was in oral form and learned from my extended families. This experience was reinforced in the classroom in elementary school. For example, students were required to draw the geography of our island. We were also required to draw details of the villages and location of each clan's community *faal* (clan meeting house) and provide a narrative of inter-clan relationships. We learned traditional war dances called *tokkie* and songs called *kolin fonou* (indigenous songs) from our region and other Micronesian regions. We also learned about *leset* (fishing) and *angangan fonou* (local agriculture). Elders were invited to our classes during social studies to reinforce our knowledge of oral history through stories and songs.

---

1   Lukunor, also known as Lekinioch, is an island in the Lower Mortlocks in the state of Chuuk, FSM.

Figure 1: Part of my island, Lekinioch, where my humble beginning started.
Source: Photograph taken by Bartol Mwarey in 2014.

My high school years were spent on different islands, which connected me to my distant relatives dispersed throughout Pohnpei and Chuuk. In contrast, the history I learned in secondary school came from textbooks written by foreigners and largely about topics unfamiliar to the life experiences of young Micronesians, such as the dawn of European civilisation. We also learned about Japanese and American activities in Micronesia, which were the main topics in my history classes. Islanders' history was not included. This trend continued during my college years in the United States (US). After leaving the US, I continued my studies in Australia. I enrolled in a Pacific history program taught by Australian academics influenced by the new historical movement, initiated by J. W. Davidson at The Australian National University (ANU) in the 1950s. In the program, Pacific Island students were given the opportunity to write history from an islander's perspective. However, Micronesia was largely missing from this program due to the lack of Micronesian expertise in Australia. I was frustrated about Micronesia being virtually absent from the whole curriculum.

I was also exposed to Aboriginal history, including Indigenous Australian interpretations of the world and engagement with colonialism. This opened up new insights for me. I began to ask questions about the notion of discovery, decolonisation, independence, identity and continuity. I was also exposed to the writings of an indigenous Pacific historian, Sione Latukefu from Tonga, and a Samoan writer, Albert Wendt, who influenced my own intellectual development. There were also non-islander scholars such as Edward Wolfers, Stewart Firth and Caroline Ralston who challenged my own indigenous perspective of history. Of particular interest was the book *The Other Side of the Frontier* by an Australian historian of European background, Henry Reynolds. Reynolds used the book to question the Eurocentric historiography of Australia. Reynolds later became one of the chief architects of the watershed case of *Mabo and Others v Queensland (No. 2) (1992)* (the 'Mabo case'). This case overturned the colonial legal fiction of *terra nullius*[2] in Australia for the first time since British settlement, and the government of the day reluctantly acknowledged Indigenous rights to land.

After my graduation from university, I returned home to teach at the College of Micronesia, Pohnpei Campus. I encouraged my students to engage in terms of their own local history. I remember my first session in Micronesian history, where I posed the simple question, 'who discovered Micronesia?'[3] No one said the Micronesians. After challenging them, the whole class burst out in laughter and guilt. Most of the students said, 'well we all know that Micronesians were here first before the Europeans arrived, but according to the textbooks they said Europeans'.[4] After two weeks of discussions, the students decided to ditch the textbooks recommended for the course. They decided to undertake projects writing about their own family or local history using oral sources by interviewing their surviving elders. They were thrilled when I also took them out to undertake fieldwork to see the areas where the 'Sokehs rebellion' took place and the old Spanish fort in Kolonia, Pohnpei.

After many years of teaching in the classroom, both in Micronesia and Australia, I decided to undertake a PhD at ANU under the wing of Pacific historian Paul D'Arcy. Not surprisingly, Micronesia by and large was a neglected discipline of study at ANU. D'Arcy kept the subject alive, having conducted research on the islands over a long period of time.

---

2   *Terra nullius* was a doctrine, and later a component of international law, that the colonial powers used to acquire new territories overseas. It entailed that if a territory did not show any signs of agricultural production as perceived by the Europeans, then the first European discoverer could claim the territory on behalf of the colonial power they represented (Ian Brownlie, *Principles of Public International Law* (5th edition), Oxford University Press, 2001, pp. 173–174).

3   My questions to my students were intended to provoke their awareness and focus on island history. I posed questions such as 'Who discovered Micronesia?', 'Who owns history?' and 'Is history written or oral?' These questions led to the students' decision to forgo the textbooks and concentrate on undertaking a personal project about the history of their local communities.

4   Students at the College of Micronesia, Pohnpei Campus, Micronesian History Class, Kolonia, Pohnpei, 1998.

He exposed me to the rigorous challenges of being an indigenous historian in academia. I was forced to think deeply about Micronesian history and its placement in academia.

My global experiences have enriched me intellectually while I have continued to explore my identity as a Micronesian. I have learned that, while oral and written history are often contradictory, in many respects they are also complementary. Micronesians used their own devices through traditional networks[5] to shield themselves and their knowledge and history, both intellectually and socially, until opportunities arose to reassert their voices.[6] I will therefore speak of my own *uruo* and how it can contribute to the enrichment of the historical dialogue between Micronesians and non-Micronesians.

I have long wondered what it would be like writing history based on oral discourses[7] versus the academic traditions of the West. Could I somehow marry the two? And what sort of historical theories could I work from to lay the groundwork for my personal thesis about Micronesian perspectives of history?[8] How would I integrate archival work into my thesis since Micronesians' main forms of communication and engagement with each other are oral? Would my personal experience as a Micronesian, data collected from my fieldwork and secondary sources satisfy academic requirements to write a Micronesian perspective of history? After spending some time pondering these issues, I decided to write this book following

---

5   The clanship network system continued to connect Micronesians during the colonisation period and remained so during the decolonisation period to create a nation for Micronesians called 'the Federated States of Micronesia'. See *The Constitution of the Federated States of Micronesia*, Preamble; Glenn Petersen, *Traditional Micronesian Societies: Adaptation, Integration and Political Organisation*, University of Hawai'i Press, Hawai'i, 2009, p. 23.

6   Glenn Petersen, 'Strategic Location and Sovereignty: Modern Micronesia in the Historical Context of American Expansionism', *Space and Polity*, Vol. 2, No. 2, 1998, pp. 200–201.

7   Micronesian history predominately takes an oral form. It has its own internal logic and can be used to determine what the 'truth is'. There are processes by which evidence can be produced to substantiate the truth. For example, language format and concepts used by orators called *itang* are used to test one's knowledge of historical events. Misstating traditional views of *itang* could bring shame to the narrators of history; that is, inventing one's position in history could cause conflict between opposing clans as historical truths determine one's standing and prestige in the community.

8   Micronesian historical theories are often left to highly knowledgeable clan historians to prove or disprove (Lin Poyer, 'The Ngatik Massacre: Documentary and Oral Traditional Accounts', *Journal of Pacific History*, Vol. 20, No. 1, 2003, pp. 4–22). For commentaries and detailed analysis of Pacific history, see Paul D'Arcy, 'Introduction', in *The Pacific World: Lands, Peoples and History of the Pacific, 1500-1900. Vol. 3, Peoples of the Pacific: The History of Oceania to 1870*, edited by Paul D'Arcy, Ashgate Variorum, Burlington, VT, USA, 2008, pp. ix–xiv.

the Western traditions but to frame it within a Micronesian perspective.[9] I decided to use a combination of thematic, linear and chronological approaches to document Micronesian perspectives of history. That is, to investigate the written history of Micronesia and, where necessary, insert Micronesian perspectives into the growing corpus of knowledge in the field. Many scholars I met along the way warned me about the huge pitfalls I would encounter and the likelihood of distorting the FSM's history in the process. Some advised me to take an easier approach by narrowing my topic to a more manageable one or fewer islands. However, as already noted in discussing my own history, regional visions and connections are fundamental to being Micronesian and understanding our history.

Naturally, I understood their reticence about my approach and appreciated their concern. However, many also encouraged me not to be distracted as my work could set the stage and encourage future indigenous scholars to write more about the Micronesian perspective of history at the regional level—something long overdue. I decided to use the Micronesian Constitution as my guiding star. The Constitution is my reference point to start my own personal journey as a Micronesian into the sea of the indigenous past in order to understand the present for the purpose of engaging the future. I chose the Constitution because it is a collection of narratives by the contemporary Micronesian leadership who framed the nation in the images of the islands' past to ensure a prosperous future outlook for *shon Maikronesia* (Micronesians).

My decision to use the Constitution as a guiding star rests much with my background in law. My decision to become a lawyer while growing up in the Mortlocks was deliberate. I realised that the law could be used as a protective shield for islanders to preserve and control their future. During the campaign for Micronesian independence, for example, it became very clear that the proposed Constitution would empower Micronesians to govern themselves and forge relations internationally based on their own understanding of who they were historically. The birth of the *Constitution*

---

9   What is 'perspective'? It is debated among scholars whether the term 'perspective' debases Micronesian history in academia as it is seen by some academics as tokenism. It is claimed that perspective allows indigenous scholars to express their point of views, yet it is not considered part of mainstream history as practiced at the academic level (Vincent Diaz, pers. comm., at Weaving the Threads of Indigenous Knowledges: Te Whare Kura Symposium, The University of Auckland: Faculty of Arts, 21 June 2013). See problems of indigenous research in academia in Linda T. Smith, *Decolonising Methodologies*, London, Zed Books Ltd, 2001, pp. 1–3.

of the Federated States of Micronesia emancipated Micronesians from colonisation and allowed their entry into the United Nations (UN) as a sovereign state.

As this book is the reflection of the past on Micronesia today, each chapter discusses the interaction between these themes as being fundamental to the Micronesian perspective of history, and as influential factors in the type of engagement possible with the outside world. Micronesians are armed with their own local strategies to facilitate the changing historical circumstances brought about by colonisation and globalisation. Local adaptation involves the process of cultural refinement through successive generations to ensure the maintenance of Micronesian identity and continuity.

This book is organised into eight chapters. Chapter 1 deals with pre-colonial Micronesian society and how Micronesians organised themselves by utilising the traditional infrastructure for the purposes of maintaining their indigenous interactions, giving rise to their identity and thus continuity.

Chapter 2 deals with the various Micronesian identities and how they played a crucial role in their engagement during the contact period in defining who they were historically. It demonstrates the extent of Micronesians' desire to be in control of their own destiny in the modern world in order to perpetuate their continuity. The principle of 'diversity in unity' reveals the depth and success of multiculturalism between the constituent groups that predated the external powers and continues into modern times.

Chapter 3 compares and contrasts Micronesian engagement with the outside world from 1521 to 1979. This is the era of Micronesian interaction with colonial powers—Spain, Germany, Japan and the US. Micronesian terms of engagement with these colonisers depended on the application of their intellectual history to manage outside influences to suit Micronesian contexts. Micronesians' historical knowledge of adaptation were used to safeguard indigenous interests despite the unequal power relations between the colonisers and the colonised. The main emphasis of this chapter is on the effective management of the four colonising powers by Micronesians to suit their own purposes.

Chapter 4 focuses on Micronesia's move towards constitutional independence in 1979 and the aftermath. Issues such as the rejection of the US's offer for Micronesians to integrate into the US political system are highlighted. The reasons for the creation of a constitution to advance Micronesian interests against those of the US will also be addressed. This chapter also deals with the Compact of Free Association as a forerunner to full independence. The Compact allowed Micronesia time to organise itself politically and economically. After 2023, financial assistance under the Compact will diminish substantially.

Chapter 5 discusses the Micronesian Constitution as the organising framework for the reproduction of Micronesian continuity as islanders adapt to the changing world. The Micronesian identity is embedded in the Constitution, which perpetuates the idea of Micronesians as a distinct group of people who share a common history. This identity is analysed in relation to the past, present and future. Micronesians are conscious of their past and strive to preserve that heritage for future generations. That heritage must therefore be protected at all costs. The Constitution is central to the preservation and maintenance of multiple identities while simultaneously superimposing a single Micronesian identity. The Constitution is a living document that speaks to the past and organises the present for the betterment of the future. Principally, it established and strengthened Micronesian institutions to deny further external usurpation of Micronesian independence as enshrined under international legal instruments.

Chapter 6 analyses Micronesian engagement with both China and the US in Micronesia's jurisdictional space and the international arena. The interaction between the two superpowers is part of the long history of colonial rivalry in the northwest Pacific. Although China is not seen as a colonial power, the implication is that the US is treating China as such because China is seen by the US as a rival. The competition is about winning influence in Micronesia and thereby gaining a strategic and economic foothold in the region.

Chapter 7 deals with climate change and its consequences in the FSM. Like colonisation, climate change is a new phenomenon emanating from external forces, in this case, industrial pollution by the world's major economic powers. The consequences of this industrial negligence are now confronting the security of the FSM in terms of its customs, identity, health, food production, emigration and sovereignty. The FSM is constantly exploring ways to maintain itself despite this new threat. Climate change is a top priority for the national agenda and will affect the FSM's future engagement with the outside world.

Chapter 8 investigates and speculates on future challenges facing the FSM. They include the Compact, climate change, the Constitution, leadership and foreign affairs. These issues are discussed in light of the political conversation between the three levels of government and how this conversation will assist the country's move towards the future. The above challenges will shape the FSM's future policies and diplomatic engagement with the external world as well as its present integrity. It will be argued that Micronesians should solve their internal problems as best they can by way of learning from the lessons of history; that is, the best method to resolve arising issues is by returning to their knowledge of history as it is at the heart of preserving Micronesian culture and identity. This is essential to the perpetuation of Micronesian future continuity in a changing world.

1

Writing Micronesian History

Setting the Context

This book examines how *shon Maikronesia* (Micronesians)[1] have dealt with and controlled varied past and present external influences, from colonial powers to modern economic forces, and environmental influences from typhoons to climate change. It is one of the first written post-colonial Micronesian beliefs and perspectives of *uruo* (history). These perspectives are enshrined in the Preamble[2] to the *Constitution of the Federated States of Micronesia*. The Constitution represents a Micronesian-centred outlook and reassertion of Micronesian heritage and independence.[3] This book reflects the author's upbringing, cultural roots and national and global identity. It traverses the space between local history and identity—as epitomised by the writer's Lekiniochian–Namoi[4] identity, national, post-colonial consciousness and international

---

1   *Shon Maikronesia* refers to the indigenous people of the modern state of the FSM. All indigenous terms in this thesis are in Mortlockese–Chuukese, with terms in other Micronesian languages indicated as such.
2   The Preamble of the *Constitution of the Federated States of Micronesia* underscores a brief historical statement of the Micronesian people in terms of their past, present and future. See the *Constitution of the Federated States of Micronesia*, fsmlaw.org/fsm/constitution/index.htm.
3   The *Constitution of the Federated States of Micronesia* is framed in accordance with Micronesian values and perspective of the world.
4   Lekiniochian–Namoi is a combined local and regional identity in reference to the island of Lekinioch, situated in the region of Namoi (now the Mortlocks) in the state of Chuuk, the FSM.

engagement as a scholar enmeshed in wider global historiography—to record in print a Micronesian perspective of history, which is absent from much of the literature.[5]

The history of Micronesians' engagement with the outside world remains an understudied area of academic scholarship. Most historians who have studied the Pacific Islands, and thus Micronesia's past, emphasise the history of outsiders' activities in the islands. As historian Paul D'Arcy observed:

> historians have been more focused on instances of rapid change ... emphasising Western influences. Not surprisingly they often reproduced the same historical views as the main reasons behind the transformation of islander communities ... indigenous relations with Europeans receive the lion's share of attention, while ongoing and new interactions between local communities tend to be neglected.[6]

Like D'Arcy, anthropologist Mac Marshall highlights the continuous inter-island connections throughout history in reference to the indigenous people of the Mortlocks region, which also resonates throughout Micronesia. As Marshall observed, 'long before ... external control was imposed, people of (the Mortlocks) maintained contact with communities on numerous other islands via sailing canoe voyages using sophisticated celestial navigation techniques'.[7] Marshall's comments counter the corpus of literature that ignored Micronesians' perspective of history; that is, Micronesians were active participants in the production of colonial history. Indeed, Micronesians continue to interact with each other today just like in the past. However, they are expanding their diaspora to far distant lands like the US, Japan and Australia to internationalise their identity in a globalised world.

---

5   I was born on a low-lying atoll, Lekinioch, and have lived in the US and Australia for many years. This has formed my deep and profound opinion and appreciation of indigenous history as contrasted with that of the colonial powers.

6   Paul D'Arcy, *The People of the Sea: Environment, Identity, and History of Oceania*, University of Hawai'i Press, 2006, p. 2.

7   Mac Marshall, *Namoluk beyond the Reef: The Transformation of a Micronesian Community*, Westview Press, USA, 2008, p. 3; D'Arcy, *The People of the Sea*, p. 2.

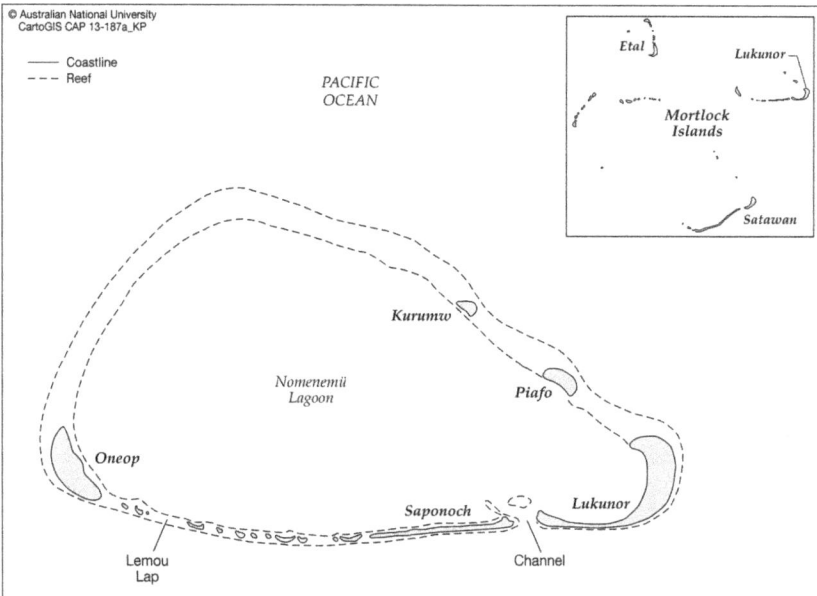

Figure 2: Map of Lukunor atoll.

Note: Oneop is an inhabited island that shares the same lagoon. There is a deep historical relationship between the two islands through the clanship system.

Source: Map produced by ANU CartoGIS.

Historian David Hanlon strongly advocates for the incorporation of Micronesian perspectives that have been missing from historical accounts for too long. This is to ensure that Micronesian voices become an enriching component of historical discourses.[8] He notes that Micronesians did not passively accept outside influence; they selected, incorporated and then manipulated what the outsiders had to offer to suit their circumstances.[9] This destroys the mainstream colonial accounts that Micronesians were on the periphery of history. To this end, the three cited scholars advocate for the inclusion of more Micronesian perspectives in the existing body of Pacific history to enhance the depth of the literature, which is currently limited by the amount of time scholars are able to spend in the

---

8   David Hanlon, 'Magellan's Chroniclers? American Anthropology's History in Micronesia', in *American Anthropology in Micronesia: An Assessment*, edited by Robert C. Kiste and Mac Marshall, University of Hawai'i Press, 1999, p. 77.

9   Hanlon, 'Magellan's Chroniclers?', p. 77.

field or archives. I seek to expand the partial truths that have emerged by presenting a more comprehensive perspective and timeframes more reflective of Micronesian experiences.

Four interrelated themes are used to construct this more comprehensive and integrated perspective of indigenous history: the law, religion, social organisation and the environment. These interrelated spheres of Micronesian actions and conceptualisation of the world in turn raise four major questions central to Micronesia's historical processes: 1) who do *shon Maikronesia* identify as the people of Micronesia, 2) how do Micronesians organise their socio-political affairs as a people, 3) what devices have Micronesians adopted to preserve their customs and identity, and 4) to what extent have Micronesians controlled the past and present for the purpose of future continuity?

Micronesianising Historiography

Uruo is perceived by those in the Mortlocks as existing in a dynamic model akin to an intricate spider web, dissimilar to Western historiography, which follows a linear model. For instance, the *sou uruo*, depending on the question at hand, has to choose a particular event in the web to begin his oral narrative. He then connects the event to other series of events surrounding the question, bearing in mind the purpose of his narrative in seeking 'the truth' while his audience of other *sou uruo* are ready to validate the narrator's historical account.[10] It is like travelling on the sea where the *palou* is surrounded by a constellation of stars in the universe. The navigator picks a particular star as a reference point at the outset of his journey. He then relates that star to other stars during the journey to reach his specific destination while being mindful of the subtleties of the waves, currents and wind, as well as observing his relationship with his crew to ensure a successful voyage.[11] The voyaging *palou* would be judged by other *palou* upon reaching the final destination—on whether he arrived in good order, became lost or showed up late, for instance.

---

10   During my fieldwork, I asked for specific dates for certain recent events. The interviewees said that they did not know the dates but remembered that someone died when the event occurred. This is the association of events, rather than the chronological ordering of events as usually practiced in Western historical discourses.

11   Destination is not so much where one ends the journey but the various points of the journey. An inter-island journey, like history, is circular and never stops completely at one particular point.

Like the navigator, my challenge is where to start to write about Micronesian history, since it is a vast area consisting of many local clans and thus histories. Naturally, the best position to start writing the history of the FSM is from my own personal experience; that is, the history of my clan and its relationship with other clans in the FSM diaspora.[12] The next step is consulting the corpus of literature to locate specific events to impart a sense of chronology to it. Most of the time-sensitive events are absent from the literature or only mentioned in passing. The war between Ettal and Lukunor, for example, which significantly influenced the history of the Lower Mortlocks, has not been discussed widely in the literature. Due to the dearth of information relating to events of significance to the indigenous community, I resorted to researching descriptive history in an attempt to follow the historical patterns that existed in the sources, while at the same time using my own sources gathered in the field, such as interviews and oral history for historical cross-analysis or references. I hope to provide a historical framework that invites future indigenous scholars to build on its foundation.

The inner core of Micronesian history is sacred. It requires painstaking attention to detail and is a delicate undertaking as it has its own *maniman*.[13] History should only be conveyed with respect and salutation to adhere to its inner principles. If one failed to honour this process, the ancestors would curse the narrator (in one form or another) for not adhering to the sacredness of the past. In the deep tradition of my Mortlockese–Chuukese–Micronesian ancestral past, it is customary for *sou uruo* (historians) to initiate their *kapasan uruo* (historical narratives) with the customary wisdom of '*tiro womi monson amusala ren ai lamelam tekia ren ia tolong lan kapasan uruo*' ('let me pay my humble respect to all historians for intruding into the subject of history'). This conveys deep humbleness, humility and respect for other historians both past and present. This is followed by an introductory remark, '*kapasan lon manimanen uruo*' ('within the spirit of history'), intended to invoke the past and also provoke the attention of the audience. This is also for the purpose of inviting the past into the present. This acknowledgement

---

12   Due to the volume and richness of its past, I cannot include the entire history of my clan diaspora.
13   *Maniman*, from a Mortlockese point of view, is a form of spiritual power. It can be used to either destroy or save a person, depending on the context of a given situation. This term is also used by Pohnpeians but with a different spelling. See Rufino Mauricio, 'Ideological Bases for Power and Leadership on Pohnpei, Micronesia: Perspectives from Archaeology and Oral History', PhD thesis, University of Michigan, Ann Arbor, 1993, p. 126; Glenn Petersen, 'Kanaegamah and Pohnpei's Politics of Concealment', *American Anthropological Association*, Vol. 95, No. 2, 1993, p. 341.

of the omnipresence of the past in contemporary discourses conveys the continuity in oral history. The narrator seeks the blessings of respected historians to protect the narrator should he misstate a particular historical event. So, in following the footsteps of my Micronesian heritage, let me also convey my own '*tirowomi sou uruo monson*' from both the distant past and the present.

Historical themes and concepts are essential elements of history production as they have specific meanings and application in connection to historical events and contexts. Their meanings need to be understood for the purposes of facilitating and validating historical processes across time and space. They are also used to identify genuine historians from non-historians. Historical truths are measured in terms of the usage of specific languages and concepts known only to a selective group of historians. These historians can then determine the narrators' intention when speaking of history, especially in community settings. For example, in the Mortlocks, and many islands beyond, historians used specific concepts to test the knowledge of those who claimed/claim to know history without question. The exchange usually takes place during inter-island meetings, where *itangs* (orators) are also involved in contesting their knowledge of history in a different form of language known only to them. History to the *itang* is about validating one's legitimate right and control of resources locally or within the clan diaspora. Many of the traditional concepts embodied in this book have special meanings.[14]

It is no accident that the conservation of the environment for survival purposes is reinforced by the traditional religious practices and historical social ordering of the islands as embodied in the *Constitution of the Federated States of Micronesia*. These practices are designed to connect the clanship system and strengthen relationships between different clans. It will be argued throughout this book that historical continuities of cultural coherence and flexibility in the face of external challenges lie at the heart of modern Micronesian identity. They are apparent throughout Micronesia's long history of adjusting to seemingly overwhelming external forces, both human and environmental. In this context, Micronesians do not perceive themselves as victims of imposed external forces in reference to, for example, colonisation, Christianisation and globalisation. Instead,

---

14 Traditional concepts are often difficult to translate into English as they have specific meanings and application. This book translates concepts into their closest English equivalents, with additional explanation provided where necessary.

they perceive themselves as challengers of these potential threats who draw strength from lessons from the past for continuity purposes. For example, during my field study, I interviewed many government officials and academics whose goal was to develop the economic system in light of its Micronesian cultures, history and geographical realities.[15] The notion that Micronesians should emulate the economic models of the developed world, especially those practised in the US, is to live in an unrealistic world that defies Micronesian traditions and relationships. Many former presidents of the FSM were keen advocates of developing the Micronesian economy in the nation's own image.[16]

History as Dynamic and Trends

Historically, Micronesians have proven to be a skilful and knowledgeable people who have managed their relationships with each other and their environment to sustain their identity.[17] They are active agents in the production and reproduction of their own history.[18] For instance, the FSM's Constitution speaks of local agencies as always being active throughout the colonial and post-colonial periods. Drafted by community representatives from across the FSM, the Constitution represents the most comprehensive statement of Micronesian history, identity and survival to date.[19]

Micronesian history, like its seas, is fluid, dynamically subtle and inherently complex, with its own undercurrents. Deep human relations and the oceanic environment are the essence of historical narratives; they embody

---

15   Mariena Dereas, Interview, College of Micronesia, National Campus, Palikir, 20 January 2011; John Haglelgam, Interview, College of Micronesia, Palikir, 11 January 2011; Peter Sitan, Interview, Kolonia, 27 January 2011.
16   Tereas, Interview; Haglelgam, Interview; Sitan, Interview; Josh Levy, 'Micronesian Nationalism Revisited: Reclaiming Nationalism for the Federated States of Micronesia', Paper delivered at Native American and Indigenous Studies Association, Uncasville, Connecticut, 5 June 2012, pp. 1–9; David Hanlon, *Making Micronesia: A Political Biography of Tosiwo Nakayama*, University of Hawai'i Press, 2014, pp. 4–5.
17   Christopher Lobban and Maria Schefter, *Tropical Pacific Island Environments*, University of Guam Press, USA, 1997, pp. 269–271, 288–294; William Alkire, 'Cultural Ecology and Ecological Anthropology in Micronesia', in *American Anthropology: An Assessment*, edited by Robert C. Kiste and Mac Marshall, University of Hawai'i Press, pp. 81–102.
18   David Chappell, 'The Post-Contact Period', in *The Pacific Islands: Environment and Society* (revised edition), edited by Moshe Rapaport, University of Hawai'i Press, 2013, pp. 144–145.
19   Paul D'Arcy, 'Cultural Divisions and Island Environments since the Time of Dumont d'Urville', *Journal of Pacific History*, Vol. 38, No. 2, October 2003, pp. 217–236; David Hanlon, 'Micronesia: Writing and Rewriting the Histories of a Nonentity', *Pacific Studies*, Vol. 12, No. 2, March 1989, p. 15.

the Micronesian history of continuity. This book adopts the Micronesian perspective of *uruo* to balance the misrepresentations and inaccurate images of Micronesians that have been manufactured, reproduced and transported in time and space by *shon liken*.

The genesis of Micronesia's historiography began with the arrival of Portuguese and Spanish explorers in the sixteenth century. The treatment and portrayals of Micronesians in the early literature focused largely on the types of responses exhibited by Micronesians to outsiders. Dumont de D'Urville, Captain Arellano and Andrew Cheyne, for instance, referred to the Chuukese as a violent and treacherous lot, the Pohnpeians as unfriendly and the Mortlockese as hospitable and considerate.[20] In Ulithi, Joao de Barros, a Portuguese historian, observed the indigenous people to be of simple rationality and still in 'the simplicity of the first age'.[21] The distorted images of *shon Maikronesia* continued to appear in subsequent literature by a host of scholars such as ethnographers, archaeologists, legal writers, economists and journalists. Literature on Micronesia is often compared unfavourably to Polynesia and Melanesia to conjure up the image of tiny islands with weak social structures. Like 'a handful of chickpeas flung over the sea',[22] the images of the micro-islands connote disconnection, isolation and deprivation. The micro-islands were imagined as a place lacking in the essential resources sought by the outside world.

The proponents of this perception are many. They include anthropologists William Alkire,[23] Ward Goodenough[24] and Sherwood Lingenfelter,[25] who described Micronesia as small islands suffering from isolation and poor soil, and depending heavily on rain to provide a subsistence life.[26] Francis Hezel, although often displaying great empathy for contemporary Micronesians and portraying them favourably, expounded on this description by reducing earlier generations of Micronesians to the lower

---

20   Mac Marshall, *The Weekend Warrior: Alcohol in a Micronesian Culture*, Mayfield Publishing Company, Palo Alto, California, 1979, p. 38; Francis X. Hezel, *The First Taint of Civilization: A History of the Caroline and Marshall Islands in Pre-Colonial Days, 1521-1885*, University of Hawai'i Press, 1983, pp. 23, 90–91.

21   Hezel, *The First Taint of Civilization*, p. 12.

22   Hezel, *The First Taint of Civilization*, p. xi; Mauricio, 'Ideological Bases for Power', p. 240.

23   William Alkire, *An Introduction to the Peoples and Cultures of Micronesia* (2nd edition), University of Victoria, British Columbia, 1977, p. 44.

24   Ward Goodenough, *Under Heaven's Brow: Pre-Christian Religious Tradition in Chuuk*, American Philosophical Society, Philadelphia, 2002, p. 29.

25   Sherwood Lingenfelter, *Yap: Political Leadership and Culture Change in an Island Society*, University of Hawai'i Press, 1975, p. 7.

26   Alkire, *An Introduction to the Peoples and Cultures of Micronesia*, p. 44.

end of the scale of human civilisation. He referred to Micronesians as 'simply living on fish and taro or breadfruit, [wearing] their traditional dress ... and [carrying] on long-distance canoe voyages for which their islands were famous'.[27] The attendant question is, who is to say that living in an oceanic environment with its own challenges is 'simpler' than living on dry, industrialised, continental land with mammoth politico-economic problems.[28] Images of Micronesia are dictated by the eyes of the observer, and their cultural baggage determines both what they see and fail to see. In portraying Micronesians as being simple people living on the margins of civilisation, outsiders ignore a deep and intricate lore designed to enable people to live in harmony with nature and a complex system of social organisation that developed to provide inter-island links. For example, in the case of a natural disaster such as a typhoon, a sophisticated organisation was needed to support a seafaring culture where many men were away for long periods. Similarly, supporting technically complex enterprises like canoe building and seafaring required deep knowledge and group involvement. European powers are assessed as organised and efficient by the degree to which they could mobilise their societies to put fleets to sea in the service of national enterprises. However, smaller Pacific societies that maintained the infrastructure to put their entire population to sea in seaworthy sailing canoes at short notice with far less resources to call on are depicted as living on the margins of subsistence.

Like elsewhere in the Pacific, many contemporary scholars have inadvertently perpetuated negative images of Micronesia as a resource-poor nation suffering from remoteness and isolation, political corruption, dependency[29] and an uninvestable environment due to its anti-foreign Constitution.[30] As political scientist Meller stated: 'Micronesia has limited living space and paucity of resources contributed to a subsistence closely bounded by the vicissitudes of nature and the ravages of human enemies'. According to Meller, it was 'goods produced elsewhere which freed [Micronesians] from the day to day dependence on the vagaries of

---

27   Francis X. Hezel, *The New Shape of Old Island Cultures: A Half Century of Social Change in Micronesia*, University of Hawai'i, 2001, p. 7.
28   Epeli Hau'ofa, *We Are the Ocean: Selected Works*, University of Hawai'i Press, 2008, pp. 30–31.
29   Francis X. Hezel, 'Micronesian Governments: A View From Outside', *Micronesian Counselor*, No. 55, April 2005.
30   *Constitution of the Federated States of Micronesia*, Article VIII, Sections 4–5.

nature'.[31] Fuelling this image, human geographer John Connell observed that nowhere else in the Pacific is the gulf between image and reality as great as it is in Micronesia:[32]

> Micronesia's image has become tarnished by a unique form of trustee military colonialism, an unusually dependent form of development, and limited prospects of achieving any degree of economic, and political independence, despite the signing of the Compact of Free Association. In a century, this strategically important region has gone from subsistence to subsidy.[33]

Connell's comments do not represent the realities of contemporary Micronesia; on the islands far from the political centres, traditional lifestyles largely untouched by American subsidies and funds remain the norm.

This book counters Connell's observation of externally imposed dependency by arguing that the current political arrangement between the FSM and US stems from Micronesian initiatives based on historical lessons to respond to contemporary international affairs on their own terms—that is, the US sought what it desired (military denial) in exchange for what the Micronesians demanded (to pay for that interest). Connell exemplifies the deep-seated, economically deterministic mentality of many contemporary commentators on the Pacific by interpreting this arrangement as being externally imposed, rather than a political stratagem. This is a shortcoming of contemporary evaluations of Micronesia: the assumption that the indigenous community holds the same worldview and political objectives as the commentator. This mentality ignores the roots of social and economic realities in Micronesia.[34] As will be argued in later chapters, these criticisms reflect externally imposed processes rather than inherent problems and solutions within Micronesian society.

The Compact is widely seen as the vehicle for Micronesians to access the US's employment market. The Compact should be more correctly seen as a lease between a landlord and tenant. The Compact monies are

---

31   Norman Meller, *Constitutionalism in Micronesia*, The Institute for Polynesian Studies, Brigham Young University, Hawai'i, 1985, Part 1, The Setting.
32   Gonzaga Puas, 'Federated States of Micronesia Still a Colony', *Pacific Daily News*, 15 January 2000, p. 19.
33   Puas, 'Micronesia Still a Colony', p. 19.
34   Many foreign observers continue to view the FSM as too dependent on the US. The question is, how does one define dependency from a Micronesian perspective? There is no literature on this topic. See Hanlon, 'Magellan's Chroniclers?', pp. 53–54.

synonymous with rent, and so the money may be spent the way the FSM desires. It is not up to outside observers to dictate the type of economic activities Micronesians should pursue, as has been attempted by American officials at various times during the Compact era.

Writing at a time before the move towards independence gathered force, political scientist Roger Gale contradicted the negative assessments of Meller and Connell. He stated that there are islands in Micronesia (e.g. Pohnpei and Kosrae) that are 'lush and verdant'[35] and provide sufficient food crops for the islanders. Moreover, to Micronesians, the soil is viewed as very rich, as it has sustained islanders for millennia. Surpluses are shared between villages and neighbouring islands. Trade is also common between islands. The size of the islands taught the inhabitants about conservation techniques and fostered an appreciation of their environment. Moreover, 'smallness' is a relative term and has its own advantages. For example, the micro-islands may have discouraged outsiders to settle permanently, thus reducing the disruption to lives that often follows and denying the negative forces and elements of the global economy that have disrupted local lives elsewhere, such as around large mining sites. Today, Micronesians continue to carry on their traditional life with manageable interruptions from the outside world. The redesignation of Micronesia's past territorial sea, which now forms its exclusive economic zone (EEZ), also speaks for itself. Micronesia's territory now dwarfs many continental nations. As in the past, Micronesians continue to perceive the sea as an extension of the land itself. The outside world is starting to appreciate this fact; it puts the concept of smallness in a different context. Outsiders are now fixated with the potential economic wealth in the FSM's EEZ.[36] Pacific Island leaders are now consistently depicting themselves as big ocean nations rather than small island nations, as will be outlined in Chapter 6.

The Micronesian perception of the land–sea continuum has not been well understood by outsiders. This point is illustrated by former US Secretary of State Henry Kissinger's response to questions about the ethics of nuclear testing in inhabited zones of the western Pacific without local consent

35 Roger Gale, *Americanization of Micronesia: A Study of the Consolidation of US Rule in the Pacific*, University Press of America, Washington, DC, 1979, p. 7.
36 Hanlon, *Making Micronesia*, pp. 170–171; Peter Sitan, 'The Development of the Tuna Fisheries in the Federated States of Micronesia', Unpublished paper presented at the Micronesian Symposium, The Australian National University, 27–28 April 2014, pp. 3–6.

being sought: 'who gives a damn there are only 90,000 people out there'.[37] Kissinger's condemnation of Micronesians and their islands reaffirmed outsiders' ignorance of the enormity of the size of the islands' resource base when including the sea, let alone the ethical issue of deciding that others should suffer nuclear testing supposedly for the 'good of humanity' and to preserve world peace, regardless of whether they consented or not.

Kissinger spoke his mind from a continental perspective. It had no bearing on islanders' perspective of their oceanic world and their place in history. Micronesia might then be more accurately described as 'Macronesia', as Hanlon once noted.[38] Perhaps the context is Micronesia's 107,000 citizens who share a sovereign territory of 1.3 million square miles of land and sea.[39] While the sea served as a unifying force for Micronesians, outsiders considered it an obstacle for the area's effective management. Outsiders perceived the sea as separating the islands rather than connecting them.[40]

The Asian Development Bank (ADB) and the International Monetary Fund (IMF) are no wiser in adopting the negative line predicting economic doom for Micronesia. For example, the IMF predicted that:

> the economy faces important risks … from a potential deterioration in the external environment and, over the longer term, the scheduled expiration of Compact grants and the continued outmigration of the working age population.[41]

---

37   Bethwel Henry, Interview, 28 June 2012. See also David Hanlon, 'You Did What, Mr. President!? Trying to Write a Biography of Tosiwo', in *Telling Pacific Lives: Prisms of Process Nakayama* edited by Brij V. Lal and Vicki Luker, ANU E Press, Canberra, 2008.
38   David Hanlon, 'Tosiwo Nakayama', paper presented in Tokyo, 2011, p. 2.
39   Sitan, 'The Development of the Tuna Fisheries', p. 3.
40   Epeli Hau'ofa, *The Ocean in Us*, University of Hawai'i Press, 1998, p. 38; *The Constitution of the Federated States of Micronesia*, Preamble; D'Arcy, *The People of the Sea*, pp. 144–146.
41   International Monetary Fund, *IMF Executive Board Concludes 2012 Article IV Consultation with Federated States of Micronesia Asia and Pacific Department*, 17 January 2013; International Monetary Fund, *Federated States of Micronesia (FSM): 2012 Article IV Consultation Concluding Statement of the IMF November 19, 2012*, www.imf.org/en/News/Articles/2015/09/28/04/52/mcs111912; Asian Development Bank, *Federated States of Micronesia: Strengthening: Infrastructure Planning and Implementation (Financed by the Japan Fund for Poverty Reduction)* (ADB Technical Assistance Report, Project Number: 44471), November 2011, p. 4, www.adb.org/sites/default/files/project-document/60497/44471-012-fsm-tar.pdf; Sione Latukefu, 'Oral Traditions: An Appraisal of Their Value in Historical Research in Tonga', *Journal of Pacific History*, Vol. 3, No. 1, 1968, pp. 41–42; Paul D'Arcy, 'The Role That Myths and Oral Traditions Should Play in the Study of Micronesian History', University of Hawai'i, 1986, p. 6 (Unpublished paper).

Many observers echoed the IMF's concern. The president of the FSM sought assistance from the ADB and other international organisations to pre-empt the negative economic outlook. However, the irony is that the ADB has patchy records about the economic history of the FSM as its data are largely based on 'fly in, fly out' consultants who remain briefly in the FSM before returning to Manila to write their reports and recommendations. For example, in the 2011 ADB report regarding technical assistance to the FSM, ADB consultants were each allocated two to three months in the FSM to complete their assignments.[42] The report did not deal with indigenous perspectives of their unique economic circumstances but focused on what the ADB believed was the way forward economically. The sea was not treated as an asset by the report either. It failed to note the importance of the sea and the increase in the FSM's income from the fishing industry. For example, the value of tuna in FSM fisheries in 2008 was estimated at US$41,818,486 compared to US$92,496,175 in 2012.[43] The industry is expected to grow further in the years ahead.

Many consultants do not understand Micronesians' current circumstances, let alone the depth of their history. Demonstrative of this point, Hezel claimed that the emergence of the cash economy has altered the fabric of Micronesian families 'almost beyond recognition during the last few decades'.[44] The reality is somewhat different. Money has been incorporated into the island system as another commodity circulating within the extended family model of *alilis* and *eaea fengan*, as Marshall diligently puts it.[45] Micronesians have not been overwhelmed by global economic forces but, rather, have incorporated these into existing mechanisms that have proven their worth over millennia. A few days in any location makes it clear that the doctrine of *alilis fengen* and the *ainang* system continue to operate and provide stability and support for clan members. In a different context, the informal economy model practised by Micronesians has never been discussed in any literature; outsiders fail to understand this model as it is hard to quantify in terms they are used to. They prefer to concentrate only on what is familiar to them.

---

42   Asian Development Bank, *Federated States of Micronesia*, p. 4.
43   Sitan, 'The Development of the Tuna Fisheries', p. 21.
44   Hezel, *The New Shape of Old Island Cultures*, p. 8.
45   Keith Marshall, 'The Structure of Solidarity and Alliance on Namoluk Atoll', PhD thesis, University of Washington, Seattle, Washington, 1972, p. 62.

Micronesian Perspective of History

My upbringing and fieldwork have alerted me to the large corpus of oral history absent from most external commentaries on FSM societies. Only a fraction has been revealed to Western researchers, and much of that has been assessed in variable ways.[46] A holistic approach is required for improving our understanding of Micronesians' perspectives of history. The increasing presence of Micronesian perspectives in published histories requires that oral history must play a greater role in academia.[47] The challenge for all historians is to be conscious of the diversities of Micronesian voices and to ensure their placement in mainstream academic discourses. As in all history, different *ainang* have the tendency to skew historical narratives to stake their own claims and interests. Academic historians can work together with their local counterparts to construct possibilities and verify the validity of competing claims.

Historians must be aware of all the available tools at their disposal to fill in the existing gaps in Micronesian historiography. Written history has been appropriated as a complementary tool for Micronesian scholars to reconstruct their histories; they are becoming more accessible for indigenous scholars to examine. This trend perpetuates Micronesians as active agents in the production and reconstruction of their historical experiences. They are redefining and reclaiming their historical past that has been misplaced, mystified and mistreated for centuries as a consequence of colonialism and its agents. A Micronesian perspective of history is gaining momentum through emerging scholars from both the islands and outside.[48]

Many non-Micronesian scholars have been supportive of situating Micronesian perspectives within mainstream academia. In their assessment, oral history is just as reliable as written history. The fact that many scholars do not have access to oral history does not necessarily mean that it is not

---

46   Negative portrayal of indigenous identity is exemplified by Poyer, 'The Ngatik Massacre', pp. 4–22; Ann Nakano, *Broken Canoe: Conversations and Observations in Micronesia*, University of Queensland Press, St. Lucia, 1983. Positive views are yet to be revealed by the new generations of indigenous scholars.

47   Micronesian historical theories are often left to clan historians to prove or disprove the validity and dynamic of events. See Lin Poyer, 'The Ngatik Massacre', pp. 20–22. For commentaries and detailed analysis of Pacific history, see D'Arcy, 'Introduction'.

48   Joakim Peter, 'Eram's Church (Bell): Local Appropriations of Catholicism on Ettal', *ISLA Journal of Micronesian Studies*, Vol. 4, No. 2, Dry Season 1996, pp. 278–280.

history per se. The debate is not which history is more credible, but how to reconcile both forms of history to increase our understanding of island discourses. Both should be treated as complementing each other for the purpose of enlarging scholarly engagement. As D'Arcy observed:

> until quite recently archaeologists and others who study pre-European history of [Micronesia] tended to treat island communities as relatively self-contained. Modern academic writings portray external contacts as being of limited significance in the development of individual islands after initial colonisation by human beings. Pre-European cultural development is usually depicted as driven by the interaction of internal processes. These include; cultural emphasis on competition: adaptation of the founding culture to a new environment; population growth on a limited land area; environmental change, both natural and human-induced, and cultural emphasis on competition for status channelled into warfare, or the intensification of production for redistribution to forge social and political obligations. The possibility of new arrivals introducing cultural innovations is not dismissed, but it is always considered of secondary importance.[49]

D'Arcy,[50] Peter,[51] Ridgell, Ikea and Uruo,[52] and Berg,[53] for example, have disproven the idea that the islands were isolated with detailed accounts of inter-island interactions across time. My clan historians also contradict this image and suggest that even D'Arcy and other Western scholars most supportive of the view of the pervasiveness of inter-island interaction are still well short of conceiving of the true extent of inter-island interaction. My clan, for instance, spoke of continuing contact between members throughout history in far more detail and intensity than is portrayed in published academic sources. Contact with and knowledge of communities in the Marshall Islands and Kiribati figures prominently in some clan traditions but is portrayed as isolated and unusual in academic literature.

---

49 Paul D'Arcy, 'Connected by the Sea: Towards Regional History of the Western Caroline Islands', *Journal of Pacific History*, Vol. 36, No. 2, 2001, p. 163.
50 For specific details, see D'Arcy, *The People of the Sea*.
51 For an indigenous perspective, see Joakim Peter, 'Chuukese Travellers and the Idea of Horizon', *Asia Pacific Viewpoint*, Vol. 41, No. 3, December 2000, pp. 253–267.
52 Reilly Ridgell, Manny Ikea and Isaoshy Uruo, 'The Persistence of Central Carolinian Navigation', *ISLA: A Journal of Micronesian Studies*, Vol. 2, No. 2, Dry Season 1994, pp. 197–205.
53 M. L. Berg, 'Yapese Politics, Yapese Money, and the Sawei Tribute Network Before World War I', *Journal of Pacific History*, Vol. 27, No. 2, December 1992, pp. 150–164.

Today, that contact remains undisturbed, especially when I travel in the FSM where relatives from different islands welcome me into their homes without hesitation.[54]

Highlighting Micronesian Perspectives

A handful of scholars from different disciplines are opening new frontiers for Micronesian historiography. Historians such as Mauricio Rufino, Joakim Peter, Paul D'Arcy, David Hanlon and Vicente Diaz, sociologist Ansito Walter and anthropologists Mac Marshall, Donald Rubinstein, Glenn Petersen and Manuel Rauchholz have made valuable contributions to Micronesian historiography.[55] This new breed of scholars have advocated a style inclusive of indigenous perspectives. In doing so, they provide a space and validity for Micronesian perspectives to be heard in a broader setting. Mauricio Rufino, Joakim Peter, Myjolynn Kim, L. J. Rayphand, Margarita Cholmay and myself represent a new and exciting wave of indigenous scholars who are decolonising their history with reference to the unique insights their cultural upbringing has given them, combined with academic lessons from external scholars open to exploring and questioning European-dominated historical sources on cultural encounters in the Pacific.[56] The only nationally prominent advocate for FSM-centred history in the previous generation is John Haglelgam.[57]

These indigenous scholars are critically engaging with Micronesia's history. For example, Mauricio noted the value of oral history in the perpetuation of Micronesian identity and continuity. Oral history, he claims, is an organising tool that can be used in conjunction with other academic disciplines to resuscitate Micronesia's past:

> oral traditions provide a comprehensive and multi-vocal narrative
> of history of the evolving [Micronesian] socio-political system.
> This narrative history is much more than a compendium of stories

---

54   This is my personal experience. Many of my relatives are unknown to me until they explain our affinity and historical links.

55   These scholars have expanded Micronesian studies by perpetrating the idea of indigenising history to broaden our understanding of Micronesian traditional societies in response to colonisation and these societies' status in the modern world.

56   New generations of indigenous scholars are currently investigating their own island histories and connection to their immediate region and beyond.

57   John Haglelgam, 'Problems of National Unity and Economic Development in the Federated States of Micronesia', *ISLA Journal of Micronesian Studies*, Vol. 1, No. 1, Rainy Season 1992, p. 6.

about past events. It also represents a structured and dynamic body of knowledge administered and managed ... and continually translates past events ... in terms of the present-day affairs.[58]

Haglelgam echoes Mauricio's view where he states that, Micronesians have:

a common and ancient heritage born from the spirit of exploration, from the skills of navigators, and the builders of the outrigger canoes. Despite the differences in languages and specific traditional practises from island to island, we have long been aware of each other, occupy similar circumstances, and have been subjected to similar influences, both natural and political.[59]

Chamorro historian from neighbouring Guam, Vince Diaz, supports Mauricio's points by raising the need to reposition history to incorporate indigenous perspectives. Hanlon referred to such repositioning as the 'decentralisation' of colonial history to treat Micronesian perspectives as history in its own right.[60] This resonates in Walter's call to dismantle the self-promoting exercise designed to perpetuate outsiders' historical interest.[61] Again, Diaz praised such an intellectual movement as remarkable and a worthy cause to eradicate colonial distortions of Micronesia's past.[62] That is to say that the colonisation process was managed by the intellectual powers of Micronesians. Micronesian intellectualism was seen by outsiders as inferior or non-existent. The inability of the colonists to recognise this drive for maintaining self-direction enabled the islanders to continue to live in a dual world while waiting for future opportunities to reassert their independence.

Hanlon reaffirms Hezel's comments, stating, 'there has always been far more to the islands' past than colonialism'.[63] There is indeed a growing admission by scholars that 'Micronesians [were the] agents, actors, negotiators, appropriators, and manipulators ... who had dealt with past colonial regimes, survived war, and now'[64] continue to challenge new sets of circumstances. The new generation is laying the foundation

58   Mauricio, 'Ideological Bases for Power', pp. 8–9.
59   Haglelgam, 'Problems of National Unity', p. 6.
60   Hanlon, 'Micronesia: Writing and Rewriting the Histories', pp. 4–6.
61   Ansito Walter, *Desirability, Problems, and Methods of Achieving National Independence: Opinions of Citizens and Senators of the Federated States of Micronesia*, Ann Harbour, Michigan, USA, 1985, p. 33.
62   Vincent Diaz, *Repositioning the Missionary: Rewriting the Histories of Colonialism, Native Catholicism, and Indigeneity in Guam*, University of Hawai'i Press, Honolulu, 2010, pp. 21–23.
63   Hanlon, 'Magellan's Chroniclers?', p. 77.
64   Hanlon, 'Magellan's Chroniclers?', p. 119.

of a new paradigm shift in Micronesian historical dialogue. It calls for a reinterpretation of history from indigenous perspectives, which has been marginalised from published works for too long.

Marshall, D'Arcy, Rubinstein and Petersen underscored the importance of the *ainang* as interconnecting Micronesian islands throughout history. Such connection continues to grow globally with the new diaspora. As Marshall observed:

> [Micronesian] culture is not bound to [an isolated] place … it is carried with [the people] as they cross borders in search of new opportunities … or safety [with their relatives] from warfare and revolution [and disasters].[65]

Marshall's comment is supported by prominent FSM diplomat James Naich,[66] who asserts that Micronesians' relationship with each other has been an essential element that has defined, shaped and sustained Micronesians as a distinct group of people who have survived centuries of external threats.[67] D'Arcy expanded on these views in commenting that the history of Micronesia is about a sea of crowded islands and open sea markers that assisted inter-island voyages,[68] allowing the *ainang* system to flourish.

The Sea as History

Development experts often neglect the importance of the sea to Micronesians. For example, the sea is viewed as an obstacle to the movement of goods and services from major world markets, while in reality, the sea is a major part of Micronesian identity. In his book *The People of the Sea*, D'Arcy outlined the importance of the sea to islanders, noting:

> People of the sea need to feel truly at home with the sea. Most of the inhabitants of Oceania lived along the coastal margins of their island homes. The sights, sounds, and smells of the sea pervaded their lives while the tastes of the sea were often on their lips.[69]

---

65 Marshall, *Namoluk beyond the Reef*, p. 10.
66 James Naich is the deputy chief of mission (DCM) at the FSM Embassy in Washington, DC. I conducted an interview with him (via Skype) on 21 December 2014.
67 Naich, Interview.
68 D'Arcy, 'Connected by the Sea', p. 165.
69 D'Arcy, *The People of the Sea*, p. 27.

This is true in the case of Micronesia, where the sea is always part of daily activities. No one can escape the sea or wishes to.

Pacific scholars such as Epeli Hau'ofa ignited a debate on external misrepresentations of the role of the sea in Pacific Island life in the early 1990s. He referred to colonisation as disrupting islanders' mobility on the seas.[70] Colonisation superimposed imaginary boundaries in Oceania as a means to divide and rule local inhabitants. Islanders were contained within the designated boundaries under the rule of various colonial powers. Hau'ofa called for a reshaping of Pacific Island history to reflect Pacific Islanders' oceanic past. As he noted:

> Nineteenth-century imperialism erected boundaries that led to the contraction of Oceania, transforming once a boundless world into the Pacific Island States and territories that we know today. People were confined to their tiny spaces, isolated from each other. No longer could they travel freely to do what they had done for centuries.[71]

Hau'ofa's view was more of a general vision of how to decolonise Pacific history than a detailed account of Pacific Islanders' use of the sea as a conduit for communication.[72] While his call for the decolonisation of Pacific history is laudable, part of that decolonisation involves correcting external images not only from Westerners but also other Pacific Islanders with different engagements with the sea. A number of Hau'ofa's assumptions are questionable, at least from a Micronesian perspective. It should be remembered that sea boundaries have always been a part of Micronesian history as they demarcated the many Micronesian identities that existed before colonisation. Demarcations defined people and space and established the norms of interaction between islands or island groups.[73] For example, in the Mortlocks, strict protocols governed fishing activities and sailing between islands. When a canoe approached an island, it had to observe protocols or the canoe would be deemed a threat. Expectation of foreknowledge of protocols by senior sailors was required to save lives, as was knowledge of the sea and landmarks, as each has a special individual

---

70 Hau'ofa, 'Our Sea of Islands', p. 34.
71 Hau'ofa, 'Our Sea of Islands', p. 34.
72 D'Arcy, *The People of the Sea*, pp. 55–56.
73 This is from my personal knowledge. See also D'Arcy, *The People of the Sea*, p. 136.

meaning. As landfall approached, they signalled when to fold the sail, to sit, paddle and wait for further signals from the hosts to approach the beach. Disrespecting protocols could mean battle.

A variety of academics have noted inter-island protocols in the much-studied *sawei* system, when canoes from the outer islands in Chuuk would sail to meet their relatives in the island chain in Yap to pay tribute and exchange gifts with the chiefs in the main island of Yap in the district of Gagil.[74] In Chuuk, protocols were also established between islands when visiting relatives or engaging in trade with each other, especially the islands in the Chuuk lagoon.[75] Island security was defined by the boundaries on the seas. The protocols endured throughout the colonial period along with inter-island exchanges, despite the best efforts of colonial authorities to assert control. Decolonisation of the FSM in my lifetime has not lifted the restrictions; rather, they sit alongside international maritime laws that recognise the post-colonial divisions.

However, just as the sea is the provider for islanders, the sea may also destroy islanders through a new form of threat, climate change. Like colonisation, climate change is foreign induced and is affecting Micronesians' traditional way of life. The existential threat that climate change poses to Micronesians and their oceanic environment represents another phenomenon that islanders must adapt to. This will be discussed in detail in Chapter 7. Meeting this new threat will require resorting to historical knowledge of adaptation in partnership with technical knowledge from the outside world. However, Micronesians will continue to engage with the sea. It must be remembered that Micronesians have been adapting to natural disasters such as typhoons, tidal waves and drought in their aquatic world for millennia. Adaptation strategies have in turn influenced the way

---

74 D'Arcy, *The People of the Sea*, pp. 146–150; Alkire, *An Introduction to the Peoples and Cultures of Micronesia*, pp. 49–52; Rosalind L. Hunter-Anderson and Yigal (Go'opsan) Zan, 'Demystifying the Sawei, A Traditional Interisland Exchange', *ISLA: A Journal of Micronesian Studies*, Vol.4, No. 1, Rainy Season 1996, pp. 4–6; Ridgell, Ikea and Uruo, 'The Persistence of Central Carolinian Navigation', pp. 197–205.

75 Felix Naich, *oral history*. Naich confirmed the trading activities between the Chuuk Lagoon and Mortlockese. During one of the trading seasons, a sailing fleet from Lukunor stopped by Losap lagoon in the Upper Mortlocks on an uninhabited island called *Piafo* ('new beach'). After they rested, the chief applied his magical chant to drag *Piafo* behind his sailing canoe to Lukunor for his son. *Piafo* is now located on the northern reef of Lukunor. The people of the Mortlocks still talk about this powerful event.

Micronesians engaged with each other.[76] Inter-island engagement prior to colonisation has refined the means and methods of travel and interaction and allowed Micronesians to adapt to new influences emanating from the outside world successfully.[77]

Outsiders continue to impose their ideologies in Micronesia through economic and political pressures. Yet Micronesian identity endures. Rather than being overwhelmed, Micronesians rearticulated colonisation through the process of accommodation and assimilation to absorb its shockwaves. For example, academics James Duane and Joakim Peter referred to the resiliency of the Mortlockese people in the late eighteenth and early twentieth centuries in adapting to Christianity on their own terms. As Duane noted, 'neither missionary activity nor the European ships which carried civilisation with them to the islands, have changed the [islanders] and their mode of living significantly'.[78] This eighteenth-century observation holds true for Micronesian engagement with outsiders today.

Since the 1950s, Pacific history has gained prominence as a specialised academic discipline advanced by James Davidson, considered the father of Pacific history. It has undergone fundamental changes as historians began to develop different approaches and methodologies in the discipline.[79] However, certain issues remain unresolved as many scholars continue the old habit of reproducing the Pacific in the image of imperial history. For example, in a recent book reviewing the sum of Pacific historiography, entitled *Texts and Contexts*,[80] edited by Pacific historians Doug Munro and Brij Lal, historians were asked to review selected books considered foundational in Pacific historiography. Each

---

76   The exchange of adaptation ideas between islands was long established before colonisation. Exchange of ideas meant social and political interaction, influencing islanders' thought processes. See the discussion on mobility in Juliana Flinn, *Diplomats and Thatch Houses: Asserting Tradition in a Changing Micronesia*, The University of Michigan Press, Ann Arbor, 1992, pp. 11–14.

77   *Pukuan* are traditional signposts that demand certain behaviours when arriving at specific seamarks or landmarks. The legendary *palou* ('navigator/s') Rongoshik and Rongelap reveal the importance of strict observation of inter-island protocols; Rongelap, who had only general knowledge of the protocols, died, while Rongoshik, who had specific knowledge of the protocols, survived.

78   Nason J. Duane, *Clan and Copra: Modernization of Etal, Eastern Caroline Islands*, University of Michigan, University Microfilms International, Ann Arbor, Michigan, 1971, p. 170; Peter, 'Eram's Church (Bell)', pp. 282–285.

79   Paul D'Arcy, 'The Teaching of Pacific History: Introduction Diverse Approaches for Diverse Audience', *Journal of Pacific History*, Vol. 46, No. 2, September 2011, pp. 197–206.

80   Doug Munro and Brij Lal, 'The Texts in Its Context', in *Texts and Contexts: Reflection in Pacific Islands Historiography*, edited by Doug Munro and Brij Lal, University of Hawai'i Press, 2006, pp. 1–11.

of the reviewers gave their impression of how Pacific history was written over time. Of particular concern was the lack of indigenous historians included in the review process, with critics such as historian Gavan Daws pointing out the shortcomings in the review. Daws[81] perceived *Texts and Contexts* as a vehicle for recycling outdated outsiders' practice of Pacific history. He questioned why indigenous historians were not selected for such a review and the reason for such a narrow selection.[82] *Texts and Contexts* should be appreciated insofar as it reflects a gazing into the past; a self-congratulatory exercise by a combined Euro-Indio vision of what constituted Pacific historiography, rather than being an example of what Pacific historiography could and should be.[83]

As part of the *Texts and Contexts* edition, Hanlon reviewed the book *The First Taint of Civilization*, authored by Hezel. In Hanlon's assessment, the book continues the old habit of reflecting negative images of Micronesians in contemporary literature: 'the overall argument of [some writers] … points to a fatality of impact that left island peoples ignorant of their past, uncomfortable with the present, and uncertain about their future'.[84] Perhaps there should be a follow-up text on 'Oralities and Contexts' to ensure a holistic trend and development of Pacific history. Diaz echoes Daws's observation, stating, 'no group of people … holds a monopoly over intellectual … access to truth … as theorised and practiced in rituals such as historical scholarship … and in things such as books'.[85] The observations made by the above historians echo similar fundamental issues in Micronesian historiography—that is, who is writing Micronesian history, for whom and for what purpose?

---

81   Gavin Daws, 'Comment: Texts and Contexts: A First Person Note', *Journal of Pacific History*, Vol. 41, No. 2, September 2006, pp. 250–252.
82   Daws, 'Comment: Text and Context', p. 252.
83   Daws, 'Comment: Text and Context', pp. 256–259.
84   David Hanlon, 'On Hezel's *The First Taint of Civilization*', in *Texts and Contexts: Reflection in Pacific Islands Historiography*, edited by Doug Munro and Brij Lal, University of Hawai'i Press, 2006, p. 207.
85   Diaz, *Repositioning the Missionary*, p. 19.

2

Pre-Colonial Society and Identity

Background

The indigenous past is in the present; it is timeless with no sense of historical evolution as the Micronesian perspective of history contradicts the idea of the linear model of history practised by Western historians. As explained in Chapter 1, the Micronesian perspective of history is dynamic and revolves around a complex web of events. To understand events of the historical past, a *sou uruo* must first isolate an event and announce it to their listeners. This is to alert other *sou uruo* to create the context of these events for the purpose of organising the relationship between such events in order to determine the validity of the historical narratives and their conclusion. In subsequent chapters, my narrative will become descriptive to allow the readers to organise their thoughts about historical parallelism since I will be following the linear model approach but will narrate the history within the context of a Micronesian perspective. No Micronesian has written a comprehensive account of the colonial and post-colonial periods in relation to how the modern Micronesian identity was formed, evolved and perpetuated for continuity purposes.

This chapter examines the processes that shaped the Micronesian identity and the reasons for its perpetuation as perceived by Micronesians.[1] It demonstrates the continuity of traditional ways of organising history,

---

1   The Micronesian perception of identity was mainly gathered in the field from those who experienced the process of independence.

society and nature that are still thriving in FSM today. By default, this subject is largely covered by academics raised and trained beyond Micronesia. I was struck by the disassociation of nature and humans in my review of the scholarly literature on Micronesian societies.[2] By and large, most academic studies of Micronesia initiate their historical discourses by describing the geography and environment of the islands. They do so before inserting the human inhabitants into the scene, as though they are removed from the environment.

The nature–culture nexus has always been an intellectual battleground between scholars. It is also a contested area between academics advocating environmental circumstances or cultural ways of viewing the world as the prime influences on human behaviour and history,[3] versus indigenous perspectives of societies, such as those in Micronesia, who consider human beings as both part of nature and influential agents in the shaping of the environment.[4] Scholars within academia are increasingly advancing the interdependent nexus between nature and culture.[5] This chapter demonstrates the large degree of continuity in social relations and human–environment relations that exists across Micronesian societies. Subsequent chapters then trace how this identity and its organising principles came about over history and how this legacy will play out in the words and actions of young people.

---

2   See e.g. Paul Rainbird, *The Archaeology of Micronesia*, Cambridge University Press, 2004; Roger Gale, *The Americanization of Micronesia: A Study of the Consolidation of U.S. Rule in the Pacific*, Washington, DC, 1979; Ward Goodenough, *Property, Kin and Community on Truk* (2nd edition), Archon Books, Connecticut, 1978; William Alkire, *An Introduction to the Peoples and Cultures of Micronesia* (2nd edition), University of Victoria, British Columbia, 1977; Kirk Gray, 'Modernization in Micronesia: Acculturation, Colonialism and Cultural Change', PhD thesis, Western Michigan University, Kalamazoo, Michigan, 1974, pp. 1–6.

3   Kerry R. Howe, *Nature, Culture and History: The 'Knowing' of Oceania*, University of Hawai'i Press, Honolulu, Hawai'i, 2000, pp. 55–57, 59–64; David W. Kupferman, 'On Location at a Nonentity: Reading Hollywood's "Micronesia"', *Contemporary Pacific*, Vol. 23, No. 1, 2011, pp. 142, 162; Jane Landman and Chris Ballard, 'An Ocean of Images: Film and History in the Pacific', *Journal of Pacific History*, Vol. 45, No. 1, June 2010, p. 4.

4   Okusi Mahina, 'The Poetics of Tongan Traditional History, Tala-e-fanua: An Ecology Centred Concept of Culture and History', *Journal of Pacific History*, Vol. 28, No. 1, June 1993, pp. 219–220; Kenneth E. Knudson, 'Resource Fluctuation, Productivity, and Social Organization on Micronesian Coral Islands', PhD thesis, University of Oregon, Eugene, Oregon, 1970, pp. 6–8; Howe, *Nature, Culture and History*, pp. 55–57, 59–64.

5   My personal experience has shown this to be the case. Academia has been slow to come to this realisation and only partially contested it.

At a number of points along the continuum between cultural determinism and environmental determinism lies the danger of Micronesians becoming exotic stereotypes, like actors in fictional Hollywood movies.[6] Some writers narrated the tropical environment with exotic images of its inhabitants to conjure up certain preconceived cultural abstracts.[7] Many scholars, for instance, refer to Micronesia as a dehumanised space to relate external myths and fantasies.[8] This exercise distorts the realities of Micronesia, a place with its own unique historical images and identities.

In reality, modern Micronesian history and thus identity are a consequence of long historical processes that have spanned centuries of indigenous development, followed by a shorter period of external colonial rule, which culminated in the indigenous desire to establish an independent *Constitution for the Federated States of Micronesia* in 1979.[9] Historians argue that all documents and perceived identities and affiliations are situated within broader historical processes and are deeply embedded in the context in which they arise.[10] Prior to colonial rule, people's identities were connected to one's village, island, lineage or the clan at the regional level.[11] Both the *ainang* system and geography defined an individual's connection to a geographical space or their place in the social system.[12] For example, one could claim to be from a kin-based social unit within a village situated on a particular island, which belonged to a particular region. That is, the islands consisted of multiple identities coexisting with each other.

The term 'Micronesia' is an externally imposed description of the scattered islands in terms of geography and as a cultural area, created to serve colonial purposes. In time, the islanders adopted the term 'Micronesian' to differentiate themselves from the outsiders and later used the term as

---

6   Kupferman, 'On Location at a Nonentity', pp. 142–143.

7   Howe, *Nature, Culture and History*, pp. 13–14.

8   Peter Hay, 'A Phenomenology of Islands', *Island Studies Journal*, Vol. 1, No. 1, 2006, p. 21; Howe, *Nature, Culture and History*, pp. 10–14.

9   It took almost 15 years after the Congress of Micronesia was established in 1965 for Micronesians to finally achieve a constitutional government (Hanlon, *Making Micronesia*, p. 100).

10   Munro and Lal, 'The Text in Its Context', pp. 1–11; Penelope J. Corfield, 'All People are Living Histories—Which is Why History Matters', *Making History*, School of Advanced Study, University of London, 2008, www.history.ac.uk/makinghistory/resources/articles/why_history_matters.html.

11   Mortlocks oral history as told by my elders (hereafter *Mortlocks Oral History*). See also Francis X. Hezel, 'The Chuuk Problem: At the Foot of the Political Pyramid', *Micronesian Counselor*, No. 50, April 2004, www.micsem.org/pubs/counselor/frames/chuukprobfr.htm.

12   Petersen, *Traditional Micronesian Societies*, pp. 22–23; Marshall, *Namoluk beyond the Reef*, pp. 8–11.

a unifying tool to fight the tyranny of colonialism.[13] The outcome of this historical discourse is the reconfiguration of the term 'Micronesian' by islanders as an identity in response to the globalised world.[14]

The decolonisation process of the 1960s and 1970s led to the emergence of Pacific identities framed within the context of self-governing nation states.[15] Many Pacific Islanders constructed their identities along the lines of their colonial experience, built on the foundation of their unique historical past. Micronesians were part of this process but were only able to exercise significant control rather late due to the prolonged control of their sovereignty by the US as a strategic UN Trust Territory of the Pacific Islands (TTPI). American rule merely delayed rather than stifled this process, however, as Micronesians later constructed their own national identity as part of the political emancipation process from external control.

The name 'Micronesia' is an example of European nomenclature based on the questionable association of the physical appearance of its inhabitants coupled with cultural similarities within a shared geographic location in Oceania alongside Polynesia and Melanesia.[16] Geographic Micronesia encompasses many island nations: Kiribati, the Marshall Islands, FSM, Palau, the US territories of the Northern Marianas Islands and Guam. However, the FSM now assumes the name Micronesia by political design.[17] Today, the FSM is recognised internationally as Micronesia, and the indigenous inhabitants are referred to as Micronesians, especially when framing themselves in political and cultural discourses. Micronesians consider themselves as a diverse and distinct group of people with a proud history and traditions. That identity derives from Micronesians' close relationship to their oceanic environment. It has already been noted that the Constitution refers to the Micronesian identity as historically deriving from the sea.[18] The sea is the prime source of livelihood and one

---

13   Robert Kiste, 'A Half Century in Retrospect', in *American Anthropology in Micronesia: An Assessment*, edited by Robert Kiste and Mac Marshall, University of Hawai'i Press, 1999, pp. 442–443.

14   Hanlon, *Making Micronesia*, pp. 5–6.

15   Meller, *Constitutionalism in Micronesia*, p. 7.

16   See the *Journal of Pacific History*'s special issue, 'Dumont d'Urville's Divisions of Oceania: Fundamental Precincts or Arbitrary Constructs?', Vol. 38, No. 2, September 2003, pp. 155–288; Bronwen Douglas and Chris Ballard, eds, *Foreign Bodies: Oceania and the Science of Race 1750–1940*, ANU E Press, Canberra, 2008, pp. 9–10.

17   Micronesia is now often associated with the FSM in many international forums. The people of Palau or the Marshall Islands identify themselves with the name of their countries—as Palauans or Marshallese, respectively. The disintegration of Micronesia can be blamed on the US as counter to the trusteeship agreement (Meller, *Constitutionalism in Micronesia*, p. 340).

18   *The Constitution of the Federated States of Micronesia*, Preamble.

that has shaped Micronesian history and identity. For example, the sea provides the space where people performed meaningful activities, where they fought wars, fished, sailed, found romance, worked and performed religious rituals.[19] These activities exemplify how islanders interact with their environment and also with each other. The sea nurtured, reproduced and transported Micronesian ideologies across space and time.

Micronesians still perceive and cherish their traditional universe as a tripartite union between *saat* (sea), *fanou* (land) and *lang* (sky);[20] these are the sacred domains where the spirits of their progenitors' dwell.[21] Inherent in these are the local guardians empowered with *maniman*[22] who instruct successive generations of Micronesians about their historical heritage. The Constitution is conceived of by many Micronesians as a canoe carved out of the progenitors' ideological images with a purpose—to transport and reinforce their history. It is the sacred vessel that beholds Micronesian identity and continuity while engaging with the changes of the modern world. Accordingly, let me then pay my deep respect to my ancestors in conveying my '*tiro lang, tiro pwel, tiro saat*[23] *and tiro nganei ash samol*'.[24] This is a special acknowledgement to the Micronesian *saat*, *fonou* and *lang*. It is an invocation honouring both the natural spaces where their ancestors' dwell and their *aramas* (people) overseas.

Former Speaker of the Congress of the FSM Jack Fritz, like many esteemed traditional leaders before him, always began his oratory speeches with a passionate delivery of the aforementioned traditional line. It reveals Micronesians' deep connection to their oceanic environment, the land and the sky. Fritz's sentiment reflects the FSM's first president Tosiwo Nakayama's instructive dictum to his people where he impressed upon them to fully embrace their customs, traditions and the god-given

---

19   D'Arcy, *The People of the Sea*, p. 32; Hau'ofa, *We Are the Ocean*, p. 32.
20   For a detailed discussion, refer to William Alkire, 'Land, Sea, Gender and Ghosts on Woleai-Lamotrek', *American Anthropological Association* (Reprinted from Special Publication, No. 25), 1989, pp. 85–86; Rainbird, *The Archaeology of Micronesia*, pp. 37–38. See also William Lessa, *Ulithi: A Micronesian Design for Living*, University of California, Los Angeles, Holt Rhinehart and Winston, Inc, 1966, pp. 56–57.
21   Lingenfelter, *Yap*, p. 80.
22   *Maniman* is the Micronesian equivalent to what Polynesians refer to as *Mana* and broadly means 'spiritual'.
23   *Pwwel* is the same as *fonou*. However, it is more appropriate to use the term '*pwwel*' when delivering a speech during community gatherings.
24   *Samol* refers to traditional chiefs. Former speaker of the FSM Congress, Jack Fritz, delivered his speeches using the tripartite connections as a sign of deep respect to the different spaces where Chuukese–Micronesians' ancestors dwell. Elders before Jack Fritz also used these opening remarks, and these are still used today by people during all sorts of meetings.

islands.[25] Micronesians, he said, should cease being afraid of outsiders who attempted to destroy their pride, dignity and self-esteem in order to steal their islands. Micronesians should also be reminded of the sea;[26] it is central to their livelihood, history and identity.[27]

Masao Nakayama, the brother of Tosiwo and a former FSM ambassador to the UN, echoed both the president's and speaker's comments when he explained what the sea means to Micronesians at the UN Convention on the Law of the Sea in 1974. He declared:

> Though essential, the land is tiny and relatively barren. It provides people with protection from the elements and a place to eat and sleep in comfort. But the real focus of life is on the sea. The sea provides food and tools and the medium to transport an islander from one cluster of humanity to another. As compared to the power and moods of the sea, the land is insignificant, humble [and] dull. The rhythm of life is dictated by the sea. The turbulence of the sea tells people when they can travel and when they can't. It controls the habits of fish and the habits of the human seeking them. The sea sustains life with the food it provides, but also carries the potential to end it in the fury of one of its periodic rages. The sea challenges people, tests their character, provides life with drama and meaning.[28]

D'Arcy also noted that 'The sea dominates the lives and consciousness of the inhabitants … as nowhere else on earth. In this ocean setting, the sea cannot be ignored'.[29]

The two Nakayamas and Fritz's prophetic statements convey Micronesians' deep relationship with the sea. As Captain David Marar alluded to, 'rematau [people of the sea] is the identity that any Micronesian can wear as a badge of honour. It evokes the unending song sung from the ocean deep to remind shon fanuash [people of our island or land] of where they came from'.[30]

---

25   David Hanlon, *Remaking Micronesia: Discourses Over Development in a Pacific Territory, 1944–1982*, University of Hawai'i Press, 1988, p. 138.
26   Hanlon, *Remaking Micronesia*, p. 138.
27   *The Constitution of the Federated States of Micronesia*, Preamble.
28   Masao Nakayama and Fred Ram, *Traditional Native Approaches to Ocean Governance*, United Nations University, 1974.
29   D'Arcy, *The People of the Sea*, p. 26.
30   David Marar (Wing Commander, Maritime Surveillance), Interview, Nett, Pohnpei, 13 January 2011; Simion Weitto (Captain, FSS Micronesia (FSM surveillance ship)), Interview, 11 January 2011. Simion is also the *makal* (traditional leader) of his island, Houk, in the northwest region of Chuuk.

Figure 3: A traditional fishing technique called *lalo*, used to catch bonito.

Note: This technique, which is still used today, involves using coconut fronds to trap fish near the beach.

Source: Photograph taken by Amanson Ansin on Lukunor Island in early 2014.

Figure 4: Another view of *lalo*.

Source: Photograph taken by Amanson Ansin on Lukunor Island in early 2014.

Joakim Peter, an academic from the FSM, summed up the pervasiveness of the sea and sea skills in Micronesian life when he described how:

> singing [represents] the use of navigation as a way of speaking ... about elements of contemporary [Micronesia]: politics, government, and Christianity ... the song cautions against bad political or social handling to enforce social order.[31]

This metaphoric song, understood only by Micronesians, continues to guide them into the future. Micronesians are creatures of the sea.

The sea has always influenced the Micronesian perception of the world, which in turn has framed their cultural identity. Historically, the term *shon metau* (people of the deep sea) has been used in reference to the low-lying islands in Chuuk and Yap, whose inhabitants' lifestyle depends on the sea. Anthropologist Lieber and historian D'Arcy discussed how the sea shapes island cultures, a theme that also resonates across the vast array of Micronesian oral histories. D'Arcy, in his book *The People of the Sea*, provides a detailed study in relation to how Pacific Islanders interact with the sea and how this interaction has shaped islanders' cultural identities.[32] Lieber's book *More Than a Living* focuses on the atoll of Kapingamarangi, where daily life and social structure depends on fishing activities. With changes in technology, new fishing practices arose as the people adapted to the changing circumstances on the atoll. New ideas were also borrowed from neighbouring islands such as the volcanic island of Pohnpei and Nukuoro atoll. However, fishing remains the central activity for the male population on Kapingamarangi.[33]

The inception of the Congress of Micronesia (COM) in the mid-1960s underscored the emergence of the modern identity and the various inhabitants' historical backgrounds. The COM was the forum for elected leaders to discuss decolonisation and independence. The concept of one Micronesian identity was a top priority for the leaders. However, this identity was under constant threat by political elements that remained favourable to Americanisation. Americanisation was unpopular among the conservative elements of the COM, who perceived that Americanisation would mean American culture and values usurping those of the

---

31 *The Constitution of the Federated States of Micronesia*, Preamble; Peter, 'Chuukese Travellers', p. 261.
32 D'Arcy, *The People of the Sea*, ch. 7, pp. 146–155. See also Hau'ofa, *We Are the Ocean*, pp. 27–40.
33 Lieber, *More Than a Living: Fishing and Social Order on a Polynesian Atoll*, Westview Press, Boulder, 1994, pp. 179–180.

indigenous population. Consequently, Micronesians would be the new minority group and inevitably treated as second-class citizens. Proponents of Americanisation included Amata Kabua[34] and Nick Bossy,[35] as well as many who suffered during WWII. They considered the threat of Cold War hostilities being played out in the Pacific to be a more urgent danger and saw the continuation of a close association—perhaps even integration—with the US to be a safeguard of Micronesian security. The administrators were unimpressed with the new Micronesian identity; they thought the quest to de-Americanise the islands was too premature, citing Micronesian experience as inadequate to form and operate a government.[36] Despite the US's roadblocks to the issue of Micronesian independence, it did not fade away. The desire for independence instead gained momentum in the early 1970s. After a series of political negotiations between the Micronesian and American parties, the issue remained deadlocked. The Micronesian leadership would not give in to the American wish to control Micronesia.[37] The pro-independence movement rallied the people with resounding support, resulting in a Constitutional Convention (ConCon) on Saipan in the early 1970s. It was a serious demonstration of the leaders' intention to define Micronesian political identity in the islanders' own image, after a long period of American rule.

Towards a New Future

The ConCon was held in Saipan in the early 1970s. Its purpose was manifold but its main focus was to debate the new Micronesian identity as premised on a proposed nationwide constitution. This was a testing time for the whole TTPI to determine whether to remain under US administration.[38] The ConCon was also the forum in which the differences between Micronesians within the American-administered TTPI emerged. For example, the districts of Palau, the Marianas Islands and the Marshall Islands decided that it was better for them to leave the proposed Micronesian union and create their own separate identities.

34 Hanlon, *Making Micronesia*, pp. 168–169.
35 Hanlon, *Making Micronesia*, pp. 174–175.
36 Glenn Petersen, 'Lessons Learned: The Micronesian Quest for Independence in the Context of American Imperial History', *Journal of the Humanities and Social Sciences*, Vol. 3, No. 1–2, December 2004, p. 53.
37 Hanlon, *Making Micronesia*, pp. 119–122.
38 Hanlon, *Remaking Micronesia*, pp. 219–223; Meller, *Constitutionalism in Micronesia*, pp. 179–182; Alkire, *An Introduction to the Peoples and Cultures of Micronesia*, pp. 92–94.

Palau and the Marshall Islands *inter alias* reasoned that they did not want to be controlled by an imposed central identity that identified them as Micronesians.[39] Further, these districts also did not want to share their revenue—from the US test missile range in the Marshall Islands, and the proposed oil super port to be constructed in Palau by Japan and Iran—with the poorer districts. The Northern Marianas Islands' greater exposure to the outside world motivated them to opt to be part of the American super identity. In employing the colonial principle of divide and rule, the US granted the wishes of Palau and the Marshalls to leave the TTPI to form their own political identities, later known as Paluan and Marshallese. The remaining districts of Ponape, Truk, Yap and Kusaie[40] decided to form the FSM, with its people now referred to as Micronesians. The Micronesian identity has been recognised by the UN. However, the identity required the forces of social valorisation for it to be embedded in everyday people's imagination. The Preamble of the FSM's Constitution became the mantra in print to perpetuate the Micronesian identity in the brave new world of autonomy and self-representation.[41]

The Constitution united the indigenous people whose political desire was to share a nation and country. Since 1979, the Micronesian identity has been universally accepted worldwide. The Constitution also bestows the identity on those who are born in foreign lands with Micronesian heritage. The FSM passport validates the Micronesian identity when one travels to different jurisdictions internationally.[42] The Constitution is also a shield[43] against outsiders' encroachment on this new identity.

---

39   Meller, *Constitutionalism in Micronesia*, pp. 178–179.

40   Kusaie was part of the Ponape district and later became Kosrae state, separated from Ponape to carry on the proposed mandate of the constitutional convention. This was to allow the Constitution to pass and thus enable the creation of the FSM (Meller, *Constitutionalism in Micronesia*, p. 9).

41   This is from my personal knowledge. In the 1970s, high school students were required to learn the preamble by heart. In my communications with many high school teachers during my fieldwork in January 2011, I found that students are still encouraged to have knowledge of the preamble.

42   Micronesians were issued passports reflecting their status within the international system as TTPI residents. However, the passport was under the control of the US Government.

43   *The Constitution of the Federated States of Micronesia.* The Constitution asserts Micronesians' rights to their islands as recognised in international law. See United Nations Human Rights, *International Covenant on Economic, Social and Cultural Rights*, Part I, Article 1, www.ohchr.org/ EN/ProfessionalInterest/Pages/CESCR.aspx; *The Constitution of the Federated States of Micronesia*, Article II, Section 1.

Local, Regional and National Identities

My personal case may be used as an example of what it is to be a Micronesian with multiple identities but with the national identity under the Constitution. I am a Lekiniochian (a person born on the island of Lekinioch) from the subregion of Mortlocks (Mortlockese) in the state of Chuuk (Chuukese) in the FSM (a Micronesian).[44] I am a Micronesian, an identity bestowed upon me by the *Constitution of the Federated States of Micronesia* to inform others of what the indigenous Chuukese, Yapese, Kosraen and Pohnpeian's collectively refer to themselves in this age of globalisation.[45] This identity reclaims Micronesia's historical past from the colonial powers. I am part of the new generation of the clan *sor*, but I am also associated with another clan as *afakiran sofa*, which entitles me to speak about my own perspective of my island and my *uruon ainang*.[46] I have lived and travelled far and wide both domestically and internationally and have always remained loyal to my identity. I was born and raised in the Mortlocks, where my perspective of the world was shaped. My progenitors travelled the Chuukese region and beyond on sophisticated sailing canoes to connect with their *ainang* members who were spread across multiple atolls and high islands. Today, I am following their footsteps and have added new experiences to enrich my own *shon metau* background as a result of my own voyages to new spaces.[47]

Travelling remains central to Micronesian history and identity. This is because it continues the traditional network system established by Micronesians prior to colonisation. Such a network transmits, sustains and transforms Micronesian ideologies within the globalisation process.[48] Although the modes of travelling have changed, Micronesians have

---

44   My personal identity is based on my island clan and the region I came from, which are rolled into the broader Micronesian identity.

45   *The Constitution of the Federated States of Micronesia*, Preamble.

46   *Sor* is my mother's clan; it is my ascribed status. *Sofa* is my father's clan, which gave me the title *afakiran*, an honorary member of the *Sofa* clan. On clan associations and relationships, see Marshall, 'The Structure of Solidarity', pp. 50–66; Duane, *Clan and Copra*, pp. 59–63.

47   Marshall, *Namoluk beyond the Reef*, pp. 98–99, 134.

48   As a member of the Micronesian diaspora, I carry my Micronesian ideologies with me as the basis of my identity in the globalised world. See also Marshall, *Namoluk beyond the Reef*, pp. 98–99, 134. Hou'ofa discussed the concept of movement of Pacific Islanders who are now part of a wider Pacific community in 'Our Sea of Islands', pp. 34–39. See also Petersen, *Traditional Micronesian Societies*, pp. 12–19, 62, 64; Oha Uman, Ferdun Saladier and Anter Chipen, *Uruon Chuuk: A Resource of Oral Legends, Traditions, and History of Truk*, Vol. 1, ESEA Title IV Omibus Program for Social Studies, Cultural Heritage Trust Territory of the Pacific Islands, Moen, Truk, July 1979, pp. 1–7.

adapted to new ways of travel to different spaces, further away from their shores.[49] They are forming new communities within a wider diaspora, carrying with them their history and identity. The new waves of followers are continuing this process. Joakim Peter, a Micronesian scholar, referred to this move as *aipwa*; that is, following the footprints of fellow islanders who are now residing elsewhere around the globe.[50] As Mac Marshall states in relation to *shon* Namoluk, 'movement, migration, voyaging beyond the horizon are nothing new to Micronesian people'.[51]

In this process, many Micronesians have now resided outside Micronesia while remaining connected to their Micronesian identity, by adapting to their new places of residence to match established ways of doing things and interacting. For example, anthropologist Lola Bautista's study of Micronesians from Satowan Island living abroad provided an insight into the Micronesian ideology of domestic space when transplanted to foreign spaces. Her research revealed that configuration of spaces used in the layout of family compounds in Satowan has been duplicated in Guam. The idea is to allow the Satowanese to continue engaging with each other as if they were on their home island.[52] She observed how the Satowanese allocated cultural spaces between genders such as *lenien maur* (sleeping quarters), *mosoro* (cooking space) and a common area to accommodate everyday interaction in order to facilitate cultural practices.[53] A separate detachment like a *faal*, if it could be afforded, would also provide cultural space for young men to interact.[54] My observations of my extended family's compound situated on what they referred to as the 'ranch' in Guam confirms Bautista's findings. My observations also indicated that my family's cultural identity remains strong despite its relocation. However, some features of cultural practices are eroding as the new generation born in Guam and elsewhere in the US are growing up in a new environment far from the centres of everyday cultural interactions.[55]

---

49   Marshall, *Namoluk beyond the Reef*, pp. 98–99, 134. See also Hou'ofa, 'Our Sea of Islands', pp. 34–39.

50   Peter, 'Chuukese Travellers', pp. 256–257.

51   Marshall, *Namoluk beyond the Reef*, p. 6.

52   Lola Q. Bautista, 'Building Sense Out of Households: Migrants from Chuuk (Re)create Local Settlements in Guam', *City and Society*, Vol. 23, No. 1, June 2011, pp. 80–83.

53   Spaces are configured to reflect the gender avoidance between sisters and brothers. See social protocols in Marshall, 'The Structure of Solidarity', pp. 54–55.

54   Interactions between brothers and sisters are still seen as taboo and so both sexes have separate spaces for interaction. This is becoming problematic with the new generation born in the US. They seem not to observe this taboo (Marshall, 'The Structure of Solidarity', p. 54; Lingenfelter, *Yap*, pp. 44–45.

55   Marshall, *Namoluk beyond the Reef*, p. 142.

Reinforcing Identity

Ainang membership and locality affiliation, citizenship and FSM constitutional rights form the foundation of Micronesian identity and the sense of belonging in the fluid modern world. For example, Article III, Section 2 of the Constitution defines Micronesians in terms of nationality and citizenship: 'a person born of parents one or both of whom are citizens of the Federated States of Micronesia is a citizen and national of the Federated States by birth'.[56] Section 3 demands the total loyalty of Micronesian citizens by prohibiting dual citizenship after a certain age:

> a citizen of the Federated States of Micronesia who is recognized as a citizen of another nation shall, within 3 years of his 18th birthday … register his intent to remain a citizen of the Federated States and renounce his citizenship of another nation. If he fails to comply with this Section, he becomes a national of the Federated States of Micronesia.[57]

A 'national' is a Micronesian by heritage but with limited constitutional rights. However, that is not to say that nationals are exempt from identifying themselves as Micronesians by virtue of ancestral connection to the FSM.[58]

Being a Micronesian involves more than conforming to legal criteria as it is deeply embedded in cultural ideology and practices. Personal identity is an ascribed status as can be seen in the *ainang* system in many parts of Micronesia. Citizenship, however, is acquired through the legal system. For example, American-born Micronesians perpetuate the Micronesian identity in a global context, though they may have no direct experience of Micronesia. The island culture, however, recognises their membership in the *ainang* system.[59] Although the offspring of mixed parental marriages who are born in other global places have less exposure to Micronesian cultural knowledge, their absence from the FSM does not deny their

---

56 *The Constitution of the Federated States of Micronesia*, Article III, Section 2.

57 *The Constitution of the Federated States of Micronesia*, Article III, Section 3.

58 There is a clash between the rights afforded to citizens and nationals, especially regarding the issue of land or title inheritance. For example, inheritance is by tradition and nothing can interfere in that process, yet the Constitution bans traditional entitlements if one loses their FSM citizenship. This is a flaw in the Constitution that urgently needs addressing.

59 People who are culturally foreign but born with a blood connection to the islands are automatically members of their clan, either as an *afaker* or other designation, depending on the gender of the parent.

permanent membership of their parent's *ainang*.[60] Membership is about connections deeply rooted in Micronesian culture for the purpose of prolonging the survivability of the *ainang* system into the future, despite one's absence.[61]

To celebrate and protect the Micronesian identity, a law was created in 2010 that designated 31 March as a national holiday known as Micronesian Culture and Traditions Day. The law states:

> most nations celebrate their cultures and traditions as an integral part of their national identity. Inherent in this practice, is the celebration of indigenous cultures [and] … the FSM is blessed with its own indigenous cultures … even in the face of globalization. [It has] retained much of [its] cultural identity through the process of assimilation, and [it] will continue to withstand continuing foreign influences into the future.[62]

For a people vulnerable to natural disasters in the oceanic environment, maintaining both intra- and inter-island connections is fundamental to the reinforcement of the social safety net.[63] This tradition is alive and well today. Displays of connections are demonstrated during public holidays to commemorate the history of each island, state and the nation. On the aforementioned 31 March national holiday, the national government invites cultural groups and dignitaries around the nation to attend the commemorative celebrations that are hosted in honour of the national holiday.[64] The states and municipalities also have their own traditional holidays celebrated every year, consisting of events that include traditional dances, displays of traditional foods and handicrafts, and speeches from dignitaries. For example, in Yap, a state holiday called 'Yap Day' is celebrated on the first weekend of March every year. They display their island wares and stick and marching dances. A canoe festival is also on display, where Yapese showcase their canoes and sailing skills rooted in the *sawei* traditions. As recently as 2010, Carolinians sailed over 756 kilometres (643 miles) from Saipan in the Northern Marianas Islands

---

60   Marshall, *Namoluk beyond the Reef*, pp. 141–142.
61   Marshall, *Namoluk beyond the Reef*, pp. 142–143; Petersen, *Traditional Micronesian Societies*, p. 82.
62   The FSM Congress, *Congressional Bill No.16-01*, which later became a law, created a national holiday to honour the cultures and traditions of the FSM.
63   See the *sawei* system discussed in D'Arcy, *The People of the Sea*, pp. 146–150.
64   This is my personal experience. Other traditional celebrations are seen during individual state's constitutional days.

to Yap.[65] It only took them a week to reach their destination. This event was used to demonstrate their navigational prowess and the value placed on this knowledge as part of their identity and historical continuity.

Pohnpei state also has a holiday to celebrate the Constitution, where the people come together to perform their dances, market their agricultural produce and display their island wares.[66] Traditional leaders make speeches emphasising the history of their islands. The Chuukese have their own constitutional holiday, with the showcasing of traditional dances, local foods and handicrafts and competitions involving traditional activities such as copra husking and spear throwing.[67] Moreover, its low-lying atolls have their own cultural and traditional day. Leaders from the national and state governments are invited to join these celebrations. These events are also repeated in Kosrae and elsewhere in the FSM.[68]

Some observers perceive the differences in cultures as an obstacle to maintaining the future integrity of the FSM. Perhaps this is so when viewed within the context of colonial discourse where external threats are always looming on the horizon, ready to rupture the nation at any moment. This discourse may be connected to the past partition of the TTPI, which saw the emergence of the various small island states out of that territory. Some claim the FSM will follow suit because of its cultural diversity. For example, Petersen claimed in 1990 that 'the FSM will break up in violence. Just as colonisation strung these islands together, islanders will undo it to suit their own circumstances as in the historical past'.[69]

---

65   If one follows the traditional sea lanes of sailing from Yap to Saipan, it should be more than the 756 kilometres—the distance from Gaferut to Guam. See D'Arcy, *The People of the Sea*, pp. 154, 158 for a map of sea lanes and approximate distances between the islands in Yap all the way to the Mortlocks in Chuuk.

66   I personally witnessed this while living in Pohnpei and teaching at the College of Micronesia, Pohnpei Campus. See Myjolynn Kim, *Into the Deep: Launching Culture and Policy in the Federated States of Micronesia*, Secretariat of the Pacific Community (SPC) and Federated States of Micronesia Office of National Archives, Culture and Historic Preservation, Pohnpei, FSM, 2011, pp. 9–11.

67   This is from my personal experience as a Mortlockese–Chuukese witnessing Chuuk Constitution Day. See also Kim, *Into the Deep*, pp. 9–11.

68   I have personally witnessed these, such as the Kosraen community celebration in Pohnpei. See also Kim, *Into the Deep*, pp. 9–11.

69   Glenn Petersen, 'Regime Change and Regime Maintenance', *Discussion Papers Number 12, Ethnicity and Interests at the 1990 Federated States of Micronesia Constitutional Convention*, The Australian National University, 1993, pp. 67–68. The Chuuk Commission has been established to manage any such disintegration in future. Lack of a coherent culture was also discussed as the basis that may break up the FSM. For further details, see Yoko Komai, 'The Failure to Objectify Culture: A Lack of Nationalism in the FSM', *People and Culture in Oceania*, Vol. 19, No. 41, 2005, p. 21.

However, Petersen's subsequent research led him to change his position.[70] He joined fellow anthropologists such as Marshall and Rauchholz to convey the local perspective that Micronesians are conscious of the fact that their similarities outweigh their differences, as forged by their common history. This historical connection has been stated in many scholarly studies of frequent canoe voyages between islands that led to the homogenisation of Micronesian cultures and traditions on many islands.[71] Seafaring was the lifeline of Micronesian islanders; it created economic opportunities, enhanced knowledge of space, connected people, strengthened relationships and initiated new alliances.[72] In Micronesia today, travelling between islands continues but with different means of transportation. Modern travelling continues to reproduce Micronesians' shared values and binds Micronesians closer together.

Oral traditions spoke of movements between Kosraens, Pohnpeians, Chuukese and Yapese that reinforced these existing connections. As Oha Uman, a traditional historian from Chuuk, said:

> *ewe samolin Ponpei a nomw a uro pwe epwe eor kinamwe lefilen [aramasan Maikronesia]. A tingei aewan Souariras [wisan epwe chok fori an epwe chok pwepweruk] nganei chuuk. Soukachaw [sou pwera] epe la mas on Kusae ren epe akaula sain Likinikechaw [shon afitikoko seni fanuan Masel] an epe tolong. A tingei Sou Yap [sou safei] Puluwat [Sou fal waa].*[73]

> The *samol lap* [paramount chief] from Pohnpei desired a united people of the Caroline Islands to live together in peace. For that purpose, he sent *souariras* [the great dancer] to Chuuk to teach the people about dancing, and the great warrior called *sou pwera* [the great fighter] to Kosrae to keep outsiders from entering the empire. He also sent *sou safei* [the great medicine man] to Yap to teach the people the art of medicine, and finally the *sou fal waa* [the great canoe builder] to Puluwat.[74]

However, before the *samol* sent his *sou* people to their destinations, he also instructed them to treat all their subjects well in accordance with established customs and traditions. Interaction between the people

---

70   Glenn Petersen, pers. comm., Micronesian Australia Friends Association (MAFA) Workshop, The Australian National University, 12 July 2014.
71   Petersen, *Traditional Micronesian Societies*, pp. 8–12; Joakim Peter, 'Chuukese Travellers', p. 258.
72   The *sawei* system is one example (D'Arcy, *The People of the Sea*, pp. 146–149).
73   Uman, Saladier and Chipen, *Uruon Chuuk*, pp. 1–7.
74   My own translation of *Uruon Chuuk*, pp. 1–7, from Chuukese to English.

between the respective areas under the *sou* was common.[75] For example, if people from *sou safei* needed to learn the art of canoe building, they would travel to the place where *sou fal waa* resided, or vice versa if people from *sou fal waa* needed to learn the art of medicine. As Joakim Peter commented, in the earlier days, frequent voyages between islands were vital to the extended *sou* system; it kept relationships alive and created opportunities for people to interact and learn from each other.[76] This interaction between Micronesians remains in place today but with additional purposes as Micronesians continue to adapt. The ongoing adaptation process binds the indigenous people in contemporary FSM.

Waa and Identity

Waa (canoe) and the *sou fal waa* (master canoe builder) represent an essential element of the Micronesian identity. That is because *waa* has sustained and transported Micronesian ideas across time and space. Specialised skills in canoe building and navigation were central to freedom of movement on the sea, which allowed islanders to restrengthen their connection, identity and continuity. Every island had *sou fal waa*. However, according to the *Uruon Chuuk*, there was a main source from which *sou fal waa* derived their knowledge. From that source, different techniques then emerged on different islands as they competed to create the best canoe model. *Waa* building was not just about cutting down a tree and carving it into a form. The *sou fal waa* had to possess multiple skills and global knowledge in relation to traditions. For example, intimate knowledge of breadfruit trees, carving techniques, special tools, measurement and people's personalities.[77] Knowing people's personalities is essential to the building of canoes as it kept the team together and maintained skills within the extended family circle.

---

75   My own translation of *Uruon Chuuk*, pp. 1–7, from Chuukese to English.
76   Peter, 'Chuukese Travellers', p. 258; Marshall, *Namoluk beyond the Reef*, p. 3.
77   I have experienced this firsthand; being an islander from Lukunor, I learned this from my elders. As a further example, I have also directly observed master canoe builders (*sou fal waa*) possess multiple skills and talents, like chanting, traditional measurement and religious practices. See also William Alkire, 'Technical Knowledge and the Evolution of Political Systems in the Central and Western Caroline Islands of Micronesia', *Canadian Journal of Anthropology*, Vol. 2, No. 2, Winter 1980, pp. 230–231; D'Arcy, *The People of the Sea*, pp. 90–91; Don Rubinstein, 'An Ethnography of Micronesian Childhood: Contexts of Socialisation on Fais Island', PhD thesis, Stanford University, Stanford, California, 1979, p. 54.

Traditional rituals are integral parts of canoe building as they signal the different stages of construction and the order in which the team needs to pay tribute to the ancestral gods to ensure success. For example, during *wiieo* ceremony, held upon the completion of the *waa*, the clan of the master builder, with his invited guests, would celebrate the event.[78] It is an opportune time to display the canoe as a showpiece to the public and allow the larger community to take notice of the clan's achievement. The *itang* (master orator) would participate in this event to bless and praise the clan in its future endeavours.

Each island retains their specific knowledge about *waa* building. There is also an exchange of knowledge between islands when specific canoe designs for specific purposes are sought. For example, D'Arcy noted that even well-resourced high islanders used a variety of methods to retain their ability to build and sail canoes after sustained Western contact.[79] The villagers of Gachpar in Yap, for example, rely heavily on Carolinian seafarers for their knowledge and skills of voyaging. These skills enabled the Yap islanders to continue to sail to Palau and the Philippines.[80]

There are many types of canoe design[81] found in the Caroline Islands, encompassing the modern states of Chuuk, Pohnpei, Kosrae and Yap. However, *ioshol* and *maisuuk* are shared Mortlockese designs. *Maisuuk* are also found in the western part of Chuuk, including the low-lying islands of Yap.[82] *Maisuuk* has the 'V' shape on both ends of the canoe, resembling the tail of the frigate bird and its speed and agility. *Palou* Sitan offered further explanation of the 'V' shape as representing the genitalia of the female body and thus life, fertility and continuity.[83] The body of *maisuuk* is painted in black and red to protect it from becoming waterlogged and the sun's heat, while *ioshol* is painted black in its entirety without the

---

78 *Wiieo* is a community gathering involving a feast and speeches to bless the completion of a canoe in adherence with custom. It is a time to display the pride of the clan's master canoe builder.

79 D'Arcy, *The People of the Sea*, p. 144.

80 Peter Sitan, Interview, 2 January 2011; David Marar, Interview, Nett, Pohnpei, 5 January 2011.

81 *Mai suk* and *ioshol* are different canoe styles. *Mai suk* are bulkier and carry more weight on the sea. *Ioshol* are used for warfare, having greater agility, speed and manoeuvrability. On Lukunor, there was another type of canoe imported from Kapingamarangi called *sain Kirinis* (lit. 'the style imported from Kapingamarangi') (Kamilo Likichimus (master canoe builder from Lukunor), Interview, Weno, Chuuk, 20 June 2013).

82 Peter Sitan, Interview, 2 January 2011.

83 During one of my personal communications with Peter Sitan at The Australian National University on 29 April 2014, he sketched the 'V' shape and exposed it from all angles. When viewed from a distance, at a 90-degrees angle, there emerged a physical imagery of the female body, a sign of sea fertility.

frigate bird tail shape at both ends. In Pohnpei and Kosrae, their present canoes have long outriggers, almost the length of the body,[84] and are used primarily for transportation around the island itself rather than between islands. They do not see the need for long-distance canoes as they are well resourced agriculturally.

Figure 5: *Maisuuk* **sailing canoe often used by some Mortlockese, people in the outer islands of northwest Chuuk and the atoll dwellers in Yap.**
Source: Photograph taken by Donald Rubinstein on Yap in 2015.

The title *palou* (master navigator) epitomises the essence of Micronesian oceanic identity. The title is bestowed upon those who have demonstrated the many qualities and abilities necessary to lead people on voyages far and wide. For instance, a *palou* must have the skills of a negotiator, an astronomer, a master chanter, a charmer, a priest of the high seas, a warrior, and, most of all, a leader with courage and patience.[85] He is almost like an *itang* in terms of the skills and knowledge he possesses and needs to master. No one questions the skills of the *palou* when on the sea as to do so would bring negative consequences. The *palou* still practise their skills and are well regarded in island communities today. Their achievements are celebrated by *po* (admission to the exclusive club for master navigators),

---

84   Segal G. Harvey, *Kosrae: The Sleeping Lady Awakens*, Kosrae Tourist Division, Department of Conservation and Development, Kosrae State Government, FSM, 1989, p. 52.
85   D'Arcy, *The People of the Sea*, p. 80.

especially in the western islands of Chuuk and the low-lying islands of Yap, for example, Pollap and Satawal.[86] In the Mortlocks, *palou* are still around, although no sailing canoes have been constructed since Typhoon Pamela destroyed all existing ones in the Mortlocks in 1975.[87]

Shaping of Identities

The FSM is a collection of many islands with different forms of landscapes, communities and traditions. The physical environment and climate influence the way space is used, conceptualised and given social identity, and also how resources are consumed and conserved. The Micronesian archipelago is made up of three types of islands:[88] volcanic high islands, like the main islands of Pohnpei, Yap, Kosrae, Weno, Fefan and Uman; low-lying atolls, such as Namonenu, Namonuito, Ulithi, Lamotrek, Mokilia and Pingelap; and standalone raised coral islands, such as Nama and Satawal. Typical atolls are encircled by coral reefs with a deep lagoon and enough vegetation to support its dwellers and biosystem, while standalone raised coral islands are completely surrounded by the sea.[89] Atoll islanders are heavily dependent on the sea because of a lack of land. Volcanic islands are typically lush with rich fauna and flora in comparison to the low-lying islands because of the presence of mountains that block moisture-laden winds off the sea, forcing them upwards to condense as rain clouds.[90] The different types of island environments have influenced varying community organisations and social identities.

Island communities are constructed and spread along the shoreline, allowing immediate access to the sea on both high and low islands. The sea provides food and sea life that can be utilised for their medicinal properties, as well as a place to perform religious activities to appease the *anun saat* (sea gods). It is also the place where young people develop and practise their skills in fishing, sailing, martial arts, swimming, weather reading, romance and leisure. All these activities are crucial in the construction of one's 'sense of belonging' to the islands or being a genuine *remetaw*.

---

86 James Naich, pers. comm. (online), 21 August 2013.
87 Jimmy Emilio, pers. comm., 5 January 2013. Jimmy is a descendant of one of the great *palou* of Ettal, Limiroch. However, *palou* Simen also possessed the art of *palou* (D'Arcy, *The People of the Sea*, p. 80).
88 Alkire, *An Introduction to the Peoples and Cultures of Micronesia*, p. 5.
89 Alkire, *An Introduction to the Peoples and Cultures of Micronesia*, p. 5.
90 Darcy, *The People of the Sea*, pp. 13–20.

The sea is also where rites of passage take place, especially for young males. In the past, an example of a rite of passage to enter manhood was a young male having to join a *fauko* (deep sea fish trap) trip where certain rituals had to be performed. His elders had to decide his fate based on his performance of the required *fauko* task. As Felik, a traditional historian once noted, 'the sea is where one is born and returns when one dies'.[91] Once a young male became a man, he was required to sleep in the *ainang's faal* (men's house) until he found a suitable wife. The chosen wife had to come from outside the clan to comply with *eoranei fel* (sacred traditions); that is, avoiding marrying his own female relatives. The *faal* was like the forum where young men undertook further training in traditional curriculum such as martial arts, dancing, mask carving, canoe building, fishing techniques and public oratory.[92] The *ainang* history was taught in detail to orient the young men about their place in the *ainang* diaspora and within the community hierarchy.

It was also a testing time for young men to hone their interests in particular sets of skills to enable them to acquire the title *sou* (lit. 'one who specialised in …'), for example, *sou set* (specialised fishermen), *sou fal waa* (specialised canoe builders) and *sou rong* (expert in traditional medicine and martial arts).[93] Steven Maipi, a former teacher from Lukunor, described what constituted a real man: 'a man must not only possess the skills required by *eoranei*, but must know when to use his internal strength as to when to fight, negotiate, and withdraw'.[94] These principles were played out in relations with outsiders, especially during the Japanese and US occupations, to protect the integrity of Micronesian cultures.

---

91   Felix Naich, or Felik as locals call him, was a historian of Lukunor Island. He was born in the early twentieth century and experienced all the changes on Lukunor Island from the German era to the US Trust Administration. I grew up listening to his histories of the island from settlement, culture and contact with the outside world. In his estimation, knowledge of history gives one identity and stability in life. Explanation of the importance of traditional history is explained generally by William H. Alkire, *Lamotrek Atoll and Inter-Island Socio-Economic Ties*, University of Illinois Press, 1965, pp. 114–119; Hanlon, 'Micronesia: Writing and Rewriting the Histories of a Nonentity', pp. 7–8.

92   Felix Naich, *oral history*. Many of the activities were still practised when I was living on Lukunor, my island home.

93   The term '*sou*' is still used in the Mortlocks to refer to people with specialised skills (Felix Naich and Kamilo Likichimus, *oral history*). I learned the history from Felix and observed Kamilo carving many canoes in the 1960s and 1970s on Lukunor Island. I also interviewed Peter Sitan at The Australian National University on 29 April 2014. The term '*sou*' is also used in Pohnpei to refer to persons with high standing in the community.

94   Steven Maipi was my teacher in the early 1970s. He came from the clan *Sor*. His sub-clan are known to have secret knowledge of paralysing people by placing pressure on specific parts of the human anatomy called *tikifel*. He explained what it means to be a real man in view of our customs and traditions.

In many parts of Micronesia, entering manhood or womanhood is an important event in a person's life as it formalises one's status in the community and creates new networks in the community by virtue of marriage outside the clan.[95] In the past, finding a suitable wife or husband involved one's participation in social events such as traditional *apwarik* (special dances).[96] *Apwarik* could be sponsored by any *samol* of a particular *ainang*. *Apwarik* often took place in the *faal* (clan's community meeting house) owned by the *ainang*. *Apwarik* was a time when relationships formed. The son or daughter of the *samol* who sponsored the *apwarik* had to pick his or her choice of partner first during the *apwarik*. *Apwarik* could take many nights and only ended when the son or daughter of the *samol* found a partner to marry. Others formed relationships during *apwarik* as well. *Apwarik* was important in the life of the community as it facilitated many important activities; it created trade, enhanced religious practices and reinforced connections between local people and others from different islands. For example, people who participated in *apwarik* had to dress up to impress their opposites. The best island attires were worn during the event, such as *urupow* (elaborate feathers), *taek* (turmeric), *lofor* (traditional perfume), *mwaremwar* or *akelet* (leis) and *toor* (traditional lavalava).[97] New dances were invented and *kapasan tong* (love poetry) composed to attract the attention of the intended partner. Many items used during *apwarik* had to be sought from elsewhere. *Wa serek* (sailing canoes) were often sent to far-off destinations to trade for the desired goods and reconnect with distant clan members.[98]

Lamelam (religious) rituals were part of the *apwarik* activities. Opposing parties who competed to win the affection of the most desired partners would call on the assistance of their ancestral gods. *Lofor me tukmaun* (potions) and *ngorongor* (chanting) were used as part of the *apwarik* rituals

---

95 Personal experience. It was explained to me that social behaviours distinguish man from woman, as well as real men from ordinary men. From early childhood, I learned how to behave accordingly.

96 Personal knowledge as taught to me by Felix Naich (oral historian).

97 *Mortlocks Oral History*. *Apwarik* was one of the big events in island life as it brought together young people and, in the process, they formed romantic relationships. The event was also used for displaying one's wealth as imported items were used for bodily decoration. Wealth connects to people's identity and social standing. Religious practices were also used as in *awar* (magic/love potion) See brief comments by Thomas Gladwin, *East is a Big Bird: Navigation and Logic on Puluwat Atoll*, Harvard University Press, Cambridge, Massachusetts, 1970, pp. 61–62. See also Goodenough, *Under the Heaven's Brow*, pp. 26–27.

98 *Mortlocks Oral History*. These Mortlockese economic activities were replicated across the Caroline Islands, especially in and among atoll communities. See e.g. Alkire, *Coral Islanders*, ch. 3, 'Daily Activities', pp. 41–68.

to increase the chances for one to capture the heart of a desired partner. The traditional historian Felik spoke of a popular legend called *pon mosor* (sweet smell of the mosor flowers) where a shy young man always hid outside the *apwarik* venue. The sweet smell of his *mosor mwaremwar* (lei) captured the imagination of the queen of the *apwarik*. The queen followed the smell and immediately fell in love with the shy young man. It was claimed that the *mwaremwar* was a love potion provided by the young man's father, assisted by the hands of an ancestral god.[99]

Continuity Under Threat

Continuity of the human–environmental relations at the heart of Micronesian identity is under threat because of climate change and illegal fishing activities by distant countries. Currently, the national government is undergoing a series of changes to implement strategies to slow down such threats, especially the impact of climate change.[100] The key question directing government strategy is, what is the best method to maintain the health of the environment to sustain Micronesian continuity? Micronesians must fight these threats to safeguard their home islands. Deep historical knowledge and reinforcement of environmental laws, both at the domestic and international level, are essential in the maintenance of the ecological system.[101] Islanders' acute awareness of their aquatic environment has enabled them to plan better for the future. This essentially optimistic local outlook is at odds with the general prognosis for Micronesia's environmental future and community sustainability as the international consensus emphasises only the vulnerability of these Pacific communities. This book seeks to overturn the marginalisation of Micronesians' knowledge of their own environment and ability to self-sustain. Continued misrepresentation has practical and far-reaching contemporary consequences.

Fanou works in sync with *saat*; they provide sustenance, stability, identity and continuity for Micronesians. The land is the provider of the daily intake of carbohydrates, which the sea complements with protein.[102]

---

99   Alkire, *Coral Islanders*, ch. 3.
100 *FSM Climate Change Policy*, Palikir, 2011, pp. 2–3.
101 Lieber, *More Than a Living*, pp. 51–59.
102 Islanders from the Mortlocks always need *salei* (protein, being meat or fish) to eat with taros and breadfruit, for example. A meal consisting only of carbohydrates is considered an impoverished meal.

Applying that concept to a Mortlockese perspective, it means the land provides *mongo* (the daily meal) and the sea provides *salei* (protein) to compliment *mongo*. One's identity is also tied to the land as it is where the *ainang* established its roots, meaning the traditional *faal* system.[103] Any person who is not connected to a *faal* would be considered a stranger from afar. However, strangers are often adopted by *mwalo*, and, as a consequence, new connections are established with the stranger's distant *ainang*.[104] New connections expand familial networks. This is important in contemporary Micronesian political discourse, especially during elections when kinsfolk are called upon to contribute to the campaign process. This in turn reinforces clan identity and networks in the island diaspora. The extended family continue to be the safety net for Micronesians. It is the foundation of the traditional economy to prevent destitution. The extended family system has increased its global connections by virtue of the new diaspora facilitated by the Compact between the FSM and US. This has expanded Micronesian identity and continuity on a global scale.

Figure 6: A clan's *faal* on Lukunor Island.

Note: This style of *faal* is common throughout the Mortlocks region. It is used by men to perform their traditional activities and serves as the meeting place for the clan.

Source: Photograph taken by Amanson Ansin in 2012.

---

103 Alkire, *Lamotrek Atoll*, pp. 28–29.
104 Goodenough, *Under Heaven's Brow*, p. 29.

Community and Gender Relations

Gender roles are typically differentiated by the complexities of the tasks and traditions of each island environment.[105] For example, in the Mortlocks region, male tasks typically involve activities requiring strength such as climbing trees, carrying heavy loads, diving, canoe building and long-distance sailing.[106] Females are assigned tasks that are considered light, such as cooking, caring for children, gathering firewood and weaving. However, there are tasks shared by both the sexes such as scraping coconuts, gathering firewood and tending the gardens. In the western part of Chuuk, cooking, seashell gathering and collecting taros are female tasks. It is also noted that, in many of the outer islands, fishing tasks are specifically assigned to males while women perform land-based tasks.[107]

However, the gendered division of labour does not mean males always have the dominant power because of physical strength. In some communities, females wield power because they control the land and maintain the clanship system where one's identity is rooted. It is also noted that gender relations are also changing because of certain features of the modern economic system, which is affecting power relations because of differences in performance in the modern education system and employment market.

Community Structure

The basic unit of an island community in the Mortlock Islands is *inepwinou* (father, mother and their children) followed by *mwalo* (sister of the same great grandmother and all their offspring). The size of each *mwalo* depends on the number of children of the sisters. Different *mwalo* are part of an *oushamw* (belonging to the *mwalo*) who share the same *faal*, which is made up a branch of an *ainang*. Members of *mwalo* share their

105 Francis X. Hezel, Edwin Q. P. Petteys and Deborah L. Chang, 'Sustainable Human Development in the FSM. Chapter 2: The People and Their Cultures', micsem.org/pubs/articles/economic/shd/frames/chapter02fr.htm.
106 Alkire, *An Introduction to the Peoples and Cultures of Micronesia*, pp. 45–46; Lingenfelter, *Yap*, pp. 19–29; Goodenough, *Under Heaven's Brow*, p. 26.
107 Alkire, *An Introduction to the Peoples and Cultures of Micronesia*, pp. 45–46; D'Arcy, *The People of the Sea*, p. 177; Lingenfelter, *Yap*, pp. 19–29; Descantes Christophe, 'Integrating Archaeology and Ethnohistory: The Development of Exchange Between Yap and Ulithi, Western Caroline Islands (Micronesia)', PhD thesis, UMI Dissertation Services, Ann Arbor, Michigan, 1998, pp. 71–72.

pei lap (estate). Each island has different *ainang*, ranked in order of their arrival.[108] Membership of an *ainang* is automatically inherited, with all the ascribed rights and privileges. The extent of an *ainang* diaspora is dependent on the *ainang's* own history. For example, in many parts of the FSM, each of these *ainang* link to a greater network dispersed throughout a designated geographical space and beyond.[109] When one arrives on an island for the first time, the question always asked of the visitor is, '*ia omw ainang or an semomw ainang?*' ('What is your clan or father's clan?'). This is to enable the receiving islanders to connect the visitor to their kinsfolk.[110]

Aterenges is the next level up, which constitutes relatives from both sides of the parents. Membership in the father's clan is *afaker* (honorary member), though with lesser rights to the father's clan properties. Members of the father's *ainang* have duties and obligations to defend their *afaker* when under threat. *Afaker* are treated with marked respect by their father's clan. For example, *afaker* can go unpunished if consuming food on the father clan's land while in different parts of an island.[111]

The *uruo* of each *ainang* is used to establish the history of each island in the FSM.[112] *Ainang* connects identity to locality and other places in a region. For example, the *ainang Sor* is widespread throughout the region of Chuuk and the low-lying islands of Yap, as Alkire suggested in his study of Lamotrek.[113] This is one of the biggest *ainang* in a wider region. The origins of other clans began in the Chuuk lagoon and extend to Pohnpei and Kosrae as suggested by oral narratives. Rauchholz noted that in pre-colonial times, there was contact between the different Trukic communities through 'family connection and commerce'.[114]

---

108 Alkire, *Lamotrek Atoll*, p. 29; *Oral history* of Lukunor Island.
109 Clan connection is now more widespread within the FSM as people are allowed (or able?) to migrate between the four states.
110 Alkire, *An Introduction to the Peoples and Cultures of Micronesia*, pp. 46–47; Rubinstein, 'An Ethnography of Micronesian Childhood', p. 90. I personally experienced this when I travelled in the Mortlocks, the Chuuk lagoon and Pohnpei.
111 *Afaker* are special to the father's clan as it is the duty of the father to protect his children (Duane, *Clan and Copra*, p. 91).
112 David Damas, *Bountiful Island: A Study of Land Tenure on a Micronesian Island*, Wilfrid Laurier University Press, Canada, 1994, pp. 18–19; David Hanlon, *Upon a Stone Altar: A History of the Island of Pohnpei to 1890*, University of Hawai'i Press, Honolulu, 1988, pp. 7–9.
113 Alkire, *An Introduction to the Peoples and Cultures of Micronesia*, p. 42 (the clans called *Saur* in Yap and *Sor* in Chuuk); Marshall, *Namoluk beyond the Reef*, p. 35; Manuel Rauchholz, 'Notes on Clan Histories and Migration in Micronesia', *Pacific Asia Inquiry*, Vol. 2, No. 1, Fall 2011, pp. 57–59.
114 Rauchholz, 'Notes on Clan Histories and Migration in Micronesia', p. 53.

Political power on each island resides with the *makal* of *ainang* who represent the first settlers; the *ainang* control land and the reef by virtue of being the first residents. The *makal* allocated ownership of land and the reef to subsequent clans who, in turn, passed on their properties through the generations. The *makal* are still recognised as the traditional spokesperson for each island, especially in the Mortlocks region. Today, the clanship network system is still in full swing and central to the Micronesian sense of social identity. The *ainang* system is a security network that constantly dislodged foreign elements that purported to rupture the longstanding Micronesian traditional societies. *Ainang* is the basis of economic production, which sustains the various social identities, which in turn collectively feeds into the larger pool of the present Micronesian sense of identity.

The inhabitants of the volcanic island of Pohnpei have developed a different social system in comparison to those found on the low-lying islands in Chuuk and Yap. Pohnpei's social structure is highly stratified, with five districts headed by a paramount chief called the *Nanmwarkhi*.[115] His 'spokesperson', the *Nahniken*,[116] is chosen from the second-ranking clan in each district. *Nahnmwarki* and *Nahniken* sit at the apex of the social pyramid, with their subordinates and the untitled people below them.[117] Their subordinates are assigned specific community tasks and maintain the specific structure of the social order. During *kamadhipw* (community feast), social ranks are displayed by the order of where individuals are seated and served in the *nahs* (traditional meeting place). The public members observe everyday rituals, especially during *kamadhipw* (feasts) where they pay their dues to the *Nahnmwarkhi* by contributing *sakau*, pigs, yams, fish and other items appropriate for the *kamadhipw*.

In the low-lying islands in Yap and Chuuk, the social structure is less stratified, with the *samol* or *tamol* responsible for each clan or sub-clan.[118] Their ranks are noted during *mweishen fanou* (island meeting). In Kosrae, the highest chiefs are called *Tokosra* (the sacred chief) and *Kanka* (secular chief).[119]

---

115 Petersen, *Traditional Micronesian Societies*, p. 144; Alkire, *An Introduction to the Peoples and Cultures of Micronesia*, pp. 60–63; Hanlon, *Upon a Stone Altar*, p. 354.
116 Petersen, *Traditional Micronesian Societies*, p. 144; Alkire; *An Introduction to the Peoples and Cultures of Micronesia*, pp. 60–63; Hanlon, *Upon a Stone Altar*, p. 354.
117 Hezel, Petteys and Chang, 'Sustainable Human Development in the FSM', micsem.org/pubs/articles/economic/shd/frames/chapter03fr.htm.
118 *Samol* is used in many parts of Chuuk, while *Tamol* is used in the outer islands of Yap.
119 Petersen, *Traditional Micronesian Societies*, p. 132.

Survival mechanisms in the FSM, both intra- and inter-island, are premised on the principle of reciprocity. At both levels, individuals assist each other when the need arises, for example, in the erection of *faal*, building of canoes and agricultural activities that require a large number of people. An individual may volunteer to trade his labour in exchange for a particular item from the other person or may be obliged to assist due to familial ties. The volunteer will, in return, expect the recipient of such labour to reciprocate when the need for future work arises, thus triggering the stimulus and response cycle.[120] This model underscores the foundation of economic modes of production in traditional Micronesian societies and further protects members of the community from exploitation.[121] This practice has continued through successive colonial periods to the present day. However, it must be remembered that the strength of traditional practices varies between the port towns and the distant islands because of the former's exposure to external influences, particularly the market economy.[122]

Colonisation has also influenced labour relations and property transactions between people. This was particularly true after WWII, when Micronesia was slowly integrated into the capitalist economy under the US.[123] Money was increasingly used as mode of exchange. Its power interfered with the existing reciprocal system, especially in the port towns where labourers were paid in cash rather than returning favours. Land, labour and Western commodities can also be bought with money, especially by the new, small business class. Money found its way into the local system during the colonisation period, but many people are mindful about its effect on communities.[124] For example, many people at the village level continue to work by the *ainang* system as it has proven many times over to be a safety net. Money does have its own value but is

---

120 David Labby, *The Demystification of Yap: Dialectics of Culture on a Micronesian Island*, University of Chicago Press, 1976, p. 20.

121 My personal experience, which includes reciprocating in village activities such as *apwipwi* (working together in a team and taking turns working each team members' land) on the taro farms.

122 Gonzaga Puas, *Labour Standards in the FSM*, FSM Department of Justice, Palikir, 12 April 2005, pp. 3–4.

123 Hanlon, *Remaking Micronesia*, pp. 73–83.

124 When I was growing up on the islands, dried copra were sold to field trip ships in return for cash. Goods were then bought and distributed within the extended family as the copra were collected from the family land. See also Marshall, *Namoluk beyond the Reef*, pp. 31–32; Labby, *The Demystification of Yap*, p. 8.

controlled by the external world. The Micronesian identity thus reflects the social dynamics of the FSM. It constantly negotiates itself in response to changes in the global system.

However, this is not to say that the social disruption brought about by the influence of the outside world has completely obliterated the Micronesian social safety net mechanism. For example, emigration, education and the legal system are playing their parts to suppress the tide of societal disruption, as alluded to in Hezel's studies. Emigration, both internally and internationally, has created more opportunities for many islanders to relocate to different places, creating a new outlet by which to understand the globalised world.[125] The educational system, especially the College of Micronesia, is equipping the new generation with the means to understand and live successfully in the new world.[126]

The style of governance at the three levels of government has allowed the new generation to engage in the democratic process. Varieties of youth and community groups have expanded in large numbers throughout the nation, thus giving rise to more opportunities for the younger generation to assist each other to be better citizens, both at the community level and through collaborating with other international youth groups. The expanding numbers of indigenous people with college degrees from many parts of the world and the perpetual rearticulation of the extended family system in the FSM is testimony to how the people have reversed the image of the FSM as the suicide capital of the world.

The Environment

Fanou and *saat* provide the basis for identity and continuity. In the pre-colonial period, the management of resources was community-based, owned and jointly managed by members of the extended *ainang*[127] (clan) or *mwalo* (sub-clan). This form of *alilis fengen* (caring for each other) and *eaea fengen* (sharing resources) bind the *ainang* members together as

---

125 *Micronesia Forum*, www.micronesiaforum.org/.
126 *Micronesia Forum*, www.micronesiaforum.org/.
127 *Ainang* is the clanship network system that has effectively been the foundation of Micronesian identity. It is one of the most important concepts to understand as we cannot comprehend the full extent of FSM history without it. Leaders continue to use this network to maintain socio-political connections (Petersen, *Traditional Micronesian Societies*, p. 23).

a social unit.[128] *Ainang* is a large extended family identified by the physical space they share with relatives in a local area or within the diaspora. Food production has always been a collective enterprise that connects the *mwalo* or *ainang*.[129] Micronesians have lived in close harmony with their *fanou* and *saat* for centuries, managing the resources to ensure continuity for future generations. Disharmony arose when the production and use of natural resources was out of kilter, for example, when recalcitrant clans sought to reorder the control of resources in territory they were not historically entitled to.

The economy and society are interconnected by the aforementioned principles, which in turn contribute to the conservation of resources. Traditional methods of environmental management are still in practice today. They include *pwau, otoul, mwanmei* and *unupwel* (restriction and offerings of coconuts, breadfruit and taro). Many of these practices are also common (but with different terms) in the Micronesian region, such as in Yap, Pohnpei and Kosrae.[130] Moreover, conservation techniques varied as these are dependent on the topography and seascape of each island.[131] For example, in the low-lying islands, *pwau* is the most effective method of conservation, restricting human activities from degrading fragile parts of the coral reef and the land along the seashores.

During *lerak*, the summer season (usually from May to September), restrictions on taro consumption may have been imposed on members of a clan by its *samol* (traditional leader). Such restrictions allowed taro to grow fully as they take three years to mature. Also, during *lerak*, when breadfruits are in abundance, members of each *mwalo* would band together to harvest them and store them underground where they ferment, preserving the breadfruit—called *mar*—for later use.[132] Restriction of movement between villages was another way to ensure maintenance of a

---

128 Marshall, 'The Structure of Solidarity', p. 55.

129 *Eaea/alilis fengen* is the principle of sharing to promote continuity (Marshall, 'The Structure of Solidarity', p. 62). For land sharing, see Petersen, *Traditional Micronesian Societies*, pp. 77–78.

130 Rubinstein, 'An Ethnography of Micronesian Childhood', p. 52; Knudson, 'Resource Fluctuation', pp. 194–195.

131 Lingenfelter, *Yap*, pp. 5–17; Margie V. Cushing Falanruw, 'Food Production and Ecosystem Management in Yap', *ISLA: A Journal of Micronesian Studies*, Vol. 2, No. 1, Rainy Season 1994, pp. 11–18; Bill Raynor, 'Resource Management of Upland Forests of Pohnpei: Past Practices and Future Possibilities', *ISLA: A Journal of Micronesian Studies*, Vol. 2, No. 1, Rainy Season 1994, pp. 49–64.

132 *Mar* is an important food item specially eaten during the *lefang* months. Relatives from the mother's side usually share the *mar*.

clan's resources. For example, members of village A may not enter village B without prior permission. This is to prevent wanderers from damaging the land or helping themselves to the resources on someone else's land.

According to oral history, coral rocks were arranged in such a way so as to facilitate the natural flow of currents and patterns of waves to minimise shore erosion. Planting of native plants such as *rakish* (seaoaks), *fash* (pandanus), *mosor* (guettarda speciosa) and *shia* (mangrove) a few feet from the shorelines was another method used, with rocks and heavy debris used to fill the gap between the shore and the native plants. This was a form of local adaptation and a mitigation strategy developed to strengthen the shorelines where they were susceptible to erosion and damage from currents and waves.[133] Since colonisation, the landscape has been altered to accommodate the needs of outsiders in the forms of docks and seawalls. This has created more problems in managing the seascape and shore erosion. Outsiders' lack of knowledge of the environment and their ignorance of local knowledge to facilitate the proper installation of the seawalls and docks are the main problems that have persisted into the post-colonial period.

These problems have been re-evaluated along with the new compound threat of climate change. Climate change is a new phenomenon caused by industrialised countries in distant lands, yet its impact is felt in the island environment. It is altering the integrity of the fragile environment, especially in the low-lying atolls. To this end, new seawall design is being used as a defence mechanism to prevent breach erosion due to climate change.[134] Moreover, traditional methods have been combined with outside engineering methods. The complementary nature of historical understanding of the environment and the use of compatible modern technology is an ongoing process, as discussed in Chapter 6.

The Constitution safeguards traditional methods of conservation of the FSM's territorial sea as recognised by international law. It also incorporates modern practices compatible with traditions. An example of this can be

---

133 Marion Henry (FSM Secretary of Resources and Development), Interview, Palikir, Pohnpei, 5 July 2013.
134 Between 22 and 26 June 2013, I travelled to Kosrae and observed a new seawall design. It promoted local adaptation to climate change using appropriate forms of technology borrowed from the outside world. The FSM's climate change policy promotes integration of modern technology to be used in the nation. See *Nationwide Climate Change Policy 2009: The Federated States of Micronesia*, 14 December 2009, p. 2.

seen in the allocation of the nation's resources between the municipality, state and national governments. For instance, marine space between these respective jurisdictions is clearly defined; ownership of reefs by different clans is acknowledged in the constitutions of the states of Yap and Chuuk. Municipalities control the areas around the reefs, often using the traditional methods of *pwau* to conserve the sea and land environment, while the states are responsible for conservation outside the municipal border to the 12-mile zone. The national government has conservational jurisdiction from the 12-mile zone to the 200-mile EEZ.[135]

Religious Practices

Lamelamen eoranei (traditional religious practices) are an integral part of Micronesian self-assurance, control and continuity. Religious practices formalised people's relationship with the environment and each other throughout history. For example, environmental conservation practices command people to treat and respect nature since it provides sustenance for life. Sacred places, such as designated special spaces, rocks, trees and places on the reef, have meaningful historical value,[136] as may be explained by the narratives of the different clans. For example, each designated space may honour the sacredness of the ancestors to that clan. Sacredness connotes restriction of access to the land and the reef, which is reserved for the members of that clan only, referred to as *aan shon ainang* (designated area for a particular clan or sub-clan).[137] People respect these reserved areas, as to dishonour such would mean violence between the extended families of the perpetrators and the guardians of the sacred areas. Respect helps maintain equilibrium between people of different clans and the environment. As in the popular traditional saying, '*liwini ngeni pwal neningeni*' (lit. 'one good turn deserves another').

---

135 *The Constitution of the Federated States of Micronesia*, Article I; *Chuuk v. Secretary of Finance*, 8 FSM Intrm. 353 (Pon. 1998).
136 Each clan sets the value and the significance of its designated spaces. It also demands that the public observe such significance. Conflict could arise from disrespecting a space's sacredness.
137 Reinforcement of sacred spaces is not confined to the clan members only, but also includes obligated *afaker* and non-clan relatives.

To seek assistance from the *leeo* (ancestral gods), *waitawa*[138] (communication between the ancestors and the living that involved the spokesperson entering into a trance of spiritual possession) is used as a medium of communication between the people and their *leoo*. The *leoo's* wisdom protects the environment by establishing the norms of conduct for the people as custodians of *fanou* (land) and *saat* (sea). Traditional concepts such as *roong* (life science), *maniman* (spiritual power), *sou safei* (medicine person), *eoranei* (traditions), *anulap* (the big god) and *anukis* (the lesser gods) are integral parts of Micronesian religious doctrines as embedded[139] in each clan's history.

Offerings are part of religious practices to ensure the ongoing special relationship between the ancestors and the people. For example, *oneiset* (first offering of fish), *mwanmei* (first offering of breadfruit), *otoul* (first offering of coconuts) and *wenipwel* (first offering of taros) are deep gestures to thank the ancestors for keeping the land and sea productive. These offerings are taken to the clan's chief, the living mediator between the clan and its *samol*. It also signifies the clan's appreciation of the public's respect in relation to the doctrine of *pwau*, which effectively allows the land or reef to recover.[140] The above connection between religious and conservation methods are still practised today. Reflecting the importance of religious practices, the Constitution recognises them as inherent fundamental rights[141] of the Micronesian people.

The extent of 'Micronesianising'[142] foreign religion can be well understood in connection to Christianity. Christianity is an alien religion, yet Micronesians have integrated it into their religious practices.[143] Micronesians inserted their own religious ideology into the

---

138 Goodenough, *Property, Kin and Community on Truk*, p. 55. Note that Goodenough used different spellings of the word '*waitawa*' (his version is '*waitawa*') but it is the same religious concept. Similarly, he used different spellings for many Chuukese words, some of which are unfamiliar to me. See also Francis X. Hezel, 'Possession and Trance in Chuuk', *ISLA: A Journal of Micronesian Studies*, Vol. 2, No. 1, 1995, www.micsem.org/pubs/articles/socprobs/frames/posstranfr.htm.

139 Religion in traditional societies was patterned along *ainang's* own *anulap* and *anukis*. This continues to be the case in many local communities in the modern FSM. See Alkire, *An Introduction to the Peoples and Cultures of Micronesia*, pp. 17–18; Francis X. Hezel, 'Spirit Possession in Chuuk: A Socio-Cultural Interpretation', *Micronesian Seminar*, Pohnpei, 1991, www.micsem.org/pubs/articles/socprobs/frames/spiritposschkfr.htm.

140 Personal knowledge. See also D'Arcy, *The People of the Sea*, pp. 98–99.

141 *The Constitution of the Federated States of Micronesia*, Articles IV and V.

142 'Mironesianising' refers to the process of incorporating outside influences into a Micronesian context.

143 Joakim Peter, 'Eram's Church (Bell)', pp. 282–285.

womb of Christianity and, over time, this gave birth to what I coin as 'Micronesianity'. Micronesianity is the appropriation of Christianity by Micronesians. Micronesianity perpetuates social cohesion through religious and community relations. For example, the use of *awosiwos*[144] is practised to receive favourable outcomes from both the traditional and Christian god in times of conflict or self-doubt. The gods share the same religious space.

Figure 7: An example of 'Micronesianity'.

Note: Here, a statue of Jesus Christ stands at the edge of Lukunor's channel, where the spirits of the ancestors continue to live in the environment—they are sharing the same space.

Source: Photograph taken by Jocelyn Rayphand in June 2014.

Freedom to practise one's belief system has long been a part of Micronesian history, as may be seen in each clan's practices. This is recognised by the Constitution and the FSM's legal codes. As declared in Article IV, Section 2 of the Constitution, 'no law may be passed respecting an establishment of religion or impairing the free exercise of religion'.[145] Section 207 of the FSM Code Title 42 states that:

> Nothing in this (title) shall be interpreted to preclude the practice of, or require medical health care licenses for, the traditional healing arts as customarily employed by citizens of the Federated States of Micronesia.[146]

---

144 *Awosuwos* is a form of traditional psychological warfare through subtle performance or songs with hidden meanings to call for spiritual support from both the ancestors and the Christian god.

145 *The Constitution of the Federated States of Micronesia.*

146 *FSM Code Title 42*, fsmlaw.org/fsm/code/index.htm.

Healing is part of Micronesian religious practices. It involves calling upon the *leoo* to assist in curing social and physical ailments,[147] for example. In this respect, traditional religious practices also serve to reinforce for social relationships.

Social Organisation

Social organisation reflects the different units of community present on each island or group of islands as patterned along the different *ainang* system. The *ainang* is a kin-based unit usually translated as a clan designed to perpetuate both local and regional continuity; it centres on social relations. *Shon ainang*[148] (members of the clan) naturally inherited their identity first from the mother's[149] *ainang* and second by the father's *ainang*. In Chuuk, and in some parts of Yap and Pohnpei, matrilineality is more dominant, but one is also connected to the father's clan as an *afaker*.[150] This dual membership passes on rights and obligations to the next generation. This in turn maintains connection with one's relatives and allocates one's rank in the islands' *ainang* system.

The degree of obligation upon individual members depends on their social position in the clan. At a minimum, one is expected to be loyal in order to have access to the *ainang's* economic resources and social status. Each member is required to defend the integrity of the clan. The people of each island created their own customary laws to safeguard their resources. The differences in social organisations are most notable between volcanic and low-lying islands. This also affected the way islanders responded to each other within the Micronesian archipelagos. For example, islanders on the small coral islands do not share many of the customs practised by islanders on the mountainous islands such as Yap, Pohnpei and Kosrae, which are more socially hierarchical because of their comparatively large land mass and greater population.[151]

---

147 According to oral history, *ruup* (yaws skin disease) was common throughout the islands in the Mortlocks and beyond. It is not known what the remedy for this skin disease was. Oral history spoke of magic men who tested the power of their magic or potion to lure beautiful women to clean the men's diseased skin.

148 *Shon ainang* means one's membership in a clan (Marshall, 'The Structure of Solidarity', p. 62).

149 As most Micronesians societies are matrilineal, the mother's clan identity is one's prime identity.

150 *Afaker* means one's associate membership in the father's clan. For more details, see Marshall, 'The Structure of Solidarity', pp. 94–95.

151 Petersen, *Traditional Micronesian Societies*, pp. 130–132.

The *ainang* system is not confined to one locale but is spread across different islands depending on their historical connection—common ancestry, marriage and trading partners. In the high volcanic islands like Pohnpei and Yap, social and political relationships are more stratified, with a greater degree of recognised hierarchy between clans (close knit and interrelated families) and lineage (a common ancestor), as in the *Nahnmwarki*[152] and *sawei* systems of Pohnpei and Yap, respectively.

In contrast, the smaller social units in the outer islands of modern-day Yap, Chuuk and Pohnpei rely on their own internal hierarchy of clans within their particular island and their inter-island relatives based largely on who arrived first, reflecting the pattern of settlement of each island or group of islands.[153] Disputes between opposing parties are referred to the social units within the local system or the larger social units between islands, depending on the complexity of the issues. For instance, stealing of coconuts would be dealt with by the heads of the village families, while killing would be dealt with between opposing clans in the islands' diaspora. However, in the modern-day FSM, a blend of the old and new is used to resolve disputes. One can choose whether to use the court system or traditional options of settlement.[154] Often, *ainang* leaders have roles in the arbitration of disputes between opposing parties. Traditionally, compensation for damages depended on the nature of the injury and the cultural geography where the injuries occurred.[155] For example, for offences such as personal injuries and property damage, the recompense was measured in material dues proportionate to the pain and suffering experienced by the victim, or the extent of injury or damage. The goal of dispute resolution was to maintain cohesion between the social entities of Micronesia.

In some instances, public shaming of the perpetrator was also warranted. However, the occurrence of a death was a complex and sensitive issue between the families of both the victim and the perpetrator. Sometimes, retribution was the only way to resolve the breach, but that had the effect of

---

152 *Nahnmwarki* is the paramount chief of the chiefdoms in Pohnpei. See Hanlon, *Upon a Stone Altar*, p. 366.

153 Personal knowledge. This is enshrined in *The Constitution of the Federated States of Micronesia*, Article XI.

154 Michael Lieber, *Using Custom in a Court of Law*, Association of Social Anthropologists in Oceania (ASAO) Conference, San Antonio, Texas, 5–7 February 2012, pp. 1–12.

155 *FSM v Mudong*, 1 FSM Intrm. 135 (Pon. 1982), fsmlaw.org/fsm/decisions/index.htm.

escalating into a vicious cycle of violence.[156] The modern legal system may interfere to prevent further violence. Violence may be confined to a local area, or could spread to a wider geographical space by dint of families' extended relations on other islands by virtue of marriage or clan connection.

In the past, revenge could restore peace when one side acknowledged defeat;[157] it was seen as a form of honouring the so-called victor. Land giving, gifting and surrendering of fishing rights to the victors were also practices used to restore peace in the community.[158] Many of these practices are still used in Micronesia but with their own subtleties. *Shon liken* (outsiders) may find it hard to comprehend customary laws in contemporary Micronesia as such understanding requires a deep connection with the local community. It is my contention that the same deep-seated continuity in traditional Micronesian societies has served as both a stabilising influence in times of external disruption and a confounder for external commentators and administrators attempting to understand the driving forces within Micronesian society.

The Law

As history is about continuity of identity, ownership of resources and relations between clans, *allik* (laws) were also needed to maintain order in the island communities. *Allik* were expressed in religious activities and environmental conservation practices and reinforced by the different social organisations as in the clan system.[159] History demonstrates the overall modes of conduct embedded in traditions as being upheld by the leaders of the different clans and their people. For example, contests over ownership of resources are often scrutinised by clan leaders. Their knowledge of history is treated as evidence. Evidence is put forth by retelling one's own history and how a clan fits into the overall socio-political structure of an island or group of islands. Final decisions are rendered by

---

156 Duane, *Clan and Copra*, pp. 141–142; Stephen M. Younger, 'Violence and Warfare in the Pre-contact Caroline Islands', *The Journal of the Polynesian Society*, Vol. 118, No. 2, June 2009, pp. 144–146. I also have personal knowledge of this, being a member of my clan *Sor* and connected to other relatives on different islands in the FSM, for example, the Mortlocks, Chuuk and Pohnpei states.

157 Goodenough, *Property, Kin and Community on Truk*, pp. 51–52.

158 Surrendering of land and/or reef to victims of violent death, called *shap* or *liwinen sha* (blood payment), is common in many Micronesian societies, and there are many oral histories that can attest to this. See also Goodenough, *Property, Kin and Community on Truk*, pp. 52–54.

159 *Mortlocks Oral History*; Francis X. Hezel, 'Congries of Spirit: The Meaning of Religion', *Micronesian Seminar*, Pohnpei, 1995, www.micsem.org/pubs/articles/religion/frames/congspiritsfr.htm.

the clans' historians, who are usually in a leadership role, and this system is often accepted as being the best mechanism of settling a dispute.[160] In my youth, I witnessed this form of dispute resolution. A particular clan claimed part of a reef as its property based on the traditional concept of *shoon wok* (reward for spears after a fight). When this claim was put under historical scrutiny, most of the historians from other clans disagreed with it. The claimant did not pursue the matter further as to do so would bring shame to the claimant. Even if it went through the court system, it was guaranteed that it would be a hopeless case as the court would also rely on the evidence from the historians of other clans.

Historically, food security reinforced clanship solidarity and has always been a major part of Micronesian conservation laws, particularly in the low-lying islands where the need to protect limited resources is foremost. *Pwau* (traditional law banning human activities) is an effective traditional conservation practice that restricts the harvesting of fish in certain areas of the reef.[161] *Pwau* serves two purposes: to honour the death of an important person in the clan and conserve the reef's resources by way of public announcement.[162] For example, when an important member of the clan who owns the reef dies, *pwau* is automatically imposed. Publicly announced *pwau* is also imposed when the clan decides to close the reef during the windy season. A big tree branch called *shell* is planted in the designated area to warn the public to stay away from the reef. The restriction is ended when the branch is removed. The community respects this form of conservation method as it benefits the island population as a whole.

Any violation of the *pwau* may lead to severe consequences including violence or even death. Oral history speaks of violent fights between the members of clans who imposed *pwau* and the violators and their relatives.[163] The violators suffered serious injuries. The dispute ended when the heads of the two opposing clans came together for settlement. *Pwau* is also practised on the land by *sou fanou* (land owners). In this

---

160 *Lukunor Oral History*; Personal knowledge from direct observation; Lieber, *More Than a Living*, pp. 4–12.
161 *Lukunor Oral History*; Personal knowledge.
162 I have personal experience of this, having routinely accompanied my father when imposing such a restriction by planting a big branch of a tree on the reef belonging to his clan, *Sofa*. See also D'Arcy, *The People of the Sea*, pp. 98–100.
163 *Lukunor Oral History*. An example would be Anaun Lengashu (a sub-clan chief of Lukunor), who gave away a big reef as a *shap* (payment of blood) to his wife's clan as he was so upset about the treatment of his young son who was killed by Anaun Lengashu's sister for breaching *pwau*. It is claimed that the reef was approximately the size of the area where the currents had carried the blood of the victim.

practice, coconut fronds are tied around a tree or the entrance to the land area to indicate that *pwau* is currently imposed. Uninhabited islands, or parts thereof, are subject to the same restrictive measures by the clan who has the traditional rights and duties as the guardians of the land. Land *pwau* fulfils the same purposes as discussed above in relation to owners of a reef. These traditional methods are examples of the laws of the land recognised by the Constitution.

The FSM is a nation with many unique forms of custom and traditions[164] that differ between its geographical spaces.[165] The variety of traditions should not be seen as an impediment to its internal coherence but, rather, a pool of shared ideas from a socio-political basket with a common goal that is resilient enough to accommodate diversity.[166] Indeed, the *Shulapan allik* (Constitution) embodies the concept of unity in diversity.[167] It is the hallmark of the modern state of the FSM and provides the framework in which the country's institutions are linked to Micronesian values, identity and continuity.

As stated in the Preamble:

> We affirm our common wish to live together in peace and harmony, to preserve the heritage of the past, and to protect the promise of the future. To make one nation of many islands, we respect the diversity of our cultures. Our differences enrich us.[168]

The preservation of heritage is protected by Article V: 'nothing in this Constitution takes away the role or function of traditional leaders as recognised by customs and traditions'.[169] Article XI, Section 11 reinforces Article V by declaring:

> Court decisions shall be consistent with this Constitution, Micronesian customs and traditions, and the social configuration of Micronesia. In rendering a decision, the Court must consult and apply sources of the [FSM].[170]

---

164 'Custom and traditions' are called *facsin* in Kosrae, *tiahk* in Pohnpei, *eoranei* in Chuuk, and *yalen* or *kafal fuluy* in Yap. See Petersen, 'Regime Change and Regime Maintenance', p. 40.
165 D'Arcy, 'Cultural Divisions and Island Environments', pp. 217–218.
166 Mac Marshall, '"Partial Connections": Kinship and Social Organisations in Micronesia', in *American Anthropology in Micronesia: An Assessment*, edited by Robert C. Kiste and Mac Marshall, University of Hawai'i Press, 1999, pp. 107–108.
167 *The Constitution of the Federated States of Micronesia*, Preamble.
168 *The Constitution of the Federated States of Micronesia*.
169 *The Constitution of the Federated States of Micronesia*.
170 *The Constitution of the Federated States of Micronesia*.

The *Shulapan allik* is connected to the globalised world as referred to in 'the Declaration of Rights' enumerated under Article IV, Sections 1–13. Articles VII–XII are structured to approximate traditional political values based on geography. For example, Article VII establishes a three-layered government and their respective branches, and allocates their roles and functions within a Micronesian context. These layers correspond to the configuration of Micronesia while integrating relevant elements of the outside world.[171] Articles VIII and IX limit the government's arbitrary power; inherent in this are the parallel powers of traditional leaders and those of present-day political leaders. The construction, scope and content of the Constitution focuses on the unique interaction between law and custom in the modern world to ensure continuity. It says, 'With this Constitution we, who have been the wards of other nations, become the proud guardian of our islands, now and forever'.[172] Nevertheless, the Constitution, by definition, is the supreme law of the land.[173]

Characterising FSM the Economy

Three theories have been proposed to describe the economic situation in the Pacific, including the FSM. It is often hoped that such theories will provide answers to improve small island economies. The three models are MIRAB (migration, remittance, aid and bureaucracy), SITEs (small islands tourist economies) and PROFIT (people considerations, resource management, overseas engagement, finance, insurance and taxation, and transportation). MIRAB emphasises foreign aid, transnational migration and remittances (where money and goods are remitted from metropolitan countries), often from the former colonial powers, to sustain small island economies like the FSM.[174] The SITEs model refers to tourism as having a dominant role in the building of island economies. SITEs aims to 'increase foreign exchange earnings to finance imports'.[175] The PROFIT model is geared towards shrewd immigration and cyclical migration policy. It aims

---

171 Dennis Yamase, *The Supreme Court of the Federated States of Micronesia: The First Twenty-five Years*, FSM Supreme Court, Palikir, Pohnpei, 12 July 2006, fsmsupremecourt.org/fsm/rules/FSMSupCt25YrsforPDF.pdf; *The Constitution of the Federated States of Micronesia*.

172 *The Constitution of the Federated States of Micronesia*, Preamble.

173 *The Constitution of the Federated States of Micronesia*, Article II.

174 Paul D'Arcy, 'The Nourishing Sea: Partner Guardianship of Fishery and Seabed Mineral Resources for the Economic Viability of Small Pacific Island Nations', *Sustainability*, Vol. 5, No. 8, pp. 33–48.

175 Riaz Shareef, *Small Islands Tourism Economies: A Snapshot of Country Risk Ratings*, Department of Economics, University of Western Australia, Perth, Australia, p. 2, www.mssanz.org.au/MODSIM03/Volume_03/B05/04_Shareef_Snapshot.pdf.

for domestic control of local resources through political processes to secure and control viable means of transportation, and through luring foreign direct investment by offering low or no taxes.[176] It thrives on the use of intensive diplomacy to achieve purposeful outcomes. It has low reliance on aid and remittances to sustain local incomes and focuses on strong financial management.[177]

The FSM economy has been characterised as mirroring the MIRAB model. This is because the FSM lacks sustained tourism, has no mineral resources, has weak financial control and its diplomacy (especially as practised in the PROFIT model) is constrained by the terms of the Compact. In alignment with the MIRAB model, the Compact allows Micronesians to migrate to and work in the US. They subsequently remit money and goods to their families on the islands. The Compact also finances the FSM government bureaucracy, the main employer in the FSM.[178] In my field interviews with government officials, many had not heard of and did not understand the MIRAB model. However, those familiar with MIRAB rejected the model because it projects a negative image of Micronesians as incapable of providing for themselves. This is at the heart of the dependency assumptions concocted by foreign economists with no expertise on Micronesia. For example, there has been no reliable data collection about the sending and receiving of remittances, and the Compact should not be seen as a form of foreign aid since it is a treaty, components of which stipulate Micronesia's right to receive money from the US.

Perhaps, one can argue that one of the best economic practices suitable to islanders is one that enmeshes the daily cultural life of the FSM, rarely acknowledged by outside commentators, and relevant elements of the modern world. Such practices revolve around the complex web of the diasporic *ainang* system (DAS) driven by its own inherent social forces reinforced by reciprocity, sharing and sustainable conservation practices.[179] DAS has its own channels of circulation and distribution of goods and monies to ensure that no one is excluded from the extended family benefits. The wealth of DAS cannot be measured in terms of statistical

---

176 Geoff Bertram, 'Introduction: The MIRAB Model in the Twenty-First Century', *Asia Pacific Viewpoint*, Vol. 47, No. 1, April 2006, p. 5.
177 Bertram, 'Introduction: The MIRAB Model', p. 5.
178 The Compact provides the main funds for the operation of the FSM Government.
179 I coined the 'DAS' term to explain the complex foundation of Micronesian societies that could be included in economic analysis to better our understanding of the islanders' economic system. Such an understanding could assist foreign consultants in working closely with Micronesians to design an economic model appropriate for the islanders. See also Marshall, 'The Structure of Solidarity', pp. 62–64; Petersen, *Traditional Micronesian Societies*, pp. 19–23.

analysis as practised by economists. That is because Micronesians' wealth is measured in terms of how many relatives one has. It is not wholly measured in terms of how the value of the dollar is distributed on a per capita basis based on a gross domestic product (GDP) abstraction, which then translates into the ranking of a country's wealth on the international economic scale. DAS is a homegrown ideology that has its own internal, self-supporting mechanism in the shaping, sustaining and positioning of the FSM in the contemporary world.

All three of the economic models discussed above are, at best, only marginally relevant in a Micronesian context. Perhaps Micronesia's future should start with its reclassification as a dual economy with the *ainang* system at its very core.[180] It has its own measures of success not yet well understood or valued by many economists of the day. MIRAB has also been challenged by Pacific scholars as nothing more than reinforcing neo-colonialism with a new image.[181] It continues to underestimate the astute judgement of islanders in pacing and framing their own economic circumstances. MIRAB reflects nothing more than the continuing belittling of Pacific Islands, as described by Epeli Hau'ofa.[182] Micronesia is refining the DAS lifestyle as it suits its social, political and economic lifestyle.

The Geography of Contemporary Micronesia

Despite the increasing globalisation of the world economy, Micronesia's current realities remain, as always, deeply embedded in the geographical realities of the local oceanic environment:

> Millions of years ago undersea volcanic activity created the islands that now comprise the Federated States of Micronesia. The vast distance from one another (one days' sail for most) and from continental land masses allowed the evolution of unique ecosystems and a large number of endemic species.[183]

---

180 Petersen, *Traditional Micronesian Societies*, pp. 19–23.

181 Laurence E. Rothenberg, *Globalization 101: The Three Tensions of Globalization*, Occasional papers from the American Forum for Global Education, No. 176, 2002–2003, webspace.ship.edu/ hliu/347/14global/3-tensions.pdf.

182 Hau'ofa, 'Our Sea of Islands', pp. 29–30.

183 Office of Statistics, Budget and Economic Management, Overseas Development Assistance and Compact Management, *Millennium Development Goals and Status Report 2010: The Federated States of Micronesia*, Palikir, Pohnpei, 15 December 2010, p. 71.

Of course, these species have been a part of Micronesians' food supply for many centuries. Today, they are threatened because of the changes in their natural habitat due to climate change and overfishing by fleets from other nations, as will be detailed in later chapters. The distance between islands also influenced the common language shared by groups of islands and the dialectical variants that evolved.[184]

The inhabitants of low-lying islands depend heavily on fishing and small-scale farming to meet their daily needs. This is supplemented by purchases of Western foods from the port towns,[185] from visiting relatives, or remittance of food or funds.[186] Small, local stores provide sources for purchasing Western foods when necessary. However, on the volcanic islands where the central port towns are located, the inhabitants, despite the abundant land to farm, prefer imported food products from Australia, Japan, China, South Korea, Taiwan and the US for their daily diet.

Non-communicable diseases such as diabetes, high blood pressure, obesity, stroke and heart problems are now common in the population because of the changes from traditional dietary habits to that of a modern diet high in refined ingredients and chemical additives.[187] The FSM Department of Health and Social Affairs is advocating a return to a more traditional diet to improve community health, which is also crucial in terms of maintaining the health of the nation. As a consequence, many islanders are replanting indigenous crops for the purpose of adhering to a healthy diet to slow down the consequences of non-communicable diseases, which have slowly spread beyond the major port towns.[188]

The FSM forms the northwest part of the region of Oceania. It lies immediately above the equator between Papua New Guinea to the south, Guam to the north, Palau to the west and the Marshall Islands to the east.

---

184 Jeffery C. Marck, 'Micronesian Dialects and the Overnight Voyage', *Journal of the Polynesian Society*, Vol. 95, No. 2, June 1986, pp. 253–258.

185 Port towns are the hubs of politico-economic activities in each of the states within the FSM. They emerged during the colonial period and remain today.

186 Hezel, *The New Shape of Old Cultures*, pp. 152–154.

187 Marcus Samo (Deputy Secretary of the FSM Department of Health and Social Affairs and Chuukese Historian), Interview, Nett, Pohnpei, 21 January 2011, Kolonia, Pohnpei, 9 July 2013; Gibson Susumu and Mark Kostka, *Federated States of Micronesia Food Security Assessment Report* (Final Draft), Palikir, Pohnpei, March 2011, pp. 18–19; World Health Organization, 'Micronesia, Federated States of', in *Western Pacific Country Health Information Profiles*, 2011, p. 219. iris.wpro. who.int/handle/10665.1/10522.

188 Kippier Lippwe, pers, comm., Department of Health and Social Affairs, 2 July 2013.

It consists of more than 607 islands[189] dispersed across a vast oceanic space. Only 65[190] of the islands are inhabited, varying in population from less than 100 in the low-lying islands to over 35,000 in the volcanic islands.[191] The islands range from small atolls that barely exceed 4 metres above sea level to many volcanic islands.[192] The total land area of the FSM is approximately 271 square miles.[193]

Figure 8: Federated States of Micronesia in relation to the world.
Source: Map produced by ANU CartoGIS.

---

189 Susumu and Kostka, *Federated States of Micronesia Food Security Assessment Report*, p. 1.
190 Office of Statistics, Budget and Economic Management, Overseas Development Assistance and Compact Management, *Millennium Development Goals and Status Report 2010*, pp. 1–2.
191 Office of Statistics, Budget and Economic Management, Overseas Development Assistance and Compact Management, *Millennium Development Goals and Status Report 2010*, pp. 1–2.
192 Rosita Henry, William Jeffery and Christine Pam, *Heritage and Climate Change in Micronesia: A Report on a Pilot Study Conducted on Moch Island, Mortlock Islands, Chuuk, Federated States of Micronesia*, January 2008, James Cook University, Townsville, Queensland, Australia, 2008, p. 7.
193 Kim, *Into the Deep*, p. 271.

The FSM has 2,978,000 square kilometres of EEZ.[194] According to the latest census published by the Office of Statistics, Budget and Economic Management, Overseas Development and Compact Management (SBOC), the FSM's population is estimated to be just over 107,000.[195] It is estimated that 49,840 of the 107,000[196] are living in the US as of 11 October 2012. Of these 49,840 living in the US, around 16,790 were born in the US[197] and are referred to as the 'Compact generation'.

There are four main native languages spoken in Micronesia: Pohnpeian, Chuukese, Kosraean and Yapese. Many linguists claim that these languages belong to the modern Trukic language, a derivative of the Malayo-Polynesian or Austronesian language family group.[198] Each of these languages has their own dialectical variants. However, English is the lingua franca of the FSM. Most Micronesians today are multilingual speakers, especially on the island of Pohnpei, where the capital Palikir is located. People from across Micronesia gravitate towards Pohnpei for tertiary education, employment and to visit relatives.

The climate is tropical and humid, with heavy year-round rainfall, especially in the eastern part of the country. The temperature is usually around 26°C, with two seasons (the dry months or *lerak*,[199] generally from May to September, and the windy months or *lefang*,[200] from October to April).[201] The FSM is located on the southern edge of the typhoon belt. Typhoons vary in intensity but usually cause severe environmental damage.[202] Climate change is also affecting the nation's environment. For example, local fishermen have observed that tropical depressions and

---

194 Paul D'Arcy, 'The Lawless Ocean? Voluntary Compliance Regimes and Offshore Resource Exploitation in the Pacific', *Asia and the Pacific Policy Studies*, Vol. 1, No. 2, 2014, p. 3.
195 SBOC, www.sboc.fm/ (site discontinued).
196 Francis X. Hezel, 'Micronesians on the Move: Eastward and Upward Bound', *Pacific Islands Policy*, No. 9, East-West Center, Hawai'i, 2013, pp. 33–34.
197 Hezel, 'Micronesians on the Move', p. 34.
198 Goodenough, *Property, Kin and Community on Truk*, p. 26; Petersen, *Traditional Micronesian Societies*, pp. 37–38; Rufino, 'Ideological Bases for Power', pp. 36–39; Alkire, *An Introduction to the Peoples and Cultures of Micronesia*, pp. 10–11; Rubinstein, 'An Ethnography of Micronesian Childhood', p. 23.
199 For an in-depth discussion, see D'Arcy, *The People of the Sea*, pp. 14–16, 152–153; Gladwin, *East is a Big Bird*, pp. 24–25; Alkire, *Lamotrek Atoll and Inter-Island Socio-Economic Ties*, pp. 44–45.
200 *Lefang* (the windy season from October to April); D'Arcy, *The People of the Sea*, pp. 152–153.
201 Goodenough, *Property, Kin and Community on Truk*, pp. 22–23. *Lerak* is referred to as the breadfruit season where an abundance of food is available. It coincides with the summer months of May to September. *Lefang* is referred to as the lean months or the windy months (October to April). Navigators called the windy months *meramen atilei fatel* (the months to rest the paddles).
202 Alkire, *Lamotrek Atoll and Inter-Island Socio-Economic Ties*, pp. 17–20.

sea surges are occurring more frequently and with increased intensity.[203] Studies on climate change conducted by Fletcher and Richard,[204] Henry, Jeffery and Pam,[205] Gibson, Wichep and Silbanuz,[206] and Keim[207] have confirmed the locals' observations. The studies indicated that rising sea levels are slowly eroding beaches and increasing saltwater incursion into wells and agricultural lands. The protection of the environment from external threats is central to the maintenance and continuity of the FSM. For example, the introduction of foreign agricultural practices not suited to local conditions, the environmental impact of WWII and now climate change increase the urgency for locals to implement traditional conservation practices in collaboration with Western technologies.

In May 1979, the FSM became a constitutional government in a Free Association transitional arrangement with the administering colonial power, the US. This transitional arrangement has been the source of increasing friction over governance and independence issues despite the close economic, migration and cultural ties between the two nations.[208] The FSM comprises four constituent states—Chuuk, Kosrae, Pohnpei and Yap—with the capital on the main island of Pohnpei. The Constitution underscored a long history of political processes stemming from Micronesians' determination to control the future of their islands. Self-preservation, control and continuity were at the heart of Micronesians' collective desire to become independent during the post-WWII decolonisation process.[209]

---

203 Interviews with locals from the Mortlocks, Sokehs, Pohnpei, 14 July 2013; Asian Development Bank, *Federated States of Micronesia Development Framework 2012. Looking to the Future: A Foundation for Discussion at the FSM Development Partners Forum*, 2012, p. 27.

204 Charles H. Fletcher and Bruce M. Richmond, *Climate Management and Adaptive Strategies*, University of Hawai'i Sea Grant College Program, 2010, pp. 4–5.

205 Henry, Jeffery and Pam, *Heritage and Climate Change in Micronesia*, pp. 38–39.

206 Gibson Susumu, John Wichep and Marlyter Silbanuz, *Preliminary Damage Assessment (PDA) Report Federated States of Micronesia: Agricultural Damage Report*, December 2009, pp. 4–9.

207 Mark E. Keim, *Sea Level Rise Disaster in Micronesia: Sentinel Event for Climate Change*, National Center for Environmental Health, Agency for Disease Control and Prevention, Atlanta, Georgia, USA.

208 Edward C. King, 'Custom and Constitutionalism in the Federated States of Micronesia', *Asian-Pacific Law & Policy Journal*, Vol. 3, No. 2, July 2002, p. 3; Clement Mulalap, 'Islands in the Stream; Addressing Climate Change From a Small Island Developing State Perspective', in *Climate Change and Indigenous People: The Search for Legal Remedies*, edited by Randall Abate and Elizabeth Warner, Edward Elgar Publishing, Cheltenham, United Kingdom, 2013, p. 386.

209 Meller, *Constitutionalism in Micronesia*, p. 7.

The different island identities are based on given groups' perceptions of themselves in relation to the sea or land. For example, the term *shon metaw* is in reference to the Mortlockese people as being from the deep seas. In some islands in the state of Yap and the northwest part of Chuuk, the term is *re-mataw*. Today, identities are based on the sub-geographical areas of the FSM, such as *mehn Pohnpei* (people of Pohnpei) or *shon Chuuk* (people of Chuuk). These identities connote people's historical past, which are now collectively under the Micronesian identity. These identities continue the historical affinity between islanders.[210]

Theories of Peopling the FSM

Micronesian identities and continuity are memorialised and celebrated in indigenous *uruon fanou* (history of the land), *pwarik* (dances),[211] *pisakin eoranei* (material cultures), *kolin fonu* (local songs), *ngorongor* (chants), *titilap* (stories and legends) and *palou* (navigational knowledge).[212] Oral history has enabled islanders to trace their places of origin and their connection to these by looking at historical continuity. This body of knowledge is largely ignored and uncited by most academic investigators of the origins of the peoples of Micronesia. Most academic theories assert that Micronesians most likely originated from Southeast Asia and Melanesia. For example, William Alkire,[213] Glenn Petersen[214] and Paul Rainbird[215] are proponents of this theoretical assumption based on archaeological, botanical, linguistic and migration interpretation.[216]

Thomas Gladwin noted that the pattern of settlement of Chuuk and Yap originated from the Marshall Islands via Kosrae, Pohnpei then Chuuk.[217] However, anthropologist Ward Goodenough referred to *kachaw* as the world with layers of heavens in his quest to represent how some Chuukese

---

210 Meller, *Constitutionalism in Micronesia*, p. 7.
211 Glenn Petersen, 'Dancing Defiance: The Politics of Pohnpeian Dance Performances', *Pacific Studies*, Vol. 15. No. 4, December 1992, pp. 13–27.
212 Peter, 'Eram's Church (Bell)', pp. 275, 279, 283.
213 Alkire, *Introduction to the Peoples and Cultures of Micronesia*, pp. 5–13.
214 Petersen, *Traditional Micronesian Societies*, pp. 39–40.
215 Rainbird, *The Archaeology of Micronesia*, pp. 97–100.
216 Alkire, *An Introduction to the People and Cultures of Micronesia*, pp. 5–13.
217 Gladwin, *East is a Big Bird*, p. 4.

perceived their origins.[218] Pohnpeian archaeologist and historian Rufino Mauricio referred to Pohnpeians as migrating from unknown islands from the east, west and south.[219] Ironically, these valuable traditions add weight to archaeological theories of migrations from Melanesia to the south as one of the sources of Micronesian settlement. Don Rubinstein noted that, according to local traditions and based on oral history of *Moyitigitig*, the island of Fais in Yap was fished up from the depth of the sea.[220] This tradition is in keeping with the Oceania-wide traditions of early founding discoverers and navigators, such as the Polynesian ancestor, Maui, fishing islands out of the sea and fixing them in place from the hitherto unknown through navigational plotting.

However, Oha Uman, Ferdun Saladier and Ante Chipen, in a detailed and valuable collection of local traditions titled *Uruon Chuuk*,[221] spoke of oral narratives of inter-island migration within Micronesia. This *uruo* was written in the Chuukese language and was based on oral narratives recorded in the 1970s. Apart from a few English translations commissioned in the late 1990s by Paul D'Arcy, it remains largely untranslated and uncited within academia. My reading of these oral narratives confirmed what I learned from my elders. For example, the peopling of the islands in the Mortlocks originated from the Chuuk lagoon. It also confirmed the pattern of contact between the Yapese, Pohnpeians and Kosraeans. *Uruon Chuuk* also contains details of the sea lanes between islands for migration purposes facilitated by the *leoo*, whose dwellings are situated at particular points in the sea. It pointed to Pohnpei and Kosrae as the point of origin of the Chuukese people.[222] Marshall confirmed the oral histories of contact between Mortlockese, Pohnpeians and the islands in the northwest of Chuuk lagoon before colonisation.[223] Despite this *uruo*, each island always resorted to its own *uruo* to trace its origin and,

---

218 Ward Goodenough, 'Skyworld and This World: The Place of Kachaw in Micronesian Cosmology', *American Anthropology*, Vol. 88, No. 3, 1986, pp. 551–568. This idea of a heaven with layers was noted as originating from Nama Island in the Mortlocks. This confirmed how some Lukunorians perceived heaven during the 1980s. For example, when I tried to explain to one of my uncles, Taichy, about the earth existing in the universe, he countered my explanation by stating that human beings live inside the earth, which has different layers where the wind comes from—*efong, eor, lotow* and *efang* (north, south, east and west)—and *lang* (heaven).

219 Mauricio, 'Ideological Bases for Power', pp. 2–7.

220 Rubinstein, 'An Ethnography of Micronesian Childhood', pp. 18, 21–22. See also Rawari Taonui, 'Polynesian Oral Traditions', in *Vaka Moana: Voyages of the Ancestors*, edited by K. R. Howe, University of Hawai'i Press, 2006, p. 30.

221 Uman, Saladier and Chipen, *Uruon Chuuk*, pp. 1–7.

222 Uman, Saladier and Chipen, *Uruon Chuuk*, pp. 1–7.

223 Marshall, *Namoluk beyond the Reef*, p. 19.

more importantly, its connection to other Micronesians. For example, the first inhabitants of my island of Lukunor in the Mortlocks region traced their origin to a village in Weno called Wichap in the Chuuk lagoon.[224] Likewise other low-lying islands in Chuuk claimed their origins in the same lagoon.[225] The islands in the Chuuk lagoon in turn spoke of Yap, Pohnpei and Kosrae as their points of origin.[226]

Moreover, Pohnpeians traced their origins to distant shores over the horizon.[227] Peter Lohn, the traditional *Wasai*[228] of the chiefdom of Sokehs, noted that some of these distant shores are Tuvalu and Kiribati.[229] Many inhabitants of the low-lying islands in Yap came from Chuuk, as evidenced by clan relationships and oral histories. Kosraeans point to the Marshall Islands, Kiribati and Yap as some of the places where they came from.[230] All in all, we can see that Micronesians perceive their origins as situated at different points within the huge area that encompasses the Micronesian region. Micronesians have argued that their own *uruo* is a science in itself; it has its own internal logic and coherency. Their historical claims therefore have the same capability as Western sciences in the determination of historical certainty.[231] For example, when looking at land cases in Chuuk, the court often looks at oral histories to determine who actually owns the land based on *ainang* histories.[232]

---

224 *Wichap* is one of the villages in Weno Island, the capital of the state of Chuuk.

225 Peter, 'Chuukese Travellers', p. 258; Eve C. Pinsker, 'Traditional Leaders Today in the Federated States of Micronesia', in *Chiefs Today: Traditional Leadership and the Pacific Postcolonial State*, edited by Geoffrey M. White and Lamont Lindstrom, Stanford University Press, California, 1997, p. 163.

226 Uman, Saladier and Chipen, *Uruon Chuuk*, pp. 1–7. However, others such as Goodenough argued that people from Weno were the descendants of the *anu-aramas*, half human, half ghost, who came from the different heavens.

227 Hanlon, *Upon a Stone Altar*, p. 42.

228 *Wasai* is the second in line to the Nahnmwarki of Sokehs (the highest traditional chief) from that district on the volcanic island of Pohnpei.

229 Oral history also connects the Mortlockese and the people from Kiribati, for example, with the clan called *tuum*.

230 Gordon, *Kosrae*, p. 6; Uman, Saladier and Chipen, *Uruon Chuuk*, pp. 1–7.

231 Oral history, according to a traditional perspective, has its own logic. It is used to validate or invalidate the processes of historical debate and pinpoint certainty. For example, members of the first clan on a particular island can shed light on the order of events by virtue of being related to the first occupants.

232 See e.g. *Mailo v Atonesia*, 7 FSM Intrm. 294 (Chk. S. Ct. Tr. 1995), CA no. 73-92.

Conclusion

As discussed throughout this chapter, the modern Micronesian identity emerged as a consequence of the colonisation process. The colonial powers attempted to reorder indigenous societies by imposing an alien system of government upon them. It did not result in Micronesians abandoning the traditional system that has served them well for many centuries. The traditional system with its own inherent adaptation mechanism perpetuates the principles of the *ainang* system, now built into the FSM's Constitution to ensure continuity. The Constitution represents the collective identities within the modern state of the FSM as deeply rooted in the nation's historical past. It also conveys resiliency and continuity.

In the globalised system, where many identities are disappearing because of the speed of new ideologies spread through technological means and unsuited to the preservation of indigenous cultures, Micronesians continue to adapt as much as possible to ensure their progress into the future. This has been possible because of Micronesia's historical strength in maintaining traditional values. The Micronesian identity is the foundation of Micronesian strength, and any questioning of its resilience stems from external perceptions of the FSM, not from the inhabitants themselves. The Constitution perpetuates Micronesians' continuity in the modern world while also safeguarding the FSM's traditions and ensuring the integrity of the islanders' values, which are discussed in the next chapter.

3

Responding to
Colonisation

The preceding chapters strongly suggested that there was greater continuity than change in indigenous survivability in Micronesia because of the strength of their traditional institutions. This suggests that colonial rule in Micronesia was relatively ineffective. The previous two chapters proposed that the reason for Micronesians' endurance stemmed from their ability to rearticulate foreign influences to suit their own context.[1] This chapter deals with Micronesian engagement with the colonial powers of Spain, Germany, Japan and the US. It will discuss how Micronesians indigenised outsiders' influences to suit local contexts despite the seemingly unequal power relations. As history is a forum of intellectual discourses, Micronesian perspectives will be emphasised since they are the least covered of the colonial era. Many of the incidents and attitudes expressed to me about the colonial era are recollections of my parents and grandparents; they are absent from published accounts of this period. By including them here alongside conventional historiography, I seek to broaden the debate and range of sources to stimulate and widen our understanding of Micronesians' perspective of history.

The colonisation process brought many foreign ideologies to the FSM. One such ideology was written history. This form of history is in and of itself a self-serving instrument in the framing and perpetuation of Micronesians as subservient to outsiders' civilisation. This is a misleading

---

1   Paul D'Arcy, 'What was the Impact of Japanese Rule on the Indigenous Population of Japan's South Seas Mandate?', University of Hawai'i, 1986 (Unpublished paper), pp. 1–21; Duane, *Clan and Copra*, pp. 200–228.

exaggeration since Micronesians continue to use traditional forms of history to educate subsequent generations about indigenous history. The post-WWII decolonisation period saw the re-emergence of indigenous history that had been suppressed by outsiders for centuries. The question is, how does one intellectually imagine indigenous history within the framework of linear history, or vice versa, since their productions and nuances are different? In other words, how does one reconcile the two different types of history? As this book is written for an academic audience, I am compelled to adopt the chronological order of history, but with relevant elements of indigenous perspectives to open up a new frontier of Micronesian historical discourses. Therefore, this chapter and subsequent chapters will follow the linear approach to hopefully bring together our understanding of how Micronesians perceived themselves during and after the colonial period.

There are many theories about the causes and effects of colonisation, ranging from exportation of European civilisation and Christianisation to economics and empire building.[2] However, for the purpose of this chapter, colonisation will be defined as an act by a foreign power of establishing a colony to assert control over the indigenous people of an area.[3] Hezel expanded on this by framing it in the context of the *terra nullius* principle, which states that:

> colonisation is the utilisation of the earth, of the flora, fauna and the above all of the human beings to the advantage of the colonising nation, and the latter is therefore obligated to give in return for the higher culture … and its better methods.[4]

At least according to their own definitions of relative worth and value.

By applying these two definitions in Micronesia's context, the process of colonisation has its genesis in the sixteenth century, when Spain declared that what is now known as the FSM was part of its colonial empire. Spain

---

2   See Peter Hempenstall, 'Imperial Manoeuvers', in *Tides of History: The Pacific Islands in the Twentieth Century*, edited by K. R. Howe, Robert C. Kiste and Brij V. Lal, University of Hawai'i Press, 1987, pp. 29–39.

3   'Colonize', *Oxford Dictionary*, www.oxforddictionaries.com/definition/english/colonize#colonize_16.

4   *Terra nullius* was a doctrine, and later a component of international law, that the colonial powers used to acquire new territories overseas. It entailed that if a territory did not show any signs of agricultural production as perceived by the Europeans, then the first European discoverer could claim the territory on behalf of the colonial power they represented (Francis X. Hezel, *Strangers in Their Own Land: A Century of Colonial Rule in the Caroline and Marshall Islands*, University of Hawai'i Press, 1995, p. 132; Brownlie, *Principles of Public International Law*, pp. 173–174).

administered its Micronesian colonial territory from Guam and later from the Philippines until the latter part of the nineteenth century. Effective rule beyond Guam was minimal until the late nineteenth century, and most Micronesian islands remained unknown and unvisited by the Spanish until then. An attempt to extend Spanish influence beyond Guam into the area of the present-day FSM saw a Christian mission established on Ulithi in the early 1730s; it was not successful.[5] Actual Spanish colonisation began in 1866 when Spanish authorities finally decided to establish their presence in Pohnpei and Yap. Micronesians' tacit consent was not just desirable but essential in the absence of effective coercive ability and the need for economic returns to justify the extra effort needed to impose colonial laws by the overstretched and underfunded Spanish forces.

General Perspectives of *Peshe Seset*

Peshe seset[6] are always looked upon with suspicion by Micronesians. Suspicion is an element of survival that allowed Micronesians to keep an eye on intruders. Such suspicion was employed during the colonial era. However, the question is, how did the colonisers perceive the indigenous population? The historical literature speaks volumes about the treatment of Micronesians in terms of derogatory language and labels such as 'savage', 'primitive' and 'uncivilised' in comparison to the outsiders' own standing on the civilisations continuum.

To the Micronesians, the outsiders were pale *peshe seset* who were arrogant and oblivious to the order of the indigenous world. This arrogance led *peshe seset* to underestimate the strength of the Micronesians. They treated the small population as too weak to mount a substantial resistance against colonial occupation. For example, small military detachments were usually deployed to guard the different colonial interests in Micronesia, only to find that their forces were insufficient in the face of serious local opposition.[7]

---

5   Hezel, *The First Taint of Civilization*, pp. 58–59.
6   The term '*peshe seset*' means 'salty feet from foreign seas'. I am using the term in reference to the colonists who were not indigenous to Micronesia and yet asserted control of the islands without permission.
7   The Spanish and Germans military detachments in Pohnpei underestimated local resistance and had to send for reinforcements from their headquarters outside Micronesia (Peter Hempenstall and Noel Rutherford, *Protest and Dissent in the Colonial Pacific*, University of the South Pacific, Fiji, 1984, pp. 109–110; Hezel, *Strangers in Their Own Land*, pp. 30–33; Hanlon, *Upon a Stone Altar*, pp. 271–273.

The *peshe seset* mistook Micronesian silence as a sign of weakness. Micronesians used a variety of survival strategies against the colonial authorities that were learned from their past historical experiences. These included open military resistance, patience, passive resistance in the form of non-compliance and political manipulation. This is part of their history—to adapt to new circumstances based on past experience and observation as to what strategies to implement for effective protection under any given circumstance. Invariably, indirect resistance rather than direct confrontation against a foe armed with modern weaponry proved most effective. At other times, Micronesians gave the appearance of patiently accepting colonial demands while covertly continuing the traditional system of authority and interactions with each other to maintain their identities and continuity.[8]

Having experienced frequent natural disasters and inter-island warfare in their oceanic environment prior to colonisation, Micronesians have developed a significant capacity to rapidly mobilise resources and defend their homes. Centuries of struggle against nature and men to preserve their cultures, regardless of any threats, left Micronesians better prepared for the new external threat of poorly resourced colonial authorities than the colonisers realised.[9] In addition, rivalries between the colonial powers and the geographical nature of the islands also made colonisation ineffective.[10] The strength of Micronesian continuity and resilience, as outlined in the previous chapter, derive principally from their social system and understanding of their oceanic environment.

Historically, the environment is susceptible to natural threats such as typhoons and drought. This has made Micronesians extremely adaptable and capable of rapidly mobilising available resources to deal with catastrophic circumstances. These threats have influenced the way Micronesians have organised their social, political and economic connections. Their organisational skills stood them in good stead for facing anthropomorphic challenges from beyond the horizon, few of which have matched the intensity of typhoons, with the possible exceptions of WWII (the typhoon of war) and some severe exotic epidemics.[11] These survival strategies have been at the heart of Micronesian adaptation

---

8   Hezel, *The New Shape of Old Island Cultures*, p. 1.
9   Hempenstall and Rutherford, *Protest and Dissent in the Colonial Pacific*, pp. 112–113.
10   Gale, *The Americanization of Micronesia*, pp. 22–23.
11   D'Arcy, *The People of the Sea*, pp. 152–153; Marshall. *Namoluk beyond the Reef*, pp. 26–27; Alkire, *An Introduction to the Peoples and Cultures of Micronesia*, pp. 6–7.

practices.[12] Prior to colonisation, the flow of information between islands was already established via the clan network between islands, which was also the source of developing islanders' diplomatic skills. That is to say that conflict avoidance was crucial to Micronesian survival.[13] The same network was also used to circulate information about the colonial powers and their activities.

Local Responses to the New Arrivals

Colonisation had both negative and positive consequences for Micronesia. Micronesian life was affected to varying degrees when outsiders started to appear on their shores. Micronesian modes of engagement with the outsiders depended on the intensity of the colonisation process as it differed between the various islands and atolls. For example, on some islands, outsiders met intimidation and violent death at their first point of contact.[14] On other occasions, islanders received the outsiders on friendly terms.[15] The type of responses exhibited by the islanders during the early engagement period signified the nature of the social system present on that island.

Many historians have claimed that the islanders' recognition of iron and other Western goods as being valuable items often created friendly conditions for encounters.[16] Metal tools were highly valued as they shortened the time required for the backbreaking traditional manual tasks. Historian Scott Russell noted the value of iron to an Ulithian man who a Spanish priest 'converted' to Christianity. The Ulithian man, after his conversion, said to the priest, 'as you long for heaven, so we long for iron'.[17] This statement demonstrates the manipulative dimensions of exchange used by islanders and the fluidity of negotiation between the

12   Rainbird, *The Archaeology of Micronesia*, p. 245; Alkire, *An Introduction to the Peoples and Cultures of Micronesia*, pp. 86–88; Knudson, 'Resource Fluctuation', pp. 4–6.
13   Gray, 'Modernization in Micronesia', pp. 59–61; Gonzaga Puas, 'The FSM Legal System: Responses to US Influence', Paper presented during the Association for Social Anthropologist in Oceania, Portland Oregon, 6 February 2011, pp. 3–4.
14   Hezel, *The First Taint of Civilization*, pp. 100–101.
15   Hezel, *The First Taint of Civilization*, pp. 96–97.
16   Hezel, *The First Taint of Civilization*, pp. 96–97.
17   Scott Russell, 'Roots of the Falawasch', Mangilao, Guam, MARC Library, n.d. (Unpublished MS paper), p. 2.

two sides to achieve their own objectives. No one knows exactly how the Micronesians came to recognise iron, though some have speculated that it was discovered in driftwood and possibly by unrecorded earlier contacts.

Unfriendly relations in early encounters may have resulted from the outsiders intruding into Micronesian spaces without prior permission, especially sacred spaces.[18] Killing was a form of eliminating threat in the local communities. The methods of killing exercised by islanders were ambush,[19] open confrontation and seeking guidance from their ancestors in terms of magic or *paut* (sorcery).[20] Selection of the appropriate security measures utilised to suppress any arising threat posed by outsiders was conditioned by the particular circumstances of each island during the contact period. For example, ambush was common in island histories as it was swift, and secretive. It warned enemies to refrain from intruding into unfamiliar spaces. Open confrontation was a display of bravery, ferocity and determination to defeat opponents and involved large-scale warfare between island alliances or extended opposing clans.[21] Negotiation was used to dissuade warring sides from taking up arms. Physical violence was used to signal to the outsiders that Micronesians were capable of mounting attacks if they were put under pressure.[22] The quick realisation that there was a mismatch between the two sides led islanders to utilise a variety of different tactics to sustain their interests. From the patchy record of first contacts, as best we can tell, the majority of first contacts in Micronesia were mainly peaceful, with sporadic violence.

---

18   My personal opinion. Outsiders may not be aware of the sacred spaces of the gods, which were and continue to be considered off limits to the public. Intrusion into such spaces could result in a fight or possibly death.

19   *Mortlocks Oral History*. Ambush is personal, however, it could develop into full-scale warfare between two extended families.

20   *Mortlocks Oral History*. Sorcery is a psychological element of warfare that involves calling upon the ancestors for support. See David Hanlon, 'Sorcery, "Savage Memories" and the Edge of Commensurability for History in the Pacific', in *Pacific Islands History: Journeys and Transformation*, edited by Brij V. Lal, Journal of Pacific History, 1993, pp. 118–119.

21   *Mortlocks Oral History*. Open warfare involved displaying one's bravery and was used as an intimidation tactic against opponents.

22   Violence took many forms, from small and personal attacks to large-scale conflict like in the Pohnpeians' violent resistance against the Spanish and Germans. See Hanlon, *Upon the Stone Altar*, pp. 287–289; Hezel, *The First Taint of Civilization*, pp. 136–144.

Sustained Contact

Having established the basic background of the islands, it should not be a surprise that outsiders were met with varying treatments during the colonisation period. The Pacific Ocean is the largest body of water in the world and promised profits for whalers. The search for more profits led many whalers to the islands in Micronesia, largely by accident. By the mid-1800s, whalers, traders and beachcombers began to arrive in large numbers. Having no whaling stations in Micronesia from which to purchase provisions, they had to rely on whichever islands and islanders they came upon. It meant the outsiders had to give in to the islanders as they controlled the land resources that they required. Pohnpei and Kosrae became known for good provisions. Subsequently, Pohnpeians and Kosreans experienced increasing numbers of visiting vessels to their shores. The islands offered necessary provisions and fine harbours for vessels to shelter during the windy months. Most of the crew members were Europeans and Americans, with a number of other Pacific Islanders among them.[23] New trade ensued between the locals and outsiders as a result of this increased contact. The high chiefs of Pohnpei and Kosrae influenced trade deals to suit local circumstances, leveraging their control of access to the provisions that the visitors required. As the volume of trade increased, there was a commensurate rise in the value of the islanders' commodities.

While in port, sailors rested and indulged in pursuits of pleasure, finding comfort in women and alcohol. The attraction of the island lifestyle encouraged many sailors to abandon their ships; they became the first beachcombers.[24] The increased traffic in whaling and trading vessels developed islanders' awareness of international commerce and politics.[25] For example, in Pohnpei, the powerful *Nahnmwarki(s)*[26] and local businessman Henry Nahnpei exploited this knowledge and manipulated the visiting vessels and foreign residents for personal interests. The *Nahnmwarki* also manipulated the beachcombers into serving them as negotiators in order to acquire more material wealth from the visiting

---

23   Francis X. Hezel, 'Book Review: *Double Ghosts: Oceanian Voyages on Euroamerican Ships*', *Journal of World History*, Vol. 10, No. 2, 1999, pp. 479–481.

24   Hanlon, *Upon a Stone Altar*, pp. 92–93.

25   Hanlon, *Upon a Stone Altar*, pp. 91–92; Hezel, *Strangers in Their Own Land*, pp. 84–85.

26   For explanation of the tile *Nahnmwarki*, see indigenous historian and archaeologist from Pohnpei Rufino Mauricio's *Ideological Bases*, p. 60. Note that there is no plural for *Nahnmwarki*, so I use '*Nahnmwarki(s)*' to refer to the various holders of the title.

vessels. This contest later played out in local politics, especially between local leaders vying to consolidate their power base. In the less-visited, low-lying islands like Ngatik (Sapwafik), Mokil and Pingelap, locals also honed their trade skills to obtain iron, clothes and tobacco.[27] Trade precipitated a notably violent massacre in which the male population of Ngatik[28] was decimated by a combined group of rogue Pohnpeians and outsiders. This reconstitution of the population demographic became the subject of an interesting scholarly study of ethnicity in contemporary Micronesia.

In Kosrae, the chiefs also exploited the imbalance in the trade relationship and did not hesitate to use violent means such as looting and burning visiting ships to keep the outsiders at bay.[29] These acts could be explained in terms of the tension between the chiefs and their subjects against the intruding outsiders. For example, local women were exploited sexually by the visiting sailors. This was unacceptable to the locals and was compounded by a handful of sailors who abandoned their ships against the wishes of the locals. In response to these affronts, violence broke out and two ships were burned and sunk by Kosraens. To avoid further conflict, captains of the visiting ships sought assistance from the high chiefs in Kosrae and Pohnpei by offering rewards for their sailors' return.

In the outer islands of Chuuk, such as the Mortlocks, whalers also occasionally sought provisions but on friendly terms. The high volcanic islands of Chuuk were avoided due to their fierce reputation as portrayed by the early explorers. In Yap, foreigners were mindful of the power of the local chiefs over their subjects and acknowledged this by appeasing them. The chiefs used their influence over their trading activities to demonstrate their power in local politics. This was to send a message to the outsiders that the chiefs were in control. Far fewer beachcombers settled in Yap than Pohnpei, demonstrating the way in which local politics differed and how that influenced the manner in which different communities addressed the common threat posed by the sailors.[30]

---

27   *Oral history* indicates that, at least in Chuuk, some of the foreigners who married locals were instrumental in educating Micronesian people about the outside world. For example, many outsiders like Jack Elhers, who married a lady from Lekinioch, mediated between outsiders and the indigenous people during the German period (Hezel, *Strangers in Their Own Land*, p. 66).

28   Known as the Ngatik massacre. See Lin Poyer, *The Ngatik Massacre: A History and Identity on a Micronesian Atoll*, Smithsonian Institution Press, London, 1993, pp. 4–22; Hezel, *The First Taint of Civilization*, pp. 120–122.

29   Segal, *Kosrae*, pp. 73–74.

30   Amanda Morgan, 'Mystery in the Eye of the Beholder: Cross Cultural Encounters on 19th Century Yap', *Journal of Pacific History*, Vol. 31, No. 1, June 1996, pp. 27–41.

Micronesianising Missionaries

Unbeknownst to the Micronesians, reports of drunken and disorderly behaviour and the sex trade in Pohnpei and Kosrae reached the ears of religious leaders in the US. The American Board of Commissioners for Foreign Missions (ABCFM) based in Boston took up the challenge to Christianise Micronesia. It was believed that the success of the ABCFM in Hawai'i could be reproduced in Micronesia.[31] However, this was not to be the case as the missionaries' lack of knowledge of Micronesian societies handicapped their efforts to convert Micronesian islanders to the Christian faith. Did the American missionaries seek permission from the Micronesian islanders to bring Christianity to their islands? What sort of reception were the missionaries expecting since they did not understand the islands' social structure?

In 1852, a group of ABCFM missionaries sailed to Pohnpei and Kosrae. Benjamin Snow and his wife, in addition to a Hawaiian couple, were permitted by the highest-ranking leader to start their mission activities in Kosrae. The rest of the American party—Dr Luther Gulick and his wife, Mr and Mrs Sturges and their Hawaiian assistant Ka'aikaula— sailed to Pohnpei.[32] Immediately upon their arrival in Pohnpei, the missionaries were at the mercy of local politics. The missionaries set up residence in the district of Kiti as encouraged by the powerful *Nahnken* who gave the missionaries land to use. The *Nahnken* took an interest in the missionaries' activities, foreseeing future benefits from hosting them.[33] In Pohnpeian society, the *Nahnken* is lower than the *Nahnmwarki* and yet the missionaries followed the *Nahnken's* demands. This immediately landed them in the middle of the internal politics of Pohnpei as there had also been ongoing problems caused by the unruly behaviours of many foreign residents. Such occurrences delayed the establishment of the Christian faith in Pohnpei.

---

31 Hanlon, *Upon the Stone Altar*, pp. 143–144.
32 Hezel, *The First Taint of Civilization*, pp. 143–144; Hanlon, *Upon the Stone Altar*, pp. 143–144. There is a discrepancy between these the two authors' comments on the pattern of missionisation in Pohnpei and Kosrae. For example, Hezel states that the missionaries landed in Kosrae first before sailing to Pohnpei, while Hanlon states that the opposite occurred.
33 Hezel, *The First Taint of Civilization*, p. 147.

Lip service was a methodology employed by the locals to convert to Christianity. To manipulate the missionaries, *Nahnken* was converted and, naturally, his followers were too. This was part of the Micronesian strategy of indirectly controlling outsiders and at the same time Micronesianising the foreigners to advance internal priorities, such as chiefly rivalries.[34] Manipulation of the missionaries meant that the missionaries had to work harder for many years before Christianity was tolerated in Pohnpei and Kosrae.[35]

Micronesianising the Spanish Rule

To prop up the Spanish ego as being one of the remaining superpowers in the Pacific, in 1886, Governor Don Isidro Posadillo and his Spanish force set foot on Pohnpei to take control of the region for the Spanish Empire. Spain claimed much of Micronesia with this move, although its actual physical presence was largely confined to the port town of Kolonia in Pohnpei. By the time the Spanish arrived, the Pohnpeians were already aware of the side effects of foreign influence as had been brought by the whalers, beachcombers, traders and American missionaries who had preceded the Spanish by 50 years.[36] The Spanish thought that controlling Pohnpei would be an easy affair. Again, like the missionaries, they did not seek permission from the locals to set up their foreign institutions and their knowledge of Pohnpeian societies was poor. What kind of reception did the Spanish think they would receive while imposing their presence in Pohnpei? They would soon find out.

The Spanish incursion in Pohnpei was subdued until Governor Posadillo tested his power over a land called *mesenieng* that was already in the possession of the ABCFM after the local ruler, the *Lepen* of Nett, granted them the right to reside on the land. The governor needed the land to establish his headquarters and looked for a way to acquire it. The governor sought the assistance of the *Lepen* of Nett to claim the land. To the *Lepen* of Nett, this was absurd. The land did not belong to any of the foreign claimants as the land system in Pohnpei did not recognise agreements

---

34 See David Hanlon, 'Another Side of Henry Nanpei', *Journal of Pacific History*, Vol. 23, No. 1, April 1988, pp. 36–51.
35 Hanlon, *Upon a Stone Altar*, p. 175.
36 Hanlon, *Upon a Stone Altar*, p. 240.

on paper under the customary system called *tiahk en sapw*.[37] Doane, one of the American missionaries who represented the ABCFM, resisted the governor's insistence, angering him in the process. Consequently, Doane was arrested and deported to the Philippines for undermining Spanish authority. Doane's deportation highlighted the power struggle between the Americans and Spanish, as well as the simmering relations with the Pohnpeians.

The Pohnpeians did not anticipate anything that would alter their perception of the new arrivals.[38] The Spanish initially did not seem to learn from the experiences of the outsiders who preceded them. The Pohnpeians were not going to succumb to the new rulers after having managed the influence of all other arrivals before them. The indigenous people adopted a 'wait and see' approach to observe what the Spanish were up to before responding. Patience is an element inherent in indigenous cultural practices to strategise during both natural disasters and man-made threats. These traits characterised Micronesian strength as weakness in the face of adversaries: outsiders only saw passivity rather than assertiveness in their culturally restricted reading of these actions.

The Spanish failed to understand the dynamics of Pohnpeian society in the late nineteenth century. Kolonia was one of the busiest port towns in the Pacific. For example, Hanlon estimated that more than 50 ships arrived during the windy months when they sought shelter from the storms.[39] During the windy season, port life centred on rum and women, much to the displeasure of the missionaries. As well as ships' crews, the community of beachcombers, traders, castaways, whalers and adventurers also threw themselves into the mix.[40] Islanders and outsiders mingled with each other seeking mutual interests. Pohnpeians understood the need of the foreigners and dealt with them accordingly. The missionaries were preaching to the locals about the bible. However, at the same time, many of the resident foreigners countered the message of the missionaries by their involvement in prostitution and heavy drinking[41] to satisfy the needs of the visiting ships' crews. Pohnpeians also cashed in on the prostitution business and traded local products for tobacco, alcohol and other Western commodities.[42]

---

37 *Tiahk en sapw* encapsules all the customary practices of Pohnpei, which defined the Pohnpeian identity (Hanlon, *Upon a Stone Altar*, p. 5).
38 Hempenstall and Rutherford, *Protest and Dissent in the Colonial Pacific*, pp. 106–107.
39 Hanlon, *Upon a Stone Altar*, p. 112; Hezel, *The First Taint of Civilization*, p. 122.
40 Hanlon, *Upon the Stone Altar*, pp. 94–95; Hezel, *The First Taint of Civilization*, pp. 110–111.
41 Marshall, *The Weekend Warrior*, p. 32; Hanlon, *Upon a Stone Altar*, pp. 155, 157–158.
42 Hanlon, *Upon a Stone Altar*, pp. 93–94.

The indigenous political system in Pohnpei was and still is structured into five chiefdoms. At the apex are the *Nahnmwarki*,[43] the paramount chiefs and their spokesperson, the *Nahnken*.[44] The paramount chief has power over the land and its people. In turn, the people worked the land and paid tribute to the *Nahnmwarki*. The *Nahnmwarki* also assigned titles to his subjects on a competitive basis, trading favours and influence for titles and status. The power of each *Nahnmwarki* is dependent on the size of the land he controls and the size of the population in his political domain. Political and economic relationships between the five chiefdoms were generally fluid but could become more rigid depending on local circumstances. Demands made by *Nahnmwarki* were often carried out by his subjects accordingly.

The relationship between Governor Posadillo and the Pohnpeians became strained when he moved to consolidate his power. Posadillo sought to increase Spanish control by developing a road infrastructure to allow free movement of Spanish officials around the island. He also sought to promote the Catholic faith and for the Spanish language to be the new lingua franca. Both moves were not well received by either the locals or the American missionaries. To make things worse, the governor called on the *Nahnmwarki* to support his ambitious plan to build the road system.[45] The governor wanted a team of men from each of the chiefdoms to be rotated on a weekly basis as labourers during the construction of the circumferential road. In addition, each *Nahnmwarki* would be required to supply food for the working teams.[46]

When the *Nahnmwarki* of Madolenihmw objected to the governor's demands, he was threatened with punishment. Further breakdown between the opposing sides ensued when the *Nahnmwarki* of Nett was ordered to clean a latrine as a form of punishment for insubordination.[47] This insult to their leader infuriated the local population as he epitomised Pohnpeian sacredness, power and identity. For Pohnpeians, to receive orders from an alien figurehead without consulting the *Nahnmwarki* was

---

43 Muricio, *Ideological Bases*, p. 60.
44 Muricio, *Ideological Bases*, p. 60.
45 Hanlon, *Upon a Stone Altar*, p. 264; Hezel, *Strangers in Their Own Land*, p. 29; Paul D'Arcy, 'Spanish and German Colonial Rule: With Reference to Spanish and German Colonial Rule in the Caroline Islands Identify the Various Parties Influencing the History of this Era? What Perceptions and Objectives Were They Motivated By?', University of Hawai'i, 1986 (Unpublished paper), p. 2.
46 Hezel, *Strangers in Their Own Land*, p. 29; Hanlon, *Upon the Stone Altar*, p. 264.
47 Hanlon, *Upon a Stone Altar*, pp. 267–268; Hezel, *Strangers in Their Own Land*, p. 29.

unthinkable, let alone to punish and humiliate someone of this rank. This gesture of arrogance brought the simmering tension between the two sides to a boiling point. The Pohnpeians rallied behind their traditional leaders by refusing to comply with the governor's demands.[48]

In response, the governor ordered the closures of schools and the ceasing of local activities like feasting until the road system was completed.[49] This only hardened the Pohnpeians' resolve to resist, and they were ready to pick up arms to retaliate against the Spanish. Things came to a head when a detachment of soldiers was sent to Sokehs to arrest the *Lepen* and *Wasai* (traditional chiefs of Pohnpei under the *Nahnmwarki*) for subverting Spanish order. The detachment arrived during a local feast and demanded that the two men be taken to the governor in Kolonia. Frustrated at the lack of immediate compliance, the detachment opened fire and killed seven Pohnpeians.[50] The Pohnpeians responded by killing 17 of the soldiers, including their leader. The *Wasai* then declared that 'it was better to die fighting rather than living as slaves', signifying a new era of engagement between the islanders and the Spanish.[51]

This incident initiated a state of war between the Spanish and Pohnpeians. The Pohnpeians took their fight to the colony in Kolonia to demonstrate their determination to subvert any further Spanish demands. Governor Posadillo's style of administration was criticised by his own Spanish priests, but this criticism fell on deaf ears. When Posadillo learned of more planned retaliation against the Spanish, he pre-empted this threat by evacuating his people to a ship anchored off the island. However, the governor and a few of his men remained in the colonial compound.[52]

To prevent the governor from escaping, the Pohnpeians posted guards in the vicinity of the compound. Fearing for their lives, the governor and his men tried to escape, but they were caught and killed. The rest of the Spanish party remained on the ship, waiting to be rescued. Help arrived when a Spanish man-of-war arrived to deliver supplies to the

---

48   Hempenstall and Rutherford, *Protest and Dissent in the Colonial Pacific*, pp. 108–109.
49   Hanlon, *Upon a Stone Altar*, pp. 267–268; Hezel, *Strangers in Their Own Land*, p. 29.
50   Hanlon, *Upon a Stone Altar*, pp. 267–268; Hezel, *Strangers in Their Own Land*, p. 30; John Fisher and Ann Fisher, *The Eastern Caroline Islands: Human Relations Area*, Files Press, Connecticut, 1970, pp. 37–38; Paul Ehrlich, '"The Clothes of Men": Ponape Island and German Colonial Rule, 1899– 1914, PhD thesis, State University of New York at Stony Brook, Stony Brook, New York, 1973, p. 71.
51   Hanlon, *Upon a Stone Altar*, pp. 267–268.
52   Hempenstall and Rutherford, *Protest and Dissent in the Colonial Pacific*, p. 109.

colony. Upon hearing of the governor's death, the commander of the ship, de la Concha, opted to remain in Pohnpei to hold the colony until reinforcements arrived from Manila.

A new governor, Don Luis Casadro y Rey, arrived a few weeks later from Manila, accompanied by three warships, 700 soldiers and two artillery batteries.[53] Immediately upon his arrival, the new governor bombarded the colony with his naval guns to intimidate the locals. It was sufficient to persuade the *Nahnmwarki* of Kiti, Madolenihmw and Uh and the *Wasai* of Sokehs to meet with the Spanish at the negotiating table.[54] The governor demanded the unconditional surrender of Pohnpeian agitators and the return of all guns and property taken from the Spanish fort in Mesening. He further demanded that *Lepen Nett* and *Wasai Sokehs* should face Spanish justice and that the rest of the inhabitants should adhere to Spanish law and order. While the people of Nett did not like the new order, *Lepen Nett*, against the wishes of his people, decided to surrender to prevent further bloodshed. The execution of the two traditional leaders was intended as a warning to the local population. However, three locals volunteered to be executed instead of the *Lepen* and *Wasai*.[55] The Spanish executed the volunteers instead of the two perceived agitators. Given that the Spanish were seeking to demonstrate their strength and supremacy, why did they agree to that deal?[56]

Believing that he had total control of the Pohnpeians after these executions, the new governor pushed for the completion of the road system.[57] He obviously had not learned from Posadillo's experience. At first, he designed a scheme to pay local people for the road construction, but the Pohnpeians remained unwilling participants. He went ahead with the road program, using whatever labourers he could muster, but it was unsuccessful.[58] Local politics also played a part. For example, in Kitti, there were two opposing factions headed respectively by the *Nahnmwarki* and the local businessman and pastor Henry Nahnpei, who the American missionaries supported. To shift the balance of power, the *Nahnmwarki* of Kitti associated himself with the Catholic Spanish. He urged the

---

53   Hezel, *Strangers in Their Own Land*, p. 32.
54   Hempenstall and Rutherford, *Protest and Dissent in the Colonial Pacific*, p. 110.
55   Hempenstall and Rutherford, *Protest and Dissent in the Colonial Pacific*, p. 110; Hanlon, *Upon a Stone Altar*, p. 274.
56   I have yet to find an answer in any literature or oral history.
57   Hezel, *Strangers in Their Own Land*, pp. 38–40; David Hanlon, *Upon a Stone Altar*, pp. 311–314.
58   Hempenstall and Rutherford, *Protest and Dissent in the Colonial Pacific*, p. 111.

Spanish governor to build a church in Kitti.[59] The Spanish saw this as an opportunity to expand their presence around the island. The church was built next to the Protestant Church and a guardhouse was also erected for Spanish soldiers, signalling a new discourse in island politics. The Spanish believed that their presence in Kitti was a success and were keen to duplicate the experience in other parts of the island.[60] The governor demanded that another Catholic Church be built in the settlement of Ohwa on the other side of the island in Madolenihmw.[61] He also ordered that a new road be constructed to connect the two churches. The proposed church in Madolenihmw was to be built within a stone's throw of the Protestant Church. The governor ignored the strong Protestant support in Madolenihmw and the advice from his own priests against such a move. Believing in his own superiority, he ordered the completion of the church to coincide with the birthday of the Queen Regent of Spain.[62] His misjudgement and overall attitude fuelled simmering tensions on the island.

Fighting broke out between the Spanish and the people of Ohwa. Many of the Spanish soldiers and workers were killed. The surviving priests were assisted by Nahnpei to escape. News of the event reached Kolonia, whereupon the governor responded by sending the warship *Manila* to bombard Ohwa. This operation failed when the gunship ran into a reef. The soldiers who were sent ashore did not have the capacity to engage in combat with the islanders,[63] and knowledge of the terrain and seashores gave the locals the upper hand. It was mentioned in local accounts that magical power was also used to ward off the Spanish aggressors.[64] The soldiers were unable to bring order to Madolenihmw and returned to Kolonia to await further orders.

It took a few more months for reinforcements to arrive from the Philippines. The new commanding officer, Colonel Isidro Guiterrez, was keen to capture the local leaders and decisively wipe out the opposition.

---

59   The ABCFM and the Spanish Catholic Church were incorporated into local politics to increase the dominance of certain leaders. For the power struggle between the leaders in Kiti, see Hanlon, *Upon the Stone Altar*, pp. 311–313.
60   Hanlon, *Upon the Stone Altar*, pp. 311–313.
61   Hempenstall and Rutherford, *Protest and Dissent in the Colonial Pacific*, p. 114; Hanlon, *Upon a Stone Altar*, pp. 314–317.
62   Hezel, *Strangers in Their Own Land*, p. 40; Hanlon, *Upon a Stone Altar*, p. 312.
63   Hezel, *Strangers in Their Own Land*, p. 40; Hanlon, 'Sorcery, "Savage Memories" and the Edge of Commensurability', p. 114.
64   Hanlon, 'Sorcery, "Savage Memories" and the Edge of Commensurability', pp. 114–115.

His plans were thwarted by his lack of knowledge of the terrain and weather conditions in Pohnpei. His humiliation at failing to quickly achieve his objective eventually led to his suicide the night before he was to launch an attack on Ohwa.[65] Fighting resumed with the Pohnpeians, who continued to resist the assaults, using their local knowledge of the terrain. After many attempts to subdue the local resistance, the Spanish retreated to Kolonia, but only after they claimed a token victory in securing an abandoned local fort in Madolenihmw. The Spanish were confined to their little compound in Kolonia, protected by what is known today as the Spanish Wall.[66] The Spaniards' lack of knowledge on local politics, geography and the traditional system doomed their attempt to build a successful colony.[67] In the end, the Spanish withdrew in humiliation from Pohnpei. The Spanish Wall still stands in the heart of Pohnpei's capital, Kolonia, and is a reminder of Spain's short history in Micronesia.

Spain also attempted to set up a colony in Yap. While they encountered American missionaries in Pohnpei, they came across the already established German commercial interests in Yap. In an attempt to counter this influence, the whole Caroline Islands were awarded to Spain by the Vatican.[68] Relations between the Yapese and the Spanish were cordial but cautious. Hezel portrayed the Yapese as 'tenacious of their beliefs and practice … and … far more discriminative of what they would accept from the outside world'.[69] The Spaniards were quick to establish open and friendly relations with the local Yapese chiefs to achieve their aims in this well-regulated society.

Yapese resistance to Spanish rule was expressed in many forms. These forms included the continued traditional practices of keeping women in the men's long house for sexual purposes against Spanish wishes and the honouring of traditional gods. The Yapese paid lip service to the newcomers' wishes while continuing to pursue their own priorities behind the backs of the Spanish. The Spanish were quick to learn that maintaining the balance of power between the village chiefs was essential to maintaining their presence in Yap. For example, the chief of Gachpar withdrew his support when he complained about the lack of Spanish benefits reaching his village. In response to this displeasure, Governor Bartola and the senior

---

65   Hanlon, 'Sorcery, "Savage Memories" and the Edge of Commensurability', pp. 319–320.
66   Hanlon, *Upon a Stone Altar*, p. 329.
67   Hempenstall and Rutherford, *Protest and Dissent in the Colonial Pacific*, p. 108.
68   Hezel, *Strangers in Their Own Land*, pp. 8–9; Hanlon, *Upon a Stone Altar*, pp. 245–246.
69   Hezel, *Strangers in Their Own Land*, p. 15.

Spanish priests travelled to Gachpar to appease the powerful chief.[70] The governor humbled himself before the chief at the meeting. Sensing this humbleness and respect, the chief welcomed the governor, which opened a new frontier of mutually beneficial relations. The governor indicated that a missionary would come and live in Gachpar;[71] the chief saw this as a means of retaining his eroding power. The encounter prevented violence and was used as an educational example for the Spanish to cement peaceful coexistence between the Yapese and themselves.[72]

In the low-lying Caroline Islands, the Spanish exercised almost no power over the outer islands, which they rarely, if ever, visited. The islands were scattered over a large expanse of water, which was almost impossible to administer.[73] The Spanish Empire was also dwindling and lacked the necessary resources to enforce its rule. The islanders continued their cultural practices as usual. The handful of German traders who occasioned the islands to gather copra for the European market did not make significant inroads into inducing change on a large scale. This history of resistance held the islanders in good stead, ready to face the challenges posed by other external powers in later years.

Engagement with Germany

Spain's loss in the Spanish–American War resulted in Spain's ejection from Micronesia. As a spoil of war, the US took over Guam as an unincorporated territory. The rest of Micronesia was sold by Spain to Germany. Micronesians had already experienced German influence since they had been allowed to conduct commercial trade during the Spanish colonial era. However, Micronesians were not consulted about these arrangements.[74] Like the Spaniards before them, the Germans did not have a coherent policy in Micronesia. Their main objective was economic: to develop the copra industry and, later, exploit phosphate when it was discovered on Fais and Angaur.[75] In terms of enhancing the social and

---

70 Hezel, *Strangers in Their Own Land*, p. 24.
71 Hezel, *Strangers in Their Own Land*, p. 24.
72 Hezel, *Strangers in Their Own Land*, p. 24.
73 Hezel, *Strangers in Their Own Land*, p. 14.
74 Gale, *The Americanization of Micronesia*, pp. 30–31; Hempenstall and Rutherford, *Protest and Dissent in the Colonial Pacific*, p. 118; Hezel, *Strangers in Their Own Land*, pp. 94–95.
75 Hezel, *Strangers in Their Own Land*, pp. 121–122.

economic welfare of Micronesians, there was nothing much to show as the German companies adopted a laissez-faire approach. This suited the Micronesians as it minimised interruptions to their traditional lifestyles.

Yap and Pohnpei became hubs for German commercial and administrative activities headed by district officers and their entourages. German traders working for the Jailut Gesselshaft copra company in Chuuk and Kosrae were appointed as German representatives. To increase the volume of its copra exports to European markets, Germany encouraged copra production in the islands. The Micronesians understood clearly that the Germans were not in Micronesia to improve Micronesian's economic conditions, but for their own interests. As Micronesian scholar Walter noted, the German 'administration did not come to … [fulfil] the wishes of the Micronesian people, but according to their own desires'.[76] In Chuuk, copra was not profitable and so individual traders were left to pursue other business activities from which they might profit.[77] Elsewhere in Micronesia, copra was profitable due to different growing techniques.

Christianity continued to be used as a tool for Western indoctrination. A buy-back scheme to control the spread of guns was instituted to minimise local conflict in the hope of centring Christianity as the new locus of a renewed colonial era that it was hoped would bring peace and prosperity.[78] The success of these measures is questionable, given the continued presence of many 'pagan' practices in this period. For example, in the Mortlocks, *waitowa* (communicating to the spirits), *apwarik* (traditional dances), *falifel* (tattooing) and *apupulun fanou* (non-Christian marriages) were revived and continued to thrive. One missionary observed in reference to the islands of Nama and Ettal, 'neither the missionary activities nor the ship[s] [that carried European] civilisation changed their concepts and their mode of living'.[79] In Yap, the Spanish Missionaries struggled to end the 'institutional prostitution', high rate of divorce, polygamy and practise of *kan* (offerings to ancestral spirits).[80] Wilhelm Friedrich (a German missionary), who worked in the Mortlocks in the

---

76 Walter, *Desirability, Problems, and Methods of Achieving National Independence*, p. 34.
77 Francis X. Hezel, 'A Brief Economic History of Micronesia', *Past Achievements and Future Possibilities*, Majuro: Micronesian Seminar, 1984, pp. 11–62, micsem.org/pubs/articles/economic/frames/ecohistfr.htm.
78 Hezel, 'A Brief Economic History of Micronesia'.
79 Duane, *Clan and Copra*, p. 170.
80 Hezel, 'The Catholic Church in Yap: A Foothold in the Carolines', *Micronesian Seminar*, 2003, www.micsem.org/pubs/books/catholic/yap/.

1930s, complained about islanders who professed themselves as being Christians and yet 'continued to make use of magic means whenever something needs to be accomplished'.[81] In other outer islands such as Satawal and Ifalik, Christianity was virtually non-existent until the 1950s.[82]

Islanders from different parts of Chuuk were recruited on minimal wages to work in the mines in Nauru and Angaur.[83] Islanders from the low-lying islands in Yap were recruited to work on German projects on the main island and were also sent to Nauru, Palau and Fais to work in the phosphate mines. Internal island politics also played a role in the Yapese recruitment system as influential chiefs used their power in the *sawei* structure to extract wages from workers. However, at the same time, workers began to disassociate themselves from the *sawei* system when they realised the exploitative nature of the labour system.[84]

In Pohnpei, the German administration attempted to establish good relations with the locals but the memories of the Spanish era were still fresh. The relationship between the two sides was cordial but changed with subsequent German administrators. The Germans reimposed labour requirements for road construction and imposed a new tax regime and an obligation to work for 15 days on public projects.[85] A new land system based on individual ownership was also introduced in an attempt to drive a wedge between the *Nahnmwarki* and their subjects. The German administrators envisioned that a private land system would be more productive instead of the commoners paying tribute to the *Nahnmwarki* in return for occupying the land.

Local politics and personalities were also involved in the political discourse, and local action at times contradicted the German's administration policy. For example, businessman Henry Nanpei, who many claimed was the instigator of the 'Sokehs rebellion', attempted to turn the southern Protestants and the northern Catholics against each other to consolidate his own personal power.[86] Nanpei was a shrewd businessman who

---

81   Lothar Käser, 'Light in the South Seas. Wilhelm Friedrich & Elisabeth Kärcher: The Life and Work of a Liebenzell Missionary Couple', Verlag Der Liebenzeller Mission (Unpublished), p. 134.
82   Hezel, 'The Catholic Church in Yap'.
83   Marshall, *Namoluk beyond the Reef*, pp. 22–23.
84   Hezel, *Strangers in Their Own Land*, p. 109.
85   Hezel, *Strangers in Their Own Land*, p. 136.
86   Hezel, *Strangers in Their Own Land*, p. 134.

benefitted from the trade boom and a key player in the Protestant Church movement. He envisioned an alternative political system in Pohnpei premised on the parliamentary model, with himself as the new ruler of Pohnpei. His naked ambition was well known to the leaders of Pohnpei and the colonial masters.[87] His machinations were unsuccessful as the traditional system continued its course on the basis of the pre-existing social and political order.

Tension between Pohnpeians and their colonial administrators grew when a new German administrator, Boeder, was appointed to oversee German interests on the island. Boeder was well known for his harsh treatment of indigenous workers; for example, he had used force to put down a labour revolt against German interests in Africa. He came from a military background and was determined to emulate the brutal policies he oversaw while in Africa. He ignored sound advice from his predecessors and executed harsh measures whenever he could to match his Protestant work ethic.[88]

In the rush to complete the road construction, he forced a labour team to build a bridge to join the island of Sokehs and the main island of Pohnpei. He miscalculated the risk the work imposed on the indigenous road workers. Violence broke out when an overseer beat a local worker almost to the point of death. The Pohnpeian response was immediate and swift, and culminated in the loss of many lives on the German side, including Boeder himself. This event was a breaking point, at which the Pohnpeians felt the need to restore their pride and honour as embedded in their local customs and traditions.[89] The outsiders were oblivious to this reality and, as a result, contributed to their own demise. Like the Spanish governors before him, Boeder's sense of superiority and misjudgement led to the loss of his life.[90] The Micronesians, like any human group, tolerated external pressures to a certain extent, but they would not tolerate subjugation that undermined the roots of their culture and traditions. Violent resistance against outsiders periodically occurred in Micronesian history, but there

---

87   D'Arcy, 'Spanish and German Colonial Rule', pp. 3–5; Hempenstall and Rutherford, *Protest and Dissent in the Colonial Pacific*, p. 118.

88   D'Arcy, 'Spanish and German Colonial Rule', p. 4.

89   Hanlon, *Upon a Stone Altar*, p. 348.

90   D'Arcy, 'Spanish and German Colonial Rule', p. 4.

were internal mechanisms to control and minimise violence. Micronesian intellectuality also played its part to restore internal coherence for the purpose of peaceful coexistence.[91]

The news of Boeder's death at the hands of a few locals from Sokehs triggered a disproportionate German response. Germany dispatched gunships with trained troops from its headquarters in New Guinea. Upon their arrival, they bombarded the island of Sokehs with cannon fire in an attempt to flush out the perpetrators. However, those responsible had already escaped before the arrival of the German force. They were scattered around the main island of Pohnpei; many sought shelter with their relatives. After an intensive search for the perpetrators, the leaders of the resistance group gave themselves up to prevent any further bloodshed. The leaders were brought to Kolonia and executed in front of a crowd in the hope of teaching the locals a lesson of the consequence of disobeying their German masters.[92] The rest of the perpetrators were deported to Palau and Papua New Guinea. After the 'Sokehs incident', the Pohnpeians went back to their normal routine, only to be interrupted a few years later when the Japanese arrived in Pohnpei to establish a new colonial rule.

The German experience in Yap was the opposite of that in Pohnpei. Yap was considered a model colony. For example, the district officers realised that the best way to implement colonial objectives was first to win the hearts and minds of the Yapese people. To do so, they needed to understand the cultural structure of the island. Social relationships were the foundation of Yapese culture, and with that understanding, the Germans were able to develop a cordial relationship with the Yapese, especially with the chiefs.[93] It was a policy of inclusion, one that was mutually beneficial. The chiefs mobilised their people to assist in the development of colonial infrastructure such as roads, docks and offices, as well as abiding by the principles of law and order. In return, the chiefs received material benefits and German recognition of their chiefly status. The personalities of the German overseers also played a crucial role in bringing both sides together.[94]

---

91 The 'Sokehs rebellion' was caused by many factors, including both intra- and inter-clan rivalries (Paul Ehrlich, '"The Clothes of Men"', pp. 159–167).

92 Hezel, *Strangers in Their Own Land*, pp. 140–141.

93 Hezel, *Strangers in Their Own Land*, pp. 264–265.

94 Hezel, *Strangers in Their Own Land*, pp. 105–106.

One can argue that there was not much difference between the Spanish and German colonial policies in the Pacific. Both were caught up in their own pursuit of being world-class powers in the Pacific, using the islands, as Hezel claimed, as 'the ornament'[95] of their colonial power. The Micronesians' traditions continued to function as usual, with the incorporation of new ideas learned from the outside world. The lack of support from the motherland countries affected the manner in which colonial policies were implemented in Micronesia.[96] By and large, the German administrators were left to finance the running of their administration of Micronesia primarily based on their personal view as to what benefits Micronesia offered to Germany. The Germans' overly ambitious plan for Micronesia and their political temperament brought complications, particularly in Pohnpei as previously discussed.

Geography and resources dictated the way the Germans implemented their colonial policies. Violence was more pronounced in the high islands, as in the case of Pohnpei, while lowkey diplomatic tactics were the main norms of engagement in the low-lying islands.[97] The Micronesians were not easy to dominate since they did not allow the colonisers to have a free hand on their islands, as in the case of Pohnpei. Further, they had seen the different demands of the outsiders who frequented their islands throughout the Spanish and German colonial times. The islanders' responses were framed within the context of survivability and continuity.[98] They understood that each colonial power had its own weaknesses and thus limitations. The change of colonial flags represented the unsettling politics of the external world, which also enabled Micronesians to frame their mode of cautious responses to the continuing colonial process. In the main, the Micronesians did not have to fight too hard as the external world was unstable and changing.[99] In the end, Germany was too preoccupied with other affairs, culminating in World War I. The defeat of the Central Powers foreshadowed their territorial concessions to the victors. Great Britain later supported Japan in the League of Nations to take over the political administration of Micronesia.

---

95 Hezel, *Strangers in Their Own Land*, p. xiii.
96 Hezel, *Strangers in Their Own Land*, p. 136.
97 Hezel, *Strangers in Their Own Land*, pp. 81–82.
98 D'Arcy, 'Spanish and German Colonial Rule', pp. 5–6.
99 D'Arcy, 'Spanish and German Colonial Rule', p. 1.

Tolerating Japanese Colonisation

Japanese merchants were not new in Micronesia as many were already working on the islands during the German administration. Many locals were already familiar with the Japanese work ethic and general attitude towards islanders. Micronesia was annexed by Japan as a Class C mandate under strict order of the League of Nations. Under the terms of the mandate, Japan's responsibilities were framed in accordance with international terms to: 1) promote the material and moral wellbeing and social progress of the local inhabitants; 2) eliminate slavery, traffic in arms and ammunition and alcoholic beverages; 3) refrain from building fortifications and military bases or from giving military aid to Micronesians; 4) permit freedom and worship and missionary activity; and 5) submit an annual accounting report to the League of Nations by way of its mandates and commission.[100]

Yet again, Micronesia was passed to another colonial ruler without any Micronesian input into the process. Japan was mindful of its mandate, but in practice, its administrators paid only lip service to their obligations. For example, economic development was for the benefit of the Japanese rather than Micronesians.

Lacking the local knowledge to form a coherent policy for the implementation of the league's instructions in the Class C mandate, scores of Japanese scholars and technicians descended on the islands to conduct economic surveys and study the cultures of the area. However, the hidden dimension was the old practice of incorporating the islands into a foreign political structure. Japan built their economic vision on the existing infrastructure left by the Germans. From 1917 to 1922, basic systems for education and health were established and Christianity continued its course. Japanese became the official language of the islands. Copra and phosphate extraction continued, while fishing and agriculture were identified as having future economic potential.[101] However, to make these industries viable required a large labour pool from Japan, which also served as an outlet to relieve the overpopulation in their country.[102]

100 Gray, 'Modernization in Micronesia', p. 40.
101 D'Arcy, 'What was the Impact of Japanese Rule', pp. 10–12.
102 D'Arcy, 'What was the Impact of Japanese Rule', pp. 3–4.

In 1922, Japan started large-scale implementation of its development plan for Micronesia. Many more Japanese were sent to Micronesia, and towns like Kolonia in Pohnpei were referred to as 'little Tokyo' due to the preponderance of the Japanese population.[103] Japan upgraded the copra and phosphate businesses left by the Germans and maximised the output of the fishing and agricultural industries.[104] It is estimated that, at its peak in 1937, the fishing industry produced approximately 6,000 tons of *katsuobushi* (dried tuna) annually. The tuna trade brought in around ¥3 million profit annually, which tripled by the end of the decade.[105] Most of the fish exports were produced in Chuuk.

Pohnpei was developed into an agricultural hub. Large tracts of land were cleared to plant crops such as tapioca, cotton, coffee, eggplants, cucumber and others. Over ¥400,000 was earned from the export of tapioca alone.[106] Phosphate production increased from 60,000 tons before 1935 to 120,000 tons at the end of the decade. Copra production increased from 4,733 tons in 1922 to 13,703 tons in 1935.[107] The economic 'miracle' was expressed in the figures from 1935, where exports totalled ¥26 million and imports ¥15 million. Export revenue increased to ¥40 million by the end of the 1930s.[108] Many Micronesians entered the workforce on their own accord to earn money to supplement their needs, although for some it was by Japanese demand.

By the 1930s, the Japanese population in the islands outnumbered the Micronesians. The Japanese reaped the benefits of the economic boom, reinforced by a racial policy that created social divisions between Micronesians and non-Micronesians.[109] The Japanese occupied the upper echelon of the class structure, followed by Okinawans and others in the middle, and the *tomin* (Micronesians)[110] at the bottom. This racial division ran deep in the education system and the employment sector.

---

103 The development plan was to benefit the Japanese, whereby they would eventually outnumber indigenous Micronesians and build Japanese commercial centres like little towns in Japan (Hezel, 'A Brief Economic History of Micronesia').
104 Hezel, *Strangers in Their Own Land*, p. 195; Duane, *Clan and Copra*, p. 216.
105 Hezel, *Strangers in Their Own Land*, p. 197.
106 Hezel, *Strangers in Their Own Land*, p. 197.
107 D'Arcy, 'What was the Impact of Japanese Rule', p. 9.
108 Hezel, *Strangers in Their Own Land*, p. 198.
109 Hezel, *Strangers in their Own Land*, p. 204; D'Arcy, 'What was the Impact of Japanese Rule', p. 12.
110 '*Toming*' is a Japanese term for Micronesians. According to Mortlockese who survived the war, it was a derogatory term distinguishing between the so-called 'sophisticated' Japanese and the low-class Micronesians at the bottom of the class structure during the Japanese era. '*Kanaka*' was a similar term.

For example, D'Arcy noted that in the phosphate industry, Japanese workers earned ¥5.7–6.5 per day, whereas Micronesians received ¥1.2–1.5 per day.[111] In the public education system, Micronesians received three years of basic education compared to the six years required for Japanese children. Physical segregation continued in the classroom, where Micronesian children were taught separately.[112] Likewise, in the health sector, Micronesians occupied the lower levels in terms of employment and received meagre health treatment compared to their Japanese counterparts.

Micronesian responses to Japanese occupation continued. This was based on traditional social networking, where circulation of material goods for survival operated and benefits were shared among families. Micronesians entered the workforce to supplement their local lifestyle. Their participation in the workforce enlarged their understanding of the new immigrants, allowing them to strategise for the future. Such strategies became important when the Japanese fortified the islands in preparation for WWII. The Japanese sense of superiority over the Micronesians was soon to be shattered when they were humiliated and forcefully ejected from the islands at the hands of another outside power, the US.

Japan and Its Iron Fist

Survivors of WWII described the Japanese occupation in Micronesia as 'harsh', 'brutal' and 'unjust'.[113] Infliction of cruel punishments, land appropriation, slave labour (which the islanders called *kinrosy*), unwarranted execution and forced prostitution are some examples of the Japanese brutalities that the islanders were subjected to. Japan's misconduct was in defiance of the instructions of the League of Nations, which was to supposedly promote the welfare of the Micronesian people. Anthropologist Lin Poyer discussed such cruelties and brutalities and noted them as deliberate aspects of Japanese intimidation, intended to

---

111 D'Arcy, 'What was the Impact of Japanese Rule', p. 11.
112 According to family history, some of my uncles attended the school catering for Micronesian students, which was equivalent to elementary level. See Hezel, *Strangers in Their Own land*, pp. 172–173.
113 *Oral history* as told by my family members about the Japanese period of administration. See also D'Arcy, 'What was the Impact of Japanese Rule', p. 19.

force Micronesians to obey Japanese policy.[114] It was a deliberate attempt to break the spirit of the indigenous people to serve the war agenda of Japan.[115] The need to survive strengthened the extended family network that was itself the social net for survival. Gale noted:

> never before in Micronesian history had the transfer of authority from one regime to another been carried out by violence ... the gradual build-up in American naval strength led to the imposition of blockade that brought severe food shortages in its wake and in some places led to starvation and Japanese atrocities.[116]

A German Missionary who was in Chuuk during WWII also stated:

> even in plain view ... Japanese soldiers commit the most gruesome atrocities against the islanders. During one of [many] air raids many women, most of whom had to serve in forced prostitution for the imperial army, flee into a roofed-over trench close to the harbor. The commander in charge fears that the invasion of the American marines is just about to take place and he also fears that the island women he abused could speak out as witnesses against him. He therefore gives orders to kill the women. He calls three corporals to the trench. These fire their machine guns through the entrance into the deep darkness inside until the screams of the women are heard no more. With the help of a flashlight they then count about seventy bodies lying there in their blood.[117]

Starvation, enslavement of islanders and cannibalism also began to emerge in Chuuk.[118]

The main Japanese naval base in Micronesia was located in the Chuuk lagoon. The US did not invade the lagoon, instead employing its air force to bomb the Japanese fleet, airports and main installations. Many lives were lost during these bombardments. In the outer islands, bombs were dropped on Japanese installations but inflicted minimal damage.

---

114 Lin Poyer, 'Yapese Experiences of the Pacific War', *ISLA: A Journal of Micronesian Studies*, Vol. 3, No. 2, Dry Season 1995, pp. 223–224, 239–241; Suzane Falgout, Lin Poyer and Laurence Carucci, 'The Greatest Hardship: Micronesian Memories of WWII', *ISLA: A Journal of Micronesian Studies*, Vol. 3, No. 2, Dry Season 1995, pp. 210–211.
115 D'Arcy, 'What was the Impact of Japanese Rule', p. 12.
116 Gale, *Americanization of Micronesia*, p. 40.
117 Käser, 'Light in the South Seas', p. 116.
118 Falgout, Poyer and Carucci, 'The Greatest Hardship', pp. 203–222. Micronesian scholar Myjoylynn and local person Chero Erwin stated that Japanese cannibalism was true in regard to a person from their village nearby (pers. comm., 20 April 2015 and 2 February 2014). Their accounts are based on family history and local connection.

Most islanders in the outer islands escaped this nightmare as they had already been relocated elsewhere as part of Japanese security measures. The memories of such atrocities are still fresh in Micronesian minds today as the stories are told and retold by subsequent generations. Micronesians today ask the question, what did the innocent Micronesian civilians do to the Japanese that warranted their massacre? Micronesian suffering was neglected or treated as secondary to the sufferings of the combatants.[119]

Subsequent generations of Micronesians still possess the historical knowledge of the Japanese activities on their islands, as passed down from their families who survived WWII. In the low-lying atolls, islanders share stories of indigenous forced labour teams called *kinrosi*. The Japanese organised these teams, and every morning, islanders had to assemble for *antere*[120] to ensure they were all were ready to execute the daily tasks. People were severely beaten even if they had an authorised break or simply stood up to straighten their back after being bent over for hours.[121] Youth groups called *sainentang*[122] were created to spread Japanese indoctrination. For example, the Japanese required islanders to bow in the direction of Japan as a show of respect to the emperor when passing particular Japanese symbols placed along the roadside. If they forgot to bow, they were beaten.

Songs were recorded and sung on special occasions, which captured the collective imagination of the new generation about Japanese ill-treatment of their forebears.[123] People in the Mortlocks, the Chuuk lagoon, Kosrae, Pohnpei and elsewhere were removed from their homes to make room for the Japanese war effort.[124] Today, the end of Japanese occupation continues to be celebrated with community holidays. For example, the people of Satowan celebrate their holiday as a reminder of the islanders'

---

119 Falgout, Poyer and Carucci, 'The Greatest Hardship', pp. 204–205.

120 '*Antere*' was a term used by the Mortlockese to refer to morning roll call before the *kinrosi* teams started work. *Oral history* indicates that if someone was a no show, Japanese guards would look for the absent person and, once they were found, punish them with brutal force. See also Peter, 'Eram's Church (Bell)', p. 283.

121 My grandmother told me about the Japanese treatment of islanders during clean up. She was one of the victims of this brutality.

122 '*Sainentang*' is a Japanese term adopted by Mortlockese to refer to youth teams graded in terms of their skills and strength. See also Hezel, *Strangers in Their Own Land*, p. 174.

123 Florian Seady, '*Eshemeto papa mama ren ar riaffou*' is a song often sung by the Satowan people, reminding them of the hardship experienced during WWII and the day they finally returned to their island after being displaced by the Japanese military. The people of Satowan celebrate their freedom from the Japanese on 1 November (*Satowan Oral History* of Japanese occupation of Satowan).

124 Hezel, *Strangers in Their Own Land*, pp. 225–226.

resilience under the Japanese regime. Despite the displacement of islanders and the slave labour system imposed by the Japanese, the Mortlockese people continued to live traditionally by way of the *ainang* system. It restrengthened their identity and continuity as a people totally separate from the Japanese.[125]

However, it should be remembered that the islanders were not merely passive actors under the Japanese rule. The Micronesians exercised discretionary measures in an attempt to neutralise the Japanese system of oppression and subjugation, at least at the psychological level. For example, when food was in short supply due to the American blockade, agricultural products were reserved for Japanese soldiers. Any islanders found taking food crops from their own land were beaten. However, such brutality did not deter Micronesians' access to their land. They organised food-raiding parties at night, many of which were successful.[126] They devised an underground network based on kinship affiliation (or just being an islander bonded by their opposition to the Japanese) to share resources and enable them to patiently sit out the war. They reinforced each other's self-esteem and spied on the Japanese activities to shield each other.[127] The Micronesians knew the war was between outsiders and would eventually come to an end. Once the Japanese were defeated, the Micronesians regathered their lives and continued to live in accordance with their traditions while awaiting the new world order and whatever new colonial power that might bring.

Engagement with the US

Micronesians who survived WWII spoke of Japan's harsh mistreatment of them, which came to an abrupt end when the US dropped atomic bombs on Japan and forced it into accepting unconditional surrender. Some accounts of Micronesian experiences were recorded by non-Micronesians during the war but these are largely still missing from the records.[128] As in the past, oral history is relied on to portray a Micronesian

---

125 I heard Satowan people's experiences during the Japanese administration from Krispin Carlos, an uncle, when he attended the Mortlocks Junior High School in the early 1970s.
126 *Oral history* and family experience recounted by Kaiko Muritok. I heard this history when growing up in the Mortlocks during the 1970s. On the Japanese's cruel treatment of islanders, see also Käser, 'Light in the South Seas', pp. 159–163.
127 *Mortlocks Oral History*; Hezel, *Strangers in Their Own Land*, p. 240.
128 Käser, 'Light in the South Seas', pp. 162–168.

perspective of WWII. Micronesians were appreciative of the Americans when they expelled the Japanese from their islands. The US was not a new interloper in Micronesia. Its interests in the islands dated back to Captain Truxton of the USS *Jamestown* who signed a treaty in 1870 with the *Wasai* of Sokehs.[129] American ideologies had also spread via the ABCFM missionaries who had earlier established themselves in Pohnpei, Kosrae and later the Mortlocks and Chuuk lagoon.

Oral accounts record that the Mortlockese composed songs to welcome the Americans to their islands. The American flag was displayed in many public spaces as a symbol to represent their newly found freedom and peace. I remember clearly a song composed for the Americans that says, '*a urute ash filaik, filaik mi kirier o parapar*' ('let us raise our flag in stripes and red'), referring to the colours of the American flag.[130] It was a time for islanders to rest, rebuild their lives and contemplate their future. While the islanders did so, the US was formulating a plan for how to acquire the islands as part of its forward strategy to defend itself in the Pacific.[131]

While the US had favoured self-determination for Micronesia, its position changed when it realised Micronesia's growing strategic importance during WWII. This position led the US to negotiate with the UN to place the islands under a strategic trust territory, later known as the TTPI. This paved the way for the US to have an exclusive free hand in the islands. Having experienced WWII, the Micronesians understood that reliance and patience was the best possible survival approach to maintain their integrity and continuity. Colonialism was an anathema to their future survival. The US was in no hurry to improve the islanders' economic situation, which had been devastated by the war.[132] There were more pressing issues on the US's Pacific agenda, like using the Marshall Islands for nuclear tests and Saipan as a CIA training camp to subvert communist activities in China. Micronesian interests were put on the political backburner.

---

129 Hanlon, *Upon a Stone Altar*, pp. 202–205; Hezel, *The First Taint of Civilization*, pp. 231–232.
130 I learned the oral history of the war from my family members who experienced the war. I grew up listening and singing the song. During the Vietnam War, US naval ships would stop by Lekinioch Island and entertain the people by playing baseball and socialising. We sang the song of the US flag, but in retrospect, I wonder whether the Americans understood the song.
131 Rinn-Sup Shinn, 'Trust Territory of the Pacific Islands', in *Oceania, A Regional Study*, edited by Frederica M. Bunge and Melinda W. Cooke, Area Handbook Series, Foreign Area Studies, The American University, 1984, pp. 303–304.
132 Hanlon, *Making Micronesia*, p. 79; Gale, *The Americanization of Micronesia*, pp. 60–61.

The thousands of American lives lost in WWII and the close proximity of Micronesia to Asia fuelled the Pentagon's desire to retain possession of the islands.[133] Since then, the Pentagon's interest has been one of the main drivers of American policy in Micronesia, featuring in successive policies of the US Government. First, the US Government required the US Navy to administer the islands immediately after WWII. The Pentagon then imposed a wall of silence by sealing off the islands from the outside world as they were considered a sensitive military zone.[134] This policy denied Micronesians access to the outside world without the US's approval. When successive American policies were no longer effective due to Micronesian political pressures, the US's final tactic was the Compact of Free Association—a document framed in military terms and created to provide the US with a foothold in the FSM in 'perpetuity'.[135]

The US Navy supplied free food, education and healthcare and imposed a system of government based on what the US thought was appropriate. Inherent in this was the three levels (municipal, district and Trust Territory Government) and branches (executive, legislative and judiciary) of government that were slowly instituted. Six districts made up the TTPI: Palau, Yap, Ponape, Truk, the Marshall Islands and the Marianas Islands. Each island in the district formed a municipality and each district was comprised of a collection of municipalities grouped together on the basis of a shared perceived culture and language similarities.

At the municipal level, especially in the outlying islands, the inhabitants continued their traditional ways.[136] That is because the field trip ships that delivered supplies from the district centres were infrequent and there was thus less reliance on them. Sailing canoes continued to be used to maintain connections between islands, especially in Yap and Chuuk. Traditional social and religious practices were in the hands of traditional elders despite the presence of Christianity and the new system of American-inspired government.[137] The land system was largely unaffected in the villages, and law and order was left to the islanders to administer. Traditional agriculture and fishing remained the primary economic mode

133 Gale, *The Americanization of Micronesia*, pp. 60–61.
134 Paul D'Arcy, 'American Administration of Micronesia: 1946–1958', University of Hawai'i, 1986 (Unpublished paper), pp. 2–5.
135 *Compact of Free Association between the Federated States of Micronesia and the United States of America*, Compilation of Documents as Amended, Palikir, Pohnpei, FSM, 2003, Title Three, Articles I, IV, V.
136 D'Arcy, 'American Administration of Micronesia', pp. 2–5.
137 D'Arcy, 'American Administration of Micronesia', pp. 4–5.

of production despite the occasional USDA assistance and the free lunch programs distributed throughout the far-flung islands.[138] In some ways, the islanders adopted the newly introduced government model, but the substance of daily life remained largely Micronesian. The ongoing adaptation process to outside influences remained at the heart of continuity; that is, the rearticulation of relevant elements of the modern world was carefully crafted to suit the Micronesian context. Although Micronesians slowly entered the TTPI government structure at every level, political power remained in the hands of Americans. This reinforced the continuing feature of the colonial system, whereby Micronesians were always rated as second-class citizens.[139]

At the district level, administrators received their orders from the US high commissioner in Saipan, who in turn received his orders from Washington, DC. The district governments ran on a shoestring budget as infrastructure for development remained a problem. People who worked in the port towns began to derive benefits from the new post-war activities, though these were unevenly distributed. For example, in the Chuuk lagoon, inhabitants of the islands close to Moen (the port town) began to receive benefits from working in the capital.[140] This was not the case in the far-off islands in Yap, Pohnpei and Chuuk. Naturally, Micronesian cultures and identity were the foundation of continuity with these islands. The US concentrated on its own interests, leaving the Micronesians to think seriously about their own future.[141] Colonisation after all was about the self-serving interests of the outsiders at the expense of the traditional inhabitants. Once again, Micronesians were aware that the external world had undergone yet another reconfiguration process after WWII.[142] Perhaps most relevantly, decolonisation was underway across the world, prompting serious thoughts of independence among Micronesians. Micronesians wanted their islands to also be free from outside control and were not afraid to govern their islands under the new international order.

---

138 My personal experience growing up in the Trust Territory era. Free lunch programs were provided to elementary schools and in the aftermath of typhoons. See also Marshall, *Namoluk beyond the Reef*, pp. 65–66; Nason, *Clan and Copra*, pp. 266–267, 276.

139 Hanlon, *Remaking Micronesia*, pp. 40–41.

140 Goodenough, *Property, Kin and Community on Truk*, p. 26. I attended high school in Weno during the 1970s. At the village level, most villagers relied on traditional food production and the sharing of this produce.

141 D'Arcy, 'American Administration of Micronesia', pp. 1–2.

142 Gale, *The Americanization of Micronesia*, pp. 60–61.

In response to the emerging decolonisation process, the US Department of the Interior (DOI) took over responsibility for the islands from the Department of the Navy in 1957. This was to create the image that the US was not another colonial power but an interim administrator, responsible for stewardship only until the inhabitants chose their own political future. American policy under the DOI was slow and cautious; it was business as usual. The DOI was oblivious to the political undercurrents gathering strength and unifying the islanders' voices in seeking an alternative to the status quo.[143] The policy of benign neglect was exposed in the 1960s when the US was criticised by the UN Security Council for the dereliction of its duties under the trusteeship agreement.[144]

Nevertheless, military interests remained influential in the formulation of policies regarding Micronesia's future. Micronesians, after a long period of waiting, took matters into their own hands. They established the COM in the mid-1960s as a forum for political dialogue between the districts in their efforts to consider different options for the future. When the US realised that the Micronesians were seriously considering their future, they pre-empted the issue by offering the Micronesians commonwealth status.[145] This offer was rejected outright and, after a series of negotiations, the US realised that it could no longer stop Micronesian leaders from pursuing independence.

To retain its strategic interests in Micronesia, the US crafted the Compact of Free Association. Under the Compact, the US proposed to have 'veto' power to override a future constitution in the event Micronesians pushed for independence, effectively continuing US administration of the islands. The Micronesian side disagreed and continued to push for full independence. Independence meant a break from its colonial past and a renewal of Micronesian freedom enshrined in international law, yet framed in terms of Micronesia's traditional past.

The islands were the sites of many fierce battles in the Pacific, where the US lost many soldiers fighting the Japanese.[146] It was this experience that prompted the US to keep the islands as part of its security zone to avert future aggression from Asia. The Pentagon was at the forefront of

---

143 Hanlon, *Making Micronesia*, pp. 161–162.
144 D'Arcy, 'American Administration of Micronesia', pp. 1–2.
145 Hanlon, *Making Micronesia*, pp. 220–221.
146 Bill Jeffery, *War in Paradise WWII: Sites in Truk Lagoon, Chuuk, Federated States of Micronesia*, Chuuk Historical Preservation Office, 2003, pp. 3–8.

this push to keep Micronesia within the US's sphere of influence. Like before, the traditional inhabitants were not consulted[147] because they were considered too weak to resist the US's wishes. While other trust territories were quickly decolonised, the TTPI was in political limbo since the US had its own plan for the territory's future.[148]

Micronesians were stateless people in the sense that the US controlled all matters concerning the governance of the territory. For example, the TTPI granted America authority over passport control and thus over the international movement of all of Micronesia's inhabitants. The passports issued to Micronesians read:

> the rightful holder of this passport is a citizen or inhabitant of the Trust Territory of the Pacific Islands under United States administration and is entitled, under Article Eleven of the Trusteeship Agreement between the United States and the United Nations Security Council … to receive diplomatic and consular protection of the United States of America. This passport is not valid for travel to the following areas under control of authorities with which the United States does not have diplomatic relations: Albania, Cuba, North Korea, and Vietnam.[149]

This restriction on Micronesian travel could only be lifted if Micronesia achieved its independence as a nation state.

Discontent towards the US increased, and the leaders of the TTPI banded together to inform the US that they wanted to run their own government in accordance with their own political design.[150] They demanded independence on the basis of the principle of inalienable human rights under international law. The question was not how Micronesians should achieve their independence but, rather, what was the quickest way to achieve this goal.[151]

---

147 Robert Kiste, 'Termination of the US Trusteeship in Micronesia', *Journal Pacific History*, Vol. 21, No. 3, July 1986, pp. 127–128.
148 Robert Kiste, 'Overview of US Policy', in *The Ninth Annual Pacific Islands Studies Conference Proceedings: History of the US Trust Territory of the Pacific Islands*, edited by Karen Knudsen, University of Hawai'i, 1985, pp. 1–4; Gale, *The Americanization of Micronesia*, pp. 60–61.
149 Gonzaga Puas, *TTPI Passport* (issued in 1982). I am still in possession of this passport, which instructs the bearer not to enter the countries listed on the passport.
150 Glenn Petersen, 'Differences, Connections, and the Colonial Carousel in Micronesian History', *Pacific Asia Inquiry*, Vol. 2, No. 1, Fall 2011, pp. 14–16.
151 Petersen, 'Lessons Learned', p. 61.

To the US, the wish was laughable; they thought the Micronesians were unsophisticated and incapable of running their own affairs either domestically or internationally, having been cocooned politically by colonialism.[152] The downside of this assumption was that the Americans did not bother to understand the Micronesians' desire. The US's resistance only hardened the Micronesian position, and TTPI leaders rejected all American offers short of independence. Faced with mounting pressure, the US caved and started negotiations for Micronesian independence.

To achieve independence, a constitution was required to attain Micronesian sovereignty, as demanded by international law. In 1979, the Constitution was finalised and became the law of the land and the basis for formulating relations with the external world.[153] Losing the islands again to a foreign power was unthinkable according to the FSM's leaders.[154] However, Micronesians were happy to retain some form of loose association with the US in exchange for assistance regarding economic development and support for international recognition of Micronesian independence. After many years of negotiations, the FSM finally gained its independence on 3 November 1986 after the UN Security Council formally terminated the trusteeship agreement with the US. This date is considered the end of colonialism in the FSM and is celebrated as FSM Independence Day.

Since independence, the Compact of Free Association has been used by the US to remain in Micronesia, with the FSM Government receiving billions of dollars of necessary funding in return. The Compact was renegotiated in 2001 and extended to the year 2023, at which time certain Compact funding will be under review. However, after 2023, the FSM will access its trust fund, set up to replace the Compact funds. It has been estimated that there will be an annual shortfall of US$600 million in the trust fund,[155] and thus a blowout in the FSM's budget unless other sources of income are found.[156] As pointed out in the DOI's report on the FSM economy dated 16 November 2011, 'the most devastating conclusion of the report

---

152 Petersen, 'Lessons Learned', pp. 17–18.
153 Puas, 'The FSM Legal System', p. 3.
154 John Haglelgam, Interview, College of Micronesia, Palikir, 7 January 2012.
155 President Emmanuel Mori, *State of the Nation Address*, Congress of the Federated States of Micronesia, Palikir, Pohnpei, 18 May 2012.
156 Pers. comm. with many officials in the FSM Government, especially in the Departments of Foreign Affairs and SBOC during field study in July 2013. President Mori's Speech, *President's State of the Nation Before the 18th Congress of the FSM*, 29 May 2014, Palikir, Pohnpei.

is FSM's 2023 estimated $265–$600 million trust fund shortfall of the $1.82 billion target' to live off during the post-2023 era.[157] These future challenges are discussed in Chapter 4.

Conclusion

Colonisation in the FSM took many forms and was dependent on the policy of the particular colonial power. Micronesian continuity relied on the strength of their customs and identity in their engagements with the colonial powers. For example, Micronesians survived by utilising their network via the *ainang* system. The colonists misunderstood this and the geography of the islands. Despite all the colonial policies implemented to disempower Micronesians, colonisation was not successful in Micronesia. Micronesians developed an understanding of the external world and the changing alliances within it as a result of their exposure to colonialism. The changing colonial masters in Micronesia were part of a bigger picture beyond the horizon—something quickly understood by the islanders. The islanders understood that they had to be patient and wait, and eventually political control would come full circle. Micronesian history is about a people with patience, respect for reciprocity, connectivity and intellectual prowess. These values formed the basis of Micronesian identity and continuity as an independent people, which will be discussed further in the next chapter.

157 Tammy Doty, 'Interior Releases Report on FSM Economy', *Micronesia Forum*, 16 November 2011, www.micronesiaforum.org/index.php?p=/discussions.

4

Negotiating Independence

Introduction

Prior to colonial rule, each island in Micronesia governed itself. However, the islands were linked via an extensive inter-island network centred on the *ainang* system. This system survived four successive colonial powers because of the limited influence of colonialism, which was largely confined to the port towns. In the 1970s, the Micronesians faced the prospect of independence framed in the image of a nation state. This chapter discusses the processes that led to the shaping of the FSM's independence post WWII and issues that arose following independence.

Three factors underpinned the people's desire for independence as promoted by Micronesia's founding fathers. The first was the US's adamant intention to fully incorporate the islands into its political sphere of influence regardless of Micronesian wishes. The second was the Micronesian leaders' own political consciousness stemming from their understanding of the new world order, which drove them to move the islands towards independence. The third was the indigenous notion of how independence should be shaped based on historical and cultural imperatives, rather than in a form imposed by outside forces. Concerns over these factors seemed increasingly justified post independence during the debate about the Compact of Free Association. A number of Micronesian leaders were especially concerned about the terms of the 'permanent denial clause' sought by the US as a restriction on the FSM's independence. Although initially agreed to by Micronesian representatives, this clause remained a concern and the Compact was amended in 2001.

Images of Micronesia Post WWII

Oral accounts from the Mortlocks recall that immediately after WWII, US military forces rounded up the Japanese garrisons in the islands and deported them back to Japan. For example, on Satowan and Lukunor islands, Japanese soldiers were disarmed and taken to the docks, where American naval crafts transported them to American warships anchored offshore to repatriate them back to Japan. During this process, the islanders would call out, '*awlela Resepan auspaw shuan no liwin*' ('go home Japanese do not come back') and sarcastically bid *saionara*[1] forever to the soldiers. However, American soldiers were welcomed with open arms.

Mortlockese people often communicate in a language of distortion called *afeliel* (hidden meanings) about issues affecting them. This is an offshoot of a special language used between *itang*.[2] Messages are delivered in a secretive mode of communication only understood by an intended audience. For example, people of Satowan Island are famous for using *kapas apiliwek* (reverse psychology) when talking between themselves.[3] A level of familiarity is required to decipher the meaning of the language during conversation. *Afeliel* and *kapas apiliwek* were used to communicate hidden messages between islanders during WWII. This provides an example of how Micronesians maintained their connection with each other during the extended colonial period.

---

1   '*Saionara*' is an adopted Japanese term meaning to bid farewell. Bidding farewell in Mortlockese is '*aulela*'.

2   '*Itang*' is a person with many talents, knowledge and skills. They can be an orator, manipulator, warrior, negotiator and historian, for example. People respect *itang* because of their wisdom and knowledge.

3   Okusitino Māhina, a Tongan scholar referred to the same in interpersonal dialogue called *helihaki* (to speak one thing but mean another). It demonstrates the extent to which communication can be manipulated in different Pacific Islands contexts. See Okusitino Māhina, 'The Poetics of Tongan Traditional History, Tala-e-fanua: An Ecology Centred Concept of Culture and History', *Journal of Pacific History*, Vol. 28, No. 1, June 1993, p. 113.

This metaphoric language is not confined to the Mortlocks but is also used in Yap and Pohnpei. For example, Glenn Petersen referred to a common practice in Pohnpei called *kanengamah*, where the indigenous people use metaphoric language to conceal real meanings in their communication with each other. Peterson notes that *kanengamah* means:

> deliberately concealing the truth about oneself or what one knows, and it is tempting to liken it to a lie. Pohnpeians do not perceive it as lying, however, concealment is different than distortion or outright falsehood.[4]

Manipulation of the local languages was necessary to transmit information between Micronesians about Japanese activities without detection. Survival strategies also included using local knowledge to secretly harvest Micronesians' own land at night. There were stories told by my elders about locals who were pursued by Japanese guards while tending the gardens at night. However, the islanders were not caught and Japanese attempts to identify the culprits floundered when they could not penetrate the solidarity of silence among extended family networks. Japanese investigations of the raids were unsuccessful due to the solidarity of the Micronesian people.

My grandfather likened Micronesia after WWII to a fatigued elderly man slow in movement but with a sharp, agile mind; retaining his intellectual wit to maintain his personal integrity, though retired from physical labour.[5] Having been a grandfather many times over, he was used to providing for his extended family with his bare hands; he did not need someone else's imposed charity. He was worried about the future of his children and, as such, instructed them politely to rely on their own capabilities and be productive if they wanted to survive. He believed that receiving charity from someone else's sweat should not be a part of their future. This personal recollection, while anecdotal, reflects beliefs common to my grandfather's generation. This chapter will suggest that this attitude

---

4   Petersen, 'Kanaegamah and Pohnpei's Politics of Concealment', p. 34; Hempenstall and Rutherford, *Protest and Dissent in the Colonial Pacific*, p. 107. Hempenstall and Rutherford referred to *kaningama* (note their different spelling) as 'a poker-faced patience in the face of life's adversities'.
5   Ring Puas was one of the leaders of Lukunor or Lekinioch Island post WWII. He was a traditional chief and the magistrate of Lekinioch Municipality. He later became an associate judge in the Truk District judiciary system and subsequently an associate justice of the state of Chuuk Supreme Court (Hanlon, *Making Micronesia*, p. 88). See also *Micronesian Reporter*, Saipan, July 1962, Micronesian Leaders Conference <001 19780700: 32 - Pacific Digital Library>; Micronesian Reporter <001 19570300: 19 - Pacific Digital Library>.

of self-reliance prevailed at this time and indeed throughout Micronesian history, and the outsiders' failure to realise this was a significant reason for the failure of colonial regimes. The Micronesians' attitude was, however, often masked behind polite smiles of silence that outsiders mistook for compliance and consent.

My grandfather's rhetoric condemned outsiders' treatment of Micronesians.[6] In his humble view, outsiders disrespected the indigenous population by reducing them to second-class citizens.[7] Despite all the adaptation, assimilation and re-contextualisation of outside forces, he thought independence should be sought through islanders' intellectual wit and built solidly on Micronesian integrity and identity.[8] He believed that it was the only way forward to restore indigenous dignity. Coincidently, his views resonated with many Micronesians, especially the leaders who fought for independence, and similar rhetoric was used to put the wheels of independence into motion.[9]

Centuries of foreign rule had left Micronesians suspicious of outsiders. Their suspicions were expressed in various forms of local resistance against the colonisation process. Memories of subjugation among Micronesians laid the foundation for Micronesian unity and political independence.[10] Independence gained momentum after WWII when the circumstances of the external world changed and the US desired outright annexation of the islands.[11] This was not acceptable to Micronesian leaders.

Micronesians' first priority was to continue to survive. The land and sea remained the sources of sustaining their livelihood. Micronesians did not conceal their genuine appreciation of the Americans who had ejected the Japanese from their islands.[12]

---

6   David Hanlon, 'Patterns of Colonial Rule in Micronesia', in *Tides of History: The Pacific Islands in the Twentieth Century*, edited by K. R. Howe, Robert C. Kiste and Brij V. Lal, University of Hawai'i Press, 1987, pp. 93–94.

7   D'Arcy, 'What was the Impact of Japanese Rule', pp. 6–7.

8   My personal knowledge. See fn. 5 for Ring Puas.

9   *Mortlocks Oral History.* Although Ring was a traditional chief, his thoughts coincided with the objectives of the FSM's leaders for independence (Hanlon, *Making Micronesia*, p. 88).

10   Hanlon, 'Patterns of Colonial Rule in Micronesia', pp. 93–96.

11   Kiste, 'Termination of the US Trusteeship in Micronesia', p. 127.

12   *Oral history* of Lekinioch Island. See also Hezel, *The New Shape of Old Island Cultures*, pp. 4–5.

Figure 9: War relics on Satowan in the Mortlock Islands.

Source: Photograph courtesy of Vince Sivas (October 2013).

Figure 10: Airplane wreckage on Satowan Island from the Japanese period.

Source: Photograph courtesy of Vince Sivas (October 2013).

Responses to the TTPI

At first, Micronesians were curious as to what the US had planned for their islands after the war. The islands were soon classified as a strategic trust territory, later known as the TTPI. Unlike the other 11 trust territories that existed after WWII, which were under the UN Trusteeship Council, the TTPI was also put under the supervision of the UN Security Council.[13] The reason for this was that the US had a veto power in the UN Security Council and could therefore control the future of the TTPI. As Roger Gale commented, the US 'created a unique entity ... different from the other trust territories in that its political status cannot be altered without the permission of the administering authority'.[14]

Under the UN trusteeship agreement, the US had responsibilities to develop the islands socially, economically and politically before the Micronesians could decide their future.[15] Like the Union of Soviet Socialist Republics (USSR) in Eastern Europe, the US drew its own iron curtain over the territory by sealing off the islands as a strategic and militarily sensitive area.[16] Outsiders, including American civilians, required permission to enter the TTPI. The 'iron curtain' years contributed to the slow economic development of Micronesia. There was not enough exposure of islanders to the outside world, and the outside world had no opportunity to learn what Micronesians were experiencing under the US. Micronesians were kept in the dark and isolated from the flow of international information. Like previous colonial practices, the inhabitants of the TTPI were not consulted about their future. It became apparent that the new administration was planning to remain in the islands, just like the previous colonial powers.

The TTPI comprised six districts: Ponape,[17] Truk,[18] Palau, Yap, the Marshall Islands and Marianas Islands. Their function was to organise services for the municipalities and implement the TTPI Government's objectives.

---

13 Gale, *The Americanization of Micronesia*, pp. 61–62.
14 Gale, *Americanization of Micronesia*, p. 12.
15 *Charter of the United Nations and Statutes of the International Court of Justice*, Chapter XII, Article 76(b), www.un.org/en/about-us/un-charter/full-text.
16 Kiste, 'A Half Century in Retrospect', p. 461.
17 Which later changed its name to its indigenous name, Pohnpei.
18 Which later changed its name to its indigenous name, Chuuk.

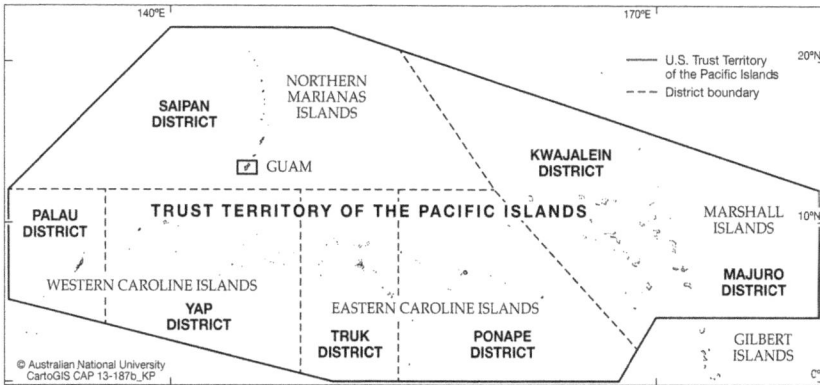

Figure 11: Map of the Trust Territory of the Pacific Islands (TTPI) prior to its break up into separate political entities in the 1970s.
Source: Map produced by ANU CartoGIS.

A high commissioner was appointed by the US president to liaise between Washington, DC, and the Micronesian people. The commissioner had the power to make decisions for the TTPI without Micronesian input. Before the creation of the COM in 1965, the US made little progress in developing the islands as required under the UN agreement.[19] It only built and maintained a skeleton infrastructure necessary to achieve its own strategic goals, seemingly oblivious to the realities on the ground.[20] For example, expenditure for the TTPI was estimated at US$5.2 million per annum during the US Navy administration. This increased to US$7.5 million[21] by the time the DOI took over. This was insufficient to meet the costs of running the territory and building effective infrastructure. As the wealthiest and most powerful nation in the world, the US's financial commitment to the TTPI was dismal.

Public buildings such as classrooms and dispensaries, as well as public homes in the district centres, were rudimentary structures of corrugated iron, plywood and whatever could be salvaged from the war.[22] The road system was in disrepair and needed maintenance. The main docks were only maintained to minimum standards to allow shipments in and out of the port towns.[23] There was also a discrepancy in salaries between

---

19   Kiste, 'Overview of US Policy', pp. 8–9.
20   Hanlon, *Remaking Micronesia*, pp. 135–139.
21   Meller, *Constitutionalism in Micronesia*, pp. 15–16; Kiste, 'Overview of US Policy', p. 10.
22   Hezel, *Strangers in Our Own Land*, p. 324.
23   I attended high schools in Weno and Pohnpei during this period and witnessed the docks.

the Americans and the local people. Americans were paid more than Micronesians with the same qualifications. Social interaction was almost non-existent as Americans had their own social spaces such as social clubs, houses and offices.[24]

In the outer islands, the inhabitants were virtually left alone and traditional lifestyles remained largely unaffected by the American presence. The municipal governments, schools, churches and the local health system were predominantly run by the few elected officials who were also traditional leaders. Sailing canoes continued to be the main mode of inter-island transportation. Inter-island contacts remained vital as economic and social interdependency continued to be maintained.[25] Decisions made in a distant land had little impact on the daily life of the inhabitants of the atolls.[26] Colonialism and WWII in particular had interrupted their lifestyle and the post-war period was an opportunity to reassert traditional ways of survival adapted to the modern world. It was understood that the Americans had their own agenda, just like the previous colonial powers. The idea of political independence was not fostered by the US but reached a crescendo at the discussion table in 1965 when the COM was formed.[27]

The ongoing importance of traditional institutions did not mean Micronesians were against change. Frustrated with the slow pace of development, Micronesians devised ways to be heard by the international community. The Micronesians expressed their concerns to the UN visiting missions as well as appearing in the UN in the early 1960s. The COM throughout the 1970s and 1980s took up the cry for independence.[28] Micronesians' push for self-determination later gained sympathy in the UN.[29] For example, the former USSR became a prominent critic of the US's performance in the TTPI. The US, for its part, continued to present

---

24 *Lukunor Oral History* told by the people of Lukunor who worked in the port town of Moen during the Trust Territory days. The issue was more pronounced on the island of Ebye, next to the military base in the Marshall Islands, where the indigenous people lived in rundown squalor. See Hanlon, *Remaking Micronesia*, p. 188.

25 Peter, 'Chuukese Travelers and the Idea of Horizon', p. 264; D'Arcy, *The People of the Sea*, p. 166.

26 *Oral History*. See also Hezel, *The New Shape of Old Island Cultures*, pp. 3–4; Kiste, 'Overview of US Policy', pp. 1–2.

27 *Oral History*. See also Kiste, 'Overview of US Policy', pp. 1–3.

28 D'Arcy, 'American Administration of Micronesia', pp. 1–2.

29 Gale, *Americanization of Micronesia*, pp. 98–99.

an image that it was working towards fulfilling its obligations under the UN agreement. The reality was different on the ground; it was business as usual, with limited development or consultation with the locals.[30]

Organising Micronesians

A UN visiting mission to the TTPI in 1961 reported that the US 'must end its neglect and undertake greater efforts to prepare the TTPI for self-government'.[31] The visiting mission also revealed that the long presence of the US in the islands had not contributed to serious development. A number of common phrases were used to describe the US's poor record in the TTPI, such as 'benign neglect', 'the Rust Territory' of the 'pathetic' islands, and that Micronesians had 'the trust' but Americans had the territory.[32] The USSR was highly critical of the US following the release of the UN visiting mission's report in 1961. The report's criticism of the US for not fulfilling its obligations under the UN agreement was echoed by the USSR and the Micronesians, who were invited to the UN General Assembly to voice their experiences of the US's failure to carry out its responsibilities in the territory.[33]

The Kennedy administration responded to the criticism by appointing Professor Anthony Solomon from Harvard University to undertake a study of the TTPI. The purpose was to provide information to President Kennedy on how the US should proceed in terms of the TTPI's future in order to avoid further political embarrassment. The professor subsequently produced the famous Solomon Report, which strongly recommended rapid Americanisation of the TTPI in anticipation of full annexation of the islands.[34]

---

30 Kiste, 'Overview of US Policy', pp. 2–4.
31 Hanlon, *Remaking Micronesia*, p. 91; Meller, *Constitutionalism in Micronesia*, p. 15.
32 During my contract work with the Congress of FSM and the Department of Justice, the terms were often used by many FSM government officials to blame the US's historical record of the lack of development in the FSM. See Peter, 'Chuukese Travellers', pp. 258, 260. Others took the opposite view, claiming that the FSM should grow up and accept its own faults on this issue. As Mariena Dereas, a senior lecturer in Micronesian Studies at the College of Micronesia said, 'let's get it right this time, and forget the old thoughts'. This seems to be the new motto for the new intellectuals who do not want to waste their energy on blaming others. I interviewed Mariena and her colleagues on 11 January 2011 in Palikir, Pohnpei.
33 Epel Illon, Interview, 13 January 2011, about his appearance in the UN in the early 1980s.
34 Hanlon, *Remaking Micronesia*, pp. 93–94.

Americanisation meant a structural reform to systematically indoctrinate Micronesians through education, law, politics and economics to embrace all things Americana.[35] To reinforce the reform agenda in the TTPI, American agents of change such as anthropologists, economists, educators and lawyers were involved in targeting the new generation of Micronesians to embrace America. The US also increased its funding to the TTPI to upgrade infrastructure and further facilitate its future objectives for the territory. For example, the budget in 1952 was US$7.5 million; this increased to US$25 million in 1967 and reached its peak of US$85 million dollars in 1977.[36] Jobs were created, new classrooms were built, free lunch programs were implemented, and the mass promotion of American culture in the public domain occurred through movies and music.

Such American action was ironically subverted when Micronesians began to attend tertiary institutions in the US and encountered the realities of Americana, including racism. These students started to question the 'American lifestyle' compared to that of their island cultures. For example, many realised that should the islands become part of the US political family, Micronesians would suffer in an American system where indigenous peoples were to be found on the lower rungs of the social ladder. This arose from their direct observations of the status and treatment of minorities such as the Chamorros, Hawaiians and the American Indians.[37]

Racism also affected Micronesian leaders' perceptions of the American system. As Bethwel Henry, former speaker of the COM, said to me during an interview, 'my experience of racial discrimination occurred during my trip to the US. I asked a taxi driver in Kansas to drive us to a hotel, but they dumped us at a hotel for coloured people only'.[38] Patsy Mink, then congresswoman for Hawai'i, favoured incorporation of Micronesia but

---

35   A. N. Solomon, *Report by the US Government Survey Mission to the Trust Territory of the Pacific Islands*, Washington, DC, 1963, vol. 2, p. 3.

36   Gale, *Americanization of Micronesia*, p. 104. Sapuro Rayphand, Interview (online), 13 December 2013. Sapuro was a qualified teacher with a master's in education from Lekinioch, who taught in many schools of the Trust Territory, including Saipan. He was told that the gap in pay between Americans and Micronesians was because American teachers needed to pay for their own accommodation and food. This was a poor excuse—why did Sapuro not receive such compensation on Saipan since he was away from home and needed to pay for his own accommodation and food?

37   Bethwel Henry (former speaker of the Congress of Micronesia), Interview, Kolonia, Pohnpei, 28 June 2012.

38   Henry, Interview, Kolonia, Pohnpei, 28 June 2012.

declared in 1971: 'It seems obvious that Micronesians will not be satisfied with anything less than independent status, and the longer a decision is delayed, the more insistent they will become'.[39]

The first generation of Western-trained intellectuals and leaders, like Bethwel Henry, Tosiwo Nakayama, Petrus Tun, John Mangefel, Jacob Nena and Leo Falcalm, were already advocating for independence for Micronesia based on their own experiences in American universities.[40] These leaders in the making became a political force of considerable influence in Micronesia. They formed a substantial lobby group to arrest the rising tide of Americanisation in Micronesia. This new phase, which arose from the new educated elite, contributed to the waning support for full acceptance of Americanisation or annexation in the islands. The waning support also stemmed from other reasons. First, Micronesians were directly exposed to a greater level of Americanisation, providing them with the opportunity to evaluate American values and culture compared to their own. Second, many of the American professionals exported to the TTPI to implement American objectives were young and full of ideals and empathy. Once exposed to the weaknesses and hypocrisies within the US's political system, many became friends of the Micronesian movement for independence.[41] Third, the Micronesian leadership made it clear to the Micronesian populace that becoming part of the US would likely see them lose their land and become second-class citizens.

Micronesian Dissatisfaction

In 1961, a UN report condemned the US for not developing the islands to a level acceptable under the trusteeship agreement. The US had breached its duties and obligations materially under the agreement, which imposed upon the US the responsibilities to develop the islands economically, socially and politically before the issue of self-determination could be decided.[42] In 1965, the COM asked the US to produce serious plans to develop Micronesia economically and politically.[43] The uneven

---

39   Gale, *Americanization of Micronesia*, p. 230.
40   Henry, Interview, Kolonia, Pohnpei, 28 June 2012.
41   Henry, Interview, Kolonia, Pohnpei, 28 June 2012.
42   Solomon, *Report by the US Government Survey Mission to the Trust Territory of the Pacific Islands*, vol. 2, pp. 3–10; Bethwel Henry (the first speaker of the Congress of Micronesia), Interview, 28 June 2012.
43   Hanlon, *Making Micronesia*, pp. 119–122.

development throughout the TTPI and the lack of Micronesian input at the top echelon of the decision-making process were key elements driving Micronesian political frustration.[44] For example, Micronesians complained about the hiring practices in the public sector, wherein Americans still occupied the best-paying jobs despite there being qualified Micronesians who could perform at that level. In a way, it was the recycling of past colonial practices where Micronesians were at the bottom of the economic ladder. Many islanders had the requisite qualifications and wanted the top positions.[45] For example, a former Micronesian teacher I interviewed said that he was receiving US$3,000 per annum in the 1960s, which increased to US$5,000 in the mid-1970s. By comparison, American teachers were paid US$12,000 annually.[46] In response, the COM legislated for Micronesians to be paid a salary based on the philosophy of 'equal work, equal pay'.[47]

The discrepancy in conditions between the district centres also became apparent. For example, Saipan, where the headquarters of the TTPI was located, continued to benefit from the US's greater presence while underdevelopment continued to be the norm in other district centres such as Yap, Truk and Ponape.[48] In the outer islands, life continued as usual. Visits to the outer islands by the field trip ships were infrequent. Health and education programs were left to the locals to organise as they had always done in the past. They continued their traditional system of governance while adapting to the new American-formed municipal governments.

In the Mortlocks, for example, history remained largely taught by the elders, Christianity and local religious beliefs coexisted, and economic activities concentrated on taro farming, fishing and breadfruit harvesting. Although there was meagre cash made from copra trading, it was often shared by the extended family.[49] It was the same pattern in the other low-lying atolls in the TPPI such as in the districts of Yap and Ponape. News of local government activities and plans could be heard on the new

---

44 Bethwel Henry (the first speaker of the Congress of Micronesia), Interview, 28 June 2012.
45 Gale, *Americanization of Micronesia*, p. 126; Hanlon, *Remaking Micronesia*, p. 102.
46 Sapuro Rayphand, Interview, Guam, 13 December 2013. Sapuro was a teacher during the Trust Territory days from the 1960s to 2010. He holds a master's in education from the University of Guam, yet was paid less than his American counterparts (see fn. 36).
47 Bethwel Henry (the first speaker of the Congress of Micronesia), Interview, 28 June 2012.
48 Hezel, *Strangers in Their Own Land*, p. 336.
49 My personal experience.

radio stations such as WSCZ in Chuuk and WSCD in Ponape. However, the locals listened to radio for entertainment rather than government policy.[50] The islanders preferred to engage in face-to-face meetings with their Micronesian leaders during field trips to the outer islands rather than listening to them on the radio.[51] Such meetings were in accordance with traditional meeting practices that aimed to build harmony within communities.

The economic situation in the TTPI was seen as heavily subsidised by the US and perceived as promoting a dependency mentality in Micronesia. The Micronesian leaders in the COM began to analyse this situation and debated how to move away from an economic model based on dependency on the US.[52] The debate on dependency rose to prominence in the 1970s as a backlash against free market development agendas espoused in development agencies dominated by US-trained economists.[53] Dependency connotes a state of helplessness, whereby Micronesians are unable to take care of themselves. This welfare theory was connected to the free feeding program (called *aikiu* by the Mortlockese) provided by the US Department of Agriculture (USDA) for schools, the elderly and following natural disasters.

There was also debate over the relative nutritional value of the food obtained from the USDA program versus local produce. For example, new categories of diseases such as hypertension, diabetes and other illnesses arose, believed to be associated with eating white rice, bleached flour, spam, chopped meat, powdered milk and shortening cooking oil. Some communities provided their schools with local agricultural products to supplement the rice and canned meat to increase the nutritional value of the meals. Many leaders such as Julio Akapito, a former congressman from Chuuk, challenged the intention of the free family lunch program as 'racially and culturally arrogant' and self-serving.[54] He declared that he had lived in Chuuk 'for the past thirty years [and had] never gone

---

50 My personal experience. On Lekinioch, people would undertake work like husking coconuts while the radio was playing. When the news came on, they would turn the radio off and have a conversation. See details in Marshall, *Namoluk beyond the Reef*, p. 32.

51 In my personal experience, the prevalence of traditions is one reason for the neglect of development.

52 Hanlon, *Remaking Micronesia*, pp. 158–159.

53 Hanlon, *Remaking Micronesia*, pp. 158–159.

54 Hanlon, *Remaking Micronesia*, p. 178.

hungry',[55] and questioned the point of the free lunch program and the other welfare programs. Nevertheless, Julio had his own critics and USDA food continued to flow to the islands.

Dependency theory, like colonialism, was a theory developed by outsiders and exported to the islands without any understanding of the structure of Micronesian economic life that had sustained the islanders throughout their history. Self-reliance is fundamental to the islanders' survival and continuity. It is argued that Micronesian economic conditions should not be measured in terms of foreign economic yardsticks such as GDP as these have no bearing on Micronesian social reality.[56] Micronesians value connections with their extended families; their individual and collective social network, wealth and mental health depend on these connections. It should be remembered that Micronesians have been governing themselves for centuries without outside help, and to be labelled as dependent on the US is at best ignorant, ethnocentric and arrogantly self-serving misinformation.[57]

Independence on the Horizon

Despite the rising tension between Micronesian leaders and the US over the political future of the TTPI, the indigenous population continued to transform their communities, using their historical skills to adapt to the new order emanating from beyond the horizon. Traditional socio-economic practices remained the mode of production to maintain the internal coherency of communities. Few were willing to wait around and depend on 'handouts'. Some Micronesians set up businesses trading Western goods in exchange for traditional goods. For example, copra was traded for items like cigarettes, candies and canned food.

However, such small businesses could not earn enough profit because of the inherent *tumunu fengen* (sharing and caring) principle embedded in the Micronesian cultural structure.[58] For example, new businesses called *koap* (the co-ops) emerged but, after a few years in operation, they collapsed as profits and goods were withered away by relatives of employees calling

---

55 Hanlon, *Remaking Micronesia*, p. 178.
56 My personal view. See also Petersen, *Traditional Micronesian Societies*, pp. 1–2.
57 Hezel, *Strangers in Our Own Land*, p. 274.
58 Marshall, 'The Structure of Solidarity', p. 62; Other leaders like Hans Williander advocated a small-scale business model based on cultural roots. See Hanlon, *Remaking Micronesia*, p. 137.

on traditional obligations to receive goods without payment.[59] Interest in Western products also faded, as islanders preferred to fish and farm within their customary practices. This basic reality of doing business in Micronesia continues to be ignored by overseas' consultants who regularly recommend beefing up the private sector as the best means for economic growth in the FSM. Foreign consultants need to alter their foreign perspective of mass consumerism to understand Micronesian modes of production and survival. In that way, collaboration can occur to undertake new forms of community production to enhance islanders' lifestyles, with due consideration also towards the business principles of credit ratios, capital reserves and earnings sufficient to cover costs and reinvest into improving the enterprise.

Micronesians who embraced Americanisation argued that it was better to live under the US because it offered a convenient way of living where individuals did not have to be accountable to the clanship system.[60] Individuals could acquire wealth and live as luxuriously as they desired. This new wealth could ease the burden of backbreaking traditional work like climbing breadfruit trees and farming in muddy taro patches, as well as procure Western-style housing that could withstand the seasonal typhoons.[61] However, after a few years, the Western houses collapsed due to lack of maintenance and USDA food programs ceased. Consequently, islanders had to revert to the traditional system as the best option for survival and continuity.[62]

The debate between the anti- and pro-independence movements could be heard during *sotang* (village meetings). For example, after Typhoon Pamela hit the Mortlocks in 1976, USDA food and other forms of American assistance were distributed to all the islands. On Lukunor, during *sotang*,

---

59 I witnessed two to three co-ops virtually disappear within a year of inception. The co-ops ranged from financing of housing to small groceries stores. One of the stores was passed on to new management but again folded within a year. This was called the Lazarus phenomena (referring to the Biblical person brought to life again by Jesus). The question is, why did the co-ops never profit as intended? Was this due to culture or lack of management skills? See Francis X. Hezel, 'Is that the Best You Can Do? A Tale of Two Micronesian Economies: The Plea to Grow Economy', East-West Centre, Hawai'i, 2006, www.micsem.org/pubs/articles/economic/frames/taleoftwofr.htm.

60 Ignacio Soumwei (Teacher at Mortlocks Junior High School, Satowan), comments in class, Semester 1, 1974. Soumwei coined the term 'chocolate cookie Micronesian', referring to individuals who looked like Micronesians but think like Americans.

61 Ignacio Soumwei (Teacher at Mortlocks Junior High School, Satowan), comments in class, Semester 1, 1974. I also personally observed this after Typhoon Pamela struck the Mortlocks in 1975.

62 Ignacio Soumwei (Teacher at Mortlocks Junior High School, Satowan), comments in class, Semester 1, 1974. I also personally observed this after Typhoon Pamela struck the Mortlocks in 1975.

many complained about the rice and chopped meat meals, which were not filling and considered tasteless.[63] Many preferred agricultural tools such as mattocks, shovels, bush knives and fishing equipment since these had more application in sustaining local production. To others, the USDA assistance promised a life that Micronesians could enjoy without exerting too much work on their land.[64] High school teachers and their students also engaged in the debate regarding the pros and cons of independence stemming from the dependency issue.[65] The ongoing debate led to the emergence of the fringe group labelled 'chocolate cookie Micronesians', referring to individuals who look like Micronesians but think like Americans.[66]

For those with higher salaries in the port towns, American materialism became very attractive. The power of money was limitless to them; it could buy whatever one desired, including land and human labour to work the land while they lived in their newly acquired luxury. They had acquired the taste of immediate gratification from the power of money. Many from the new generation also fell into this economic trap since they had never experienced the harsh realities of life, for example, under the Japanese rule.[67] They wanted the US to protect the islands from slipping into the hands of the new 'evil empire', the USSR.

Security was foremost in their calculations and they wanted the best of the American system. This group of people were referred to as 'the sell-out' or *sokon remirika*.[68] They dreamed of an American lifestyle but had no

63   My personal experience during village *sotang*. See Marshall, *Namoluk beyond the Reef*, pp. 65–66; William Lessa, 'The Social Effects of Typhoon Ophelia (1960) on Ulithi', in *Peoples and Cultures of the Pacific: An Anthropological Reader*, edited by Andrew P. Vayda, The Natural History Press, New York, 1968, p. 59.

64   Hanlon, *Remaking Micronesia*, pp. 172–177.

65   Meller, *Constitutionalism in Micronesia*, p. 318. Secondary schools like Xavier and Truk high schools were engaged in the debate for a new political status for Micronesia.

66   Ignacio Soumwei (Teacher at Mortlocks Junior High School, Satowan), comments in class, Semester 1, 1974; Teachers and village elders during *sotang* (observed by me on Satowan Island). Ignacio Soumwei coined this term.

67   Ignacio Soumwei (Teacher at Mortlocks Junior High School, Satowan), comments in class, Semester 1, 1974; Teachers and village elders during *sotang* (observed by me on Satowan Island).

68   Ignacio Soumwei and his cohorts referred to *sokon remirika* as consisting of many of the recipients of the Basic Educational Opportunity Grant (BEOG), students who studied in the US, those harbouring anti-Japanese sentiments and many big business owners in favour of integrating with the US. John Haglelgam gave the example of pet projects by congressmen and their cohorts who diverted funds into the erection of seawalls while pocketing substantial amounts for themselves (John Haglelgam, Interview, College of Micronesia, Palikir Campus, 11 January 2011). Many leaders benefited from the TTPI purse and advocated close relations with the US.

means to convince others about how to achieve it. They included many politicians, returned college students, teachers and the few petty capitalists who owned small retail outlets in the port towns.[69]

Other supporters of the money economy who came from the outer islands flocked to the port towns to find work and send goods to their families on their home islands. This group contributed to the increased population in the port towns. For example, in Ponape, the capital Kolonia had a population of less than 2,000 in 1963, which grew to over 2,800 by 1970.[70] In Moen, Truk, the population of 5,687 in 1967 grew to 9,562 in 1973. In Yap, the population of the Rull and Weloy municipalities increased from 1,741 in 1963 to 2,482 in 1973.[71]

The Road to Independence

After the long decades of what many called the era of benign neglect, the issue of independence went public, driven by the leaders of the six districts who came together to create the COM. The leaders petitioned the high commissioner to create a nationwide forum where Micronesian leaders could meet and discuss matters of concern regarding their islands. At first, the US was reluctant to recognise the Micronesians' request. However, under constant pressure, the US relented and created the bicameral COM in September 1964, consisting of 12 senators in the House of the Senate and 21 members in the House of Representatives.

The COM became the voice of the people, signalling a new era in Micronesian political history. One of its prime purposes was to accelerate the process of decolonisation. This happened in 1966, when House Joint Resolution No. 47 was adopted, expressing that 'this generation of Micronesians should have an early opportunity to determine the ultimate constitutional and political status of Micronesia'.[72] In 1967, the US president sent a proposal to the US Congress to study the future of the TTPI and how 'to consult with the people of Micronesia'.[73] The US

---

69 My personal experience regarding relatives who operated small stores to earn a few dollars.
70 Hezel, *Strangers in Their Own Land*, p. 323.
71 Gale, *Americanization of Micronesia*, p. 128.
72 *Summary of the Political Status Talks of the Joint Committee on Future Status*, Congress of Micronesia, Saipan, 1973, p. 1.
73 *Summary of the Political Status Talks of the Joint Committee on Future Status*, p. 2; Meller, *Constitutionalism in Micronesia*, p. 52.

Congress did virtually nothing. It made no recommendations and did not investigate the issue as requested by the COM. The US Congress did set up a committee, which produced no tangible result.

In response, the COM adopted Senate Joint Resolution No. 25, creating its own future political status without input from the US. The resolution demanded the following: 1) that the COM develop a process for political education in Micronesia; 2) that Micronesians choose their future political status; and 3) that Micronesians undertake 'a comparative study of how Puerto Rico, Western Samoa, Cook Islands and other territories have achieved their self-government, independence, or other political status'.[74]

The US, having been pressed by the COM to come to the negotiating table, reluctantly participated in a series of negotiations with the Micronesians. Four options for Micronesians were proposed by the Micronesian representatives during these negotiations: independence, free association, integration with another sovereign power or continuation of the status quo. In response, the US offered commonwealth status, which meant becoming an unincorporated territory of the US.[75] This proposal failed as it did not meet Micronesian expectations. The US was also criticised by the UN for not honouring the trusteeship agreement, which allowed the people of the TTPI the choice of determining their own means of self-determination. Micronesians were more politically astute, determined and angrier than the Americans realised.[76] The central question thus became what sort of political independence would be suitable for all six districts. The Micronesian leaders also proposed the Compact of Free Association as an alternative to independence. The US found this proposal acceptable but operated on the assumption that the Compact should be negotiated on their terms.

These issues were the subject of the ConCon that brought Micronesia's political and traditional leaders to Saipan in the early 1970s.[77]

---

74 Meller, *Constitutionalism in Micronesia*, p. 2.
75 Meller, *Constitutionalism in Micronesia*, p. 2.
76 Hanlon, *Remaking Micronesia*, pp. 136–139.
77 The issue was which type of government model best suited the people of the TTPI.

The Constitutional Convention

The ConCon brought together the educated elite and traditional leaders of the six districts of the TTPI. It was a forum designed for Micronesians to discuss their political future. Norman Meller, the main advisor to the ConCon, described it as the forum where the TTPI leaders gathered to demonstrate both their differences and similarities. For example, the Palau delegation came to the ConCon with an arrogant attitude, demanding certain conditions and proclaiming that if the ConCon disagreed, then Palau would withdraw from the ConCon.[78] Palau demanded that the capital should be situated in Palau, and each state should be allowed to withdraw from the proposed federation after eight years of joining. Further, Palau envisaged a decentralised form of federation, where the central government acted only as a facilitator, and foreign aid should be divided equally between the states.[79] Palau's proposals were virtually ignored by the rest of the delegates at the ConCon.[80]

Meller noted that Palau's position seemed to signal that the ConCon was destined to fail. Palau's aggressive stance related to their belief that Palauans were more sophisticated and politically astute than other Micronesians.[81] The Palauan delegates believed that they would be better off economically without the proposed federation. A proposed joint venture between Japan and Iran to build a super oil storage port in Palau played a major role in Palau's decision to steer clear of any proposed federation. The Palauans thought that they would pocket millions of dollars from this port and did not want the other states to share in this benefit.[82]

The Marianas and Marshallese delegations had their own reservations about the federation. Like Palau, they considered that their own interests might not necessarily benefit from federation. The Mariana Islanders had greater exposure to the outside world, which motivated them to continue the consumer culture and cash economy they had become accustomed to. Some viewed their position as being politically engineered by a minority elite.[83] The Marshallese, on the other hand, had experienced the economic

---

78   Hezel, *Strangers in Their Own Land*, pp. 351–353.
79   Meller, *Constitutionalism in Micronesia*, pp. 176–177.
80   Meller, *Constitutionalism in Micronesia*, pp. 184–188.
81   Hezel, *Strangers in Their Own Land*, pp. 351–352.
82   Meller, *Constitutionalism in Micronesia*, pp. 175–176.
83   Hanlon, *Remaking Micronesia*, pp. 220–221.

benefits arising from the US military installation in Kwajalein. The chief architect of the Marshallese separation movement was Amada Kabua, one of the paramount chiefs of the Marshall Islands.[84]

Opposing factions of pro-federalists and separatists dominated the political landscape in Palau, the Marshall Islands and the Marianas Islands. Their own domestic referendums were decisively in favour of separating from the TTPI. The disintegration of the TTPI was blamed squarely on the US as it allowed the other districts to negotiate for separate political status, contrary to the UN-imposed requirement of deciding the political future of the territory as a single entity.

The delegations from the conservative states of Truk, Pohnpei and Yap, who favoured retaining much of their traditions while joining the international community of nations, would not allow the fragmentation to sway them from their objective of achieving an independent nation for the rest of the Micronesians. Their leaders were instrumental in ensuring they remained together as a political unit. For example, the first president, Tosiwo Nakayama, and his political cohorts were instrumental in uniting the leaders of Yap and Chuuk. Nakayama belonged to an extended clan network that spanned from Chuuk to the outer islands of Yap. Many of these islands are part of the traditional *sawei* system.[85]

The only obstacle to the adoption of the Constitution was to fulfil the requirement in the proposed Constitution that three-fifths of the voters in a majority of the remaining four states approved the Constitution. Since half of the districts had already left the TTPI, the district of Kosrae was created to satisfy this legal requirement and thus allow the majority of the states to adopt the Constitution by referendum—that is, three-fifths of the voters in the majority of the remaining four districts in the TTPI approved the Constitution.[86] These districts, now called the states of Chuuk, Pohnpei, Yap and Kosrae, became constituted as the FSM in accordance with the majority vote of the people.[87] In 1979, the FSM declared itself an independent constitutional government. The Constitution as carried

---

84 Hanlon, *Remaking Micronesia*, pp. 220–221, 226.
85 Hanlon, *Remaking Micronesia*, pp. 25–27.
86 Meller, *Constitutionalism in Micronesia*, pp. 329–330.
87 Meller, *Constitutionalism in Micronesia*, pp. 329–330; Hanlon, *Remaking Micronesia*, p. 174.

by the majority requirement affirmed the historic commitment of the common wish of the people to live in harmony with each other. It also legitimised the FSM as a new, self-governing nation.[88]

The Debate Over Disintegration

Some questions about the legalities of the US's conduct surrounding the disintegration of the TTPI remain unanswered. In particular, the question of whether the US violated the terms of the trusteeship agreement. The terms of Article 83 of the UN Charter as applied to a strategic trust territory stipulated that:

1. All functions of the United Nations relating to strategic areas, including the approval of the terms of the trusteeship agreements and of their alteration or amendment which shall be exercised by the Security Council.

2. The basic objectives set forth in Article 76 shall be applicable to the people of each strategic area.

3. The Security Council shall, subject to the provisions of the trusteeship agreements and without prejudice to security considerations, avail itself of the assistance of the Trusteeship Council to perform those functions of the United Nations under the trusteeship system relating to political, economic, social, and educational matters in the strategic areas.[89]

There is a strong case for arguing that the US's conduct contradicted the terms of the agreement. For example, Section 1 of Article 83 indicated that any 'alteration or amendment to the TTPI agreement shall be exercised by the Security Council'. The US did the opposite by facilitating the disintegration of the TTPI into four independent parts, Palau, the Marshal Islands, the Northern Marianas Islands and the FSM, without the UN Security Council's prior approval. The US's conduct constituted an alteration of the TTPI agreement because it engaged in negotiations with districts within the TTPI rather than engaging with the TTPI representatives as a whole.

---

88 *The Constitution of the Federated States of Micronesia*, Article I.
89 *Charter of the United Nations and Statutes of the International Court of Justice*, Article 83.

The fragmentation of the TTPI, supported by America's conduct, violated the UN precedent in relation to the doctrine of territorial integrity of a non-self-governing territory.[90] One issue was whether the FSM was required to continue their negotiations with the US given that the TTPI had disintegrated. The FSM was no longer a constituted part of the TTPI as agreed to under the terms of the trust territory agreement.[91] In hindsight, perhaps the FSM could have taken a different path to ensure the realisation of its economic goals under a different political arrangement, with or without the US.

Anthropologist Robert Kiste argued that there were no specific procedures regarding the termination of the TTPI agreement and, in the absence of such, both the FSM and US ended it on their own terms. An alternative view is that the principles within UN Resolution 1514 (XV) could have been applied to terminate the TTPI agreement[92] rather than a simple agreement between the US and Micronesia. The TTPI agreement specifically granted the UN Security Council the final power to terminate the agreement. One can also question why Micronesia was subject to US approval to terminate the TTPI, given that the TTPI as originally formed no longer existed.

It can also be argued that there was a:

> material breach of the trusteeship agreement on the part of the USA. That is because it failed repeatedly to satisfy the terms, which were to develop the islands economically and politically towards self-government or speed up the process of independence as may be appropriate to the particular circumstances of the Trust Territory and its people before the Constitutional Convention.[93]

Further, the chief advisors to the Micronesian ConCon, Norman Meller and Leonard Mason (an American anthropologist with deep knowledge of the islands), also advised the US not to divide up the trust territory as it would contradict the UN agreement. They were ignored.[94] As Petersen stated:

---

90 Meller, *Constitutionalism in Micronesia*, p. 325.
91 Personal argument based on what constituted the TTPI.
92 Brownlie, *Principles of Public International Law*, pp. 170–173. Resolution 1514 referred to the former South West Africa (now Namibia), which involved the Security Council being required to apply the provisions of the said resolution in relation to Article 83 of the UN Charter. The same principle could have also applied to the case of Micronesia.
93 *Summary of the Political Status Talks of the Joint Committee on Future Status*, p. 1.
94 Meller, *Constitutionalism in Micronesia*, p. 324.

At the time of the 1975 ConCon the US was engaging in political status negotiations with individual [districts] as a means of overcoming the Congress of Micronesia's resistance to American demands for the permanent control over Micronesian lands.[95]

Perhaps the US should not shoulder all the blame since the Micronesian leaders should have been aware of the issue and responded to it legally. However, the above exercise demonstrated the contradictions in international law, whereby the most powerful countries can ignore or manipulate the UN to suit their own purposes.[96]

Independence and the Constitutional Convention

Various issues concerning independence continued to be raised during the ConCon. What sort of independence was appropriate to the new state of the FSM? What government structure should the leaders strive towards since Micronesia is a diverse collection of islands and cultures? While the Micronesian leaders debated the issues, the US was studying the Compact. It emerged that there was a conflict between the proposed Compact of Free Association and the newly drafted Constitution.[97]

The Compact, as perceived by the US, should have overriding power over the Constitution;[98] that is, the Constitution should literally restate the language of the Compact, with the Constitution having a secondary role. This position was seen by Micronesian leaders as a deliberate attempt by the US to undermine the sovereignty of the FSM and its people.

To respond to the US's tactic, the president of the ConCon, Tosiwo Nakayama, cleverly said:

> it will be best to draft a constitution without knowing what is in the draft compact, because in working on the constitution, we are dealing with the interests of the people and we should not be concerned with trying to protect the interests of [an outside power] in Micronesia.[99]

---

95   Glenn Petersen, *Federated States of Micronesia in Pacific Ways: Government and Politics in the Pacific Islands*, edited by Stephen Levine, Victoria University Press, 2009, pp. 47–48.
96   Contradictions in international law that the super powers always exploit.
97   Hanlon, *Remaking Micronesia*, pp. 25–27.
98   Meller, *Constitutionalism in Micronesia*, pp. 317–318.
99   Meller, *Constitutionalism in Micronesia*, pp. 317–318.

The draft Constitution was sent to Washington, DC for American comments. The US responded by citing the inconsistencies between the draft Constitution and the Compact. The US insisted on the Compact as having an overriding power in relation to the Constitution.[100] The Micronesian negotiators responded by saying, 'while the Constitution may be inconsistent with [the US] interpretation of free association, it is not inconsistent with [the Micronesians]'.[101]

It took many more negotiations before the US finally faced the fact that Micronesian independence could no longer be denied. The US opened new rounds of negotiations, focusing on the 'permanent denial clause' of the Compact that gave the US unilateral power to refuse any third party from accessing FSM territories for military purposes and sole responsibility for the defence of the FSM.[102] The FSM's interpretation of the Compact is that the US's rights derive from the Compact and end when the Compact ends. The concept of the permanent denial clause contravened the FSM's sovereignty as upheld in its Constitution.[103]

Figure 12: The official flag of the Federated States of Micronesia.

Note: The stars represent the four states. The blue colour represents the ocean from which Micronesians derive their identity.

Source: Image courtesy of the FSM Government.

---

100 Meller, *Constitutionalism in Micronesia*, pp. 317–318.

101 Meller, *Constitutionalism in Micronesia*, p. 319.

102 Who are the enemies of Micronesia that the US wants to defend the FSM against?

103 The 'permanent denial clause' in the Compact pertains to the principle of a permanent agreement between Micronesia and the US. Changes within could be negotiated but the compact remains as is. It is based on the philosophy that US security in the northwest Pacific should be protected forever (Stewart Firth, 'Sovereignty and Independence in the Contemporary Pacific', *The Contemporary Pacific*, Vol. 1, No. 1 & 2, Spring/Fall 1989, pp. 79–83).

The 15-Year Life of the Compact

The FSM stood firm in refusing to recognise the permanent denial clause but agreed to a variation, whereby the denial clause would only last the 15-year duration of the Compact, after which the Compact would be subject to renegotiation. This was done by the FSM's negotiators on the basis of pragmatism rather than acquiescence; they saw that the Compact needed to be signed quickly so that the US could terminate the UN trust agreement.[104] The FSM could then join the UN and forge diplomatic relationships with other nations for the purpose of enhancing its economic and political position.

The Compact was then framed on the basis of a bilateral treaty with the US, providing US$3.4 billion dollars to the FSM Government in exchange for the US being granted the right to exercise power to deny third party states access to the islands if such access was deemed contrary to the US's interests.[105] The Compact was renegotiated in 2001 and extended to 2023. However, it is still debated as to whether the 'deniability clause' will have any validity after 2023.

Despite arguments by political scientists that the FSM has lost its sovereignty because of the security arrangements under the Compact, it can be argued that the denial clause does not and cannot usurp the FSM's Constitution. The Constitution's Preamble states, 'We, the people of Micronesia, exercising our inherent sovereignty, do hereby establish this Constitution of the Federated States of Micronesia'.[106] Section 1 of Article II then reaffirms Micronesian sovereignty by declaring:

> This Constitution is the expression of the sovereignty of the people and is the supreme law of the Federated States of Micronesia. An act of government in conflict with this Constitution is invalid to the extent of conflict.[107]

---

104 The Compact needed to be signed quickly to trigger the process of recognition by the international community (Meller, *Constitutionalism in Micronesia*, pp. 317–318).

105 *The First and Amended Compact of Free Association Combined*, www.fsmitha.com/world/micronesia.htm.

106 *The Constitution of the Federated States of Micronesia*, Preamble.

107 *The Constitution of the Federated States of Micronesia*, Article II.

Therefore, any act of Congress, including the signing of a treaty, cannot be contradictory to the Constitution; if it is, then the act is made without power to the extent of its conflict with the Constitution. Congress is not empowered to sign away the FSM's sovereignty.

The Compact restates the language of the FSM's Constitution by stating that the US recognises that the Compact:

> entered into force on November 3, 1986 ... based upon the International Trusteeship system of the UN Charter, and in particular Article 76 of the Charter ... the people of the Federated States of Micronesia...and in the exercise of their sovereign right ... have adopted a Constitution appropriate to their particular circumstances ... the Compact terminates the Trusteeship and establish a government-to-government relationships ... [however] the people of the Federated States of Micronesia have and retain their sovereignty.[108]

Title I, Article I, Section 3 reaffirms this, stating: 'The people of the Federated States of Micronesia, acting through the Government established under the Constitution, are self-governing'.[109] The two documents are clear on the matter that sovereignty rests in the hands of the Micronesian people. Nothing can usurp such a power, except by constitutional means—that is, by a referendum.[110]

The Micronesians accelerated the process of approving the Constitution by sidelining the debate on the Compact. The people approved the Constitution in 1979 by a referendum, without delay. Tosiwo Nakayama's tactic worked as the Compact was then required to be derived from the Constitution. The US had no choice but to acknowledge the superiority of the FSM's Constitution over the Compact.[111]

The Compact has been perceived as creating problems for the FSM, affecting FSM–US bilateral relations. At the heart of the problem are the issues of sovereignty and dependency. Since the implementation of the amended Compact in 2001, Micronesian observers and leaders have expressed their disappointment in the way the US has been meddling

---

108 *Compact of Free Association between the Federated States of Micronesia and the United States of America*, p. 55.
109 *Compact of Free Association between the Federated States of Micronesia and the United States of America*, Title I, Article I, Section III, p. 55.
110 *The Constitution of the Federated States of Micronesia*, Article XIV.
111 Gale, *The Americanization of Micronesia*, p. 241.

with the internal affairs of the FSM. For example, the Joint Economic Management Committee Office (JEMCO), which consists of five members (three of whom are American), is now becoming the 'fourth branch' of government by controlling how Compact funds are utilised. An example of JEMCO's heavy-handed tactics is the delayed implementation of the education sector grant to Chuuk State in 2008 when Chuuk disagreed with the US on priority needs in its education system. The US refused to budge when the Micronesians vehemently objected to JEMCO's assertion that, as the Compact funds are paid for by US taxpayers, the US has the right to interfere in the FSM's internal affairs to ensure the funds are implemented as allocated.[112] The FSM Congress has questioned this approach, but their concerns have so far been ignored. By setting up an absolute 3:2 American majority in JEMCO, the Compact has effectively become a tool for the US to pressure the FSM Government to comply with US demands or suffer financial consequences.[113] The issues surrounding the Compact are yet to be settled, with the 2023 end date fast approaching.

The Compact and Economic Development

It can be argued that the Compact should be viewed as a transitional vehicle or an experimental tool to allow the islanders to measure the success and failure of various economic strategies advocated by foreign experts.[114] Others see Compact funds as 'rent money' paid by the US

---

112 Carl Apis, pers. comm., FSM Department Foreign Affairs, Nett, Pohnpei, 2012. I also discussed the issue with Epel Illon, who was one of the negotiators from the FSM side. He noted that the right for the US to interfere in the implementation of the Compact funds in the FSM was agreed to from the start. The US left the FSM to do the implementation for the first 15 years. However, when the Compact was amended, the US saw the need to interfere to ensure the funds were appropriately implemented. He also said that it was agreed to that the US Department of the Interior was granted the right by the FSM to audit the funds in the FSM. The question of sovereignty includes the right of the FSM to forgo some of its rights, according to Epel Illon. See also *The Constitution of the Federated States of Micronesia*, Article IX, Section 4, for approval of treaty delegating power to another sovereign power. This section seems to be deliberate as the Compact and the Constitution were drafted and negotiated concurrently in the 1970s and 1980s.

113 JEMCO has two members from the FSM and three from the US. The FSM is always outvoted on issues the American members do not want to implement.

114 The Compact is considered a transitional economic vehicle to test whether it would satisfy Micronesian development circumstances. For a brief discussion, see John Fairlamb, *Office of Compact Negotiations, U.S. Department of State Compact of Free Association Negotiations: Fulfilling the Promise*, A Paper Originally Presented to Island State Security Conference Asia-Pacific Center for Security Studies, Honolulu, Hawai'i, June 2001, www.fsmgov.org/comp_per.html.

for wanting to exclusively maintain the islands as part of the American security zone in the Asia-Pacific region. As such, Micronesians have the right to use the rent money as they desire because such a rental is an implicit acknowledgement of their sovereignty.[115] The supporters of this position have questioned the mindset of the tenant (the US) in believing they have the right to tell their (Micronesian) landlord how to spend the rent money. They argue that Micronesians should stand up and move forward by devising their own economic plan while only paying lip service to the US's economic strategies.[116] Why should they be pushed by someone else's demand?[117]

Since the termination of the TTPI in 1986, the FSM's development programs have been restricted by the terms of the Compact. The Compact's main premise is to stimulate economic activities such that Micronesia will be able to sustain itself economically in the future. For example, in the first 15 years of the Compact, the US provided around US$1.5 billion to the FSM Government.[118] The funds were used for general government operations in health and education, economic development, capital improvements and other special purposes.[119] Sixty per cent of this amount was spent on operational costs and the remaining 40 per cent on capital investment.[120] Micronesians looked forward to an improvement in their living standards as measured by economic indicators. It was likened to the *lerak* season, the season of plentiful food, where money was in abundance. The perception was that Micronesians would be bathing in this newfound wealth and not worrying too much about the future, since the money would be coming from somewhere else. However, this ray of economic sunshine was grossly insufficient for its stated purpose of establishing an independent economic base beyond the Compact era for a nation of over 103,000 citizens whose multi-island nature makes the provision of services

115 James Naich, *Sustaining the Spirit of the Compact Partnership: Comments on the US Report on the First Five Years of the Amended Compact of Free Association*, Embassy of the Federated States of Micronesia, Washington, DC, October 2010, pp. 1–10.

116 The US has suggested various models of economic development, none of which have been very successful. The debate continues as to why. See The Micronesia Forum; Hanlon, *Remaking Micronesia*, pp. 146–148.

117 Hanlon, *Remaking Micronesia*, pp. 146–148.

118 *Report to Congress on the Compact of Free Association with the Federated States of Micronesia (FSM) and the Republic of the Marshall Islands (RMI) for Fiscal Year 2006*, Washington, DC, 2006, p. 3.

119 *Report to Congress on the Compact of Free Association with the Federated States of Micronesia (FSM) and the Republic of the Marshall Islands (RMI) for Fiscal Year 2006*, p. 3.

120 Francis X. Hezel, 'Rough Seas Ahead: The FSM Economy During Compact II', *Micronesian Counselor*, No. 44, January 2003, www.micsem.org/pubs/counselor.htm.

problematic. Corruption also greatly reduced the effectiveness of the funds. For example, the 60 per cent earmarked for necessary infrastructure at the state and municipal government levels was siphoned off by politicians and their cohorts. Congressional appropriations were used for pet projects[121] to appease politicians' electorates by providing them with community halls, motorboats, fishing gears, cars and food. Municipal monies were squandered on superfluous projects that could not be sustained, like purchasing inter-island ferries that were not seaworthy. Many politicians spent money just on looking for boats outside the FSM, with the expenses being categorised as a holiday.

In 1987, the amount of Compact money spent per person per annum was approximately US$1,357. In 1993, this figure decreased to around US$996 per person per annum. This decline in relative per capita funding has continued in subsequent years. It is predicted that per capita funding will decrease to US$562 by 2023 under the amended Compact.[122] These figures do not mean much to many citizens, who do not benefit directly from the pet project appropriations. Each congressman and their cohorts control the funding of 'infrastructure projects' in their states and municipalities, presenting opportunities for corruption and personal enrichment. In the mid-2000s, investigations and subsequent criminal action was undertaken against three powerful congressmen who were later convicted of corruption. (They have since been pardoned but are permanently banned from running for Congress.) Corruption continues to be a major problem, as discussed in the Chuuk Reform Agenda public forum[123] and a report by the Office of Public Auditing in 2014.[124]

---

121 William Cook, 'U.S. Department of State Diplomacy in Action: Executive Summary', Washington, DC, June 2014, p. 8; Henry Asugar, *Congress Bill No. 13-76*, A Bill For an ACT, 'To grant amnesty to certain classes of people who are now being accused, or yet to be accused, or who have been prosecuted of certain types of crimes against the sovereignty of the Federated States of Micronesia but not yet convicted, and for other purposes', 20 January 2004.
122 David Gootnick, director of International Affairs and Trade, *Micronesia Faces Challenges to Achieving Compact Goals: Testimony before the Insular Affairs Subcommittee, House Resources Committee, U.S. House of Representatives: Attachment III: Estimated FSM Per Capita Compact Grant Assistance, Fiscal Years 1987–2023*, United States Government Accountability Office, Washington, DC, 10 June 2008.
123 Chuuk Reform Agenda, www.chuukstate.org/; Office of the National Public Auditor, FSM, *CFSM Public Projects and Social Programs: 1.6 Million Approved without Clear Criteria. Audit Report Number 2015-04*, 2014, www.fsmopa.fm/files/onpa/2014/Audit%20Report%202015-04.pdf.
124 Vid Raatior, 'Audit Confirms That FSM Congress Misuse of 1.6 Million of Public Funds', Chuuk Reform Coalition, 10 February 2015, www.chuukstate.org/audit-confirms-that-fsm-congress-misuse-1-6-million-of-public-funds/; Office of the National Public Auditor, *CFSM Public Projects and Social Programs: 1.6 Million Approved without Clear Criteria. Audit Report Number 2015-04.*

In denying the ongoing issue of corruption, the speaker of Congress claimed that the Office of Public Auditing was intentionally engaging in politics and recklessly misleading the public.[125]

The issue of corruption raises the question of how Micronesians will sustain themselves amid the projected decline in living standards after 2023. The US has encouraged the FSM Government to address the shortfall by tapping into different revenue sources outside of the Compact. The FSM is engaging with China to explore opportunities to expand its revenue base. It is unclear as to whether China will be receptive to the FSM's overtures. If so, can China match the magnitude of assistance provided by the US under the Compact? Otherwise, it is not known how the US$600 million shortfall will be met.

Pessimists perceive the Compact as nothing more than a vehicle for facilitating the US's recolonisation of Micronesia. Although the objectives of the Compact are well intended, at least at the theoretical level, its application can be seen as undermining the FSM's sovereignty.[126] Some observers have claimed that the US is using the Compact as a power by proxy through a backdoor approach to reassert its dominance over the FSM.[127] For example, JEMCO, which has a majority of American members, dictates how Compact funds should be used despite Micronesian objection. In doing so, JEMCO is effectively pressuring the FSM to conform to an American vision of the FSM's future, with the implicit threat of withholding funds. For example, President Mori objected to two resolutions by JEMCO that demanded:

> an incremental $700,000 annual reduction of Compact funding to the College of Micronesia [COM] beginning in 2013 until the College's funding is peaked at $1 million per year … and by 2023 approximately $25 million will have been subtracted [by this reduction].[128]

---

125 'Speaker Halbert Responds to Audit Report', *The Fourth Branch*, www.tfbmicronesia.com/articles/2015/2/16/speaker-halbert-responds-to-audit-report.
126 The JEMCO is controlled by its American members who often make decisions based on their perception of what development ought to be (Fabian Nimea, *Federated States of Micronesia: National Assessment Report. Support for the Formulation of National Sustainable Development Strategies in the Pacific Small Island Developing States*, Palikir, Pohnpei, June 2006, p. 34).
127 A popular issue of public debate is whether the FSM is experiencing the same treatment by the US as it did in the Trust Territory days.
128 FSM Information Office, 'President Mori Expressed Serious Concern Over JEMCO Draft Resolutions', *Press Release No. 0911-04*, Palikir, Pohnpei, 6 September 2011, p. 1.

The same resolution rejected US$8.4 million in funding to improve infrastructure for the College of Micronesia over the next four years. JEMCO also demanded a US$1.8 million reduction in scholarships, which would reduce funding by US$18 million over the remaining Compact period.[129] In the state of Chuuk, the government asked JEMCO to spend money on improving the physical structure of classrooms; the US said that improving teacher qualifications and the purchase of new textbooks were more important and thus the priority for new expenditure.[130] This has created friction between Chuuk and JEMCO, leading to a resurfacing of old colonial tensions regarding America's paternalistic attitude towards Micronesians. In my interview with the current chairman of the Chuuk Education Committee, Mr Walter, he said, 'let the USA push its own agenda as we know 2023 is not that far [away]'.[131] JEMCO's bellicosity exemplifies the extent to which the US is prepared to demonstrate its power over Micronesian financial affairs under the Compact, as well as the short sightedness of this policy in not anticipating local opposition. The FSM president has demanded that JEMCO conduct formal, public consultations about funding for all public programs before implementing new measures that could be seen as being against Micronesian interests. His request has been ignored. Micronesian leaders can protest against JEMCO's actions but, legally, there is nothing much they can do if JEMCO's decision in the 'best interests of Micronesians' differs from what Micronesian leaders perceive to be in the best interests of Micronesians.[132] It remains to be seen what the FSM's leaders will do before the 2023 expiration of the Compact.

Supporters of the Compact welcome American involvement regarding financial oversight, viewing this as a means by which the misspending of funds earmarked for the private sector, social programs and public infrastructure can be prevented.[133] The US has made good on its promise to audit the Compact funds, and will continue to withhold funds until the FSM has put its house in order. For example, per David Gutnik, director of International Affairs and Trade, US Government Accountability

129 FSM Information Office, 'President Mori Expressed Serious Concern Over JEMCO Draft Resolutions', p. 1.

130 Nimea, *Federated States of Micronesia National Assessment Report*, p. 35.

131 Inos Walter, Interview (online), 3 April 2013. His comments alluded to 2023 when the FSM will change the way it conducts business internationally.

132 Nimea, *Federated States of Micronesia National Assessment Report*, pp. 34–35.

133 Francis X. Hezel, 'How Much is Enough? US Aid and Free Association', *Marianas Variety*, Saipan, 22 March 1985. www.micsem.org/pubs/articles/economic/frames/howmuchfr.htm.

Office, 'prior to the annual awarding of compact funds, the FSM must submit a development plan that identifies goals and performance objectives for each sector',[134] such as education, health, and private and capacity-building programs. There have been repeated failures on the part of the FSM Government to comply with JEMCO's demands. Gutnik claims that 'numerous factors have negatively affected the use of the compact grants for FSM development goals'. The FSM's grant allocations have reflected Compact priorities by targeting education, health and infrastructure. However, as of April 2008, the FSM had completed only three infrastructure projects and approximately 82 per cent of the US$82.5 million in infrastructure funds remained unexpended. Lack of progress can be explained by entrenched disagreement between national and state governments over infrastructure priorities, problems associated with the project management unit and Chuuk's inability to secure land leases.[135] Other problems with the FSM's development programs include the inflated public sector, limited tax revenues, reliance on external finance assistance (amounting to 65 per cent of the FSM's GDP), lack of expertise and lack of development in the fishing and tourism sectors.[136] It seems as though Gutnik, the ADB and their cohorts consider the FSM's future to be rather bleak, especially in light of the looming 2023 Compact end date. It remains to be seen whether the Compact will be renegotiated for a third time and, if not, what new form of engagement will develop between the FSM and US.

Optimists perceive the Compact as a means of maintaining a very important connection between the US and FSM. They align with the view that the FSM should not 'cut its nose off to spite its face' even though the Compact's goals have not been met,[137] arguing that the Compact is a safety net that has assisted in building the nation's political and economic capacity (despite the slow progress). The FSM's association with the US has brought stability to the nation and regional security. Further, the Compact allows Micronesians to live, work and seek education in the US. It has provided excellent opportunities for the increasing number of Micronesians migrating to the US. An associated benefit has been the

---

134 Gootnick, *Micronesia Faces Challenges to Achieving Compact Goals*, p. 6.
135 Gootnick, *Micronesia Faces Challenges to Achieving Compact Goals*, p. 3.
136 Gootnick, *Micronesia Faces Challenges to Achieving Compact Goals*, p. 6; Asian Development Bank, *Federated States of Micronesia Partnership Strategy*, www.adb.org/countries/micronesia/strategy.
137 Nimea, *Federated States of Micronesia National Assessment Report*, pp. 34–35.

economic benefit provided to Micronesian families through remittances.[138] The reduction in FSM citizens' living standards under the Compact has prompted massive emigration to greener pastures in the US. However, if the Compact restricts emigration in the future, what opportunities will there be in the FSM[139] for its citizens who have come to expect and enjoy a more Westernised lifestyle?

Dependency and the Economy

Dependency theories are many and dominate the public debate. Many advocates of these theories characterise Micronesians as relying too much on the US's generosity. This perpetuates the previous era of American influence and stifles the urgency of seeking alternative funding sources.[140] Dependency is seen as synonymous with the Compact and necessary to enable Micronesians to survive. There have been considerable statistical data generated over the past 20 years that indicate that billions of dollars have been poured into the islands without a significant return, as judged by the economic modelling favoured by economic statisticians.[141] There have been many workshops, economic summits and discussions about economic strategies that could be appropriate for Micronesia; however, positive results have yet to be produced.[142]

Part of the FSM's unsuccessful economic story has been blamed on Micronesians themselves. This has stemmed from reports asserting that the Micronesian leadership is not equipped with the requisite economic knowledge to competently develop Micronesia.[143] For example, during my fieldwork and in discussions on the Micronesia Forum, many participants blamed their congressmen and the executive branch of government for misappropriating Compact funds to serve their own interests.[144] Others

---

138 Naich, *Sustaining the Spirit of the Compact Partnership*, p. 5.
139 Glenn Petersen, 'Routine Provocation and Denial from the Tonkin Gulf and Hainan to Kyoto and the Pacific Islands', in *Security in Oceania in the 21st Century*, edited by Erie Shibuya and Jim Rolfe, Asia-Pacific Center for Security Studies, 2003, pp. 210–212. Lorin Robert also confirmed Petersen's point on the FSM as the 'hole in the donut', referring to it strategic value (Interview, Palikir, Pohnpei, 7 January 2011).
140 It is known to many Micronesians that 'dependency' is not a real economy.
141 Pers. comm. with many citizens during field research in 2010–2013.
142 Nimea, *Federated States of Micronesia National Assessment Report*, pp. 13–14.
143 Raatior, 'Audit Confirms That FSM Congress Misuse of 1.6 Million of Public Funds'.
144 Bill Jaynes, 'Cabinet Member to Stand Trial on FSM Criminal Charges', *Kaselehlie Press*, 13–26 April 2015, p. 3.

blamed the Micronesians' lack of expertise, which limits their ability to effectively scrutinise[145] advice provided by foreign consultants (who have also benefitted from Compact funds). It is also based on the belief that the FSM continues to emulate economic strategies that are unviable in Micronesia due to the small domestic market, limited access to overseas markets, transport costs to market and limited output/ability to satisfy big market demands.[146] Some observers seriously question whether the FSM negotiators involved in the Compact negotiations undersold the islands, as the funding level was only enough to build a skeleton infrastructure.[147]

Micronesians have seen the rise and fall of all the colonial regimes and various business models brought to their shores. Businesses were set up for the benefit of outsiders. To the local people, it is a cycle of economic antagonism, wherein outsiders exploited the lands, sea and islanders themselves. Scores of consultants have descended on the nation, proposing new ideas of what economic development ought to be. The ideas ranged from cooperative models, to the creation of both public and private corporations, to individual trading stores, to partnerships with outsiders. The main emphasis is on stimulating the private sector, a concept deeply entrenched in the idea of capitalism. It should be remembered that Micronesians continue to practise their traditional economic mode of production, which has served them well for millennia, and have used the introduced foreign economic system to enhance their lifestyle and continuity.

Globalisation

Globalisation is becoming the new economic mantra in the FSM, yet the term is elusive because it connotes many things, which islanders need to comprehend before acting on it. Globalisation can be defined in many ways; this chapter adopts the definition of:

---

145 Gootnick, *Micronesia Faces Challenges to Achieving Compact Goals*, pp. 1–4; Bill Jaynes, 'GAO Official Says Compact Impact Reporting is Not Reliable or Consistent', *Kaselehlie Press*, 29 July 2013.
146 Nimea, *Federated States of Micronesia National Assessment Report*, p. 17.
147 There is a section of the public that is critical of the FSM negotiators for accepting the composition of the JEMCO when it was initially created (Nimea, *Federated States of Micronesia National Assessment Report*, pp. 34–35).

a process driven by international trade and investment and aided by information technology. This process has effects on the environment, on culture, on political systems, on economic development and prosperity, and on human physical wellbeing in societies around the world.[148]

Micronesian leaders believe that opening up the FSM to global influences is the economic road to prosperity. However, there are dangers in rushing to embrace this idea. For a start, the FSM must diligently study what globalisation entails and what consequences it may have on Micronesians.[149] For example, what are the costs and benefits of integrating Micronesia into the global structure? Will the benefits outweigh the costs? Historically, Micronesians have always looked beyond the horizon, as their world is connected within a large region with its own mini globalisation that predates colonisation. The region had its own communication and trade routes where goods and ideas were often exchanged.[150] This past must be understood to enhance Micronesian engagement with each other and outsiders. For example, is globalisation a new idea or a reconceptualised notion of the colonial past dressed up in modernity? What historical lessons can islanders learn from the past in terms of colonisation before jumping on the globalisation bandwagon? These questions may enable Micronesians to better frame their future, given that globalisation has the propensity to erode the island lifestyle faster than one can imagine.[151]

It is no secret that the world is divided unevenly in terms of the distribution of wealth. To the West, which incorporates elements of Marxism, social democracy and the free market, the touted best solution for advancing the standard of living is through the creation of wealth measured by individual and corporate acquisition of materials and money.[152] This is possible through the utilisation of the capitalist mode of production, wherein individuals pursue their own objectives at the expense of the masses. Profit is the main goal and success is measured by the size of individual bank accounts.

---

148 Rothenberge, *Globalization 101*.
149 The debate is ongoing and discussion can be found in the Micronesia Forum: www.micronesia forum.org/.
150 Marshall, *Namoluk beyond the Reef*, p. 3.
151 Globalisation is an ongoing debate in the FSM, especially among the educated elite. See the Micronesia Forum for some of the current debates: www.micronesiaforum.org/.
152 James M. Boughton, 'Globalisation and the Silent Revolution of the 1980s', *Finance and Development*, Vol. 39, No. 1, March 2002, www.imf.org/external/pubs/ft/fandd/2002/03/bought.htm.

Human exploitation is part of the capitalist system.[153] In order to maximise profit, the few owners of wealth require more workers to create more wealth for them. In return, workers receive wages from the owners for their labour. This creates a cycle of dependency between the wage earners and the owners of wealth.[154] As owners become richer, they gain control of the labour market that the wage earners depend on. Since the owners control the labour market, they are also selective as to who and how many workers they will employ or make redundant.[155] This is the heart of the idea of dependency—not the kind of relationship that the FSM has with the US under the Compact. The issue is that workers in the capitalist system will not survive without wages if the labour market suddenly collapses because of a downturn in the economy, as has been seen numerous times throughout the twentieth and twenty-first centuries.

This is not the case in the traditional Micronesian economic model as the *ainang* system is the basis of individual survival. Micronesians are well aware of the changing circumstances in their islands caused by the introduction of capitalism. The US will continue to inject more funds into the FSM under the Compact in order to buy Micronesian acquiescence for the implementation of American economic practices.[156] The key question is, how does one measure the standard of living under the Compact compared to the traditional model that has been the provider of Micronesian continuity and predates colonialism?

Micronesians are a separate and independent category of people different from Americans, as based on their deep historical connection and unique identity. The answer lies in the Micronesian understanding of their history and how to exploit the lessons of their past to engage in the larger sphere of international relations. This is the subject of subsequent chapters.

---

153 Chrisoula Andreou, *Philosophy of Economics: In Defense of Marx's Account of the Nature of Capitalist Exploitation*, www.bu.edu/wcp/Papers/Econ/EconAndr.htm.
154 Albert Einstein, 'Why Socialism?', *Monthly Review: An Independent Socialist Magazine*, Vol. 61, No. 1, May 2009, monthlyreview.org/2009/05/01/why-socialism/.
155 Art Perlo, *Capitalism and Unemployment*, 17 October 2011, peoplesworld.org/capitalism-and-unemployment/.
156 US$2.5 billion annually is provided to the FSM under the Compact, yet the FSM remains economically stagnant. Many Micronesians wonder why.

Conclusion

Independence from colonial rule did not come easily for Micronesians. Autonomy and respect for the sovereignty of local social and political entities have always been part of Micronesian history, prior to, during and after colonisation. Successive, poorly resourced colonial regimes left many communities beyond administrative centres relatively free to pursue their own priorities and objectives, which continued to revolve around *ainang* solidarity and support. Micronesians' political astuteness and negotiation skills have thus far thwarted American attempts to retain political control over the FSM. The FSM's leaders ensured that the Constitution was ratified prior to the Compact so as to ensure the relatively inferior position of the Compact and thereby promote Micronesian priorities ahead of American interests. Upon the ratification of the Constitution, the US's push for the supremacy of the Compact over the FSM's sovereignty was no longer viable—the Constitution was formally established as the supreme law of the land and the Micronesian people. Today Micronesians continue on their historical path to ensure the existence of their identity and continuity. These are essential to the management of superpower rivalries in FSM's territory, which will be discussed in the next chapter.

5

The Constitution and
Post-Colonial Identity

The backdrop to the constitutional philosophy of the FSM reflects the dynamics of history as a circular web of social connections. This chapter deals with the *Shulapan allik*[1] (Constitution) of the FSM as the embodiment and perpetuation of *shon Maikronesia* history, identity and continuity, while acknowledging the relevant elements of colonial history. The *Shulapan allik* reconciles internal differences and asserts a distinct politico-cultural perspective and personality.[2] To understand how this perspective developed requires an investigation of four interwoven processes. First, what historical precedents motivated the diverse Micronesian population to share a nation state? Second, what historical factors inspired Micronesian leaders to convince the indigenous population that a constitution was necessary to regain control of their islands? Third, why did the leaders advance the concept of constitutional independence while sidelining economic development as a secondary issue? Fourth, how do Micronesians perceive themselves after the adoption

---

1   The concept of *Shulapan allik* is a Mortlockese–Chuukese term referring to the Constitution as the backbone of all laws in relation to the modern FSM state. For an in-depth discussion of modern forms of constitution and theories, refer to Tony Blackshield and George Williams, *Australian Constitutional Law and Theory: Commentary and Materials* (2nd edition), The Federation Press, 1998, pp. 4–20. For a specific discussion on FSM Constitutional Federalism, see John Haglelgam, 'Federalism and Multiculturalism. Federalism in the Federated States of Micronesia', Asian Resource Centre for Decentralisation, 2006, pp. 125–138, localgov.up.edu.ph/federalism-and-multiculturalism-haglelgam-federalism-in-the-federated-states-of-micronesia.html.

2   See *The Constitution of the Federated States of Micronesia*, Preamble, which conveys the distinct Micronesian identity and perspectives in view of the many islands.

of the Constitution in terms of the ongoing debate between economic and political development as well as jurisdictional issues between the federal and state governments?

These four interrelated questions are central to any discussion of Micronesian identity in a post-colonial era as they facilitate our understanding of Micronesian opposition to the long occupation of Micronesia by foreigners. As will be demonstrated, the ongoing, contested interaction between internal Micronesian priorities and actions on the one hand and external influences on the other continued well after the Constitution came into force. With recourse to detailed legal analysis supplemented by cultural observations, this chapter explores the Micronesian perspective from the dawn of fledgling independence to the FSM's future prospects. It is generally accepted among constitutional law specialists that a constitution is a written document designed to provide the socio-political framework by which a nation is governed. It defines power relations between government organs and the people, as well as the manner in which the constitution can be amended to alter those power relations.[3] The general objective of a constitution is to prevent government tyranny against its people.[4] Colonial tyranny was the backdrop to Micronesians' push to establish a constitution to protect their future interests in line with international standards and to assert the FSM's status as an independent nation, with all the rights afforded to that status. It was reassuring for Micronesians to use the Western concept of a constitution. The FSM's Constitution then became a framework to harmonise and project a united voice for Micronesians. It was also a concept recognised by external powers and presented legitimacy for Micronesian sovereignty.

The Constitution is a living document that reminds the people of their historical past and shields them from emerging threats to their sovereignty. As constitutional scholars Tony Blackshield and George Williams comment, 'if a constitution is written, then, with the passing of time … the living constitution inevitably comes to be related much as the past is related to the present'.[5] In reflecting the historical past and geographical realities of Micronesia, the Constitution established a government structure referred to as coordinate federalism. This entails that both the states and national government are sovereign within their

---

3   Blackshield and William, *Australian Constitutional Law and Theory*, pp. 5–7.
4   Peter Hanks, Deborah Cass and Jennifer Clarke, *Australian Constitutional Law: Materials and Commentary* (6th edition), Buttersworth, Sydney, 1999, p. 8.
5   Blackshield and William, *Australian Constitutional Law and Theory*, p. 5.

respective areas of power, 'each is to be free to perform its functions without hindrance by the other governments … except in the case of concurrent legislative powers (where the national government) prevailed over the states' if state laws are inconsistent with national laws.[6] Political scientist Peter Larmour credited the successful constitution-making in the Pacific Islands to the pre-existing cultural conditions that facilitated the transfer of colonial institutions into the hands of indigenous Pacific Islanders.[7] The Micronesian experience fits Larmour's observations.

Colonisation underscored the uneven power relations between *shon Maikronesia* and the colonial powers. Colonial authorities ignored the rights of the indigenous people as first settlers of the islands and instead annexed the islands into their own externally imposed political structures. The consequence of this alien imposition was the development of a sense of Micronesian unity as a separate, distinct group of people. This shared feeling intensified post WWII, when Micronesians realised that the US's control of Micronesia was perpetuating colonial attitudes and behaviours similar to those experienced prior to the war. The universal awareness that decolonisation was a fundamental right of indigenous people fuelled Micronesians' desire to emancipate themselves from further external control. However, to do so required a constitution for the purpose of gaining international acceptance.

The Essential Elements of the FSM's Constitutional Model

The search for a constitutional model befitting Micronesians' outlook became the task of the emerging Micronesian leaders post WWII. The leaders envisioned a constitution embedded in *eoranian fanou* (cultures of Micronesia) and supported by international standards.[8] Historically, Micronesians did not have a written legal code. Codes of conduct were handed down orally and enforced through the generations via a system of culture, and post-colonially, through the adopted legal

6   Leslie Zines, *The High Court and the Constitution*, Butterworths, Sydney, 1981, p. 1.
7   Peter Lamour, *Foreign Flowers: Institutional Transfer and Good Governance in the Pacific Islands*, University of Hawai'i Press, 2005, pp. 36, 41, 70.
8   Post WWII brought dramatic changes in the world order. Micronesian experiences of colonisation were more acute than before, and thus the desire to control their own destiny was also more acute. For general discussion, see David Hanlon, 'Magellan's Chroniclers?', pp. 53–54; Gale, *Americanization of Micronesia*, pp. 67–73.

system. Violations of socially sanctioned behaviours were dealt with in accordance with community standards. The FSM's Constitution acknowledges the various *eoranian fonou* while also providing the legal structure for their reinforcement in the modern world.[9]

The success of the *Shulapan allik* rests on the adaptability of the traditional socio-legal system to deal with the import of modern legal doctrines. The *Shulapan allik* defines who Micronesians are as a people, designates their territorial home and provides the structure and manner of government.[10] The Constitution's ultimate aim is to perpetuate the principles of peaceful coexistence within the FSM's territory and promote the new Micronesian identity internationally.[11] In reflecting the historical past and contemporary realities, the Constitution superimposed a coordinated federalism as the principal form of governance. Under the Constitution, each island (municipality) and island group (state) are free to form their own constitutions without hindrance by the federal government, except in circumstances of concurrent powers, in which case the *Shulapan allik* can be negotiated or else prevails.[12]

The establishment of the *Shulapan allik* meant that the FSM fulfilled the four internationally accepted requirements to become a sovereign nation: 1) a Constitution to protect its population's interests, 2) a population whose desire is to share a common identity, 3) a territory for its residents to live as a free a people and 4) a nation state fully recognised by the international community.[13] The first three elements are explicitly stated in the Constitution's Preamble:

> We, the people of Micronesia, exercising our inherent sovereignty, do hereby establish this Constitution of the Federated States of Micronesia. With this Constitution, we affirm our common wish to live together in peace and harmony, to preserve the heritage of the past, and to protect the promise of the future ... We extend to all nations what we seek from each: peace, friendship, cooperation, and love in our common humanity.[14]

---

9   *The Constitution of the Federated States of Micronesia*, Article II, Section 1.
10   Blackshield and William, *Australian Constitutional Law and Theory*, pp. 5–7.
11   Hanks, Cass and Clarke, *Australian Constitutional Law*, p. 8.
12   Zines, *The High Court and the Constitution*, p. 1.
13   The Trust Territory agreement ended in 1986, and the FSM was admitted into the UN in 1991. However, per the terms of the Compact, the FSM is free to have dialogue with the international community to pursue its own political interest, but this must be in line with US interests (Epel Illon, Interview, Palikir, Pohnpei, 13 January 2011).
14   *The Constitution of the Federated States of Micronesia*, Preamble.

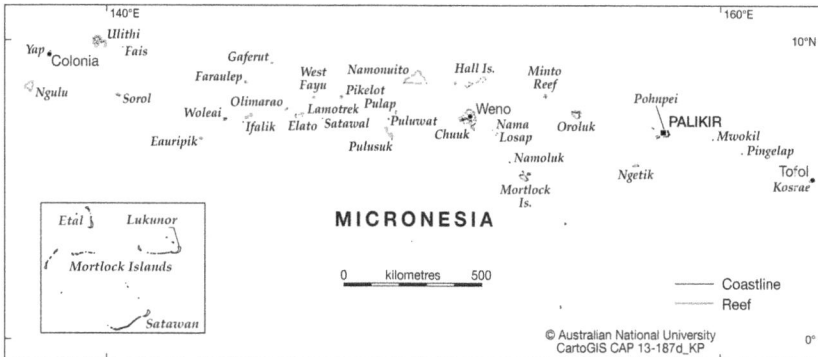

Figure 13: The islands of the Federated States of Micronesia.
Source: Map produced by ANU CartoGIS.

The FSM's Constitution is *sui generis*[15] as it puts Micronesian customary values at its very heart for the purpose of protecting the integrity and sovereignty of the traditional inhabitants. For example, the *Shulapan allik* obliges the courts to take account of customs and traditions by following the 'geographical and social configuration principle' when handing down decisions.[16] Each municipality is encouraged to maintain their cultural practices as rooted in their historical past.[17] It also acknowledges the hierarchical power structure within local communities and beyond. Devolution of power as traditionally practised is also emphasised with the demarcation of responsibilities between the municipalities, national government and states.[18] The *Shulapan allik* also allocates power to each of the three branches of government (executive, legislative and judiciary) so as to maintain political and social cohesion.

The states and municipalities manage their own affairs by the power of their own constitutions in relation to the national government. The national government in turn represents the states in matters of international concern.[19] Article XIII, Section 3 of the FSM's Constitution requires the state and national governments to cooperate with each other in maintaining the integrity of the Federation:

---

15   '*Sui generis*' is a legal term meaning 'of its own kind' or 'unique'.
16   *The Constitution of the Federated States of Micronesia*, Article XI, Section 11.
17   Haglelgam, 'Federalism and Multiculturalism'.
18   The demarcation principle approximated the grouping of islands. See Haglelgam, 'Problems of National Unity', pp. 5–12; Petersen, *Traditional Micronesian Societies*, pp. 12–13.
19   The FSM Government was modelled on the US Constitution while its features are largely of Micronesian construction. See King, 'Custom and Constitutionalism in the Federated States of Micronesia', p. 3.

it is the solemn obligation of the national and state governments to uphold the provisions of [the] Constitution and to advance the principles of unity upon which [the] Constitution is founded.[20]

The Constitution is the supreme law of the land. No laws, foreign or domestic, usurp its sovereign power.

The Constitution and the Environment

As previously explored, the Micronesian people live in an oceanic environment where they share common historical experiences. Their national identity comes from the sea. Their territorial seas have been recognised by the international community and must be protected at all times from unscrupulous external threats exploiting their resources. The Constitution is thus the legal instrument that shields Micronesian interests. The Constitution makes it clear that Micronesians are the custodians of their oceanic environment and its resources.[21] Their history is testimony to such a claim, which fundamentally advocates the doctrine of interdependency between the people, sea and land.[22] Micronesians conserved and preserved the environment, which in return provided sustenance for survival. This doctrine influenced Micronesians' social, economic, religious and political affairs. The people derived their sense of identity through genealogy by tracing this identity to specific spaces within the oceanic environment, such as the locales where their clans or extended families originated.[23] Genealogy in turn influenced the way each island conducted its affairs locally, regionally and nationally. These interrelationships collectively shaped how Micronesians engaged with each other.

The national Constitution embraces the preservation of the sea and asks the international community to observe this practice. It speaks of unity, identity and continuity: 'the seas bring us together, they do not separate us. Our islands sustain us. Our island nation enlarges us and makes us

---

20   *The Constitution of the Federated States of Micronesia*, Article XIII, Section 3.
21   *The Constitution of the Federated States of Micronesia*, Preamble.
22   The concept of interdependency is widespread in the FSM as the clanship system acts as the people's social security web (Petersen, *Traditional Micronesian Societies*, pp. 22–23).
23   The term '*shon ainang*' is used to trace one's local identity and within the clanship system. See Hanlon, *Upon a Stone Altar*, p. 353; Marshall, 'The Structure of Solidarity', p. 55; Duane, *Clan and Copra*, pp. 59–60.

stronger'.[24] The sea is intimately linked to Micronesian identity, and the Yapese and Chuukese call themselves *remetaw* or *shon metaw* (the people of the deep sea).[25] Micronesians have lived together in harmony within the seas. Colonisers misunderstood the special relationship between Micronesians and the sea. For example, Micronesians were discouraged from sailing during colonial times to prevent the need for costly rescue efforts,[26] prevent warring between islands[27] and divert men's attention from sailing towards land-based food production. However, Micronesians continued to sail the seas despite such restrictions because the sea and seafaring was an essential part of their identity and way of being.[28]

Customary rights of the seas are protected by the Constitution. For example, ownership of reefs and fishing rights beyond the reefs and within the lagoons are traditionally demarcated. These are provided for under Article V, Sections 1–3. Section 1 states:

> nothing in this Constitution takes away a role or function of … custom and tradition, or prevents a traditional leader from being recognized, honoured, and given formal or functional roles at any level of government as may be prescribed by this Constitution or by statute.[29]

Section 2 states:

> the traditions of the people of the Federated States of Micronesia may be protected by statute. If challenged as violative of Article IV, protection of Micronesian tradition shall be considered a compelling social purpose warranting such governmental action.[30]

---

24 *The Constitution of the Federated States of Micronesia*, Preamble.
25 Mortlockese called themselves *shon metaw*, which is the same as *re-mataw* often used by the people of the northwest of Chuuk and some of the low-lying islands in Yap. These terms are in reference to people of the sea as emphasised by Paul D'Arcy in his *The People of the Sea*.
26 Hezel, *Strangers in Their Own Land*, p. 108; D'Arcy, *The People of the Sea*, p. 164.
27 Flinn, *Diplomats and Thatch Houses*, p. 25; D'Arcy, *The People of the Sea*, p. 164.
28 In the 1960s and 1970s, sailing canoes were still travelling between islands in the Mortlocks. I have personal experience of this. See also Gladwin, *East is Big Bird*, pp. 134–144; Duane, *Clan and Copra*, p. 258.
29 *The Constitution of the Federated States of Micronesia*, Article V, Section 1.
30 *The Constitution of the Federated States of Micronesia*, Article V, Section 2.

Section 3 ensures that customs and traditions are protected under the guidance of the indigenous leaders:

> the Congress may establish, when needed, a Chamber of Chiefs consisting of traditional leaders from each state having such leaders, and of elected representatives from states having no traditional leaders. The Constitution of a state having traditional leaders may provide for an active, functional role for them.[31]

Framing of Identities to Constitutionality

Pre-existing regional and local identities are recognised by the FSM's Constitution with the provision for three layers of government, the federal, state and local or municipality. At the municipal level, residents of each island community elect their own government officials and recognise their traditional leaders to ensure harmonious coexistence between municipal ordinances and customary laws. This duality is typified by the constitutions of Lekinioch Municipality (in Chuuk) and the state of Yap.

The Lekinioch Constitution empowers *sou eak* (traditional leaders) to ensure imported laws are compatible with local customs. Its Constitution declares:

> *Oolap V, Okisen 1 a apasa, ei chulap mi amafila me apechakula eoranei, nonnoon aramas, samolen eoranei me pechakilen soupisek. Tumwunen limaach, osupwangen aramas, are afefeitan tufich epwe ffor pwal itei pwungen alluk. Okisen 2. Soueak a auwennam on tumunen me apechakkulen eoranei.*[32]

> the Constitution shall reinforce the traditions of the people, recognise their traditional leaders, and customary ownership of properties. The maintenance of traditional community health and prevention of poverty shall be reinforced by the municipal's ordinances.

Section 2 further states that 'traditional leaders shall be the guardians and reinforcers of traditions'.[33] The Municipality of Namoluk's Constitution similarly reinforces its customs and traditions: 'the people of Namoluk

---

31 *The Constitution of the Federated States of Micronesia*, Article V, Section 3.
32 *The Constitution of Lekinioch Municipality*, Lekinioch Island, 17 August 1996, Section 1-2.
33 *The Constitution of Lekinioch Municipality.*

… affirm our desire to respect and uphold our traditions and customs, protect and promote our natural heritage and social bonds we have as a people, now and forever'.[34]

Traditions and customs are also constitutionally protected in the neighbouring state of Yap. For example, Article III, Section 1 of that state's Constitution expresses that 'due recognition shall be given to the *Dalip pi Nguchol*[35] and their traditional and customary roles'.[36] Section 2 states:

> there shall be a Council of *Pilung*[37] and Council of *Tamol*[38] which shall perform functions which concern tradition and custom. Due recognition shall be given to traditions and customs in providing a system of law, and nothing in this Constitution shall be construed to limit or invalidate any recognized tradition or custom as articulated by section 3.[39]

The state of Chuuk also ensures that traditions and customs are fully safeguarded in its Constitution. Article IV, Section 1 states:

> existing Chuukese custom and tradition shall be respected. The Legislature may prescribe by statute for their protection. If challenged as violative of Article III, protection of Chuukese custom and tradition shall be considered a compelling social purpose warranting such governmental action.[40]

Section 2 states:

> nothing in this Constitution takes away the role or function of a traditional leader as recognized by Chuukese custom and tradition, or prevents a traditional leader from being recognized, honoured, and given formal or functional roles in government.[41]

---

34 Marshall, *Namoluk beyond the Reef*, p. 6.
35 The *Dalip pi Nguchol* are the paramount chiefs of Yap State. See Donald Rubinstein and Clement Mulalap, 'A Proposed Chinese Mega-Resort in Yap: Vulnerabilities, Opportunities, and Pacific Geo-politics', Paper presented at Micronesian Symposium 'Micronesia in Focus', The Australian National University, Canberra, 28–29 April 2014, p. 9.
36 *Yap State Constitution*, Article III, Section 1, fsmlaw.org/yap/constitution/index.htm.
37 *Pilung* refers to the three pillars of traditional wisdom and power. See Pinsker, 'Traditional Leaders Today in the Federated States of Micronesia'.
38 *Tamol* refers to the traditional chiefs of the outer islands in Yap. In Chuukese, they are called *samol*.
39 *Yap State Constitution*, Article III, Section 2.
40 *Chuuk State Constitution*, Article IV, Section 1, fsmlaw.org/chuuk/index.htm.
41 *Chuuk State Constitution*, Article IV, Section 2.

Section 3 allows the state legislature to appropriate funds annually for a traditional leaders' conference. Section 4 ensures that 'traditional rights over all reefs, tidelands, and other submerged lands, including their water columns, and successors' rights thereto, are recognized. The Legislature may regulate their reasonable use'.[42]

Article II, Section 1 of the Kosraen State Constitution affirms that:

> except when a tradition protected by statute provides to the contrary:
>
> (a) No law may deny or impair freedom of expression, peaceable assembly, association, or petition, and
>
> (b) a person may not be deprived of life, liberty, or property without due process of law, or be denied the equal protection of the laws.[43]

The Pohnpeian Constitution, Article 5, Section 1, 'upholds, respects, and protects the customs and traditions of the traditional kingdoms of Pohnpei'.[44] Section 2 states:

> the Government of Pohnpei shall respect and protect the customs and traditions of Pohnpei. Statutes may be enacted to uphold customs or traditions. If such a statute is challenged as violating the rights guaranteed by this Constitution, it shall be upheld upon proof of the existence and regular practice of the custom or tradition and reasonableness of the means established for its protection, as determined by the Pohnpei Supreme Court.[45]

Section 3 seeks to 'strengthen and retain good family relations in Pohnpei, as needed' by recognising and protecting 'the responsibility and authority of parents over their children. This Constitution also acknowledges the duties and rights of children in regard to respect and good family relations as needed'.[46]

42 *Chuuk State Constitution*, Article IV, Section 4.
43 *Kosrae State Constitution*, Article II, Section 1, fsmlaw.org/kosrae/constitution/entire.htm.
44 *Pohnpei State Constitution*, Article IV, Section 1, fsmlaw.org/pohnpei/index.htm.
45 *Pohnpei State Constitution*, Article IV, Section 2.
46 *Pohnpei State Constitution*, Article IV, Section 3.

Prelude to the Creation of the Constitution

The FSM's Constitution was negotiated during the ConCon and adopted by Micronesian representatives in the early 1970s. During the negotiation process, each state delegation expressed what needed to be included in the proposed constitution. The essential features were related to the harmonisation of the variety of cultures in the structure of the proposed government. The key question was how should the constitution be framed to accommodate the issues? Recognising their differences, the delegations agreed on traditions and local environmental issues to be left to the state and municipal governments,[47] while foreign relations were delegated to the national government. The Yapese and Pohnpeian delegations wanted their paramount chiefs to have a role at the national level. The delegation from Chuuk disagreed with this idea as the Chuukese have no paramount chief; each village or island in Chuuk has its own *samol*, and it would be hard to nominate a paramount chief from the pool of *samol* to represent Chuuk at the national level. Kosrae had lacked paramount chiefs since Western diseases reduced the population in the nineteenth century. An agreement was reached between the delegations that a chamber of chiefs should be created constitutionally,[48] with the decision on how to select chiefs to represent them at the national level left to each state to decide. To date, the provision relating to the creation of a chamber of chiefs remains dormant as there has been no move to activate it. At the state and municipal levels, however, chiefs continue to play essential roles in protecting cultures and traditions.[49] It is very possible that the ongoing power struggle between the executive and legislative branches of the national government may precipitate the need for the chamber of chiefs to intervene. This suggests that traditional chiefs can assist in shaping the nation's future.[50]

---

47 For an in-depth discussion, see Meller, *Constitutionalism in Micronesia*, pp. 261–281.

48 *The Constitution of the Federated States of Micronesia*, Article V.

49 *The Constitution of the Federated States of Micronesia*.

50 Political leaders of the FSM need to understand the purpose of traditions as included in the Constitution as an alternative to legal dispute. The Chamber of Chiefs is meant to serve this purpose. See the *Constitution of the Federated States of Micronesia*, Article V, Section 3.

Connecting the Constitution and Micronesian History

The FSM's Constitution underscores the continuity of Micronesian history and belief in the ongoing value of unity in the face of challenges presented by the modern world. It empowers Micronesians to wear the Micronesian identity as a personal badge of honour as they carry their passports, crisscrossing the globe.[51] The assertion of Micronesia's place in history is noted in the Preamble:

> with this Constitution, we affirm our common wish to live together in peace and harmony, to preserve the heritage of the past, and to protect the promise of the future. To make one nation of many islands, we respect the diversity of our cultures. Our differences enrich us. The seas bring us together, they do not separate us. Our islands sustain us, our island nation enlarges us and makes us stronger. Our ancestors, who made their homes on these islands, displaced no other people. We, who remain, wish no other home than this. Having known war, we hope for peace. Having been divided, we wish unity. Having been ruled, we seek freedom. Micronesia began in the days when man explored seas in rafts and canoes. The Micronesian nation is born in an age when men voyage among stars; our world itself is an island. We extend to all nations what we seek from each: peace, friendship, cooperation, and love in our common humanity. With this Constitution we, who have been the wards of other nations, become the proud guardian of our own islands, now and forever.[52]

While it is easy to dismiss these as statements of desire rather than reality, the values espoused above are culturally valued and historically proven pillars of Micronesian identity. They were inserted into the Constitution to help restore Micronesian memories of values suppressed by colonial rule and permanently embed them into the national psyche for the purposes of perpetuating the Micronesian identity and continuity. While framed by colonial boundaries, a deeper reading of Micronesian history and nation

---

51   *The Constitution of the Federated States of Micronesia* was constructed based on Micronesian historical experience in response to the changing international circumstances. As the Preamble states, 'to preserve the heritage of (Micronesian) past and to protect the promise of the future … to make one nation of many islands, we respect the diversity of our cultures. Our differences enrich us'.
52   *The Constitution of the Federated States of Micronesia*, Preamble.

building reveals the FSM was born from Micronesians' own historical consciousness stemming from their deep affinity with each other prior to and after colonialism.[53]

Oral history and linguistic evidence suggests that the configuration of the FSM approximates the pattern of past boundaries.[54] The *sawei* system,[55] which centred on inter-island connections between the volcanic island of Yap and its low-lying islands in the western part of Chuuk, is a reminder of the extensive connection between the central and eastern parts of the FSM. This connection also served as a form of insurance to ensure the survivability of the people who depended on each other in an environment prone to natural disasters such as typhoons, ocean surges and famine. The FSM is located in what is known as typhoon alley. Typhoons or *melimel* (strong storms) frequent these islands every year. They can devastate islands and deprive the islanders of their food supply. Historically, in such instances, the high volcanic islands of Yap and Chuuk would provide assistance to the low-lying islands as their larger land area and high ground meant that they could better withstand typhoon damage. Assistance was distributed through the established *sawei* network, with an associated regular voyage of outer islanders to Yap to acknowledge the latter's parental kin relationship. Yapese hosts benefitted from the prestige of this off-island recognition of their authority, which made them willing to give far more than they received in the material exchanges between low and high islands that took place during outer islanders' stays on Yap.[56]

---

53 Historian Hanlon argued that Micronesia is a colonial construct and only exists in people's imagination. However, anthropologist Glenn Petersen claims that while this may previously have been so, the people of Micronesia now have a sense of their historical connection as united by the name 'Micronesia'. Thus, this is no longer a figment of imagination and is a reality in the contemporary FSM. See Hanlon, 'Magellan's Chroniclers?', pp. 53–54; Petersen, *Traditional Micronesian Societies*, pp. 12–13.

54 The FSM is part of the Trukic geo-linguistic group prior to the arrival of the colonists. See Rauchholz, 'Notes on Clan Histories and Migration in Micronesia', pp. 54–55.

55 William Alkire, 'Traditional Exchange Systems and Modern Political Developments in the Yap District of Micronesia', in *Persistence and Exchange: Papers from a Symposium on Ecological Problems of the Traditional Societies of the Pacific Region*, edited by Ronald W. Force and Brenda Bishop, August–September, 1979, pp. 16–18; William Lessa, 'Ulithi and the Outer Native World', *American Anthropologists*, Vol. 52, 1950, p. 32; D'Arcy, *The People of the Sea*, pp. 146–147; Hunter-Anderson and Zan, 'Demystifying the Sawei', pp. 4–6. The *sawei* system was a tribute system between the volcanic island of Yap and the low-lying islands to east of it and the northwest Chuuk. It was seen as security insurance for all involved.

56 D'Arcy, *The People of the Sea*, pp. 146–150.

Similar networks are found in the islands of present-day Chuuk and Pohnpei states. In the Mortlocks, for example, the *ainang* system imposes duties and obligations to provide food to its members in the island chain during famine or when a member travels between the islands.[57] Pohnpei's oral history also speaks of a network system between its low-lying islands surrounding the volcanic main island. These network systems are still in existence, but with evolving dimensions as they incorporate new elements of the modern world.[58] Pohnpei and Kosrae were also linked, for example, by the exchange of ideas in the design of their architecture. Kosraean structures have similar designs to Nan Madol in Pohnpei, suggesting cultural links.

Reconnecting Islands

The sea remains central to Micronesian survival. It serves as the highway for inter-island communication and trade throughout the Micronesian archipelagos.[59] Although modern modes of transportation have replaced sailing canoes, the sea routes remain known to Micronesians today. The modern economy is increasingly focused on marine resources. Micronesians continue to retest their knowledge by retracing their ancestral voyages on sailing canoes and open motorboats using traditional navigation techniques. For example, in June 2013, a traditional *palou* from Poluwat named Soste and his relatives sailed from his island to Guam using traditional methods of navigation.[60] Likewise, Peter Sitan, a traditional *palou* from the Mortlocks, tested his skills on the sea as recently as 2008 using an outboard motor skiff to travel from his island of Ettal in Chuuk to the main island of Pohnpei.[61] Soste's and Sitan's actions served as a reminder of the ongoing links to and value placed on sea navigation by Micronesians. The Constitution's Preamble states

---

57   Marshall, *Namoluk beyond the Reef*, pp. 39–40; Flinn, *Diplomas and Thatch Houses*, p. 141.
58   My personal knowledge. The descendants of Mortlockese people who migrated to Pohnpei after the 1907 super typhoon that devastated the Mortlock Islands hold some traditional titles bestowed upon them by the traditional chiefs of Pohnpei, especially the chiefdom of Sokehs. This is in recognition of their contribution to *tiahk en sapw* (Marshall, *Namoluk beyond the Reef*, pp. 40–42; Goodenough, *Property, Kin, and Community in Truk*, p. 86).
59   D'Arcy, *The People of the Sea*, pp. 144–145; Duane, *Clan and Copra*, pp. 120–123; Marshall, *Namoluk beyond the Reef*, pp. 8–10.
60   Phillip H. Blas, 'Traditional Chuukese Sailing Canoe Reaches Guam: Crew Navigated 500 Miles without Using Modern Technology', *Pacific Islands Report*, 19 June 2013, www.pireport.org/articles/2013/06/19/traditional-chuukese-sailing-canoe-reaches-guam.
61   Peter Sitan, Interview, Pohnpei, 20 January 2011; Blas, 'Traditional Chuukese Sailing Canoe Reaches Guam'.

that Micronesian history 'began in the days when man explored seas in rafts and canoes. The Micronesian nation is born in an age when men voyage among stars'.[62] This suggests that Micronesians still honour their ancestral ways to perpetuate islanders' continuity, as demonstrated by the above two navigators. It is worth noting that Sitan is the president of the National Fisheries Corporation and applied his traditional knowledge of the sea to return the FSM's fishing fleets to profit and sustainability. Micronesians are in touch with their deepest past while simultaneously mastering the modern world.

The *Ainang* System

The *ainang* system has been central to Micronesian relationships across the horizon. For example, the *kachaw* clan in Chuuk has its origin in Kosrae and Pohnpei.[63] Likewise, some Yapese clans' origins extend to the islands of Chuuk and vice versa.[64] Today, the indigenous people continue their relationship with each other via the *ainang* network. Linguistic evidence also suggests a shared Micronesian connection through a common language called Chuukic that encompasses the Mortlock Islands in the eastern part of the former Caroline Islands to the western end of the island chain in Palau.[65] This is evidenced by the fact that many of the low-lying islanders in Yap can converse with the people in the western part of Chuuk and the Mortlocks region.[66] Connection between Micronesians through this common language remains strong, and the Constitution has provided opportunities for more interaction.[67] For example, any citizen of the FSM can travel and reside anywhere in the FSM, and most migrate if they have kin connection in a new place.

Since Micronesian people are historically mobile, they naturally continue to transplant themselves further afield. This is made possible by the global transportation system and political links with former colonial powers. Current estimates indicate that under the Compact, more than 20 per cent of the Micronesian population now resides outside the nation,

---

62 *The Constitution of the Federated States of Micronesia*, Preamble.
63 Uman, Saladier and Chipen, *Uruon Chuuk*, pp. 1–7; Kim, *Into the Deep*, pp. 6–7.
64 Alkire, *Lamotrek Atoll and Inter-Island Socio-Economic Ties*, p. 10.
65 Rauchholz, 'Notes on Clan Histories and Migration in Micronesia', pp. 54–55; Kim, *Into the Deep*, pp. 6–7; Alkire, *Lamotrek Atoll*, pp. 28–30.
66 Marck, 'Micronesian Dialects and the Overnight Voyage', pp. 253–258.
67 *The Constitution of the Federated States of Micronesia*, Preamble.

particularly in the US.[68] This new diaspora will continue to expand as a result of the globalised world and the inherent urge of the Micronesian people to travel to join their families now searching for opportunities outside Micronesia. It is argued that a consequence of this process is the exportation of Micronesian ideologies to the new spaces in order to facilitate Micronesians' transition to their adopted environment while maintaining a connection to their island homes.[69] The *ainang* system is the glue that links geographically dispersed clan members to each other and their nation state.

Forever mobile throughout their long past, Micronesians are adapting quickly to their new globalised lifestyle. As Captain Marar notes, 'Micronesians are genuinely great navigators; they continue to explore new stars to sail in the new globalised sea of the globalised world to reconnect with their history and new experiences'.[70] Despite the movement of Micronesian people beyond the horizon, the *Shulapan allik* recognises their citizenship. For example, Micronesians living abroad continue to participate in national elections; their votes are sent back to the FSM to be counted. Further, their interests in land over non-citizens are legally protected by the Constitution.[71]

The Legal System in its Micronesian Context

While reflecting Micronesian history and values, the FSM's Constitution is still derived from an American model. This provides an inherent tension between American and Micronesian jurisprudence.[72] This tension was naturally present from the outset as US judges dominated the court system. Legal precedents were framed in the image of American judicial precedents. For example, lawyer Brian Tamanaha argued that US judges used their knowledge of the US legal system when interpreting Micronesian cases due to their unfamiliarity with Micronesian traditions,

---

68 SBOC, www.sboc.fm/ (site discontinued).
69 Marshall, *Namoluk beyond the Reef*, pp. 144–145.
70 David Marar, pers. comm., Nett, Pohnpei, 20 January 2011.
71 *The Constitution of the Federated States of Micronesia*, Article XIII, Section 4.
72 There is often tension between FSM and US interpretations of the law, especially when the issue of culture is involved. Although some cases have been settled, it is debated whether the decisions were conclusive. See *FSM v Mudong*, 1 FSM Intrm. 135 (Pon. 1982); *FSM v Tammed*, 5 FSM Intrm. 426 (Yap 1990).

despite being constitutionally mandated to consider these traditions.[73] However, former Associate Judge Dennis Yamase asserted that this is no longer the case as more Micronesian judges have entered the court system and are shaping it in accordance with Micronesian jurisprudence.[74] The court system has matured legally and is promoting constitutional principles immersed in traditional practices, such as alternative dispute resolutions among communities.[75] However, one still wonders about the validity of Yamase's claim, particularly when most Micronesian judges are educated at institutions that teach American jurisprudence.

It is understood that at the time of the FSM's independence there were no qualified indigenous lawyers certified by competent law schools to organise and develop the legal system and a Micronesian-based jurisprudence. Consequently, US judges were appointed to undertake the task. The judges' landmark decisions essentially reinforced non-Micronesian legal principles, which promoted the interests of the state and the universal rights of a person as an individual. This line of thought and priority contradicted traditional values despite the Constitution's recognition of the importance of cultures and traditions in the courts' decisions.[76] This is still a matter of controversy and the subject of ongoing debate between the black letter approach and the radicals who seek a wider and fuller interpretation of the Constitution, including the application of customary laws. The key legal question is, what constitutes 'the law' from a Micronesian perspective?[77]

Jurisprudential debate has been central to Micronesian independence, identity and continuity. This has raised the issue of whether the FSM's legal system is genuinely constructed by local values or whether the system has been utilised by outsiders to reimpose their values under a different guise.[78] Is the lack of understanding of Micronesian cultures an appropriate defence on the part of foreign judges when rendering decisions contrary to indigenous cultures?[79] Foreign judges presiding over FSM courts immediately after the implementation of the Constitution have been

---

73 Puas, 'The FSM Legal System'.
74 Yamase, *The Supreme Court of the Federated States of Micronesia*, pp. 36–38.
75 Yamase, *The Supreme Court of the Federated States of Micronesia*, pp. 36–38.
76 Puas, 'The FSM Legal System', pp. 11–12.
77 No one has raised the issue and it needs to be addressed. See Puas, 'The FSM Legal System', pp. 11–12.
78 Puas, 'The FSM Legal System', pp. 11–12.
79 Puas, 'The FSM Legal System', pp. 11–12.

regarded as the main architects of FSM's jurisprudence. The established precedents and their rulings have provoked debate between two opposing camps within the FSM legal fraternity.[80] One view is that the decisions of the foreign judges have been admired and recognised as developing the legal landscape in the fledgling nation. This is because their decisions were seen as endorsing black letter law and the primacy of the individual in any contest involving customary law.[81] This perspective has been supported for providing certainty by not having to determine customary issues in key cases and leaving behind a solid legal system. The alternative view is that the US judges left behind a half-baked legal system almost devoid of Micronesian perspective or input.[82] This is evident from their narrow interpretation of the Constitution from the outset, which arguably put the legal system on an inappropriate footing for developing an independent and locally responsive legal system.

Values and Identity in the Legal System

Micronesian criticism of the narrow interpretation of the Constitution in decisions made by US judges can be seen in cases such as *FSM v Mudong* (Pon. 1982),[83] *FSM v Alaphonso* (Truk 1982),[84] *Semens v Continental* (Pon. 1986)[85] and *FSM v Tammed* (Yap 1990).[86] The courts' decisions in these cases and subsequent similar cases constituted a systematic promotion of American social values at the expense of Micronesian cultural values. The decisions effectively moulded the FSM legal system in the image of American jurisprudence, rather than developing a Micronesian legal system based on the goals articulated during the ConCon.[87] The basis of

---

80 My personal observation as a trained lawyer who has frequently worked with lawyers within the FSM over the last 11 years. There has been ongoing debate about legal precedents left by foreigners that are still followed by Micronesian judges. Micronesian legal scholars have not extensively written on this subject.

81 My personal observation.

82 Brian Tamanaha, *Understanding Law in Micronesia: An Interpretive Approach to Transplanted Law*, Studies in Humanities (series), Center of Non-Western Societies, Leiden University, The Netherlands, 1993, pp. 59–67; Discussions with colleagues at the FSM Supreme Court, Palikir, Pohnpei, January 2010 during contractual employment at the Congress of the FSM.

83 *FSM v Mudong*.

84 *FSM v Alaphonso* (Truk 1982), fsmlaw.org/fsm/decisions/index.htm.

85 *Semens v Continental*, 2 FSM Intrm. 200 (Pon. 1986), fsmlaw.org/fsm/decisions/index.htm.

86 *FSM v Tammed*, 5 FSM Intrm. 426 (Yap 1990).

87 Meller, *Constitutionalism in Micronesia*, pp. 340–341.

this harsh assessment is that, constitutionally, court decisions must first look at *eoranian fanou* in the FSM.[88] In the case of *Etpison v Perman* (Pon. 1984), for example, it was stated by the court that:

> the FSM Supreme Court may look to decisions under the United States Constitution for guidance in determining the scope of jurisdiction since the jurisdictional language of the FSM Constitution is similar to that of the United States.[89]

In re Sproat (Pon. 1985), again the court said, 'the jurisdictional language in the FSM Constitution is patterned upon the United States Constitution'[90] and the implementation of US legal concepts. In *FSM v Alophonso*, the court reasoned:

> most concepts and many actual words and phrases in the FSM Constitution [as in] … the Declaration of Rights came directly from the [US] Constitution … Bill of Rights. In the two Constitutions, the language … is nearly identical.[91]

Therefore, it was only logical that the court establish a precedent based on the import of American laws.[92]

A comparison of the US and FSM constitutions reveals obvious differences. They have a different history, textual language, structure and underlying philosophy.[93] Even if the Micronesian Constitution was patterned on the US Constitution, it does not necessarily follow that a court must transplant US precedents to decide cases arising in a Micronesian context. The court could have made a greater effort to accommodate Micronesian *eoranien fanou* by seeking the advice of scholars or Micronesians knowledgeable in the matters before the court.

Conflict between a narrow interpretation of the law and *eoranian fanou* was initially tested in the cases noted above. Because the courts lacked the depth of knowledge in relation to *eoranien fanou*, they inadvertently derailed the development of a fully-fledged Micronesian jurisprudence.

---

88 *The Constitution of the Federated States of Micronesia*, Article XI, Section 11.
89 *Etpison v Berman*, 1 FSM Intrm. 405 (Pon. 1984), fsmlaw.org/fsm/decisions/index.htm.
90 *In re Sproat*, 2 FSM Intrm. 1 (Pon. 1985), fsmlaw.org/fsm/decisions/index.htm.
91 *Alaphanso v FSM*, 1 FSM Intrm. 209 (App. 1982), 209, fsmlaw.org/fsm/decisions/index.htm.
92 *Alaphanso v FSM*.
93 It seems that Edward C. King contradicted himself when discussing the differences between the *Constitution of the Federated States of Micronesia* and the US Constitution. Yet he preferred to follow the US approach in deciding the law. For further discussion, see King, 'Custom and Constitutionalism in the Federated States of Micronesia', pp. 2–3; Puas, 'The FSM Legal System', p. 13.

This could be considered a revival of the colonial years when black letter law was perceived as superior to customary law.[94] This argument treats the two judges as facilitators of an American 'judicial activism' that further diluted Micronesian customs and traditions for the purpose of maintaining American interests in the FSM.[95] Micronesia requires judicial decisions that seriously consider customary law and deliver inclusive, holistic and harmonious judgments to Micronesian communities. It is not accepted that customary law operates 'outside' the constitutional legal system. In fact, many municipal-level courts ignore the formal legal system and use traditional methods of settling disputes.

The case of *FSM v Mudong* highlighted the conflict that could arise when interpreting the Constitution from an individual rights perspective in a case enmeshed in customary and traditional issues. In that case, the two appellants asked the court to dismiss the case as the issues had been resolved through *tiaken Pohnpei*, a Pohnpeian customary apology.[96] The court denied the defendants' motion, citing 'prosecutorial discretion' and referring to custom as insufficient grounds on which to call a halt to and dismissal of criminal proceedings.[97] The court indicated that:

> the customary effect upon court proceedings of a customary forgiveness is not self-evident, and the defendants offered no evidence to establish that dismissal of a court proceeding is one of customary [law].[98]

However, it should have been self-evident to the court that it would be impossible to find precedents that could establish that the dismissal of court proceedings was available under customary law given that there was no court system in customary law.[99]

---

94   The law provides mechanisms for judges to use expert witness when customary practises are involved. Justice King ignored such an avenue. See *National Judiciary Act, Public Law No. 1-31* (FSM).
95   Puas, 'The FSM Legal System', pp. 21–22.
96   Customary apology in Pohnpei involves bringing together the families of the opposing parties over *sakau* and making apologetic speeches evoking traditional connections. See the case of *FSM v Mudong*.
97   It is often a risk when prosecution discretion is exercised by outsiders as they lack the depth of knowledge of Micronesian customs. Today, it is a policy to hire Micronesians first. Foreigners may be hired if a position cannot be filled by indigenous professionals.
98   *FSM v Mudong*.
99   *Amicus curiae* (lit. 'friend of the Court') refers to experienced, retired lawyers familiar with the court system and the law who may be called on by the court to offer expert advice on issues before the court. See *National Judiciary Act, Public Law No. 1-31* (FSM).

In support of the prosecutorial discretion argument, the court reasoned that 'the National Criminal Code does not grant the prosecutor authority to dismiss an existing prosecution on the basis of customary law'.[100] The court further reasoned, *inter alia*, that customary law and the Constitution perform different functions.[101]

The court could have considered the alternative, that 'those customs that have the status of customary law are a source of law and should be recognised by the Court as such, without evidence having to be adduced'.[102] That is, evidence of Pohnpeian practice should have been sufficient without the appellants requiring 'expert' evidence from a foreign anthropologist. Pohnpeian custom should have been self-evident as it is uniform practice on the main island. Perhaps the court could have called upon its *amicus curaie*[103] to assist it in establishing the proper interpretation and thus application of Pohnpeian traditions. Moreover, an assessor could have been appointed by the court as subject to the National Judiciary Act, Public Law No. 1-31. As Section 12 of that Act states, the court is authorised:

> to appoint assessors to advise about local law or custom … any Justice of the Supreme Court may appoint one or more assessors to advise him at the trial of any case with respect to local law or custom or such other matters requiring specialised knowledge. All such advice shall be of record and the assessors shall be subject to examination and cross-examination by any party.[104]

This misinterpretation of the FSM's Constitution by US judges may be considered as undermining the development of the FSM justice system, arguably weakening the FSM's unique cultural identity. In doing so, precedents were set that differentiated the law from custom, with the view that it would be easier for subsequent judges to concentrate on a precedent-based system. However, this has made it difficult for subsequent Micronesian judges to reset the system to include both the law and custom.

---

100 *FSM v Mudong.*
101 It is undoubtedly true that the US Constitution differs from the *Constitution of the Federated States of Micronesia* as they have had different roles based on the different histories of their respective countries. The *Constitution of the Federated States of Micronesia* values customs as part of the judicial process, especially when issues of the social configuration principle are involved. The issues could be generally settled if the court looks at *The National Judiciary Act, Public Law No. 1-31* (FSM).
102 Tess N. Cain, 'Convergence, or Clash? The Recognition of Customary Law and Practice in Sentencing Decisions of the Courts of the Pacific Islands Region', *Melbourne Journal of International Law*, Vol. 2, 2001, p. 51.
103 See the principle of *amicus curiae* in fn. 99.
104 *FSM v Mudong.*

There is still a significant tension between custom and the court system within the FSM. It can be argued that the Constitution should not control but recognise custom as it plays an important role in disputes, violence, or wrongdoing in the Pohnpeian community.[105] Many independent Pacific Island nations' constitutions and legal systems effectively recognise customary law within their procedures.[106] The FSM's Constitution can and should recognise customary means of dispute resolution within criminal proceedings. However, per established legal precedent:

> [Micronesian custom and] the constitutional legal system established by the people of the FSM, flow from differing premises and traditions. They serve different purposes … Customary law de-emphasises notions of individual guilt, rights and responsibility, and places greater stress on the groups to which the individual accused and victims belong. The Constitutional … system concentrates upon smaller and larger units than those immediate groups emphasised by customary law.[107]

Yet, the Constitution provides the solution to this tension between custom and court legal procedures. The root of the problem lies in the interpretation of the Constitution within the court system, rather than in the Constitution itself. The Constitution does not set up dual independent systems of law as suggested in the above court cases; indeed, to the contrary, the Constitution intended the courts to take customs and traditions into account in all decisions, as set out in Article XI, Section 11. These words should be accorded this recognition during the court process and not diluted so as to promote individual rights in all contexts.[108] As sociologists MacIver and Page comment:

> customs support the law and without such it becomes meaningless. Custom establishes social order of its own so that conflict arising between custom and the law is not a conflict between law and lawlessness, but between the orders of reflection [customs] and the order of spontaneity [law]. In general, customs regulate the

---

105 *The Constitution of the Federated States of Micronesia* specifically indicates that judges should be mindful in their decisions when customary matters are involved. See *The Constitution of the Federated States of Micronesia*, Article XI, Section 11; *Etscheit v Santos*, 5 FSM Intrm 35.38 (App. 1991); *Rosie v Healy-Tibbets Builders*, Inc, 5 FSM Intrm. 358, 361 (Kos. 1992).
106 Lamour, *Foreign Flowers*, pp. 15–17.
107 *FSM v Mudong*.
108 Daniel P. Ryan, *Essential Principles of Contract and Sales in the Northern Pacific: Federated States of Micronesia, the Republics of Palau and the Marshall Islands and US Territories*, iUniverse, USA, 2009, p. xxiii.

whole social life of man. Law itself cannot cover the whole gamut of social behaviour. It is the customary practices that contribute to the harmonious social interactions in a society.[109]

This combination of law and custom working in tandem towards the same objective of consensus-based social harmony is essential in the Micronesian context.

It is clear that the US judges meant to elevate the status of individual rights over those of the group and justified this position by claiming that the rights of 'immediate groups' fall within the purview of customary concern. This reasoning does not reflect the reality of life in the FSM. As noted earlier, Micronesians belong to an extended *ainang* diaspora dispersed throughout the islands. They are not divided into isolated clans that can be left alone to perform their own customary duties.[110] Customary law is part of the Constitution and should have been considered holistically by the courts as a valid means of resolving disputes and bringing peace back into the community—surely the ultimate intention of the Constitution.[111]

Familial relations are equally as important as *ainang* relationships within Micronesian custom. It is undoubtedly true that familial relationships are at the very core of Micronesian society and are the source of numerous rights and obligations that influence practically every aspect of the lives of individual Micronesians. These relationships are an important component, perhaps the most important component, of the custom and tradition referred to generally in the Constitution (Article V) and specifically in the National Criminal Code, which states, 'this Court has no desire to disregard or minimise the importance of such relationships'.[112]

In *FSM v Tammed*, the court noted:

> the duty of a national court justice [is] to give full and careful consideration to a request to consider a particular customary practice or value in arriving at a decision requires careful investigation of the nature and customary effect of the specific practice at issue, a serious effort to reconcile the custom and tradition with other

---

109 Robert MacIver and Charles Page, 'Custom', *Sociology Guide*, sociologyguide.com/basic-concepts/Custom.php.
110 The extended *ainang* family.
111 See *The Constitution of the Federated States of Micronesia*, Article XI, Section XI.
112 *FSM v Tammed*.

constitutional requirements, and an individualised decision as to whether the specific custom or tradition should be given effect in the particular contexts of the case before the court.[113]

Further complicating the issues of custom, the court stated that 'the party asserting customary law has the burden of proving by a preponderance of the evidence the existence, applicability and customary effect of such customary law'.[114] The key issue at stake here is who should be recognised as having the authority to provide that evidence to the court to ensure that Micronesian values are not eroded.

Conflict between the FSM's Constitution and State Traditions

In 1990, a consolidated appeal case went before the court as a test case between the primacy of the Constitution and state traditions. The case was *FSM v Tammed*, where two separate appellants were charged with rape. However, before they were arrested or charged, they were caught and beaten by the relatives of the victims, with both sustaining serious injuries and one requiring hospitalisation. Both defendants were convicted of the charges but disagreed with the sentencing and appealed.

Both appellants argued that the 'trial court erred in not giving mitigating effect to the beatings each had received when it handed down their respective sentences'.[115] The Appellate Court faced the dilemma as to whether the customary beatings could be considered as mitigating factors in sentencing. The chief justice reasoned:

> the record reflects no serious effort by any party in either case to establish the precise contours of customary punishments. There are contentions that some aspects of the beatings were violative of customary procedures, there seems to be general agreement that these beatings have 'substantial customary' and traditional implications.[116]

---

113 *FSM v Tammed*.
114 Ankush Sharma, 'Customary Law and Received Law in the Federated States of Micronesia', *Journal of South Pacific Law*, Vol. 10, Issue 1, 2006, www.paclii.org/journals/fJSPL/vol10/7.shtml.
115 *FSM v Tammed*.
116 *FSM v Tammed*.

This ruling came in the face of pre-sentence reports for one appellant, whose relatives accepted that the beatings were derived from customary practices. The government's counsel suggested:

> as a matter of customary law, the beating may have restored the defendants fully to the community, not only reducing or obviating the need for further punishment, but entirely cleansing him of liability … because of the customary nature of the punishment, then no prosecution was ever initiated against any of those who attacked either of the defendants.[117]

However, the court had to draw a line between custom and the law in order to render its decision. The dilemma was to balance the customary practice of the beating of a wrongdoer against the constitutional right of an individual not to be assaulted.[118] The court did not want to encourage violence against the individual. Yet, if the court condemned beatings as merely a customary practice devoid of legal standing, this would devalue customary law and thus deny the rights of families under customary law as raised in the *Mudong* case. The court issued a decision that the beatings had some mitigating effect but without having any regard to their customary implications or their compatibility with the criminal law or civil rights.[119]

It can be argued that the court in *FSM v Tammed* made its decisions on the basis that the state and the individual have greater rights than traditional interests. Further argument suggested that perhaps some consideration with respect to international law could have been explored to moderate the American perspective of the law by way of balancing it with certain articles in the *International Covenant on Economic, Social and Cultural Rights*, the *Universal Declaration of Human Rights* and other relevant international instruments.[120] There have been decisions in other jurisdictions where judges have drawn on international instruments to resolve problems in domestic jurisdictions. In the alternative, judicial decisions about customary law could have been sought from other Pacific

---

117 *FSM v Tammed.*
118 Sharma, 'Customary Law and Received Law in the Federated States of Micronesia'.
119 Many traditionalists argued that cultural beating is compatible with the Constitution in view of Article V, Section 2.
120 *Semens v Continental.*

jurisdictions such as Vanuatu, Samoa or Tuvalu,[121] as discussed in *Semens v Continental*. In this case, Justice King acknowledged the possibility that 'when constitutional and statutory provisions, customs, and traditions fail to furnish a full solution to issues the Court will look to common law applied in the United States and elsewhere'.[122] However, Justice King applied American precedents and did not consider other Pacific Island states.[123]

Some indigenous lawyers have rejected the above analysis by the court in *Mudong* on the basis that the Constitution has highlighted the importance of custom in the justice system, as reflected in Articles V and XI. The notion that customs and the Constitution flow from 'differing premises' is to narrowly interpret the Constitution if the effect is to ignore customs, except in cases where the court thinks it applies to 'those immediate groups emphasised by customary law'.[124] The distinction between custom and individual rights is not made explicit in the Constitution as the intent was that they both be considered in decision-making (judicial and otherwise).

In addition, the concept of the individual in many Micronesian customs is hard to determine as the individual is considered inseparable from their *ainang* group.[125] The decision that the rights of an individual are paramount when compared to an *ainang* group, as held by the court, contributed to the devaluing of Micronesian custom by removing the rights of the extended families to settle their own disputes, a central tenet of traditional community justice. Such a practice could alienate the individual, with devastating consequences for both the family and community at large. In this regard, it should be noted that the FSM has

---

121 *Semens v Continental*. Justice King said to look at the South Pacific to borrow precedents of common law but then drew on US law instead. It was a contradiction that demonstrated the inconsistencies in the law as handled by outsiders.

122 For example, *sakau* is a ceremonial drink in Pohnpei, used during community gatherings like funerals, feasts or customary apology. It is made from the root of the pepper tree (*Piper methysticum*).

123 *FSM v Mudong*. The prosecutor lacked knowledge of custom and so to deny Mudong's request to drop the case meant that Pohnpeian custom was secondary to the law in view of the outsider.

124 During my contract work as a lawyer at the FSM Congress and Department of Justice in 2005 and 2010, I discussed the matters with the Micronesian lawyers in government.

125 Individuals are part of the *ainang* system and there is no private individual in many parts of the FSM. One person's problem becomes the affair of the whole extended family in land disputes and death. Perhaps the court could have adopted the doctrine of 'circle sentencing' (restorative justice). This is prominent in many Australian jurisdictions involving Australian Aboriginals, where the court can determine the question of law but Aboriginal Elders decide on the sentencing of the individual offender.

one of the highest suicide rates by *amwinimwin*.[126] Traditional remedies play a crucial role in the maintenance of *eoranian fanou*, the foundation of local identity and continuity.

Tamanaha and his supporters have accused the court of Americanising the judicial system through what many call 'creative legalism';[127] that is, judges give lip service to custom and ignore other jurisdictions in the Pacific whose treatment of custom in their legal system could provide a model, instead preferring to cherry pick US cases. This is not an entirely unreasonable stance, given that the judges are more familiar with US law. This has raised questions as to the capacity of foreign judges to be involved in matters concerning customs and the law. For example, Tamanaha has argued that Congress should consider introducing legislation requiring all foreign judges and lawyers to undertake workshops in Micronesian customs and traditions.[128] This would increase their capacity to deal with the difficult issues concerning customs and the law to safeguard the continuation of Micronesian values.

The Law as a Reinforcer of Identity

Brian Tamanaha, a US lawyer who worked in Yap and later wrote a book about his experiences titled *Understanding Law in Micronesia*, is a critic of the primacy afforded to American jurisprudence and case law in matters before FSM courts. He has criticised Justice King for his selective approach in favouring American legalism, which had no direct connection to the laws and values of Micronesia.[129] Tamanaha has argued that outsiders created their own brand of what the law 'ought to be' rather than what 'the law is', particularly from a Micronesian perspective.[130] He further argued that the suggestion by Justice King that Micronesians knew what they were in for when ratifying the Constitution as a basis for strengthening his own analysis (e.g. in *FSM v Alophonso*) was not a defence to the criticism of King's decisions. Tamanaha asserts that even though a high percentage of the population ratified the Constitution, this

---

126 *Amwinimwin* is a form of psychological punishment imposed on parents and close relatives who, in the eyes of the victim, wrongly punished him or her. See Francis X. Hezel, 'Cultural Patterns in Trukese Suicide', *Ethnology*, Vol. 23, July 1984, pp. 193–206, www.micsem.org/pubs/articles/suicide/frames/cultpatfr.htm. I use a different spelling of the term.
127 Tamanaha, *Understanding Law in Micronesia*, pp. 59–67.
128 Tamanaha, *Understanding Law in Micronesia*, pp. 59–67
129 Tamanaha, *Understanding Law in Micronesia*, pp. 59–67.
130 Tamanaha, *Understanding Law in Micronesia*, pp. 59–67.

does not mean that the voters understood the constitutional text in its entirety.[131] Tamanaha is not alone in his view. This is a part of the ongoing debate between the opposing factions within the FSM legal profession as to whether a Micronesian perspective of the legal system has been fully represented by outsiders. Many indigenous lawyers have since entered the legal profession and brought with them different perspectives to the debate. Many have questioned both Tamanaha's and King's perception of Micronesian law and traditions as both are outsiders.

Conclusion

The administration of the Constitution as discussed in the above cases has been a challenge to Micronesians. This is especially so because the law itself cannot be purely based on imported legal concepts but must fit local customs to sustain continuity. Since coming into contact with the outside world, Micronesian customs and traditions have adapted and maintained their integrity in the globalised world. The management and administration of the law are the responsibility of each state and municipal jurisdiction, in conformity with the national Constitution. At the municipal level, methods of settling disputes continue to be largely led by the heads of the extended family or traditional village leaders of each clan in conjunction with the court system. The FSM honours its Constitution and the culture it safeguards. Like any newly independent nation, the FSM faces tension between its traditions and imported laws. This can be seen in the cases outlined earlier, where US judges implemented precedents that often contradicted local understandings of effective ways of adjudicating and resolving disputes.

The judges' lack of understanding of Micronesian custom and cultures should not be used as a defence of their judgments. The Constitution is clear on the issue of customs and traditions having primacy in judges' decisions. Additionally, there were mechanisms available for the judges to seek assistance on cultural issues. These avenues were ignored. This resulted in legal precedents that continue to promote outsiders' influence in Micronesia. However, Micronesian judges are entering the constitutional system to restrengthen constitutionally defined Micronesian jurisprudence based on historical experience to ensure the indigenous continuation of the Micronesian identity.

---

131 Tamanaha, *Understanding Law in Micronesia*, pp. 59–67.

6

Engaging with China and the US

Introduction

Independence has meant that the FSM's external relations have moved from essentially bilateral relations with colonial powers to multilateral relations with the international community at large. The world's two largest economic powers, which are also military superpowers, China and the US, are potentially heading towards a battle for influence in the western Pacific. The challenge the FSM now faces is managing the US and China under the new global regime in order to promote its own interests. This chapter will demonstrate that the FSM has handled this challenge in a skilful and considered way that has served its best interests.

Far too often scholars have falsely argued that since the colonisation period, Pacific Islanders have been largely lost to the overwhelming forces of outside powers, almost to the point of extinction.[1] It has been claimed that local religious practices have been absorbed into Christianity, traditional social organisation has transformed into a Western style of government, codified laws have replaced common laws, and land has been appropriated by a capitalist mode of production. A litany of misguided comments added to this misinterpretation, suggesting that Micronesians succumbed to the 'first taint of civilization', which reduced them to

---

1   Hanlon, 'Micronesia: Writing and Rewriting the Histories', pp. 1–3; Roland W. Force and Maryann Force, 'Political Change in Micronesia', in *Induced Political Change in the Pacific: A Symposium*, edited by Roland W. Force, Honolulu, Hawai'i, 1961, pp. 1–6, 8–10; Petersen, 'Lessons Learned', pp. 45–63.

'strangers in their own land' because they could not withstand 'the winds of change' in their 'broken canoe'.[2] Such assertions of collapse fail to address how one accounts for the rich and dynamic Micronesian cultures that survived over 100 years of colonisation and still exist today.

The FSM under the Spotlight

The FSM is shaping up as the next potential flashpoint in Chinese–US relations in the northwest Pacific because of its strategic position in the Asia-Pacific region. Currently, it is going through an intense economic and political transition in preparation for the scaling down of the Compact of Free Association in 2023. The Compact is a bilateral treaty between the FSM and the US, forged as a result of their common historical experience and interests post WWII. It was first implemented in 1986, renegotiated in 2001 and extended to 2023. The US has provided just over US$7 billion to the FSM Government in return for America having exclusive use of the islands for military purposes.[3] Already, the US is scaling down its Compact assistance. As a consequence, questions have been raised about the FSM's ability to survive economically in the post-2023 era. China, some observers argue, is likely to partially fill the gap by increasing its engagement with the FSM due to its own interests in the region.[4]

Located in close proximity to Asia, the US military base in Guam and the missile range in the Marshall Islands, the FSM must tread cautiously and exercise due diligence in its foreign relations because of its geopolitical position. For the FSM to maintain its position of strategic importance, it must learn from the lessons of WWII and balance the presence and scope of influence of each of these superpowers in the region. China's

2   These are titles from Francis X. Hezel's books, except for *Broken Canoe* which was written by Ann Nakano. The titles connote ethnocentrism as still part of Micronesian scholarly discussion.

3   Paul D'Arcy, 'The Role of the Tuna Fishery in the Economy of the Federated States of Micronesia', *Pacific Economic Bulletin*, Vol. 21, No. 3, 2006, pp. 75–87. During my interviews with them, government officials openly voiced and accepted the fact that the US will use the Compact to question the FSM's motives for dealing with countries viewed as unfavourable by the US. For example, an incident occurred over the introduction of an FSM Congress resolution that favoured granting China exclusive rights to fish in the FSM's EEZ. It was speculated by many that after the US objection to the resolution, the FSM Congress quietly withdrew the proposal. Additionally, the public at large opposed the resolution, especially supporters of the US both in the FSM and the US.

4   My experiences while working in Congress in 2010, interviews with many of the congressmen (e.g. Lorin Robert (Secretary of Foreign Affairs), Interview, Palikir, Pohnpei, 7 January 2011) and the adoptions of various resolutions (discussed in this chapter) are good indications of the FSM's positive engagement with China based on Micronesians' own understanding of the new global order.

increasing presence in the FSM raises concerns among some political observers over China's long-term objectives. The FSM has stated on many occasions that its relationship with China is based purely on economic interests. Notwithstanding this, the US may decide to invoke its right to deny certain external relations under the Compact if it perceives its interests are under threat.[5]

The undermining of Chinese activities in the FSM has already been attempted. For example, China proposed to loan the FSM Government US$22million to fund the overhaul and refurbishment of Micronesian fishing facilities. A US fishing company called Oceania then attempted to undermine this offer. In its letter of memorandum to the FSM Congress, Oceania complained about China's move to overhaul the fishing facilities in the nation, stating in part that China's fishing infrastructure proposal:

> does nothing to create additional industries, promote economic projects, or even guarantee a sustainable revenue basis. The difference between [the] Chinese proposal and Oceania's detailed comprehensive plan is the latter includes university economic study … Oceania's plan also comes with its own financing; there are no loan requirements or guarantees incumbent upon the FSM.[6]

It went further, asserting that the 'PRC [People's Republic of China] participates only in projects that benefit [itself]; and maintain its interests only to the extent the needs of PRC is met'.[7] The question of what benefits the FSM will continue to receive once loan monies have been exhausted is unclear.[8] As yet, there has been no government-to-government confrontation between China and the US over their interests in the FSM.

---

5   Carl Apis, pers. comm. (online), 3 July 2012.
6   Bob D. Rosen, 'Oceania Memorandum to Speaker of the Congress of the Federated States of Micronesia', Issac Figir, 7 January 2011, p. 2; Nick Solomon (chief executive officer, National Fisheries), Interview, Kolonia, Pohnpei, 17 January 2011.
7   Rosen, 'Oceania Memorandum', p. 2; Solomon, Interview.
8   Rosen, 'Oceania Memorandum', p. 3; Solomon, Interview.

The FSM and the Pacific Region

In 2007, University of the South Pacific academic Ron Crocombe noted the fast-growing involvement of Asia in the Pacific and strongly suggested that Pacific nations should take serious notice of this influence.[9] The rippling effect of the economic influence wielded by emerging powers like China, Japan and South Korea would mean positioning Pacific interests to optimise engagement with these countries.

Political scientist Terence Wesley-Smith has observed that China's growing engagement in the Pacific region is part of its own rise as a new economic and political global power, reaching out to the developing world with similar initiatives in Asia, Africa, Latin America and the Middle East.[10] It is a new opportunity for Pacific Island nations to explore new possibilities instead of being trapped in an outdated system that often undermines their own interests.[11] The Pacific consists of many independent nations, and they possess the right to exercise their choice as to which countries they engage with.[12]

The FSM is conscious of other Pacific Island nations' engagement with China and the resulting reconfiguration of Oceania's collective engagement with the rest of the world. For example, former US Secretary of State Hillary Clinton, during her trip to the Pacific Forum meeting in the Cook Islands in 2012, said that the US would remain active in the South Pacific for the 'long haul' as the region is big enough for all interested parties, including China.[13] Beneath this diplomatic rhetoric lies genuine American concern about the threat of China's growing influence in the Pacific. Australia and New Zealand's heavy-handed response to the 2006 Fijian coup resulted in the island nation strengthening ties with China. It is seen as an example of US apprehension about the Pacific becoming a non-Western lake.[14] Moreover, Clinton's comments were one-

---

9   Ron Crocombe, *Asia in the Pacific Islands: Replacing the West*, University of the Pacific, Suva, 2007, pp. 213–220.

10   Yongjin Zhang, 'A Regional Power by Default', in *China in Oceania: Reshaping the Pacific?*, edited by Terence Wesley Smith and Edgar A. Porter, Berghahn Books, USA, 2010, pp. 60–61.

11   Zhang, 'A Regional Power', pp. 60–61.

12   Peter Christian, 'Patriot Games: Island Voices in a Sea of Contest', *Pacific Institute of Public Policy*, Discussion Paper No. 21, June 2012, p. 2.

13   Jenny Hayward-Jones, 'China No Rival in the Battle for Island Influence', Lowy Institute, 17 May 2013.

14   Fergus Hanson, 'Don't Ignore the Big New Player in Fiji', *The Sydney Morning Herald*, 9 May 2008, pp. 1–2, www.smh.com.au/articles/2008/05/08/1210131163040.html.

sided as the tone did not include the perspective of the Pacific Island nations and neglected to consider how they play an important role in maintaining stability in their own region.[15]

The FSM is learning from other Pacific Island nations to better position itself in regard to relations with China without offending the US. Its diplomatic relations with China have been maintained for more than 20 years, while its longstanding relationship with the US is under review. Its relationship with China has been the subject of debate over the years, with critics claiming that China is using the FSM as part of a moving frontier into the northwest Pacific. This is not so according to supporters of China, as the FSM has a constitution that defines its foreign policy; China is a part of this policy by Micronesian design.[16] Moreover, the FSM has been benefiting from China's assistance, so this relationship remains firm, particularly in view of the scaling down of the US's Compact monies since 2003. Many Micronesians are suspicious of China's foreign aid programs; they perceive China as slowly gaining ground in the northwest Pacific.[17] The US may exercise the option under the Compact to unilaterally dislodge China should it perceive China as a threat. However, such an action would raise the issue of violating the supremacy of the FSM's Constitution[18] and relevant international laws of non-interference in the sovereign affairs of other nations.

Contact with China

The FSM's initial contact with China dates back to when it was still part of the US-administered TTPI. The traditional inhabitants had waited patiently for the transition to independence following the decolonisation of the other trust territories around the world. However, the US was not in a hurry to forgo its interests in the islands. China, as a member of the UN Security Council, was aware of the US's tactical move in slowing

---

15   Jenny H. Jones, 'Big Enough for All of Us: Geo-strategic Competition in the Pacific Islands', Lowy Institute, 16 May 2013, www.lowyinstitute.org/publications/big-enough-all-us-geo-strategic-competition-pacific-islands.
16   *The Constitution of the Federated States of Micronesia*, Article II, Section 1.
17   Bill Jaynes, 'FSM Congress Pushes for Exclusive Fishing Rights: Single Foreign Country Would Have Access to Grounds', *Kaselehlie Press*, 26 July 2010, p. 1.
18   *The Constitution of the Federated States of Micronesia*, Article II, Section 1.

down the process of terminating the trusteeship agreement.[19] In an effort to gain support in the UN Security Council for the purpose of ending the trusteeship agreement, the FSM contacted Chinese diplomats in the UN. To demonstrate its support for the FSM's anticipated independence, China invited the leaders of the FSM to Beijing for political discussions and to initiate diplomatic relations. A delegation from the FSM, headed by the FSM's first president, Tosiwo Nakayma, and first secretary of the Department of External Affairs (now Department of Foreign Affairs), Andon Amaraich, visited China in the early 1980s to gain more knowledge about China as a developing nation.[20] According to former FSM President John Haglelgam, the US was not fully aware of all the discussions that took place between the FSM and China.[21] At the time, Haglelgam perceived the trip as a sign of the FSM leaders' growing confidence to engage with other countries in the international arena.

The Road to Control

The transition to independence remained slow as the US was still studying the details of its relationship with the FSM under the Compact. However, China and the USSR reminded the US of its obligations under the trusteeship agreement to honour the demands of the FSM people to pursue their goal towards self-determination. Again, Haglelgam noted, 'the Americans and Europeans were too legalistic in their approach to strictly follow the text of the decolonisation process',[22] which would take time to unfold, while China often opted for more flexible diplomatic dialogue in dealing with the issue. China's support for the FSM struck a chord with Micronesian leaders. In response, the FSM pledged to honour the 'One China Policy' when it became a member of the UN.[23]

---

19   John Haglelgam, currently a professor at the College of Micronesia, was the second president of the FSM. He had direct contact with Chinese diplomats during his term in Congress and as the second president. I interviewed him and others about these issues: John Haglelgam (professor), Interview, College of Micronesia, National Campus, Palikir, Pohnpei, 11 January 2011; Epel Illon (special advisor to SBOC and former secretary of the Department of Foreign Affairs), Interview, Palikir, Pohnpei, 11 January 2011; Lorin Robert (secretary of the Department of Foreign Affairs), Interview, Palikir, Pohnpei, 7 January 2011.

20   Haglelgam, Interview.

21   Illon, Interview; Lorin Robert, Interview.

22   Haglelgam, Interview; Illon, Interview; Lorin Robert, Interview.

23   Haglelgam, Interview; Illon, Interview; Lorin Robert, Interview.

Since then, the relationship between both nations has been built on trust, respect and mutual cooperation.[24] The One China Policy remains at the heart of the diplomatic relationship between the FSM and China.

However, China's presence in Micronesia has lately been under scrutiny by critics. They question China's sudden interest in the FSM, a region it had not shown much interest in before. They speculate that China is positioning itself to become a major influence in the Pacific area.[25] China's intention, according to these critics, is to create a climate of mistrust, which is likely to evolve into a new Cold War front in the Pacific. This Sinophobia may be a new phase in Micronesian politics, but many see it as a continuing legacy of the Cold War period when the USSR and the US were at each other's throat.[26]

In the case of the FSM, this underlying fear of China is externally derived; it is connected to the colonial history of the islands. This antagonism towards China is part of a concerted effort by the former colonial powers of the Pacific, who remain the leading aid donors to the region, to continue their dominance in the Pacific, including the FSM. Micronesians were indoctrinated to support the Western style of political philosophy by successive Western colonisers and the entrenchment of Western governance.[27] When one takes a closer look at Micronesia, however, one can discern some socialist features present in the island's traditional social superstructure. For example, the inter-island extended family has socialist elements based on the principle of *eaea fengan*.

The undermining of socialism as alien to island cultures has been facilitated by Christian and colonial agencies. These twin forces attempted to dissuade islanders from getting too close to socialism.[28] Islanders were taught that democracy and Christianity were precursors for a tranquil world, as opposed to the antagonistic and godless socialism. They were also taught that any doctrine that undermined the fundamental principles of

---

24   Haglelgam, Interview; Illon, Interview; Lorin Robert, Interview.
25   Rachel Reeves, 'China Not Threatened by U.S. Presence at Pacific Forum. Vice Foreign Minister: Clinton's Visit Not Attempt to Override Influence', *Pacific Scoop*, 2 September 2012.
26   My personal experience when growing up in the FSM was that communist countries like Russia and China were frowned upon by many Micronesians as being untrustworthy and to be feared because of their undemocratic practices.
27   Gonzaga Puas, 'Is China a Threat in the Pacific? The Case of Micronesian Experience', Paper delivered in the Pacific Islands Political Science Association (PIPSA), Apia, Samoa, 2012, pp. 20–21.
28   Florian Seady, *Church Song: Moun Russia*, Satawan Island, 1974; Crocombe, *Asia in the Pacific*, p. 340.

democracy and Christianity was inherently bad and not conducive to the sustainability and survivability of Micronesians. For example, I remember my high school years, when discussion on the future political status of the FSM was in full swing. The students were taught that if they rejected American democracy, an evil empire would take over the islands and impose its evil wrath on Micronesians, worse than the Japanese during WWII. This was supported by the Catholic faith, which propagated socialism as naturally evil because of its opposition to biblical scriptures. Christians and non-Christians would be slaughtered by the socialist states should they allow socialist ideologies to take root on their islands.

Anti-Chinese sentiment is part of the contemporary socialism versus capitalism debate in the FSM. For example, many Micronesian soldiers who serve in the US military strongly support American democracy and have spoken against China's growing influence in the nation.[29] They claim that the FSM is treading on dangerous ground in allowing Chinese influence to rise in the region, and is undermining US interests in doing so. To date, however, the Chinese have been extremely cautious about challenging or upsetting US interests in the western Pacific. In my interviews with the Chinese ambassadors to the FSM in Pohnpei in 2011 and 2013, they emphasised China's support for the FSM as a developing country, like China.[30] China wants to learn more about Micronesians as a people, including their cultures and history.[31] On these points they expressed their frustration at not being able to locate materials written from a Micronesian perspective.[32] They also emphasised the point that they are not in the FSM to antagonise the US but to assist the FSM in whatever capacity possible.[33] However, it remains to be seen at what point the US will object to the diplomatic relationship between Micronesia and China, especially in relation to the end of the current Compact in 2023.

---

29   Haglelgam, Interview. Professor Haglelgam explained that the Micronesians who joined the US military forces are the promoters of US interests in the FSM. He referred to them as a fifth column and as Micronesian super patriots of Americanism. No statistics are available yet as to the number of Micronesian citizens in the US armed forces.
30   Yongjin Zhang (Chinese ambassador to the FSM), Interview, 13 July 2013, Palikir, Pohnpei; Zhang Weidong (Chinese ambassador to the FSM), Interview, Palikir, Pohnpei, 19 January 2011. Both ambassadors commented on the Compact of Free Association as being a major part of FSM foreign policy.
31   Zhang, Interview; Weidong, Interview.
32   Zhang, Interview; Weidong, Interview.
33   Zhang, Interview; Weidong, Interview.

Micronesians have always adapted successfully to foreign influences and have managed and lessened the impact of such incursions through a number of strategies. Currently, the emergence of the internet and globalisation have enabled the FSM's citizens to learn more about the outside world for the purpose of contextualising such externalities from their own perspective. Micronesian educational institutions have also heralded a new period of intellectual discourse to respond effectively to the major foreign players who are trying to control their islands. At the forefront of this discourse are the challenges the FSM needs to consider in relation to its future development in search of an economic model that complements its present social order. Additionally, the FSM diaspora has been growing tremendously over many decades, and their economic knowledge of the outside world has contributed enormously to the development of the FSM. The FSM also has a constitution that outsiders need to respect if they want to retain their interests in the FSM's jurisdiction. Finally, under its constitution, the FSM has the right to forge relations with any country of their choosing, including China.[34]

The FSM–US Connection

The FSM–US connection was forged after WWII when the US took control of the islands as their last colonial master. As noted in the previous chapter, the US consolidated its power by registering the islands in the UN as a trust territory, the TTPI. The TTPI was the only trust territory placed under the jurisdiction of the UN Security Council, because of its strategic value to the US, pursuant to Chapter XII, Article 83 of the UN Charter.[35]

The process of independence took a long time as negotiators on both sides sought to secure optimal outcomes in their country's best interests. The key issue for Micronesians was why was the FSM pressured to gain political independence prior to economic development?[36] In weighing the options, Micronesian leaders decided that economic matters should be negotiated under a Compact of Free Association and kept separate

34 *The Constitution of the Federated States of Micronesia.*
35 *Charter of the United Nations and Statutes of the International Court of Justice*, Article 83 of Chapter XII.
36 This was the Congress of Micronesia's response to the US's foot-dragging approach towards Micronesian independence. Nevertheless, political freedom was the priority. See Hanlon, *Making Micronesia*, p. 95.

from political issues. Political independence only was therefore sold to the Micronesian people and accepted in 1979. However, formal termination of the TTPI awaited US approval in the UN Security Council.

The UN trusteeship agreement came to an end in 1986, followed immediately by the formalisation of the Compact, although not without controversy.[37] At the heart of this ongoing controversy is the 'permanent denial clause', which is interpreted by critics as providing the US with permanent and exclusive rights to use the islands for military purposes. Many supporters of this interpretation claim that, although the financial assistance ends in 2023, the security provision remains in American hands indefinitely. This view was rejected by most FSM government figures interviewed during my fieldwork as being without any basis. The denial clause, they argued, only survives for the duration of the Compact. Further, the Compact can be unilaterally terminated as subject to Title IV, Article 4, Sections 441, 442 and 443.[38] However, Section 443 must be scrutinised closely because it requires a constitutional process (i.e. a referendum) for final termination of the Compact by the FSM.[39] This places the burden of terminating the Compact on the Micronesian side, as holding a referendum is costly and time consuming to administer across all the islands. It is obviously designed to make the Compact difficult to be unilaterally terminated by the FSM. However, the US cannot prevent the FSM from terminating the Compact by other means if provided for by the Micronesian Constitution, which supersedes the Compact as subject to Article 2, Section 1.[40]

Dishonouring the Compact

A political outburst by Senator Dan Inouye of Hawai'i and his supporters in the US Congress exemplified the continuing paternalistic attitude of many US officials towards Micronesians. In 2012, the senator wrote a letter to

---

37   Lorin Robert, Interview.
38   *Compact of Free Association between the Federated States of Micronesia and the United States of America.*
39   *Compact of Free Association between the Federated States of Micronesia and the United States of America.*
40   My personal interpretation (as a lawyer). Lorin Robert said that the Compact derives from the FSM's Constitution, so it is secondary to the Constitution. There has been an ongoing debate as only the financial parts of the Compact are subject to renegotiation, with the military part remaining in perpetuity (Lorin Robert, Interview).

the US secretary of state expressing dissatisfaction over the influx of FSM immigrants to Hawai'i, Kansas and the US territories of Guam and the Northern Marianas Islands. The senator claimed that immigrants from the FSM were draining the states' and territories' financial resources despite the Compact money to compensate their costs.[41] This led to tension and resentment between the new immigrants and many US citizens of these states and territories. Senator Inouye advocated for all Micronesians to be screened before entering the US to determine whether they were able to support themselves independently. Such a demand ignores a basic feature of Micronesian social organisation—they are not individualistic; they rely on the support of the family system, so any individual assessment at entry masks kin support networks in place upon arrival. Such demands also ignore the tax payments Micronesians inject into the US economy. As taxpayers, they are surely entitled to receive medical attention and social welfare.

The senator's letter was also sent directly to the president of the FSM, something seen by both the FSM's people and leaders as disrespectful and lacking the courtesy of international protocol. For example, Senator Inouye is not the US president and should not have dealt directly with the FSM's head of state. Inouye's actions were perceived as nothing more than a continuation of the belittling of Micronesian leaders as being inferior to their US counterparts.[42] This attitude needs to be curtailed by the top tiers of the US Government as the Compact was negotiated between the sovereign governments of the FSM and US, not the states of Hawai'i and others.[43] Micronesia is an independent nation with its own identity. It is not part of the US's domestic jurisdiction.

The FSM Congress's Resolution No. 17-61[44] was tabled in response to the US Senate Committee for Appropriations, chaired by Senator Inouye, directing the Department of Homeland Security to implement 'all legally allowable grounds of inadmissibility under the Compact which apply to

---

41   Giff Johnson and Bernadette Carreon, 'Micronesia's Access to U.S. under Review', *Marianas Business Journal*, 18 July 2011; Giff Johnson, 'US Lawmakers Seek Limit on Micronesian Migrants: Marshall Protests, Cite Compact Terms', *Marianas Variety*, 23 May 2011; Bill Jaynes, 'Senate Appropriations Committee Takes Concrete Steps to Begin Barring Some FAS Citizens from Entry to the United States', *Kaselehlie Press*, 19 September 2011, p. 1.
42   Reactions to Inouye's comments were widespread on the *Micronesian Forum*; Inos Walter (Chuuk State legislator and Chuukese historian), Interview, 10 December 2012.
43   Walter, Interview.
44   *FSM Congress Resolution No. 17-61*. It was introduced by Senator Peter Christian of Pohnpei to terminate the Compact by 2018.

nationals from the (FSM) … to establish … advanced permission for prospective travellers from the (FSM) to enter the United States'.[45] Many Micronesians regard Senator Inouye's action as the branding of FSM citizens as terrorists.

The FSM's response to Senator Inouye's letter was swift and deliberate, with strong overtones expressing the FSM's dismay and disgust. The new generation of FSM leaders like David Panuelo responded to the letter by expressing outrage at Inouye's insensitivity in treating Micronesians as scapegoats for domestic Hawaiian problems, which could affect the historical relationship between the US and FSM. In his letter, Congressman Panuelo (and like-minded colleagues) stated that:

> the U.S. can no more unilaterally create a bottleneck for FSM citizen's right to freely travel and work in the United States, than the government of the FSM can revisit the defence provisions of the Compact. Aren't the veto powers over the waters and air space of the FSM that the two countries agreed to in the Compact a security and strategic lifeline for the U.S.?[46]

These comments were supported by many FSM leaders and also reflected the sentiment of educated members of the public. For example, the Micronesian Seminar website received many comments from the FSM diaspora reminding the US that if it changed the terms of the Compact unilaterally to the detriment of FSM citizens, the FSM might see fit to terminate the US's interests in its territorial jurisdiction.[47] The political tension between the two congressmen may produce negative consequences, but it effectively demonstrated the extent to which the FSM has come of age and is able to deal with matters of international concern on its own terms. Congressman Panuelo represents a new style of leadership that puts the FSM first, and he sincerely articulated the Micronesian perspective without fear of political repercussions.[48]

Two resolutions introduced by the two longest serving FSM congressmen, Peter Christian and Dohsis Halbert, provide good examples of how the FSM was considering terminating the Compact. Christian's Congressional

---

45   Jaynes, 'Senate Appropriations Committee', p. 1.
46   David Panuelo, 'Where Did Our Real Friends Go?', *Honolulu Civil Beat*, 5 April 2012, www.civil beat.org/2011/08/12669-where-did-our-real-friends-go/.
47   Panuelo, 'Where Did Our Real Friends Go?'.
48   My personal reflection based on analysis of his background. He has held many positions in the FSM and Pohnpei governments.

Resolution No. 17-61 asked the FSM president to terminate the Compact early, in 2018 rather than 2023, while Halbert's Congressional[49] Resolution No. 16-89 proposed granting China exclusive fishing rights in the FSM's EEZ. In return, the FSM sought higher fishing fees from China and guaranteed that it would effectively patrol its EEZ and arrest ships not displaying the Chinese flag.[50]

China also expressed its interest in redeveloping the FSM's fishing facilities and increasing its fishing activities in FSM waters through a US$30 million soft loan and other assistance packages aimed at filling the gap in the FSM's fishing capacity. As previously noted, an American company, Oceania, torpedoed the plan.[51] The US objected to the resolutions and cautiously reminded the FSM about its obligations and duties under the Compact. The response from the FSM Congress was that the resolutions were economic in nature and fell outside the Compact's denial clause, thereby rendering the US's claim as being without legal effect.[52] The above concerns have prompted the FSM to seriously reconsider its foreign policy vis-à-vis the Compact.

The actions of the US-dominated JEMCO have also raised questions about the US's intent to continue to honour the Compact in good faith. Critics perceive the Compact as nothing but a vehicle for facilitating the recolonisation of Micronesia.[53] JEMCO, which has a set majority of American members, dictates how Compact funds are to be used, even if there are objections from the Micronesian members. This was seen in the dispute over the spending of funds earmarked for the Chuuk education sector, discussed in Chapter 4.

As US financial contributions under the Compact dwindle, the FSM has to find ways to sustain itself. US ambassador to the Marshall Islands Martha Campbell noted the grim reality in 2010:

---

49   Jaynes, 'Senate Appropriations Committee', p. 1.
50   Hers, 'US Congress Pushes for Limits on FAS Entry to the US', April 2011, www.micronesia forum.org.
51   Hers, 'US Congress Pushes'.
52   Sitan, Interview, Kolonia, Pohnpei, 27 January 2011.
53   *FSM Congress Resolution No. 17-61.*

> [there is a] dangerous belief that the U.S. will extend more aid
> when the current Compact of Free Association grant package ends
> in 2023[54] ... there is no intention on the part of anyone anywhere
> in the government of the U.S. to extend Compact funding
> past 2023.[55]

This stance poses two key dilemmas for the US and FSM. Will the US allow increased Chinese funding to replace its own diminishing funding in the FSM leading up to 2023 and beyond? If not, what other means will the US use to persuade the FSM to circumvent China's rise in the Micronesian region and Oceania if it determines not to extend its rent for influence? These issues are increasingly germane in view of the FSM's close proximity to Guam, the Northern Marianas Islands and the Marshall Islands, all of which host US military installations and bases.[56] The question of influence will continue to escalate before 2023 while the FSM is calculating its future economic interest and viability.

Managing the US and China

The FSM's diplomatic relations with China and the US remained essentially bilateral and separate until 2006 when China's foreign aid to the FSM increased, particularly in light of the watershed announcement of Chinese President Hu Jintao in Fiji in April 2006 of a dramatic increase in Chinese assistance to Pacific Island nations.[57] President Hu announced a package of US$300 million in preferential loans and other aid to expand trade, investment and infrastructure development.[58] As a result of this, the FSM will secure a significant increase in Chinese aid and may exhibit less care in undertaking actions that could be construed as antagonistic towards the US.

Chinese assistance has resulted in the construction of a series of infrastructure projects, especially public buildings, development projects in farming and fisheries, and a series of smaller targeted grants to assist

---

54   Giff Johnson, 'No More Compact for the RMI', *Pacific Islands Report*, 5 November 2010, pidp.
eastwestcenter.org/pireport/.
55   Johnson, 'No More Compact'.
56   Lorin Robert, Interview.
57   Olivier Wortel, 'China Increasing Its Presence in FSM in Big and Small Ways', *Kaselehlie Press*,
7 February 2007, www.fm/news/kp/2007/feb07_3.htm. The following details on China's aid program
are based on Wortel's extended interview with Ambassador Liu Fei.
58   Wortel, 'China Increasing Its Presence in FSM'.

local community project infrastructure.[59] These projects have largely been based in and around the state capitals like Kolonia in Pohnpei and Weno in Chuuk. For example, in 2006, the use of Chinese aid money resulted in the construction on Pohnpei of the Western Pacific Tuna Commission headquarters and official residences for the nation's president, vice president and speaker of congress. School buildings have been constructed for Kosrae State, while Yap and Chuuk states have benefitted from the delivery of two custom-built cargo and transport vessels for the far-flung islands. The Chinese are also keen to further assist each of the four state governments in their future infrastructure projects.[60] Although Chinese assistance is well received by the FSM, the US remains the largest contributor to Micronesian development programs.[61] However, China's policy of political non-interference in the FSM's governance, unlike the US (exemplified by JEMCO), has led to FSM leaders embracing China's presence in the FSM.

China's consultative approach in providing infrastructure as requested by national and state governments is a dramatic contrast to the previously discussed American domination of the budget and aid allocation of Compact monies. Chinese Ambassador Liu Fei has had a number of Pacific postings and earned a reputation for being sensitive to local needs and respectful of Micronesian aspirations as a developing nation. The ambassador notes that China is also a developing nation, and characterises her country's aid policy as 'very open and practical'.[62] She notes that, in addition to providing requested infrastructure, China's aid is aimed at assisting economic ties, trade and investment between China and the FSM, and giving people a better and more positive understanding of China.[63] The latter objective figures prominently in small-scale aid projects for individual institutions below the level of national and state governments, such as providing libraries with books on China. Another example is the first wave of these small-scale aid projects including new computers for the FSM Congress and a donation of over 200 books on Chinese subjects

---

59 Weidong, Interview.
60 My personal notes on *WikiLeaks Documents*. China's assistance to the FSM since the two countries opened diplomatic relations with one another is estimated to be over US$170 million. Compare this to the over US$7 billion provided by the US. See also Philippa Brandt, 'The Geopolitics of Chinese Aid', www.lowyinstitute.org/publications/geopolitics-chinese-aid.
61 My personal notes on *WikiLeaks Documents*.
62 Wortel, 'China Increasing Its Presence'.
63 Wortel, 'China Increasing Its Presence'. The Chinese ambassador said the people of the FSM should know more about China than what is reported in the media.

to the Pohnpei Public Library and College of Micronesia. Chinese library collections are available for many other educational institutions, such as Kosrae and Xavier high schools.[64]

Educational exchange programs for students and high-ranking officials are also an important part of China's policy of enhancing understanding of its culture and intentions in the Pacific Islands, as a means to counter the generally negative reporting in Western media and academic analysis. Examples of this include collaboration between Zhejiang College in southern China and the College of Micronesia, including learning exchanges and scholarships in marine science. Chinese scholarships offered to FSM citizens jumped from two to three per year before 2006 to 17 in 2006 and have continued to increase. In April 2014, Chinese Ambassador Zhang Lianyuen stated that 'over 100 FSM students [were] granted the full government scholarship to study in China'.[65] In the health sector, two groups of Chinese medical experts have visited FSM and offered precious services to local people, and 'China will continue to offer its sincere assistance within its ability to help FSM achieve sustainable development and enhance its people's living standards'.[66]

China is increasingly involved in the FSM's agriculture and fisheries sectors as an aid donor, trainer and participant. China has developed a large pilot farm in Madolenihmw District, Pohnpei, growing a large variety of vegetables. A large tuna fishing fleet and operation, Luen Thai, from Hong Kong, is also based permanently in Pohnpei, and has plans to significantly increase the size of its fishing fleet.[67] China also assists the FSM trade schools on Pohnpei by offering training in trades such as carpentry, plumbing, washing machine repairs and electrical repairs. The Chinese acknowledge the merit of developing primary industries that add value to locally produced foods such as noodles made from taro, breadfruit or banana flour, which Ambassador Liu notes are 'healthy, balanced, [and] cheaper' than imported foods.[68]

---

64   Wortel, 'China Increasing Its Presence'.
65   Zhang Lianyuen, '25 Years' Run toward Amity and Prosperity. Commemorating the 25th Anniversary of Diplomatic Relationship between China and FSM', *Kaselehlie Press*, 6 April 2014, p. 8.
66   Lianyuen, '25 Years' Run toward Amity', p. 8.
67   Peter Sitan (president of the FSM National Fisheries Corporation), Interview, Micronesian Symposium, The Australian National University, 28 April 2014.
68   Lianyuen, '25 Years' Run toward Amity', pp. 8–9.

China has been sensitive to American and Micronesian critics. China is at pains to emphasise that its aid program in the Pacific Islands is far smaller than those of the US, Japan and Australia. China's aid to the Pacific Islands amounted to US$850 million in 2006–2011,[69] compared to Australian aid of US$4.8 billion in the same period.[70] China desires collaboration with other donors and denies it is ratcheting up aid in direct competition with other donors. Ambassador Liu emphasises that China sees itself as filling a supporting role to the region's big three aid donor nations. She notes:

> We are very keen on helping the education, private, and infrastructure sectors, as well as trade and investment and the other areas that have been outlined in the country's Strategic Development Plan. We are very much the same in focusing on the key sectors here … we actually are on the same policy with the U.S. Government in this regard. … If the U.S., Australian, and Japanese Embassies want to work with me, I always welcome them.[71]

The Exhibition Travel Group

A new tourist project proposed by the business group Exhibition Travel Group (ETG) seems at odds with Ambassador Liu's statements. The project is massive and has deeply divided local communities. The company is still negotiating with the Yap Government and landowners. Initially, ETG planned to build a mega-tourist resort with 10,000 hotel rooms and associated infrastructure, such as expanding the airport and constructing docks, a golf course, roads, hospitals, shopping centres and beaches.[72] The company anticipates direct flights to the FSM and large profits, although tourism is a fickle market dependent on the buoyancy of the home economy of travellers and jet fuel prices. The ETG project will not compete with the nearby tourist industry of Guam and Saipan since it is anticipated that direct flights from China will become the norm, sidestepping US security checks and delays in Guam.[73]

69   Brandt, 'The Geopolitics of Chinese Aid'.
70   Brandt, 'The Geopolitics of Chinese Aid'.
71   Gonzaga Puas, 'Micronesia and the Rise of China: Realpolitik Meets the Reef', Paper delivered to the Pacific History Association, Taiwan, 3 December 2014, pp. 20–22.
72   Rubinstein and Mulalap, 'A Proposed Chinese Mega-Resort in Yap', pp. 8–10.
73   Rubinstein and Mulalap, 'A Proposed Chinese Mega-Resort in Yap', pp. 8–10.

However, there has been controversy about the scale of this mega tourism project, prompting voices of concern from within the FSM and the international community. Many have condemned the size and the impact it will have on the pristine Yap environment. A recent study conducted by anthropologist Donald Rubinstein and attorney Clement Mulalap indicated the polarisation of views in the Yapese community. For example, anti-ETG proposal citizen groups such as the state legislature, Yap Women's Association and Catholic Church are at odds with pro-ETG proposal lobby groups such as the executive branch of government, the business community and certain traditional leaders.[74] The anti-ETG forces claim that the proposal is unrealistic and unsustainable, while the pro-ETG forces argue in favour of the development on the basis of the enormous financial windfall that the project could bring to Yap. Rubinstein and Mulalap raised two important questions about ETG's intentions. First, 'what is China's real purpose in building a billion-dollar resort complex in Yap'?[75] Second, why is Yap still considering the project in light of ETG Chairman Deng Hong being remanded in jail in China for alleged corruption since March 2013?[76] Despite this, China's government has no plan to slow down its diplomatic relations with the FSM, although there is no evidence that the mega-resort has any political motive behind it. If the Yapese people approve the project, the FSM will become a tropical playground for Chinese tourists and other Asian nationals, as well as for tourists from the US and Europe.

It is anticipated that Micronesian scholars and professionals trained in Chinese higher education institutions will benefit the FSM's future. An association between the citizens of China and the FSM, the Micronesia–China Friendship Association, was established in early 2011.[77] Its first president was the highly esteemed Micronesian scholar Professor Haglelgam. He possesses a vast wealth of knowledge on China due to his previous position as the second president of the FSM. The association's stated aim is to promote greater contact between the citizens of both countries through education and cultural programs.[78] Direct business contact between citizens is also encouraged.[79]

---

74 Rubinstein and Mulalap, 'A Proposed Chinese Mega-Resort in Yap', pp. 8–10.
75 Rubinstein and Mulalap, 'A Proposed Chinese Mega-Resort in Yap', pp. 11–12.
76 Rubinstein and Mulalap, 'A Proposed Chinese Mega-Resort in Yap', pp. 8–10.
77 Haglelgam, Interview.
78 Haglelgam, Interview.
79 Haglelgam, Interview.

In 2009, the FSM and China celebrated the twentieth anniversary of their friendship. Chinese President Hu Jintao and FSM President Emmanuel Mori exchanged congratulatory notes praising the hard work of their countries in maintaining their ongoing friendship based on a model of mutual respect. President Hu indicated that China and the FSM have maintained 'a good momentum of reciprocal cooperation' that has 'delivered real benefits' to both nations and 'promoted stability' and prosperity in the region.[80]

President Mori's speech highlighted the 'growing bonds' that exist between the two nations and noted that the FSM is 'looking to the challenges ahead'.[81] The FSM will continue 'to count on the strength of the partnership and friendship' between the two countries. He further noted that the FSM has 'greatly benefitted' from the assistance provided by China.[82] Although China is a recent actor in FSM politics, the island people consider China as a new addition to Micronesia's list of diplomatic friends. This is part of the FSM's diplomatic adaptation to the external world to assert its identity and continuity.[83]

On 24 March 2014, China's ambassador to the FSM again reinforced China's growing relationship with the FSM, noting:

> China and FSM offer each other unfailing support in their own capacities and with sincerity. In the past 25 years, the bilateral trade volume between our two countries rose from nearly nothing to 15 million dollars last year.[84] The pilot farm donated and constructed by China has successfully run for 18 years and quite a number of biogas generators have been set up in local farmers' homes. The two cargo-passenger vessels donated by China are playing vital roles in Chuukese and Yapese people's daily life. The fruitful outcome of our practical cooperation can also be easily seen around us, like China-FSM Friendship Sports Centre in Pohnpei and High School Building in Kosrae. More and more FSM people begin to appreciate Chinese culture and see China as a genuine friend ... China will continue to offer its sincere assistance within its ability to help FSM achieve sustainable

---

80   'The FSM President Hu and President Mori Exchange Congratulation Letters to Celebrate the 20th Anniversary of China-FSM Relations', *FSM Information Service Press Release*, Palikir, Pohnpei, 1 September 2009.
81   'The FSM President Hu and President Mori Exchange Congratulation Letters'.
82   Lianyuen, '25 Years' Run toward Amity', p. 8.
83   Lianyuen, '25 Years' Run toward Amity', p. 8.
84   Lianyuen, '25 Years' Run toward Amity', p. 8.

development and enhance its people's living standards. And there are more exciting new projects under detailed discussion and are making important progress. Great potential also lies in tourism, infrastructure, transportation and fisheries, etc.[85]

Epel Illon, a former negotiator for the Compact, former secretary of the Department of Foreign Affairs and currently senior advisor for SBOC, commented on how China can deliver benefits to the FSM: 'China can buy up all FSM exports overnight and that will be a great benefit to the FSM. Can you imagine that?'[86]

Is China a Threat?

China's growing influence in the FSM has been met with optimism at the top level of the FSM Government. However, others continue to speculate that China is using the FSM as a means to develop its strategic presence in the region.[87] China dismisses this claim, stating that its presence in the FSM is based on mutual respect and common interests as developing nations. In my interview with China's ambassador to the FSM on 15 July 2013, he cited the Preamble of the FSM's Constitution as part of China's foreign policy: 'We extend to all nations what we seek from each: peace, friendship, cooperation, and love in our common humanity'.[88] China shares this goal with the FSM.[89] The FSM is part of the Pacific region—a region of competing interests between external powers—and so too is China because of its strategic interests. China has been unfairly demonised as the red dragon ready to create disequilibrium in the region.[90]

---

85   Lianyuen, '25 Years' Run toward Amity', p. 8.
86   Illon, Interview. Illon said China is economically important to the FSM. For example, China could buy up all the FSM's export commodities within one hour. The FSM private sector can benefit immensely from China's assistance.
87   The FSM is the only country among the Compact nations with diplomatic relations with China. There are suspicions and speculations regarding China's presence and intentions in the FSM. In my personal communications with many FSM government officials and diplomats, many stated that China is not in the FSM for military purposes. Many of them support the idea of the US engaging with China rather than fearing it. However, many did not want to be identified as they fear repercussion for making comments contrary to official FSM Government policy. The two Chinese ambassadors I interviewed claimed that there is a strong relationship between the US and the FSM and that China is in the FSM for reasons other than military (e.g. for mutual diplomatic and cultural assistance) (Zhang, Interview; Weidong, Interview).
88   *The Constitution of the Federated States of Micronesia*, Preamble.
89   Zhang, Interview; Weidong, Interview.
90   Terrance W. Smith, 'China in Oceania: New Forces in Pacific Politics', *Pacific Islands Policy*, No. 2, East-West Center, Hawai'i, 2007, pp. 13–19.

The FSM seeks friendship with all powers in order to develop itself and its interests. This principle will be tested by circumstances where friendly powers act in ways contrary to the FSM's perceived interests. For example, the Chinese fishing vessel *Ping Da 7* ran aground on Nankapenparam Reef in Pohnpei State in December 2013. A state of emergency was declared out of concern for the environmental threat to the reef and its marine life posed by leaking fuels and chemicals from the vessel. The ship's owner, Jianghai Ping, indicated that he had no intention of taking full responsibility for salvaging the boat, much less collaborating in undertaking preventive measures against environmental harm.[91] This kind of response will jeopardise relationships between the two nations. The bottom line is that it is for Micronesia to decide its own future, including which countries to associate or disassociate with. China and the US are not immune from such a decision-making process.

Conclusion

The FSM does not believe that it will sink into oblivion without Compact funding.[92] The economic wealth of the FSM is yet to be tapped because of the vastness of its EEZ and lack of technology and investment. Many suspect that vast mineral deposits and marine resources exist in its EEZ. The FSM has been bleeding economically because much of its fishing harvest has been stolen due to illegal fishing activities or foreign fleets paying a mere fraction of the sale value for fishing licenses.[93] Exploitation of and profits from the FSM's marine resources will depend on the FSM's understanding of international business practices and diplomatic relations within the global community.

Already, many Pacific nations are forming new regional organisations to protect the potential economic wealth in their EEZs, demonstrated at a meeting of Pacific Island leaders in the Cook Islands on 15 May 2014.[94]

---

91 FSM Updates, 'President Mori Declares "State of Emergency" as Ping Da 7 Post Greater Threat Sitting on Nan Kepkepin Param Reef in Pohnpei', 23 January 2014, myfsm.blogspot.com. au/2014/01/president-mori-declares-state-of.html.
92 Interviews with many FSM officials during my fieldwork in 2011–2013. They did not believe that the FSM would sink into oblivion without the Compact funds. The question is, how did Micronesians survive for centuries? Did they need the Compact?
93 D'Arcy, 'The Lawless Ocean?', pp. 4–5; Peter Wilson, 'A Tuna Industry in Micronesia?', *Micronesian Counsellor*, No. 66, April 2007, pp. 1–4.
94 Ben Chapman-Smith, 'Income from Sea Bed Mining in Cooks Could Eclipse Tourism and Cook Islands has "World Class Resource" Worth "a Vast Sum"', *Cook Island News*, 15 May 2014.

Harmonising environmental laws and claiming a bigger share of profit from future seabed mining are top priorities for Pacific Island states. This emergence of big ocean nations in the Pacific to control their potential wealth will bring about a new perspective of the Pacific. The FSM is taking the same steps to exploit the potential wealth in its EEZ to become self-reliant and ensure its continuity.

Roger Gale has noted that Micronesia will always be in someone else's strategic plan.[95] This sums up why the FSM must be mindful of its history and identity. The FSM's future security will depend on understanding how valuable it is to the outside world, and how empowered it is to engage in mutually respectful dialogue in the present environment of competitive bidding for engagement.[96] Much of that value lies in the natural resources in its territorial seas and seabed. Yet, the greatest immediate threat to the FSM derives not from superpower strategic rivalry in the western Pacific but, rather, from the climatic consequences of the race to modernise by means of industrialisation and its polluting residue. Its future is threatened by the consequences of climate change, including increasingly frequent and destructive typhoons and rising sea levels, as will be discussed in the next chapter.

---

95   Gale, *Americanization of Micronesia*, p. vi.
96   Paul D'Arcy, 'Leading by Example: Micronesians and the Sea as World's Best Practice', paper delivered at the Micronesian-Australian Friends Association (MAFA) Symposium, The Australian National University, 28 April 2014.

7

Managing Climate Change

Introduction

This chapter deals with climate change and its impact on Micronesia's food security, health, territorial integrity and adaptation policies. Effective management of the impacts of climate change may be possible if future scenarios are modelled properly. To this end, the low-lying islands in the Mortlocks will be used as a case study since they are already suffering the consequences of rising sea levels due to climate change. Their experience will be extrapolated to the other low-lying islands[1] in the states of Yap and Pohnpei and the coastal areas of Kosrae. Traditional environmental knowledge is being used to counter the impact of climate change, but is also an example of the persistence, strength and ongoing relevance of Micronesian ways of organising and interacting with their environments.

Micronesians derive their livelihood from the oceanic environment. The ocean occupies a larger space than their land. In that respect, the land must be integrated with the ocean in terms of managing resources to create balance in nature. For example, specific types of agricultural production must be in sync with the seasons of the year. *Lerak* is the season when food is in abundance. Breadfruits are harvested and stored away in *mar* pits. Catching fish is also easier, and they are salted and dried in the sun for the lean *lefang* season. Taro production is left to allow the taros to grow. When the *lerak* season ends, people survive on what they stored during

---

1   For descriptions of low-lying islands in the FSM, see Alkire, *An Introduction to the Peoples and Cultures of Micronesia*, pp. 44–48; Marshall, 'The Structure of Solidarity', pp. 12–20. For the names of low-lying islands in Yap and Chuuk, see D'Arcy, *The People of the Sea*, pp. 151–152.

the *lerak* season, supplemented by taro farming. The rhythm of nature shapes the islanders' environmental conservation practices. It also dictates the type of social activities undertaken on each island and inter-island events. The reliance on integrated social and environmental practices adopted by islanders prior to colonisation has endured to the present day. The Mortlockese are part of this social endurance.

The Mortlock Islands

The Mortlock Islands are situated in the southern part of Chuuk State and are all low-lying atolls. The distance between Weno, the capital of Chuuk, to the southern tip of the Mortlocks is roughly 273 kilometres (170 miles). It takes around 12 hours by cargo ship to reach the southern end. The Mortlocks are divided into three subregions, the Upper, Middle and Lower Mortlocks. The Upper Mortlocks are near the port town of Weno and consist of three islands, Nama, Losap and Pis. Namoluk, Ettal, Kuttu and Moch islands make up the Middle Mortlocks. The islands of Satawan, Ta, Lekinioch and Oneop comprise the Lower Mortlocks subregion. They range from less than 1.6 kilometres (1 mile) to 8 kilometres (5 miles) in circumference.[2]

Their elevation is around 3–4 metres above sea level.[3] Because of their vulnerability to sea level rise, they will be among the first to be submerged if climate change–induced sea level rise scenarios eventuate. Relocation will be the last option, but many islanders have stated that it is not an option for them at all. For example, during my field interviews, many interviewees described being unable to foresee living in a different environment, even if it was on another island, where their life would be subject to someone else's dictates. They prefer to remain on their islands and die rather than subject themselves to an alien space somewhere beyond the horizon.[4]

---

2   Marshall, 'The Structure of Solidarity', p. 14. Marshall's description of the Namoluk Isles reveals similar features to other islands in the Mortlocks.

3   Henry, Jeffery and Pam, *Heritage and Climate Change in Micronesia*, p. 7.

4   Many elders from Lukunor islands said they would rather remain on the island and die (Notes from interviews during fieldwork in 2011–2013).

Identity and Natural Disasters

The FSM is located on the southern edge of a typhoon belt, with typhoons regularly causing severe damage to the environment and threatening human life. Two patterns of typhoon are common in the FSM. The first one usually originates in the southern part of the Mortlocks region and slowly intensifies as it moves westward towards Yap and the Philippines. The other pattern is usually generated in central Yap and moves northward towards Guam and Japan.[5] However, regardless of their origins, typhoons have often inflicted colossal and unforgiving injuries to humans and the environment in the Pacific. They have also left significant scars on Micronesian history.[6] However, natural disasters have taught Micronesians to be resilient and enhanced their adaptation skills. The recent looming threat to Micronesia is climate change. Recent studies have indicated that climate change is increasing the frequency and intensity of typhoons and tropical depressions.[7] Sea level rise is also presenting new sets of challenges for Micronesians. Adapting to climate change as resiliently as possible is urgent since the prospect of Micronesians continuing without their islands—a source of their identity—is questionable.

Like other Micronesians, the Mortlockese are natural conservationists; they have a deep understanding of their fragile environment, having made the islands their home for many centuries. They understand that their environment demands constant care to conserve the islands' natural resources. For them, conservation means having a holistic understanding of human behaviour towards the physical environment, an intricate knowledge of the weather system, and an ability to utilise the best available practices compatible with the survivability of Micronesians. Adaptation to climate change has once again required Micronesians to resort to their traditional knowledge of conservation. Current government policies at the national level are supporting local strategies to form the frontline of climate change defences.[8]

---

5   Alkire, *An Introduction to the Peoples and Cultures of Micronesia*, pp. 6–7; D'Arcy, *The People of the Sea*, p. 15.
6   Dirk H. R. Spennemenn, *Melimel: The Good Friday Typhoon of 1907 and its Aftermath in the Mortlocks, Caroline Islands*, Albury, NSW, 2007, pp. 15–18.
7   Joahnnes Berden (manager of the Weather Station in Chuuk), Interview, 21 June 2013; Local fishermen such as Tonio Muritock, Lewis Estep and Kauten Kandy, pers. comm. on different occasions in Palikir, Pohnpei; Weno, Chuuk; and Lukunor Island, 2001, 2008, 2013. All stated that it has been getting difficult to predict the seasons due to the changes in weather patterns.
8   *Nationwide Climate Change Policy 2009*, pp. 1–7.

Historically, the Mortlockese divided their atoll islands into common zones, from the ocean side to the middle of the lagoon or vice versa. The zones differ slightly from those on the volcanic islands and standalone islands due to differences in topography.[9] An outline of the different zones is provided in Table 1.

Table 1: Common zones in the Mortlock Islands

Name of zones	Environment	Activity
Lematau	The deep ocean near the horizon	Deep water fishing/trawling
On mong	Behind the crashing waves	Underwater spearfishing
Likin ounou	The exposed reef system	Shellfish finding
Fan ounou	Where the waves crash	Pole and net fishing
On alang	Shellfish area	Shellfish and sea crab gathering
Fan Net	Beach at the ocean side	Gathering plants for medicines and picnicking
Ilik	Inland breadfruit trees	Breadfruit farms
Lenunu	Where tall coconuts grow	Build gardens
Lepwel	Taro farms	Taro farming
Imor	The edges of taro farms	Coconut planting and gardening
Leal	The lagoon side road system	Inter-village road system
Roro	The foreshore	Small-scale gardening
Leppei	The beach	Leisure activities
Lemoshiset	Swimming zone for children	Spearfishing
Lein imwmwimw	The sea grass zone	Line fishing
Wenen	The exposed lagoon side	Path for canoe transportation
Lepweshepwesh	Swimming zone for adults	Spearfishing
Mesenpal	The sloping part of the lagoon	Underwater spearfishing
Lelol	The first deep part of the lagoon floor	Bottom line fishing and turtle hunting
Lekung	Invisible depth of the lagoon	Deep bottom line fishing
Lenomw	The centre of the lagoon	Big fish trapping

Note: These zones are used as part of cultural maintenance. They can also be used to monitor climate change impact on the total environment in the low-lying islands.

---

9   This was taught to me on the atoll where I grew up. I learned from my uncles about the zones, their relationship within the ecosystems and the importance of knowing the zones. For fishing zones in the low-lying islands in Pohnpei, see Lieber, *More Than a Living*, pp. 51–59. For Yap, see Alkire, *Lamotrek Atoll*, pp. 19–22. For Yap Island, see Samuel T. Price, 'The Transformation of Yap: Causes and Consequences of Socio-Economic Change in Micronesia', PhD thesis, Washington State University, Ann Arbor, Michigan, 1975, pp. 54, 57–60. For a general outline of the Pacific Islands, see D'Arcy, *The People of the Sea*, pp. 21–23.

The purpose of these zones is for cultural maintenance, conservation and communication. The zones are vital for everyday communication between the residents of each island because they pinpoint space, events and time; that is, zones specify where people are during the day in terms of work and leisure activities. For example, a person may be working at the *lepwel* (taro farms) or fishing in the *lenomw* (lagoon centre) and remain there until the sun reaches the height of *lenunu* (tall coconut trees). Communication with the ancestral gods is an important part of island life as it provides vital information to resolve problems or predict likely future events. As Victor Puas, former mayor of Lekinioch Municipality alluded, 'environmental zones are like our traditional library as they provide useful information about nature and our relationship with it'.[10]

Moreover, the zones are crucial environmental references to those who have specialised skills, for example, for *sou safei* (traditional doctors), *sou set* (fishermen) or *sou fal waa* (canoe builders) to locate the resources that their professions require. For example, *sou safei* only need to locate specific zones to collect the ingredients for medical remedies, or to train students as to what particular fauna or flora grow in each zone to treat specific ailments. Island priests also rely on the zones to determine which ancestral gods to pray to or direct their *waitawa*[11] to when the need arises.

Islanders have developed deep knowledge of the zones and an understanding of the interdependency between the species in the food chain hierarchy. Changes in any of the zones may be a warning sign of a threat to certain species, which would affect the food chain system or the entire environment the islanders depend on. It would therefore require the islanders to react quickly and implement remedies to curtail such a threat. The zones provide information regarding the habitual behaviour of species, allowing the indigenous population to locate them easily.[12] Likewise, knowledge of the 30 stages of the moon, such as *sikauru* or *wereian anu* (visible to ghosts), *eling* (visible to human) and *meseling*

---

10 Victor Puas, pers. comm., 2 July 2013, Palikir, Pohnpei. See Segal, *Kosrae*, pp. 212–215, 218–220; Andrew L. Debuce, *Cultural Change in Horticultural Practices on the High Island of Kosrae - Micronesia*, University of Oregon, 1996, pp. 58–59.

11 This is according to the *oral history* of Lekinioch Island. *Waitawa* means channelling to communicate with the ancestors. See Peter, 'Chuukese Travellers', p. 264.

12 My personal experience. For zones in the volcanic islands such as Yap, see Falanruw, 'Food Production and Ecosystem Management in Yap', pp. 5–22. For zones in low-lying atolls, see Duane, *Clan and Copra*, pp. 28–33. For specific fauna and flora, see Marshall, 'The Structure of Solidarity', pp. 16–19.

(all can see),[13] are also crucial to the ecosystem as they influence the behaviour of species. For example, during a full moon in the Mortlocks, land crabs migrate en masse to the beach to lay their eggs. The islanders only need to go to the beach and wait for them at midnight when the high tide is in to collect the crabs for food.

Certain schools of fish such as *momishik* (island sardines) and *kish* (squirrel fish) are caught only at certain times during *lefang* and *lerak*. Moreover, *souset* have developed a sophisticated regime in calculating when and how to harvest the fish. Religious rituals in the form of *ngorongor* (chants) are also part of fishing activities to lure other types of fish like *angerap* (bonitos or skip jack) close to the beach for *lalo* (encircled traps made from coconut fronds) or *maaii* (fish weirs). *Ngorongor* are chanted before, during and after the fishing activities to pay respect to the ancestral gods. Each clan has a specific system of *ngorongor*, which is passed down through the generations for the purposes of continuing the clan's history and safeguarding its reputation.[14]

The impact of climate change on these zones has been affecting the livelihood of islanders over the years, with the effects becoming more pronounced over the past few decades. For example, saltwater incursion on land due to ocean surges is changing the dynamic of both the fauna and flora ecosystems. Islanders are devising ways to adapt to this threat by studying the new life dynamics in the zones. Only time will tell as to whether they will find new solutions to maintain the health of the environment, hopefully by collaborating with climate change experts from the international community.

Climate Change Background

Climate change is a complex phenomenon with numerous different causes and associated impacts varying from country to country and region to region.[15] It is a worldwide phenomenon affecting all of humankind. It is no

---

13   Kamilo Likichimus (master canoe builder and oral historian from Lukunor Island), Interview, Weno, Chuuk, 20 June 2013. See also Uman, Saladier and Chipen, *Uruon Chuuk*, pp. 359–361.

14   Being a member of an *ainang* is permanent and demands your total loyalty. Emotional attachment to one's *ainang* is strong as it is tied to one's personal identity and history.

15   Christopher B. Field, Vicente Barros, Abdrabo Mohamed A. K. et al., *IPCC: Intergovernmental Panel on Climate Change. WGII AR5 Phase I Report Launch. Climate Change 2014: Impacts, Adaptation, and Vulnerability Summary for Policymakers*, 31 March 2014, pp. 4–9; Climate Institute, *Sea Level Rise: Risk and Resilience in Coastal Cities*, www.climate.org/topics/sea-level.

longer defensible to blame natural processes as the main cause of climate change. Increasingly, scientists from across the world have identified anthropogenic activities as a significant accelerator of climate change.[16] A rise in sea levels is one of the consequences of climate change and has already affected islands and coastal regions around the globe.[17]

Since data collection on climates began in 1880, the temperature of the earth's surface has increased, especially from the 1970s onwards. For example, satellite images indicate that the ice sheets in Greenland and Antarctica are melting faster than predicted, with an especially noticeable acceleration from April 2002 to February 2009.[18] Such acceleration has been largely caused by the increasing amount of greenhouse gases collectively produced by industrialised economies.[19]

It is a slow process, but the steadily increasing volume of water in the ocean caused by ice melting is causing sea levels to rise. This has significant consequences for the low-lying islands of the Mortlocks, which are only 3–4 metres above sea level. Climate change is also affecting the dynamics of the Pacific Ocean in terms of the El Niño[20] and La Niña[21] weather patterns and marine life due to the increased level of acidification.[22] It is hoped that the advanced economies will reduce their greenhouse gas emissions sufficiently to keep the temperature rise below 2°C so as to slow the impact of climate change on low-lying islands in the Pacific and elsewhere.

A study conducted in the FSM, the Marshall Islands and Palau over a 50-year period (1951–2010) provided convincing evidence that weather and environmental changes have occurred throughout most of the Micronesian region. For example, these islands have experienced

---

16 Field et al., *IPCC*, pp. 4–9.
17 Field et al., *IPCC*, pp. 4–9.
18 Fletcher and Richmond, *Climate Management and Adaptive Strategies*, p. 6.
19 Gillian Cambers and Paul Diamond, *Sandwatch: Adapting to Climate Change and Educating for Sustainable Development* (revised and expanded edition), United Nations, Educational, Scientific and Cultural Organization, France, 2011, p. 15.
20 D'Arcy, *The People of the Sea*, pp. 16–18.
21 D'Arcy, *The People of the Sea*, p. 17; Francis X. Hezel, 'High Water in the Low Atolls', *Micronesian Counselor*, No. 76, 2009, p. 2, www.micsem.org.
22 Radio Australia (Melbourne), 'Fish Losing Survival Instinct Due to Climate Change: Study Research on PNG Reefs Says Fish Behavior Becoming Riskier', *Pacific Islands Report*, 15 April 2014.

a significant to moderate rise in temperatures and a decrease in rainfall over the 50-year period.[23] The study is one of many confirming that the temperature of the earth's surface is rising, which is causing droughts and sea levels to rise.

The increase in the earth's temperature is impacting the atolls, as seen in the unusual sea surges witnessed by Micronesians in 2007 and 2008.[24] Sea surges have occurred before with varying degrees of intensity, for example, in the 1970s[25] to 1990s, but these were nowhere near as devastating as the events in 2007 and 2008. The 2007 and 2008 surges affected 50–75 per cent of the land used for food production.[26]

The first National Communication to the United Nations Framework Convention on Climate Change (UNFCCC) in 1999 noted the increase in:

> the frequency, duration and intensity of El Niño droughts, and the need to enhance capacity to address El Niño and La Niña events. Accelerated sea level rise was identified as a concern over the longer-term…[other] concerns were noted as being [the] coral reef ecosystems, coastal zones, waste management … agriculture and water supply.[27]

23   Maria Ngemaes, Johannes Berdon et al., 'NOAA: Republic of Palau, The Federated States of Micronesia and Republic of the Marshall Islands', Paper presented in Noumea, 3–4 July 2013; Johannes Berdon (director of Chuuk Weather Station), Interview, Weno Island, 4 April 2015.
24   Hezel, 'High Water in the Low Atolls', pp. 2–3; Fletcher and Richmond, *Climate Management and Adaptive Strategies*, pp. 8–9; Gaynor Dumat-ol Daleno, 'High Seas Flood Tiny Lekinioch, Chuuk', *Pacific Daily News*, Guam, 3 May 2007; Kauten Kandy (local fisherman), Interview, Likie, Pohnpei, 28 June 2013; Paulis Chol (local fisherman), Interview, Sokehs, Pohnpei, June 2012. Kauten and Paulis were among the many from Lekinioch who witnessed firsthand the sea surge and its impact on 5 March 2007.
25   I personally witnessed the sea surge in 1971 (which was not caused by a typhoon). It destroyed almost half of the taro farms in my village, Rewow. Other surges occurred afterward, but on a small scale and only affected the shoreline. Unfortunately, there are no documents about these events.
26   Susumu and Kostka, *Federated States of Micronesia Food Security Assessment Report*, p. 22; Fletcher and Richmond, *Climate Management and Adaptive Strategies*, p. 9.
27   Mulalap, 'Islands in the Stream', pp. 382–383, 386.

Figure 14: *Puron sat* **(sea surge) on Lukunor Atoll in 2007.**
Source: Photograph taken by Kanrina Puas.

Figure 15: *Puron sat* **(sea surge) in Kosrae 2007.**
Source: Photograph courtesy of Abraham Simpson.

Territorial Integrity and Climate Change

Micronesia's territorial integrity and sovereignty are defined by its constitution and in compliance with international laws. Article 1, Section 1 of the FSM's Constitution states:

> The waters connecting the islands of the [Micronesian] archipelago are internal waters regardless of dimensions, and jurisdiction extends to a marine space of 200 miles measured outward from appropriate baselines, the seabed, subsoil, water column, insular or continental shelves, airspace over land and water, and any other territory or waters belonging to Micronesia by historic right, custom, or legal title.[28]

Yet, the FSM's islands and surrounding waters are being slowly affected by climate change. Both citizens and climate change experts have noted the effects of climate change in Micronesia.[29] The legal implications of submerged islands in regard to territorial sovereignty have still not been seriously considered.

Like colonisation, climate change can be considered a result of foreign state actors, particularly the industrialised nations of Japan, China, India, Brazil and the US. Their industries have high rates of fossil fuel consumption and are largely dependent on these resources. One of the consequences of this is the trapping of heat in the atmosphere, resulting in melting ice caps and ice sheets at the poles and, in turn, sea level rise.[30] The resulting damage has already affected many Micronesian communities, and they have started to adapt to this new phenomenon as best as they can. However, new studies need to be conducted to further Micronesians' understanding of climate change in order for them to meet the challenges of adaptation effectively.

---

28   *The Constitution of the Federated States of Micronesia*, Article 1, Section 1.
29   This is my personal observation following interactions with the local people on Kosrae in 2012. I also interviewed people from the various low-lying islands in the FSM. See also Henry, Jeffery and Pam, *Heritage and Climate Change in Micronesia*, pp. 7–9, 37–38; Hezel, 'High Water in the Low Atolls', pp. 1–3; Fletcher and Richmond, *Climate Management and Adaptive Strategies*, pp. 8–10.
30   R. Warrick and J. Oerlemans, 'Sea Level Rise', in *Climate Change: The IPCC Scientific Assessment*, edited by J. T. Houghton, G. J. Jenkins and J. J. Ephraums, Cambridge University Press, Cambridge, 1990, pp. 263–267.

The FSM Government has adopted a policy that articulates survivability as an uncompromising priority. In its official policy statement, the national government stated that its role is 'to mitigate climate change especially at the international level, and adaptation at the national and (local) levels to reduce FSM's vulnerability to climate change's adverse impacts'.[31] In this context, the FSM reaffirms its right to exist as a nation under international law, particularly in view of the debate on sovereignty as a result of possible reconfiguration of island territories if some islands become totally submerged in the future.[32]

For the FSM Government, mitigation means, among other things, the promotion of a 'post Kyoto carbon dioxide emission reduction that will maintain temperature rise as advocated by the "Tuvalu Deal"'[33] at the Copenhagen climate summit. For adaptation purposes, the national government has required all development activities to take into account new recommendations for project design[34] in compliance with its Strategic Development Plan, use ecosystem-based approaches to encourage and strengthen the application of (local) knowledge and conservation practices, and implement strategies as soon as possible to improve food production.[35]

The Impact of Climate Change in the Mortlocks

The Mortlockese have already anticipated changing their agricultural practices and fishing techniques to adapt to the effects of climate change.[36] The islands are very small in land size and completely flat. One can stand

---

31   *Nationwide Climate Change Policy 2009*, p. 1.
32   *Nationwide Climate Change Policy 2009*, pp. 1–2.
33   The Tuvalu Deal refers to maintaining a less than 1.5°C rise in world temperature to ensure the survivability of the low-lying islands in the Pacific (*Nationwide Climate Change Policy 2009*, pp. 1–2; Masao Nakayama, 'Statement before the Committee of Religious NGOs and the United Nations. The Last Push Before Copenhagen: Defining Positions Strategies and Goals on Climate Change', New York, 10 November 2009).
34   Fletcher and Richmond, *Climate Management and Adaptive Strategies*, p. 17; Henry, Jeffery and Pam, *Heritage and Climate Change in Micronesia*, pp. 38–39.
35   Hezel, 'High Water in the Low Atolls', pp. 18–19, www.micsem.org/pubs/counselor/pdf/mc76.pdf; Susumu and Kostka, *Federated States of Micronesia Food Security Assessment Report*, pp. 5, 27.
36   Gibson Susumu and Mark Kostka, *Food Security Vulnerability Assessment Report*, Palikir, Pohnpei, 2012, p. v.

on the beach and survey the islands from one end to the opposite end.[37] There are no forests, only dense bushes and a few gigantic breadfruit trees and coconut trees. *Nu* (coconuts), *fash* (pandanus tectorius), *rakish* (sea oak tree) and a variety of waterfront bushes usually surround the beach areas and the shorelines, especially on the ocean side. Further inland, islanders' houses are built with their usual surrounding household gardens. Swampy taro patches, breadfruit trees, coconut trees and thick bushes are located in the interior of the islands.[38]

The Mortlocks do not have massive agricultural lands suitable for large-scale rice cultivation or cattle rearing (both of which produce methane), thus their greenhouse gas emissions are negligible. Deforestation is not applicable in the Mortlockese context given the lack of forests. Moreover, the FSM as a whole does not have large-scale factories or heavy coal-burning industries, and cars are largely confined to district capitals. What the islanders are aware of is that the emissions from the aforementioned activities are caused by the lifestyle and activities of the 'West' and the emerging economic powers from the developing world, and that this affects their traditional economic and ecological systems via accelerating the process of climate change.[39] The combined impact of the economic practices of the outside world on the earth's climate is forcing the Mortlockese to find effective adaptation strategies to grow traditional crops in the face of intensified droughts and sea level rise.[40]

Climate change is one of the biggest threats currently facing the FSM. It poses severe risks to health, agriculture, water and food security, and political relations. It is destroying coastlines, corals, coastal fisheries, taro patches and breadfruit trees. If there is no significant reduction in greenhouse gases in the next 15 years, 'climate models predict that low lying islands in the Pacific may become uninhabitable within the next 50 years'[41] or towards the turn of the century. This includes the Mortlocks and the low-lying islands in Yap and Pohnpei.

---

37   Gonzaga Puas, 'How Could the Agricultural Sector Become More Conducive towards Climate Change Mitigation and Adaptation?', Paper presented to CliMates International Student Organisation, Paris, France, April 2012, p. 5.
38   Puas, 'How Could the Agricultural Sector', p. 5.
39   Mulalap, 'Islands in the Stream', pp. 382–383, 386.
40   Local adaptation strategies are being utilised, including assistance from the national government (*Nationwide Climate Change Policy 2009*, pp. 1–3).
41   Barry Pittock, cited in Henry, Jeffery and Pam, *Heritage and Climate Change in Micronesia*, p. 7.

Seawalls

In the late 1960s, seawalls were considered to be the best approach to fight shoreline erosion in the Mortlocks.[42] However, many local elders were against their erection. They opposed the construction because seawalls required the clearing of native trees and bushes on the shorelines, which naturally prevent coastal erosion.[43] Many seawalls fell apart within a few months due to changing near-shore currents, as predicted by the local elders. In response, government officials claimed that the seawalls were not installed properly. A new engineering approach was recommended and the seawalls again erected. After the completion of the so-called 'well engineered seawalls', local people started to complain again about resulting changes in the seascape around the shorelines. For example, the usual habitats of certain schools of fish were interrupted, causing their migration to different parts of the islands. This caused tension between clans as certain fish belong to particular clans by tradition, and the seawalls forced fish into different shoreline zones owned by other clans.[44] This is a sensitive cultural issue, with the tension between clans caused by both the effects of climate change and attempts to mitigate these effects. This needs to be resolved to bring the communities back together.

The result of this erosion has been the shifting of some beach sand to different parts of the shorelines. It has also confirmed the elders' suspicion about the seawalls. It was not until the late 1970s when Typhoon Pamela hit the Mortlock Islands that the folly of the seawalls was extensively revealed to the public.[45] The typhoon completely destroyed the seawalls, and saltwater soon found its way into the taro patches, devastating people's livelihoods.

---

42   Seawalls were built based on a model erected at the channel by the Japanese. Unfortunately, they were not successful in preventing shoreline erosion.

43   This is according to Ring Puas and Alfonis Buluay, who were present at the debate on seawall erection in 1972–1973 during a *sotang* (village meeting) in Relong village. See also Marshall, *Namoluk beyond the Reef*, p. 68.

44   I watched village elders debate the issue during the early 1970s. It became apparent in later years that the seawalls were politically motivated, and so many called seawalls the 'political wall'. Today, seawalls are still required due to clearing of vegetation near the coast, but they must be carefully designed according to the topographical features of the coastline.

45   Typhoon Pamela destroyed many seawalls in the Mortlocks (Marshall, *Namoluk beyond the Reef*, p. 68).

Figure 16: Old-style seawall constructed in the 1970s on the island of Lukunor.

Note: This seawall, like many others in the Mortlocks, fell apart shortly after its construction due to various environmental factors that were not accounted for due to the elders' lack of involvement in the project.

Source: Photograph courtesy of Inos Walter (2012).

Many local people suspected that the erection of the seawalls was politically motivated.[46] It was alleged that the seawall project was part of several municipality capital improvement projects used to disguise corruption. The process of allocating funds was controlled by powerful political figures, with funds channelled to relatives at the local level. The construction of seawalls was not properly planned and lacked input from professional engineers.[47] The overall result was that the funds earmarked for these walls were used for political reasons, rather than to properly safeguard the shorelines.[48]

---

46   I observed this public reaction and discussed it with Haglelgam during my fieldwork interviews. Haglelgam, Interview.

47   Saltwater was mixed with cement, gravel and sand. When the concrete dried, it took only a few days to crack and fall into the water. A similar experience occurred in the Solomon Islands according to Terry Brown, 'Small Island States and Global Warming', *Anglican Communion News Service*, Niagra, Canada, 5 June 2014.

48   Haglelgam, Interview; Congress of the FSM, *Public Law No. 3-12*, First Regular Session, 1983.

Today, the debate over seawall construction is still dividing island communities.[49] In my interview with Marion Henry, a traditional leader from the island of Oneop and national secretary of the FSM Department of Resources and Development, he stated that:

> seawalls contradicted traditional wisdom because they interrupt the natural flow of ocean currents around the islands which deposit sand on different shores and thereby increase beach erosion rather than preventing it.[50]

He argued that native bushes and trees should have been left alone.

More people are becoming receptive to such traditional wisdom. However, others dispute this view and believe seawalls are still necessary, but that their design must be compatible with the topographical configuration of the islands.[51] In Kosrae, for example, a new design of seawall has been implemented with some success. The seawall was built on a beach, with solid concrete blocks lined in a pattern that hugs the natural configuration of the local foreshore area. In my discussion with some of the locals, they said the seawall has prevented beach erosion and withstood big tides and strong storms.[52] To this end, it should be up to each island to adopt specific designs that suit their local areas, with the support of the national government.

Seawall technology is a modern form of defence that could assist the islanders in their fight against the effects of climate change. However, collaborative approaches using local and outside experts are required for the purpose of implementing the appropriate solutions to suit local requirements.[53]

---

49 Elders and officers of Lukunor Municipality, Interview, Pohnpei, 26 January 2014. This is an ongoing debate.
50 Marion Henry (secretary of Resources and Development), Interview, Kolonia, Pohnpei, 18 July 2013 (he is also a local *samol* from the Island of Oneop); Haglelgam, Interview; Congress of the FSM, *Public Law No. 3-12*, First Regular Session, 1983; Marshall, *Namoluk beyond the Reef,* p. 68.
51 Personal observation of seawall in Kosrae, 22 June 2013.
52 Personal observation of seawall in Kosrae, 22 June 2013.
53 *Nationwide Climate Change Policy 2009*, p. 2.

Figure 17: New seawall design in Kosrae to prevent beach erosion.
Source: Photograph taken by author on 23 June 2012.

Traditional Foods

The main food staples in the Mortlocks and the low-lying islands in Yap and Pohnpei are taro, breadfruit, coconut, banana and resources obtained from the sea. Farming activities involve land clearing and planting of traditional crops such as taro, breadfruit, coconuts, papayas and pandanus for consumption. Taro is available year round, while breadfruit is in abundance during the summer months, usually from May to September. Preservation of food such as *mar* (preserved breadfruit) is still observed but is practised using new methods.[54]

Resources from the sea are also in abundance and harvested year round. Meat sources are coconut and land crabs, pigs, dogs and chicken. Imported food products such as rice, flour, canned goods, sugar and salt are also

---

54 *Mar* (preserved breadfruit) are now stored in big iron cooking pots called *kama* above the ground and kept in the outdoor cooking house. It is now more accessible and can be eaten anytime of the year rather than waiting for the lean months when it has to be dug up from the ground. See D'Arcy, *The People of the Sea*, p. 155.

consumed alongside a traditional diet. Mortlockese employed in the port towns also send foreign food products to their families.[55] Traditional food crops are constantly under threat from the impacts of climate change. The low-lying islanders are improvising their traditional practices to limit the intrusion of saltwater onto agricultural land along with new methods of preserving food.

Vulnerability to Climate Change

While advanced economies abroad accelerate the process of climate change, the Mortlockese are constantly studying ways to adapt to the changes in their environment. The national government has required:

> all development activities … to take into account projected climatic changes … in compliance with its strategic development plan … use ecosystem based approaches, encourage and strengthen the application of [local] knowledge on conservation practices, and implement strategies to improve food production.[56]

The Nationwide Climate Change Policy has yet to be translated into specific defence strategies.

National legislation[57] was adopted in February 2013 to further reinforce the policy. Its purpose is to provide a Nationwide Integrated Disaster and Climate Change Policy, with relevant departments such as the Department of Resources and Development, Office of Environment and Emergency Management, and Department of Transportation obligated to implement the policy. It requires that:

> every year … the President of the Federated States of Micronesia shall submit a report to Congress on the progress of the implementation of the Climate Change Policy, and recommend additional legislation where applicable and necessary.[58]

---

55 It is an established custom that relatives send assistance to those in trouble during natural disasters. See Marshall, *Namoluk beyond the Reef*, pp. 26–27; Spennemann, *Melimel*, p. 6; Lessa, 'The Social Effects of Typhoon Ophelia (1960) on Ulithi', p. 369.
56 *Nationwide Climate Change Policy*, 2009, p. 2.
57 Congress of the FSM, *Public Law No. 18-34*, Second Regular Session 2013, Palikir, Pohnpei.
58 Congress of the FSM, *Public Law No. 18-34*, Second Regular Session 2013, Palikir, Pohnpei.

This illustrates the seriousness of the FSM Government's resolve to tackle climate change by creating a legal framework for the nation to actively measure its adaptation strategies. As the policy states:

> in order for the FSM to successfully achieve its objectives the policy requires ... [the] support of all levels of governments in the FSM, the civil societies, the private sector, [local] communities and traditional leaders.[59]

The FSM is also seeking assistance and support regionally and internationally to ensure that its adaptation goals are systematically implemented to increase the likelihood of achieving positive outcomes. Geologists Charles Fletcher and Bruce Richmond suggested that adaptation within the FSM may be facilitated by a two-step approach of 'forming international partnerships to aid adaptation efforts, and continuing the development of internal policies focused on building resilient and sustainable communities'.[60] International partnerships will adhere to local needs based on discussions from both sides but within a domestic policy framework, which will lead to appropriate decisions being made, for example, planting more pandanus, sea oaks and mangroves around island shores as has been done in other Pacific Islands. Advanced technology seawalls should also be part of the adaptation strategies adopted, where appropriate. Although there are new concepts for creating floating and artificial islands and barrier reefs, many are too costly for the government to fund. Perhaps they will become a reality if the potential resources from the nation's EEZ are able to be exploited.

Observations of Ecosystem Alterations due to Sea Level Rise

Mortlockese fish behaviourists have deep knowledge of the sea environment. Since the 1990s, they have noticed changes in the behaviour of certain kinds of fish.[61] They no longer reside in specific habitat zones due to changes in the weather patterns that have affected water temperatures. Fish with a low tolerance of temperature variation

---

59   *Nationwide Climate Change Policy 2009*, p. 4.
60   Fletcher and Richmond, *Climate Management and Adaptive Strategies*, pp. 11–12; *The Nationwide Climate Change Policy 2009*, p. 2.
61   Interviews with many fishermen from the Mortlock Islands during my fieldwork.

such as *angarap* (bonitos), *momoshik* (island mackerels) and *sarikai me til* (anchovies) are now hard to locate. Their migratory habits have become difficult to predict, and islanders have difficulty catching them in schools using *lalo* (coconut fronds to trap the fish) or *maii* (fish weirs).[62]

During one of my visits to the Mortlocks in the summer of 2001, the fishermen informed me that the low tide no longer exposed the reefs where fish used to congregate in abundance. I used to join the fishermen of my village on the reefs, where I learned about fish behaviour. I can no longer predict their movements based on my past knowledge. The indigenous people are readjusting to the new circumstances in the sea environment.[63] For example, they are developing new observation strategies to understand the behaviours now exhibited by the local fish populations. I hope to learn this new adaptive knowledge from my villagers soon. For example, *sarikai* have moved to different depths and zones along the shorelines. *Momoshik* (owned by my father's clan) now appear in different months, making it harder to pinpoint when to catch them in weirs.[64]

In recent years, islands in the Micronesian region have suffered serious damage due to wave surges, saltwater inundation and drought. Traditional methods are being utilised to minimise their impact, particularly saltwater incursion into taro farmland. An example of this is new canals being dug, following the land's topography, to provide an environmentally conscious way to drain the saltwater out of affected taro plots.[65] Constructing barriers to resist the flow of saltwater into gardens is another example. Just as in the past, Micronesians continue to adapt and seek new methods to prolong their survivability and continuity.

There have been a handful of studies conducted in the Mortlocks on the effects of sea level rise. Most of these studies noted the real vulnerability of beach erosion due to high tides as being an ongoing issue.[66] The intrusion of saltwater into taro patches is also becoming a major problem. For example, in 2007, the Mortlocks was inundated by saltwater caused

---

62   Interviews with many fishermen from the Mortlock Islands during my fieldwork.
63   Interviews with many fishermen from the Mortlock Islands during my fieldwork.
64   My personal experience. Elders from *Sofa* and *Soumosh ainang* complained about *momoshik* appearing in different places.
65   When an ocean surge hit Lukunor in 2007–2008, the youth groups dug canals to drain saltwater from the taro patches.
66   Inos Walter (mayor of Lukunor), Interview, February 2011 (he assessed the damage of the sea surge during his time as mayor); Kandy, Interview (he witnessed the event); Chol, Interview (he witnessed the event).

by king tides,[67] which infiltrated the taro farmland and drinking wells. Other crops such as bananas, papayas, pumpkins and sweet potatoes were destroyed.

On Lekinioch Island, more than half of the island's taro farms were decimated by saltwater incursion in 2007.[68] It took approximately two years for taro crops to regrow. Youth groups from the island were organised into groups to dig canals to release the saltwater from the taro patches and other affected areas. People survived because of the extended family system, which is relied on during natural disasters as it was in the past. Other relatives from throughout Micronesia and the new diaspora in the US also remit assistance to their families. The quick action by the youth groups prevented further destruction of the taro farms. The islanders continue to observe wave patterns and signs of nature that will alert them to oncoming meteorological events. New adaptive strategies are being monitored, and the islanders must adopt new methodologies for farming to protect their taro farms and other agricultural land against further saltwater intrusion.[69]

Some suggested farming alternatives include hydroponics and vertical farming. Others have recommended the erection of hollow, soil holders built well above the ground.[70] They can be filled with soil and perhaps enhanced with the use of fertilisers, allowing food crops to be grown and harvested year round.[71] New plant species such as saltwater-resistant taro[72] have been experimented with to supplement the anticipated reduction in food supply. New varieties of crops that can be rotated throughout the year and harvested in a shorter period are also being explored.

67   Interviews with other witnesses, December 2011; Keim, *Sea Level Rise Disaster in Micronesia*.
68   This was told to me during interviews with many people from Lukunor, including the mayor of Lukunor (who assessed the damage of the sea surge) and Kauten and Paulis who witnessed the event (see fn. 207). See also Mark, *Sea Level Rise Disaster in Micronesia*.
69   Hezel, 'High Water in the Low Atolls', p. 18.
70   Hezel, 'High Water in the Low Atolls', p. 18.
71   Gibson Susumu, Interview, Palikir, Pohnpei, 13 July 2013.
72   The State of Kosrae, and other islands in Chuuk and Yap, are experimenting with saltwater-resistant taros (Gibson Susumu, Interview, Palikir, Pohnpei, 13 July 2013).

Recent Research on Climate Change

Research undertaken on climate change in the Mortlocks confirm what the islanders have already witnessed or experienced. For example, a study conducted by Australian academic Rosita Henry and her team on Moch Island found that many Mortlockese are aware of climate change. When the islanders were questioned about their views on the causes of the rise in sea level, one local person claimed, 'to my own understanding and word by mouth from some people, the iceberg at the North and South Pole start melting and cause this sea level rise'.[73]

Others linked the concept of global warming to global issues and human activities such as pollution, airplane emissions and greenhouse gases. These responses are not confined to Moch Island but are widespread throughout the Mortlocks. Their awareness of climate change has been heightened by the recent installation of internet networks, by radio announcements, by networks of students in the diaspora and by engagement with officials at the national level.[74] Indeed, Micronesians are placing responsibility for global warming on the larger economic structures of bigger nations.[75]

Another study conducted by Fletcher and Richmond noted that in 2007 and 2008:

> [FSM] communities were flooded by large high tides … that eroded beaches, damaged roads, intruded in aquifers and … and inundated communities. Seawater flowed into coastal wetlands and surged up through the water table killing taro, breadfruit, and other food crops. Fresh water [wells] turned brackish and [have not fully recovered]. Crop sites in use for generations were physically and chemically damaged or destroyed on approximately sixty percent of inhabited atoll islets. Again, food and drinking water were in short supply. A nationwide state of emergency was announced on December 30, 2008, and food security was declared the top priority in the nation.[76]

---

73 Henry, Jeffery and Pam, *Heritage and Climate Change in Micronesia*, p. 21.
74 This is based on my personal observations and interviews with Micronesians at home and abroad.
75 Henry, Jeffery and Pam, *Heritage and Climate Change in Micronesia*, p. 21.
76 Fletcher and Richmond, *Climate Management and Adaptive Strategies*, p. 9.

A study of the same event by Mark Keim[77] on Lukunor and Oneop islands corroborated Fletcher and Richmond's views. However, Keim (a medical doctor) went further, cautioning authorities to be mindful of the health issues that can arise from climate change due to water and food shortages.

The FSM Government has appointed a team of field observers to collect information to assist in the implementation, monitoring and reporting of observable impacts from storm surges, beach erosion and saltwater inundation in taro patches.[78] The observers are also charged with educating locals in relation to the newly adopted national government policy. Fundamental to the observers' task is to detail local knowledge of adaptation strategies to be integrated into the Western methods of research studies. For example, during my interview with one of the project coordinators, Gibson Susumu, he commented on how the local people resorted to traditional food items that were typically only eaten during drought.[79] These strategies need to be recorded as they form the foundation of any first response strategy to be implemented while waiting for further assistance to arrive.

Food Production Strategies

The *Food Security Vulnerability Assessment Report* authored by two FSM agricultural specialists, Gibson Susumu and Mark Kostka, indicated that agricultural production is declining due to poor soil conditions caused by exposure to saltwater. They stated that 'the biggest threat to food security is the impact of climate change. Over forty-five atolls in the FSM continue to be affected by the sea level rise'.[80] Taro patches are the major problem as local inhabitants are either abandoning them because they have become unproductive or waiting for rain to dilute the saltwater before re-farming the land (which takes considerable time to return to full production).[81]

The government has set up a national food security committee, the FSM Food Security Steering Committee, whose role is to enhance coordination and cooperation of food security for the nation and oversee the effective

---

77   Keim, *Sea Level Rise Disaster in Micronesia*.
78   Susumu, Interview.
79   Susumu, Interview. Drought foods include parts of the coconut and banana trees, shrubs and small land and sea creatures.
80   Susumu and Kostka, *Food Security Vulnerability Assessment Report*, p. v.
81   Susumu and Kostka, *Food Security Vulnerability Assessment Report*, p. v.

implementation of future initiatives.[82] Again, in my interview with Susumu, he noted that during a trip in 2012 to the low-lying atolls in Chuuk, many people were close to starvation due to the failure of food crops affected by saltwater. He estimated that close to 70 per cent of all the islands he visited in Chuuk alone were affected by food insecurity, and safeguarding effective and consistent food production stood out as the main challenge for the islanders. Many of the low-lying islands in Yap and Pohnpei were experiencing the same difficulty.[83]

The FSM Government has been working hard on its adaptation policies for food security and environmental management, with the following strategies suggested to sustain food production:

- switch to different cultivars
- improve and conserve soils
- increase water supply by using groundwater and by building reservoirs and rain catchment areas
- improving watershed management to assist in desalination
- improve or develop water management
- alter system operating rules (e.g. pricing policies and legislation)
- improve coastal zones and marine ecosystems
- protect the environment, including via building seawalls and beach nourishment
- research/monitor the coastal ecosystem.[84]

According to Susumu and Mark, new 'concept projects' have been put to the national government to consider.[85] If the government accepts the proposals, they will be shared with both the state and local governments. The concept projects include the following recommendations:

82   Australian Aid, *Food Security: Securing Food Resources in the Federated States of Micronesia* (Pacific Adaptation Strategy Assistance Program (PASAP)), Commonwealth of Australia, 2013, terranova. org.au/repository/paccsap-collection/securing-food-resources-in-the-federated-states-of-micronesia.
83   Susumu and Kostka, *Food Security Vulnerability Assessment Report*, pp. iii–v.
84   Susumu and Kostka, *Food Security Vulnerability Assessment Report*, pp. iii–v.
85   Susumu and Kostka, *Food Security Vulnerability Assessment Report*, pp. iii–v. New concepts of farming (e.g. the saltwater-resistant taro project in Kosrae) were also mentioned by Gibson during my interview with him in Palikir, Pohnpei, 13 July 2013.

- Household food security to create awareness in the community about the importance of food security and the need for people to eat more indigenous food. This will involve the restrengthening of food production systems through the supply of root crops, with vegetables, breadfruit, coconut and fruit trees to be integrated into the agroforestry system.
- Integrated atoll farming system and capacity building. This will involve the planting of traditional food crops, home gardening, establishment of plant nurseries, hydroponics and hands-on technical training.
- Integrated coconut development. This project targets the rehabilitation and replanting of coconut trees.
- Fisheries and aqua culture to carefully assess locations suitable for the production of fish, seaweed, sea cucumber and other sea food resources.
- On the atolls, traditional practices such as restricting fishing activities on the coral reefs for a number of months or even years have been explored. This practice will allow further observation of the reef ecosystem and allow repopulation of fish stocks.
- Building of fishing weirs to farm fish in the lagoon.
- Renewed use of breadfruit ground pits (a hole dug in the ground to store preserved breadfruit for future consumption). Many islanders now use above-ground storage units in the form of large cooking pots to preserve breadfruit and other crops, and these are vulnerable to disasters such as floods and typhoons.
- Reducing family size to lessen food demands as climate change threatens to curtail food production.
- Use of traditional fishing canoes as these are less harmful to the marine environment compared to motorboats that use fuel and pollute the water.[86]

I noted other food production strategies during fieldwork in the islands that can be included in the above list:

- Utilising *peiel* (coconut fibre)[87] to absorb water and constructing stone walls and pre-dug canals to use the land topography to deviate water flow. This has been done on my island, Lekinioch.[88]

---

86   Susumu and Kostka, *Food Security Vulnerability Assessment Report*, pp. iii–v; Gibson, Interview.
87   *Peiel* is the fibre enclosing the copra. The fibre is separated from the copra by using a big, sharp stick called *anget*. Piles of the fibre are used to encircle crops to slow the flow of water to the crops.
88   Personal recommendation based on my experience growing up learning the traditional methods of environmental conservation.

- Small family farms for growing coconut trees and land crabs. This will involve locating appropriate inland areas where both species can survive and thrive.[89]
- Barter. This will encourage local people to concentrate on planting traditional crops and reduce the importation of junk food, which is causing all kinds of health problems for the local population.[90]
- Develop marine farms for octopi and clams, as well as the reintroduction of traditional weirs that can be used for both the growing and catching of specific fish species.[91]

The rapidly growing body of evidence documenting the adverse impact of global warming on small island states has prompted the FSM Government to undertake an active role in the international arena to call on industrialised nations to cut greenhouse gas emissions.[92] The FSM has signed international agreements related to climate change including the UNFCCC, Kyoto Protocol, Vienna Convention and Mexico City Pact. It has also signed and ratified other major conventions concerning environmental issues.[93]

The FSM is also part of a subregional agreement called the Green Micronesia Initiative. This subregional agreement, which is spearheaded by the chief executives of the various regional governments in Micronesia, seeks to increase energy efficiency by 20 per cent, increase energy conservation by 20 per cent and expand renewable energy to 30 per cent of power generation[94] by 2020.[95] However, Mr Soram, the national government's spokesperson for climate change, has stated that the FSM is not committed to the COP15 (Copenhagen). It has signed the COP16 (Cancun) agreement but is still in the process of studying the agreement before implementation. As for the COP17 (Durban), the FSM is still

---

89   Personal recommendation based on my experience growing up learning the traditional methods of environmental conservation.
90   Personal recommendation based on my experience growing up learning the traditional methods of environmental conservation.
91   Personal recommendation based on my experience growing up learning the traditional methods of environmental conservation.
92   *Nationwide Climate Change Policy 2009*, pp. 2–3.
93   Jackson Soram (head of Climate Change Advisory Body to the FSM Government), Interview, 21 January 2011.
94   Office of Statistics, Budget and Economic Management, Overseas Development Assistance and Compact Management, *Millennium Development Goals and Status Report 2010*, p. 74; Benadette H. Carreon, 'Pacific Leaders Launch Green Initiative', *Marianas Variety*, 11 August 2010.
95   Office of Statistics, Budget and Economic Management, Overseas Development Assistance and Compact Management, *Millennium Development Goals and Status Report 2010*, p. 74.

considering some of the issues before committing itself fully.[96] However, the FSM's participation in international climate change forums cannot solve all its local issues.

Initiating Environmental Strategies

The FSM's environmental strategy began in 1999 during the nation's second economic summit. It called for the establishment of 'a network of effective, community managed, ecologically sustainable agricultural practices, in order … to safeguard the nations' precious natural heritage'.[97] This strategy was refined further in different action plans over the first decade of the twenty-first century. These plans include the National Biodiversity Strategic Action Plan (2002), Blueprint for Conserving the Biodiversity of the FSM (2003), state-specific Biodiversity Action Plan (2004), FSM Strategic Development Plan (2004–2023) and National Environment Sector Plan (2009).[98] The biodiversity reports identified that the biological resources of both the nation and the states are faced with existential biological and anthropogenic threats.[99] The development plan looks at strategies to optimise economic output in light of future threats and the scaling down of Compact funding.[100] The report on the national environment identifies strategies that can be implemented to protect the nation's environment, on which much of the country's economic output relies.[101] The national government is seeking funds to implement the recommendations of these reports. It remains to be seen how long it will take for implementation to occur.

In 1994, the FSM prepared a baseline assessment of its greenhouse emissions. It noted total emissions as expressed in CO_2 equivalents were 246.01 gigagrams per year.[102] Almost all of the emissions (98 per cent) came from the energy sector, with only a small contribution from the

---

96   Jackson Soram (deputy assistant secretary, Foreign Affairs, International Division), Interview, Nett, Pohnpei, 10 October 2012.

97   Office of Statistics, Budget and Economic Management, Overseas Development Assistance and Compact Management, *Millennium Development Goals and Status Report 2010*, p. 72.

98   Office of Statistics, Budget and Economic Management, Overseas Development Assistance and Compact Management, *Millennium Development Goals and Status Report 2010*, p. 72.

99   *The Blueprint for Conserving the Biodiversity of the Federated States of Micronesia*, 2003, pp. iii–iv.

100   *The Blueprint for Conserving the Biodiversity of the Federated States of Micronesia*, p. 8.

101   *The Blueprint for Conserving the Biodiversity of the Federated States of Micronesia*, pp. 3–5.

102   Office of Statistics, Budget and Economic Management, Overseas Development Assistance and Compact Management, *Millennium Development Goals and Status Report 2010*, p. 74.

agricultural sector. It is important to note that these emission volumes are minute on the global scale. However, as a member of the international community, the FSM is committed to reducing its domestic emissions.

Similarly, industrialised countries need to commit themselves to reducing their own emissions if humanity is going to survive the impacts of climate change. The FSM is a supporter of the 'Tuvalu Deal',[103] which advocates the reduction of emissions to keep global temperature rise below 1.5°C to curtail sea level rise.[104] Other considerations involve getting the major international 'emitters' to adhere to their suggestion to set aside funds for vulnerable countries in the Pacific and Indian oceans for immediate adaptation projects to safeguard their future.

Saving the Environment

Ensuring a sustainable environment rests on the nation's development goals, which are ultimately geared towards improving adaptation techniques. Development, to the Mortlockese people, may be measured in terms of the application of local knowledge coupled with skill-based imported technology able to be used to enhance islanders' adaptation strategies.[105] For example, the main food supplies for islanders are from the sea and the breadfruits and taros they harvest from their land. Islanders have designed new methods to preserve breadfruits by putting them above ground in large pots instead of preserving them in underground pits to prevent saturation from seawater floods.

Modern technologies such as refrigerators, freezers and ice plants are also used to prolong the storage of fish and other perishable local foodstuffs. Solar panels have been introduced, especially on the low-lying islands, to enable the use of refrigeration technology and connection with the

---

103 The Tuvalu Deal emerged during the Copenhagen Climate Change Conference, where it was put to the member states attending that Tuvalu will be unable to maintain itself if global temperature rises by more than 2°C. See also Masao Nakayama, 'Statement before the Committee of Religious NGOs and the United Nations'.
104 *Nationwide Climate Change Policy 2009*, p. 1.
105 *Nationwide Climate Change Policy 2009*, p. 2.

international community through the use of computers, radios and televisions.[106] The communication links provided by this technology have enhanced the islanders' understanding of climate change issues.[107]

The adaptation policy published by the national government has not yet sufficiently filtered down to the local level to have a comprehensive local impact. Part of the problem is the lack of trainers to educate the local population on policy issues. The Mortlockese are doing the best they can to protect their land while waiting for further research findings and welcoming the knowledge of climate change scientists and international aid. Local communities have implemented programs based on local knowledge, such as the planting of native plants with big roots such as *shia* (mangroves), *fash* (pandanus) and *rakish* (sea oaks) that have the ability to prevent soil and beach erosion. Adaptation remains a matter of life and death to the Mortlockese and has higher priority than large-scale economic development.[108]

Development and Climate Change

A 2006 report titled 'Federated States of Micronesia: National Assessment Report' discussed sustainable development strategies. Written by FSM economist and financial expert Fabian Nimea, it indicated that there is not a single comprehensive National Sustainable Development Strategy (NSDS) for the nation. However, there are disparate pieces of information and plans that could and need to be put together to formulate an overall NSDS plan. Any such NSDS should be accompanied by supporting mechanisms for the purpose of implementation and reinforcement.[109] This will include policy development and a legal framework. As Nimea noted, 'sustainable development planning [will] … better manage the process [of] development, implementation and improvement'.[110] However, missing from this report is a specific economic model that the

---

106 Larry Bruton, 'Successful Renewable Energy Projects in the FSM', Paper presented at the 26th Pacific Islands Environment Conference, 22–25 June 2009, Saipan, CNMI.

107 Stephen J. Winter, 'Water for an Island', The FH Foundation, Long Beach, California, 1995.

108 According to a local source in the atolls, the most important thing in their lives is maintaining local production to sustain their livelihood as they have been doing for many centuries. However, imported goods are shared to supplement local diet. See also Gonzaga Puas and Anelita Puas, 'How Can Development be Linked to Climate Change Adaptation Policies?', CliMates- International Student Organisation, Paris, France, December 2012, pp. 4–5.

109 Nimea, *Federated States of Micronesia: National Assessment Report*, p. iii.

110 Nimea, *Federated States of Micronesia: National Assessment Report*.

Mortlockese can utilise to sustain their livelihood instead of perpetuating outsiders' perceptions of development, which are often unsuitable for an island lifestyle.

Ten key objectives, ranging from establishing a comprehensive system of environmental law and good governance to strengthening the knowledge base of the local people, were key factors in formulating sustainable development strategies 'that will be evolutionary, adaptable, and sustainable for all generations', according to Nimea.[111] Despite all the suggested frameworks identified in the report, the proposed NSDS fell short of 'linking and integrating them with socio-economic priorities' for the FSM.[112]

In 2009, the FSM Government produced its own Nationwide Climate Change Policy that incorporated the objectives of Nimea's report. This policy document identified some major issues that the national government needed to inform its people about, such as the importance of combating the impacts of climate change within the framework of sustainable development. This policy document was compiled using mainly international adaptation instruments and needs input from local inhabitants to ensure the complementary policy of 'act locally, think globally' is enacted. Thus, the overall statement of the policy should be for the FSM Government to participate globally in the mitigation of climate change while promoting adaptation at the domestic level to ensure the survivability of its people into the future.[113]

At the international level, the FSM Government is actively involved in lobbying the world's largest economies to be mindful of their practices that are destroying the livelihoods of Micronesians. The FSM is also part of the Small Island Developing States organisation and regional organisations such as the Pacific Forum whose purposes include promoting their collective interests, including the addressing of climate change. At the domestic level, local knowledge should be the main driver while new partnerships are sought with the international scientific community. Partnership means ensuring the preservation of natural heritage and natural resources in all the islands.[114] It also means requiring all development activities to take into account 'projected climate change

111 Nimea, *Federated States of Micronesia: National Assessment Report*, pp. iii–iv.
112 Nimea, *Federated States of Micronesia: National Assessment Report*, pp. ii–iv.
113 Nimea, *Federated States of Micronesia: National Assessment Report*, pp. 35–36.
114 Nimea, *Federated States of Micronesia: National Assessment Report*, pp. 35–36.

design and implementation of [the] strategic development plan, such as the use of eco-based approaches, and the implementation of strategies to sustain food production'.[115]

Self-Reliance

Food security presents one of the main challenges to the FSM Government. The *Food Security Vulnerability Assessment Report* (authored by agriculturalists Susumu and Kostka in 2012) gave a snapshot of what the FSM may look like in the future. The authors characterised the FSM's economy as aid dependent, wherein the FSM relies primarily on money provided by the US under the Compact and from other donor countries like Japan, China and Australia. The authors found that the Compact's funding accounts for about 65 per cent of national government revenue and 75 per cent of state government revenue. The FSM economy remains in negative growth today.[116] A shift to local thinking is required to ensure self-sufficiency remains an objective for the nation, especially in the coming years when the effects of climate change are predicted to become more severe.

Additionally, construction methods for public buildings and private dwellings need to incorporate changes in the local environment, such as variations in temperature and topography caused by climate change.[117] The best possible design for these buildings is one that uses local knowledge and materials, in addition to weather-resistant imported materials and engineering models from the global community. For example, *shoon fash* (pandanus leaves), *shoon nu* (coconut leaves), *sopon mei* (breadfruit trunks), *sopon nu* (coconut trunks), *shia* (mangrove), *mosor* and *shokis*[118] are best suited to the island environment. They can withstand the tropical weather longer than materials imported from China or Japan, for example. Moreover, local products are cheaper than the inflated prices charged for

---

115 Office of Statistics, Budget and Economic Management, Overseas Development Assistance and Compact Management, *Millennium Development Goals and Status Report 2010*, p. 3.
116 Susumu and Kostka, *Food Security Vulnerability Assessment Report*, p. 3.
117 Islanders also need to observe temperatures caused by climate change to give them ideas about their fishing activities (Walter, Interview).
118 *Shokis* is a very strong tree that is grown in saltwater on the shoreline. Its branches, which can last for many years, are used in traditional house construction, especially for pillars, and for fish traps.

imported materials. Local knowledge should be incorporated into high school or post-secondary trade qualifications to encourage sustainable building practices.

Sustaining the Seas and Agriculture

The fishing industry has been targeted as part of the FSM's self-sufficiency blueprint for survival in the future. The FSM's EEZ is about 2.9 million square kilometres and considered one of the most productive tuna fishing areas in the world. It is estimated that the FSM is capable of sustaining a yield of well over 100,000 tons annually; however, it lacks the capabilities to exploit this potential.[119] Its fishing zone benefits outside countries like Japan, Korea and Taiwan who pay a fishing license fee to the FSM Government that is less than 10 per cent of the sale value of the fish caught. Aquaculture has the potential to be a productive industry, and the government is exploring this option. Aquaculture and marine farming trials have commenced in Pohnpei but require skilled workers to maintain them. The National Fishing Corporation is also involved in a joint venture to maximise the EEZ's potential. Already, there has been an increase in the National Fisheries Corporation's profit.[120]

Local agricultural production for domestic consumption is another priority for food security and self-reliance. However, the budget set aside to encourage local people to engage in agricultural programs has been disappointing. For example, Susumu and Kostka noted that in '2004 to 2005 only 1.8 per cent of the national budget (the budget was US$63 million in total)[121] was set aside for agriculture'.[122] Many argued that the locals' lack of interest in engaging in agricultural activities stemmed from the following. First, the younger generation considers agriculture to be a 'dirty' business, and so it is not a priority for them. They prefer to engage in white-collar employment where the pay is higher than other local options. Second, agriculture is not widely promoted in the educational curriculum. Third, the younger generation does not see

119 Peter Sitan, pers. comm., Micronesian Australian Friends Association Research Symposium, The Australian National University, 29 April 2014. Peter Sitan is the president and chief executive officer of the National (FSM) Fishing Corporation. The shortcomings in the FSM's capacity to maximise its fishing potential is also discussed by D'Arcy, 'The Lawless Ocean?', pp. 3–5.
120 Sitan, 'The Development of the Tuna Fisheries'.
121 Susumu and Kostka, *Food Security Vulnerability Assessment Report*, p. 5.
122 Susumu and Kostka, *Food Security Vulnerability Assessment Report*, p. 3.

the need to enlarge the scope of agricultural activities as they consider it to be for local consumption only, rather than for commercial sale to attain large profits.[123]

With the onslaught of climate change, the attitudes of many in the younger generation is that, if the soil cannot be saved from erosion and the impact of sea level rise, what is the point of agriculture if it is a doomed enterprise? Why concentrate on agriculture if many people will likely be leaving their homes in the future due to climate change? There is an urgent need for education about options for climate change mitigation and adaptation for young Micronesians so they do not abandon hope.[124]

Policy Formulation

The mobilisation of government field officers to collect data to provide an overall picture of the impacts of climate change on the nation is ongoing. Evidence suggests that there is a heightened awareness shared by islanders in relation to soil erosion and sea level rise, most notably regarding the intrusion of saltwater onto farmland.[125] Some islanders have expressed anxiety in relation to the gloomy predictions about their possible relocation, which seems to become more certain as the years go by. There are already people moving to join their relatives on the volcanic islands. However, others, determined to 'keep up the battle' to ensure that future generations will have homelands where the ancestral ways are preserved, have accepted the risks of climate change.[126]

To complement its climate change adaptation policy, the FSM Government produced yet another document in 2010, the 'Millennium Development Goals and Status Report'. This report was in response to the UN's eight Millennium Development Goals, alternatively known as the 'Millennium Declaration', which was supposed to be finalised

---

123 Susumu, Interview.
124 Marcus Samo (deputy secretary of the FSM Department of Health and Social Affairs and Chuukese Historian), Interview, Palikir, Pohnpei, 21 June 2013.
125 Susumu, Wichep and Silbanuz, *Preliminary Damage Assessment*, pp. 14–16. For further assessment and discussion, see Fletcher and Richmond, *Climate Management and Adaptive Strategies*; Henry, Jeffery and Pam, *Heritage and Climate Change in Micronesia*, pp. 5–15; Hezel, 'High Water in the Low Atolls'.
126 Interviews with Mortlockese people during field research in Pohnpei, 5–12 January 2011.

in 2015.[127] In 2003, the FSM completed a 20-year Strategic Development Plan that reflected the input of over 400 participants, representing a broad range of perspectives including government, traditional leaders, industry and civil society.[128] The report identified priorities for the promotion of sustainable development objectives.

The objectives included good governance, coordinated nationwide sustainable economic development with inputs from grassroots organisations and state governments, encouragement of a private sector–led economy, development of technical know-how by merging traditional and outside knowledge, investment in relevant infrastructure to combat the adverse effects of climate change, and implementation of long-term environmental protection and sustainability. The report declared that the link between the Millennium Development Goals and the Strategic Development Plan could be achieved by a coordinated approach between the national and state departments, offices and agencies, the private sector, NGOs and civil society organisations.[129]

While the report identified the areas of development priorities for the nation, it remains to be seen how this will translate into concrete action. Take, for example, goal number seven. Its objective is to 'ensure environmental sustainability to integrate the principles of sustainable development into … policies and programs; reverse loss of environmental resources by 2015'.[130] To achieve this objective by 2015 was unrealistic as the FSM Government did not have the capacity to implement it. Perhaps it should be left to each country to set its own implementation deadlines. Alternatively, the FSM should not be obliged to implement a UN goal that is outside its capacity. There are inherent flaws in the FSM Government's policies as it is paying too much attention to dictates from the outside. The report is therefore a symbolic statement that does not reflect the realities of Micronesian modes of production, their environment and their social system.[131] These are the backbone of their identity and continuity.

---

127 Office of Statistics, Budget and Economic Management, Overseas Development Assistance and Compact Management, *Millennium Development Goals and Status Report 2010*, pp. 8–9.
128 Office of Statistics, Budget and Economic Management, Overseas Development Assistance and Compact Management, *Millennium Development Goals and Status Report 2010*, p. 7.
129 Office of Statistics, Budget and Economic Management, Overseas Development Assistance and Compact Management, *Millennium Development Goals and Status Report 2010*, p. 2.
130 Office of Statistics, Budget and Economic Management, Overseas Development Assistance and Compact Management, *Millennium Development Goals and Status Report 2010*, p. 72.
131 See Rich Harris and Clare Provost, 'The Millennium Development Goals: Big Ideas, Broken Promises?', *The Guardian*, 24 September 2013.

Resiliency and Local Communities

The FSM must continuously explore its economic potential in terms of its own resources to deliver important services to its people.[132] The national government advocates for the introduction of all development activities that take into account projected climate change design and implementation of its Strategic Development Plan, such as the use of eco-based approaches and strategies to improve local food production, as being fundamental to the nation's adaptation policy.[133] Adaptation is therefore about the maintenance and preservation of Micronesian cultures through locally based education and combined efforts with outside agencies as a model of preserving the history of Micronesia, which continues to be threatened by the impact of climate change.

Capacity building and training involves developing a coordinated system of educational and instructional programs in order for the FSM to be able to respond to the impact of climate change issues as they arise. The first priority is to implement local knowledge as a first line of defence.[134] In order to deliver effective programs, the national government has teamed up with its state counterparts in designing and developing strategies to ensure that people at the grassroots level are aware of new information about climate change. Human resources for the purpose of collection and analysis of data for enhancing adaptation policies are already in place but require more personnel. Of course, many foreign governments and institutions are present in the FSM, but they are there to assist in the implementation of policy practices and community-based climate change projects initiated locally, rather than being the main drivers of the initiatives.[135]

Adaptation and Island Development

The Mortlockese people have adapted to their local environment and utilised local knowledge to provide for their needs for centuries.[136] When one speaks about development in the Mortlock Islands, the islanders

---

132 Nimea, *Federated States of Micronesia: National Assessment Report*, pp. 1–10.
133 *Nationwide Climate Change Policy 2009*, p. 2; Susumu, Wichep and Silbanuz, *Preliminary Damage Assessment*, pp. 15–16.
134 *Nationwide Climate Change Policy 2009*, pp. 1–3.
135 *Nationwide Climate Change Policy 2009*, pp. 1–3.
136 *Mortlocks Oral History*; Petersen, *Traditional Micronesian Societies*, pp. 3–5.

often react by asking, 'development for who?' Such a reaction reflects the long history of colonialism in the FSM and Mortlockese suspicion of outsiders' influence in their attempts to reshape the region according to foreign plans or models. The Mortlockese are always aware of their economic circumstances due to the limited modern technology they have. Further, the Mortlockese consider that developing their islands should be done according to how locals envisage their island, and at their own pace.

The interconnection between extended families, which has been in place for many centuries, acts as a safety net for islanders' ongoing survival. It maintains the fabric of the islands' social wealth, which feeds into the larger economic system.[137] Today, this infrastructure continues to be at the heart of the islanders' continuity. The extended family model has increased its connection globally by virtue of the new diaspora under the Compact. Islanders continue to adapt to an increasingly globalised world to ensure the survival of future Mortlocks generations.[138]

Micronesians understand the benefits that derive from retaining their connections within the diaspora. They also understand the benefits that can derived from engaging experts from a variety of international channels in designing a unique, locally based economy for the proper conservation of their environment in anticipation of climate change challenges. The education curriculum should also play its part in teaching the younger generation about local knowledge so that they can appreciate their environment and transmit both traditional skills and relevant modern skills from the outside world to the next generation.

Adaptation is a priority not just for the Mortlockese but throughout the FSM and the Pacific Islands. Individual scientists and groups are partnering with community-based groups in the FSM to collaborate on the best options to fight the impacts of climate change. The Nationwide Climate Change Policy's overall objective is to harness all traditional practices from all low-lying and volcanic islands to form the basis of a Micronesian 'first line of defence' against the encroaching sea level rise. Field officers are monitoring environmental changes and educating islanders from low-lying atolls. In Pohnpei, for example, the island of Pakin has recently planted pandanus trees on its shorelines, borrowing

---

137 *Mortlocks Oral History*; Petersen, *Traditional Micronesian Societies*, pp. 3–5.
138 For discussion on Micronesian global movement, see Marshall, *Namoluk beyond the Reef*, pp. 113–130.

the idea from Mokil and Pingelap islands. Likewise, many islands are circulating new ideas regarding the idea of creating a first line of defence by utilising new engineering projects like the seawall in Kosrae and above-ground farming in Yap. Islanders will continue to adapt as they always have done.

Conclusion

Climate change issues are the responsibility of the three branches of government in the FSM. However, each level of government works within its own jurisdiction, as defined by the nation's constitution. The president, Department of Foreign Affairs, Department of Resources and Development, and Office of the Environment and Emergency Management are working together with their state counterparts and historical preservation offices.

Climate change adaptation ranks as one of the top priorities of the nation, and newly introduced laws have been enacted to support government policies that address this issue. National government officials have been conducting field studies and engaging in discussions with the populations of all the islands, where there is strong support for implementing climate change adaptation strategies.[139] The FSM's climate change policy is evolving to meet the challenges of its changing environment, although obstacles remain. These include a lack of human resources development, infrastructure building capacity and funding.[140] However, at least the people of the FSM understand that their government is trying as best as it can to link the issues of development with its climate change adaptation policy. In the Mortlocks region, economic development emphasised sustainability practices and discouraged reliance on foreign assistance (except in the use of new technologies) to fight the effects of climate change.

Sea level rise is not only affecting the islands' fragile arable land but is also disturbing fishing activities. Beach erosion and intense sea currents are interrupting the flow of nutrients to feeding grounds. Oral testimonies from fishing communities have indicated that many species of fish are migrating to different parts of the shorelines or lagoon. Schools of fish

---

139 Susumu, Interview.
140 Susumu, Interview.

such as *sarikai, umulo* and *iketor* that were once found in the shallow water have disappeared and it is not clear whether they will return to their original habitats, especially with the changes in the shoreline zones due to climate change.[141]

From the 1970s to the mid-2000s, the Lower Mortlocks were hit by unusual tides.[142] Locals have observed the increase of saltwater inundation in food crops as a result of king tides. Due to the volume of saltwater, it remains on the farms for many weeks. Luknunor Islanders have had to dig new canals to drain the saltwater. They have even caught fish in the taro swamps, and it was also claimed that they encountered new fish species never before seen by locals.

This is a grim reminder of what the islands will experience in the future without effective adaptation strategies developed in conjunction with the international community. Micronesians' first priority is to maintain self-sufficiency to ensure continuity. The land and the surrounding seas sustain Micronesians' livelihoods. They must be prepared to face this challenge as a priority in order to continue as a people with a distinct history in a unique place where past generations lie buried. The future is unpredictable and challenging, but Micronesians have overcome climate-related obstacles in the past. How Micronesians might best face this uncertain future is the topic of the next chapter.

---

141 This observation stems from my personal experience growing up on Lukunor, listening to local fishermen discuss issues about fishing.

142 Kandy, Interview; Chol, Interview. My interviews with many Mortlockese confirmed the unusual weather patterns in the Mortlocks.

8

Contemporary Challenges

Introduction

This chapter deals with the challenges currently facing the FSM. The main obstacles include the reduction in funding from the Compact of Free Association, climate change, promoting economic development to increase the sources of funding, education, health, the Constitution, foreign relations, customs and traditions, the EEZ and leadership issues. I will discuss these challenges within the context of how Micronesians have previously dealt with and are continuing to respond to these issues, including what sort of self-reliant practices and external assistance the FSM requires to overcome these challenges. Should there be a particular timeframe to address these challenges in light of the imminent end to Compact funds post 2023? Is the *ainang* system strong enough to withstand the increasing impact of the globalised world?

Compact of Association or Disassociation?

The FSM is going through an intense economic and political transition in preparation for the reduction of Compact funds post 2023. Since the implementation of the Compact in 1986, the US has provided over US$2 billion dollars to the FSM Government in return for granting the US power to deny access to the islands to third parties, ostensibly to preserve regional security but, in reality, a strategic denial to potential enemies of US national interests.[1] The scaling down of American financial assistance to the FSM may open up opportunities for other regional powers to extend their influence in the region. A trust fund was set up for the FSM under the Compact, supposedly to replace Compact funds after 2023. However, it is uncertain whether the proceeds from the trust fund will be enough to sustain the FSM.[2] There is speculation that China is likely to pay more attention to the FSM post 2023 due to its own interests in the region. As was noted in previous chapters, China has been assisting the FSM in many areas such as the building of infrastructure, educational scholarships, training for FSM citizens to learn the Chinese language and social system, concessional loans and small-scale grants for community development.[3] For the FSM, the key concern will be preserving and extending its autonomy in these circumstances. The Compact has been the major source of the FSM Government's income since 1986. It is often referred to as being a double-edged sword. On the one hand, it is seen as a saviour in that it prevents the FSM from bleeding to death from economic collapse; however, on the other hand, it is seen as handicapping the FSM's progress both internationally and domestically by creating dependency on Compact monies. Despite this, Micronesians are aware of the fact that reliance on someone else's money is not economically viable in the long term. The nation is embarking on a balancing act to ensure its future economic survival.[4]

The supporters of the amended Compact (2004) have welcomed US oversight of the distribution of funds, with the hope that this will stop the misspending of funds earmarked for essential sectors such as the private sector, education, health and public infrastructure.[5] JEMCO has conducted audits of the Compact funds and, on occasion, withheld certain

---

1   Since WWII, US interest in the FSM has always been of strategic military interest. The Compact was negotiated in relation to such an interest. See *Compact of Free Association between the Federated States of Micronesia and The United States of America*, pp. 93–101.

2   It is predicted that there will be a shortfall of the trust fund by 2023. This has put stress on the leaders of the nation, which prompted Chuuk to seek independence in order to handle its own financial affairs. See President Mori, *State of the Nation Address*, 18 May 2012, p. 8.

3   Weidong, Interview.

4   Debate on the Compact and whether it has been beneficial is an ongoing issue. Epel Illon (advisor to the president of the FSM), Interview, Palikir, Pohnpei, 13 January 2011; Lorin Robert (secretary of Foreign Affairs), Interview, 7 January 2011.

5   See Debate on the Compact on Micronesia Forum under the heading 'The Compat is a Done Deal – Our Leadership Should Start Thinking About Economic Development', www.micronesia forum.org/.

funds, pending their satisfaction that the necessary checks and balances have been put in place by the FSM Government. With this new auditing measure, both sides are studying their next move before the year 2023. It remains uncertain as to whether the Compact will be renegotiated/extended for a third time.

Optimists perceive the Compact as a means of maintaining the important connection between the US and FSM. They feel the FSM should not 'cut its nose off to spite its face' even though the US has been unwilling to compromise on many occasions. The Compact, they argue, is a safety net as it has provided the financial means to enable the building of the nation's political and economic capacity.[6] The US's presence in the FSM has brought stability to the nation and regional security. Moreover, it has allowed Micronesians to live, work and seek education in America—a good opportunity to release the population pressure through emigration, an additional benefit of which has been remittances.[7]

The FSM is weighing its options and ability to tap into alternative sources of funding to replace the Compact funds. Many observers have predicted that the FSM is heading towards economic hardship in the years ahead, with a reduced living standard compared to that currently enjoyed under the Compact. Many Micronesians I interviewed over a two-year period (2011–2013) expressed concerns as to what will happen after 2023. Some want to revert back to traditional subsistence using the sea and land from which they have been sustained historically. Others have expressed the desire to look for employment overseas or to join their families who have already established themselves in the US.[8] The challenge is whether the FSM will survive politically without economic assistance from the US.

Facing Climate Change

The leading threats that arise from climate change are coastal erosion, freshwater pollution, crop destruction due to salination and sea level rise. Micronesians' ability to sustain environmental resources for future generations depends on careful stewardship that reinvigorates traditional

---

6   Naich, *Sustaining the Spirit of the Compact Partnership*, pp. 5–6.
7   Naich, *Sustaining the Spirit of the Compact Partnership*, pp. 5–6.
8   Naich, *Sustaining the Spirit of the Compact Partnership*, pp. 5–6; Elizabeth Grieco, *The Federated States of Micronesia: The 'Push' to Migrate*, Migration Policy Institute, 1 July 2003, www.migration policy.org/article/federated-states-micronesia-push-migrate.

conservation practices and merges these with modern scientific principles. Most of the islands in the FSM are low lying. A further rise of 2 metres in the sea level would overwhelm the islands and require the relocation of the inhabitants. The Tuvalu Deal[9] is seen as a lifesaver for islanders if it is adopted by the major international polluters.

Climate change is an ongoing challenge for the FSM. As was detailed in the previous chapter, this new threat is already affecting the nation, especially those on the low-lying atolls. For example, strong storms, typhoons, sea surges and droughts have become more frequent and intense. From the 1960s to 1990s,[10] these events have been of concern but remained on the margins of political debate, the reason being that climate change was not well understood by a large number of Micronesians, especially at the local level. Information about climate change has largely only been accessible to the few government officials who attended overseas conferences in relation to the issue. Until recently, there were no major studies undertaken on climate change events in the FSM. The only relevant information provided to the public were the daily reports regarding weather forecasts.

The atolls in the FSM are far from the major port towns, and there has been no face-to-face education programs provided to the atoll communities to enable them to better understand the issues relating to climate change. For example, when I was teaching at the College of Micronesia in the late 1990s, the Mortlockese were complaining about serious foreshore erosion, especially on the ocean side of the lagoons. A team of assessors was dispatched to the Mortlocks but could not stay long enough to conduct in-depth studies, as the only means of transportation available, the inter-island ship, had to be shared by the many outer islands. This inevitably resulted in short and infrequent visits, as this transport was routinely subject to change.

Many Mortlockese have heard about climate change but do not understand the process fully, such as the causes of the extreme sea surges, although they may see the effects. What they know is that they are witnessing unusual changes in their environment. For example, weather patterns are not as predictable as they have been in the past. Summer months have come late

---

9   See fn. 33.
10   *Mortlocks Oral History* and personal experience. Transportation between Weno, the capital, and the outer islands was infrequent and, as such, studies were not properly conducted.

or too early. This has affected the pattern of their fishing activities and the cultivation of crops. They have also observed that breadfruit trees (one of the main staple crops) are producing fewer fruits. The Mortlocks region is not an isolated case as these experiences are shared with its neighbouring islands and other parts of Chuuk and the atolls in Pohnpei and Yap.

There have also been changes on the volcanic islands, though with less impact due to the elevation of the islands. The FSM Government is slowly developing policies to engage the public about how to respond to climate change. The policies are ad hoc owing to the lack of local expertise in the field, and the national government is still amassing resources to deal with the effects of climate change. From the mid-2000s onwards, major studies began to appear detailing the causes of the sea surges and the changes in the seasonal cycle impacting the outer islands in Pohnpei, Chuuk and Kosrae.[11] Today, many local and national organisations have been established for the purpose of educating the public about this threat and monitoring the progress of climate change in the FSM. Historical knowledge is also integrated into these educational programs, such as traditional food storage, building materials and methods of protecting shorelines from saltwater incursion.

Education and Health

Education and health are major challenges, particularly in terms of non-communicable diseases. The national government is mindful about its responsibilities and obligations to provide quality education and health services to its citizens. This follows the constitutional mandate of Article XIII, Section 1:

> the national government of the Federated States of Micronesia recognizes the right of the people to education, health care, and legal services and shall take every step reasonable and necessary to provide these services.[12]

---

11   Some reports are Fletcher and Richmond, *Climate Management and Adaptive Strategies*; Henry, Jeffery and Pam, *Heritage and Climate Change in Micronesia*; Susumu and Kostka, *Federated States of Micronesia Food Security*; Keim, *Sea Level Rise Disaster in Micronesia*.
12   *The Constitution of the Federated States of Micronesia*, Article XIII, Section 1.

According to the FSM Government, there have been improvements in these two areas. For example, total youth literacy was at 95 per cent according to a report in 2000.[13] However, the relevance of the type of education offered to young people remains to be seen. For example, is education targeting the development of individuals to be good citizens or the acquisition of skills and knowledge for the competitive job market both at home and overseas? The College of Micronesia has dealt with this issue and offered both academic degrees and vocational certificates.[14] Many students have attained qualifications and either moved to the US to find work (where the wages are more attractive) or continued their education. Many have followed their families to start their high school years in the US and continued on to American colleges.[15] Those who choose to remain in the FSM seek employment in the domestic market and continue to live a more traditional lifestyle. Therefore, the challenge is for educators to implement the best practices in education for the nation's future.

A report entitled *Health Progress Report: 2008–2011*, authored by Assistant Secretary of the FSM Department of Health and Social Affairs Marcus Samo, indicated a marked improvement in the department's capacity to collect and analyse data for the purposes of monitoring and responding to emerging health issues over the three-year period under review.[16] The report further acknowledged an increase in the availability of medical, pharmaceutical and biomedical assistance to the hospitals in the FSM.[17] An increase in funding was also noted as essential for the department's achievements. It should be noted that there is a need to improve the health of the population, especially in the areas of non-communicable diseases such as diabetes, hypertension and lung cancer, which require special equipment.[18] It must also be remembered that

---

13   SBOC, www.sboc.fm/ (site discontinued).
14   My personal knowledge as the program coordinator and curriculum designer at the College of Micronesia, Pohnpei Campus in 1998–2001. See also Henry H. Kellam, *Social Sector: Education, Part I: Education: Background Analysis: Understanding the Educational System in the FSM*, September 2001, pp. 10–12.
15   My personal knowledge as the program coordinator and curriculum designer at the College of Micronesia, Pohnpei Campus in 1998–2001. See also Kellam, *Social Sector: Education, Part I*, pp. 10–12.
16   Marcus Samo, *Health Progress Report: 2008–2011*, Palikir, Pohnpei, 1 January 2012; Gonzaga Puas, *Review of the Current Health Protection Practises in the FSM: Law, Regulation and Policy Regimes*, Palikir, Pohnpei, 30 July 2013.
17   Samo, *Health Progress Report*, pp. 32–33.
18   Samo, *Health Progress Report*, pp. 32–33.

a healthy nation depends heavily on the enhancement and enforcement of its laws, policies and regulatory regimes governing the delivery and maintenance of both its social and health protection programs. Health and education responsibilities are shared between the states and the national government. They are thriving on the philosophy that a healthy nation depends on the quality of social services and the education of the population. Traditional lifestyles and diets can significantly reduce these non-communicable diseases. New programs aimed at educating the population on the benefits of local foods are in progress.[19] However, ongoing success depends on local attitudes as Western foods are seen as a sign of prosperity and monetary wealth. This is a big challenge in the areas of education and health at the grassroots level.

Foreign Relations

Foreign relations is one of the key indicators of FSM's success as it will define the extent to which Micronesia interacts with the outside world and the benefits that flow from such interactions. For example, opportunities for capacity building provided by other governments, particularly in the areas of technology and economic development assistance, need to be maintained. However, Micronesia will only deepen its relations with countries empathetic to Micronesian causes such as the impact of climate change on the islands, respect for the FSM's EEZ and airspace, and a commitment to the principle of non-interference in the FSM's internal political affairs.

At this stage, there are still some outstanding legal issues that need to be resolved before the FSM can conduct itself effectively and independently on the international scene. The ongoing debate between US and FSM leaders over the issue of the security of the US in the Asia-Pacific region under the terms of the Compact will remain a challenge.[20] However, it needs to be noted that in recent years, the primacy of the FSM's Constitution over the Compact has not been fully articulated by FSM officials when the Compact is at issue. Further, the FSM Congress at times usurps the function of the executive branch in terms of foreign relations. For example, Congress was involved in the renegotiation of the Compact,

---

19   Island Community Food Community of Pohnpei, *Let's Go Local: Culture, Health, Environment, Economy and Food Security*, Koloia, Pohnpei, 2013, www.Islandfood.org/index.html.
20   Naich, *Sustaining the Spirit of the Compact Partnership*, pp. 1–6.

which was seen as a responsibility of the executive branch. The function of the executive branch is expressed in Article X, Section 2(a) and (b), which stipulate that the president is assigned 'to faithfully execute and implement the provisions of [the] Constitution and all national laws' and 'to conduct foreign affairs and the national defense in accordance with national law'.[21]

Conversely, it has been argued that the above sections contradict provisions of the Compact. For example, Article II, Section 123(a) of the Compact states:

> in recognition of the authority and responsibility of the Government of the United States under Title Three [Defense and Security Relations], the Government of ... the Federated States of Micronesia shall consult, in the conduct of their foreign affairs, with the Government of the United States.[22]

Section 123(a) is being used by the US to assert its right to veto decisions by the FSM Government in relation to the conduct of its foreign affairs if the decisions are not seen to be in the interests of the US. This is an area of significant debate and tension between the two governments.

The Constitution states that a:

> treaty is ratified by vote of 2/3 of the members of Congress, except that a treaty delegating major powers of government of the Federated States of Micronesia to another government shall also require majority approval by the legislatures of 2/3 of the states.[23]

The Compact is a treaty delegating major authority over the FSM's defence to another country, the US, which has been permitted under the Constitution. It is within this legal context that the US asserts the primacy of the Compact over the Constitution and, in particular, the US's right to veto decisions by the FSM Government in relation to third parties that are perceived to threaten US security. However, one can argue that the US cannot blindly rely on the Compact to pursue its objectives at the expense of Micronesian sovereignty and national interests. This is because the Constitution can limit the power of the Compact if the Compact exceeds

---

21 *The Constitution of the Federated States of Micronesia.*
22 Refer to the original *Compact of Free Association between The Federated States of Micronesia and the United States of America*, uscompact.org/files/index.php?dir=FSM%20Publications%2FCompact%20 Documents.
23 *The Constitution of the Federated States of Micronesia*, Article XI, Section 4.

the power bestowed upon it by the Constitution. Should there be a need to terminate the Compact, Article XIV, Section 1 maybe invoked.[24] The FSM Foreign Affairs Department will have to monitor its duties under the Constitution and escalate issues when any violation arises to ensure Micronesians stand firm on the issue of sovereignty. Micronesia's image in the international community will be judged on how it conducts itself based on self-respect and respect of others.

The EEZ

The FSM's EEZ remains the biggest single hope for the nation's future, particularly at the end of Compact funding in 2023. The EEZ covers an area of 2,978,000 square kilometres.[25] It has significant wealth in marine biota and likely mineral resources under and on its seabed. In 2007, Peter Wilson, a fisheries expert whose consultancy work includes work for the governments of Papua New Guinea and the former TTPI, conducted a study of the tuna industry worldwide. He estimated that approximately 60 per cent of the total tuna harvest in the world comes from the western Pacific nation states of Palau, Kiribati, the Marshall Islands, Tuvalu, Papua New Guinea and the Solomon Islands.[26] The FSM contributes 28 per cent of this harvest. Wilson noted that the main beneficiaries of the fishery harvests were Japan, the Philippines, Taiwan, the US and South Korea, while the European Union market is a growing beneficiary.

The tuna fishing industry, according to Wilson, continues to grow on a yearly basis. Russia and the Arab League are also expressing interest in the Pacific Islands commercially, particularly to access the tuna industry, and diplomatically, by fostering new relations with Pacific nations.[27] Like many Pacific Islands countries, the FSM faces problems of illegal fishing in its EEZ by foreign fishing vessels. To combat this problem, the FSM has joined with the Marshall Islands and Palau to pool their resources to more effectively patrol their waters. The Australian Government has provided patrol ships and been involved in the ongoing training of maritime surveillance activities with these three nations.[28]

24   *The Constitution of the Federated States of Micronesia*, Article XI, Section 4.
25   D'Arcy, 'The Lawless Ocean?', p. 3; *Commercial Fisheries in the Federated States of Micronesia*, www.fsmgov.org/nfc/.
26   Wilson, 'A Tuna Industry in Micronesia?'.
27   *Pacific Islands Report*, East-West Center, Hawai'i, 24 June 2010, p. 1.
28   Marar, Interview.

According to the president and chief executive of the National Fisheries Corporation, Peter Sitan, the fishing industry is the main FSM resource capable of replacing some of the financial shortcomings in the Compact.[29] Tuna fishery licensing fees are being adopted, but those fees need to be increased substantially to turn sufficient profit for the nation. It is argued that there should be a correlation between the license fees and market value of the fish caught in the FSM's EEZ.

Micronesian fishing analyst Paul D'Arcy agrees with Sitan and suggests that another way of developing the indigenous fishing industry is value-added processing in the country.[30] However, the FSM requires partners to assist with technical knowledge and capital to develop a viable fish processing industry. This could be achieved by entering into joint ventures with outside fishing nations so that the FSM can maximise its earnings from fishing resources.

Notwithstanding the possible future directions, illegal fishing remains an ever-present financial drain on the FSM's limited resources both in terms of policing and lost marine resources. Surveillance needs to be strengthened in order to deny foreigners the opportunity to steal from Micronesian waters.[31] In addition, there needs to be more effective enforcement when vessels are caught in the EEZ, including confiscation of the vessel and its haul. As D'Arcy noted:

> Offshore fishing fleets from larger and wealthier Pacific Rim nations regularly violated Pacific Island EEZs in the absence of local monitoring. The same lack of resources to monitor offshore waters also meant that Island nations could not develop effective fishing fleets and were forced into fishing access agreements that returned a mere fraction of the value of the catch at market.[32]

Foreign fishing companies haul in hundreds of billions of dollars' worth of fish caught in the Pacific Islands' EEZs; yet only a fraction of their profits are received by the island states. Again, D'Arcy conservatively estimated that in 1998 Pacific Island nations received approximately US$60 million

---

29 The fishing industry in the FSM has the potential to replace most of the funding under the Compact. See Sitan, 'The Development of the Tuna Industries', pp. 17–19.
30 D'Arcy, 'The Lawless Ocean?', pp. 3–4.
31 D'Arcy, 'The Lawless Ocean?', pp. 3–4.
32 D'Arcy, 'The Lawless Ocean?', pp. 3–4.

in fishing access fees from fleets that declared an annual catch sale price of approximately US$1.3–1.9 billion.[33] This shortfall between actual and potential income for the host country is staggering.

The United Nations Convention on the Law of the Sea (UNCLOS III, 1982) established the legal regimes that protect the rights of coastal nations, like Micronesia, from unscrupulous illegal harvesters.[34] The regimes cover the exploitation of economic resources within the designated EEZ, which covers 200 nautical miles (370.4 kilometres) from the shores of the islands that form the outer limit of the archipelagos. The economic resources include fishing and extraction of mineral resources both on and beneath the ocean floor, bearing in mind the sustainability of the resources.[35] Notwithstanding these international legal principles, illegal fishing by foreign fleets continues. Palau is in the process of exploring for oil in its EEZ, and if it is successful, the FSM may do the same. Perhaps mineral extraction activities will be easier to monitor compared to fishing activities because the activity will occur within designated zones. It will be easier to observe the amount and manner of extraction to ensure adherence to restrictive environmental laws.[36] With these challenges and potential benefits looming, the FSM needs to seek new international partnerships for the purposes of expanding its capacity to build its future economic and social programs.

Leadership Issues

Unified leadership is fundamental to the integrity and future development of the FSM. Leadership comes in many forms in the FSM. Traditional leaders are confined to specific geographies of the nation, but their roles in the national political process need to be revisited. Political leadership spans all three levels of government: national, state and municipal. There is often a conflict between leaders of these jurisdictions over decisions made by the national government. One area of great conflict is the power relationship between the leaders of the legislative branch versus the executive branch of the national government.[37] The basis of this

---

33   D'Arcy, 'The Lawless Ocean?', pp. 3–4.
34   D'Arcy, 'The Lawless Ocean?', pp. 3–4.
35   D'Arcy, 'The Lawless Ocean?', pp. 3–4.
36   D'Arcy, 'The Lawless Ocean?', p. 1.
37   Francis X. Hezel, 'Chuuk Independence: Why and How?', *Pacific Institute of Public Policy*, 2 March 2015, pacificpolicy.org/2015/03/chuuk-independence-why-and-how/.

conflict is constitutional in nature. For example, the president is selected by the members of Congress, rather than by voters. This has caused much public discord whereupon many citizens have claimed that the president is basically the puppet of Congress since it is Congress that installs the president. The president is elected by the 13 members of the Congress instead of by the people under Article X, Section 1 of the Constitution:

> the executive power of the national government is vested in the President of the Federated States of Micronesia. He is elected by the Congress for a term of four years by a majority vote of all the members. He may not serve for more than two consecutive terms.[38]

The lack of participation by women in the highest decision-making process in the nation is another issue of concern in the leadership of the national government.[39] Many observers advocate that women should be a part of the decision-making process as they can offer different perspectives than men. Moreover, Micronesian communities are largely based on 'matrilineality', and so it is only natural that women should be involved at the highest levels of government. This is true in Micronesia and other Pacific nations. To address this concern, a Congressional Bill, C.B. No. 16-10, January 2010, was introduced to bridge the gap between the genders. The Bill states:

> to propose an amendment to the Constitution of the Federated States of Micronesia, for the purpose of increasing the representation of women in Congress by increasing the number of at-large seats in Congress, and reserving said seats for women, and for other purposes.[40]

This Bill was defeated for many reasons, ranging from sexism to outside intervention.[41] The response of those opposed to the Bill was that the Constitution already provides for women to run for Congress, thus making the Bill unnecessary. Federal politics is dominated by males, a post-colonial construct that does not take into account the role of women in traditional communities and elsewhere in other government

---

38 *The Constitution of the Federated States of Micronesia.*
39 Fifteenth Congress of the Federated States of Micronesia: *5th Special Session 2008.*
40 Sixteenth Congress of the Federated States of Micronesia, *First Regular Session 2009, C.B. No. 16-10.*
41 Peter Sitan (chairman), *Judiciary and Government Operation, Standing Committee Report No. 16-10,* January 2010.

branches and departments. Many have claimed that old fashioned male chauvinism still reigns, just under a different guise. Others claim that Congress is not the venue for gender balance to be addressed.[42]

However, anecdotal evidence suggests that increasing numbers of women are in key government positions, such as ambassadors, heads of departments and agencies. Women's associations in some states and an office in the national government have been created to monitor women's rights for the purpose of improving their participation in the political process. It is in the best interests of the nation that women should be involved in the decision-making process as their contribution to their communities is significant and deeply rooted in Micronesian traditions.

There is an emerging view that the FSM has been suffering from a lack of leaders representing the new generation. The old leaders continue to rotate through government seats. They are not in tune with the latest best government practices that would assist in taking the nation into the future. Retiring older leaders may provide opportunities and openings for the next generation, including women, to take up future challenges.

Constitutional Issues

The Constitution is under pressure to accommodate changes that have been evolving since independence and threaten the FSM's integrity and continuity. Micronesians must continue to cooperatively harness their strength to deflect such pressures from rupturing the nation's unity. Micronesian unity is framed and promoted by Article XIII, Section 3 of the Constitution, which states:

> it is the solemn obligation of the national and state governments to uphold the provisions of this Constitution and to advance the principles of unity upon which this Constitution is founded.[43]

It is only proper that the maintenance of this constitutional philosophy should be taken seriously, otherwise Micronesians will once again be subject to outside dominance, as they were in their colonial past.

---

42   Bill Jaynes, 'Special Seats For Women', *Kaselehlie Press*, 25 September 2012.
43   *The Constitution of the Federated States of Micronesia.*

The Constitution is the legitimate source of power and a reference for the citizens when confronted with complex issues from both within and outside the nation. It is expected that differences in opinion between the state and national governments will continue for some time, maintaining the old political wounds over jurisdictional issues. Various secession movements since independence continue to threaten the Federation, especially over the allocation of national funds. The secessionist movement in Chuuk State is the latest threat that may rupture the Federation. It is driven by leaders from the trust territory days and centres on their belief in allocating the budget between states on the basis of population, noting that Chuuk is by far the most populous state in the FSM.[44] These older leaders also blame the lack of Chuukese funds on other states for draining the nation's purse through chronic mismanagement. One consequence of this is that the new generation is increasingly disillusioned by this political rhetoric, used by many leaders stir up public opinion and maximise their votes.[45]

The Chuuk State Legislature recently introduced Bill No. 11-12-08, which later became law, creating the Future Status Commission:

> to review and recommend possible political status suitable for long term financial survival of Chuuk State after the economic assistance provided under the amended Compact between the FSM and US expires in 2023, and for other purposes.

This particular move contradicts the spirit and language of the Constitution. For example, the Constitution promotes the concept of unity in diversity, and the Compact should not be seen as the source of Micronesian survival, since Micronesians' continuity is dependent on the *ainang* system. *Ainang* binds people together and survives on the principles of reciprocity and sharing as deeply rooted in Micronesian traditions and cultures, like the *sawei* system in Yap. To divide the Federation would mean disaster. The FSM could become a softer target for transnational crime as

44   Hezel, 'Chuuk Independence: Why and How?'.
45   The ongoing feuding among political leaders at all levels is affecting the new generation in terms of their future as the year 2023 is not too far away. See Heather Jarvis, 'Voices of Young Women Need to Be Heard, Says Micronesian Youth Leader, Interview with Lucille Sain', *ABC Radio Australia*, 11 March 2014, www.radioaustralia.net.au/international/2014-03-07/voices-of-young-women-need-to-be-heard-says-micronesian-youth-leader/1265114.

law and order would be compromised.[46] Political observers see Chuuk's move as a teething problem, a typical symptom of a young nation finding its way to maturity. Moreover, those in the secessionist movement need to understand that to secede requires jumping many complex hurdles. One of the hurdles is compliance with the constitutional process that protects the nation's political integrity. The process for splitting the Federation is subject to Article IV, Section 1, which states:

> an amendment to [the] Constitution may be proposed by a constitutional convention, popular initiative, or Congress in a manner provided by law. A proposed amendment shall become a part of the Constitution when approved by 3/4 of the votes cast on that amendment in each of 3/4 of the states. If conflicting constitutional amendments submitted to the voters at the same election are approved, the amendment receiving the highest number of affirmative votes shall prevail to the extent of such conflict.[47]

Domestic debates are fundamentally important steps towards developing the FSM's social and political health; they provide opportunities for self-evaluation and thus the resolution of complex issues. The political discourse between the federal government and its constituents is subject to Article VIII, Section 1, which states, 'a power expressly delegated to the national government, or a power of such an indisputably national character as to beyond the power of a state control, is a national power'.[48] The state governments have consistently held the position that anything that is not specifically provided for in the Constitution falls withing the bounds of state jurisdiction. Lawyers and academics have been exploring specific measures to pre-empt jurisdictional rifts arising between the disputants. One suggestion is that they negotiate outside the Constitutional Court on the basis of Micronesian cultural principles of fairness and equity.[49] This is because if the national governmental continues to assert control over matters that are not clearly defined as its prerogative, it may antagonise the states and undermine solidarity. Instead, the issue should be premised on

---

46 Michael Yui, 'Border Security: Transnational Crime in Micronesia. Part 3: Micronesia and Its Law Enforcement Problems', 6 March 2012, www.asiapacificdefencereporter.com/articles/216/Border-security-Transnational-crime-in-Micronesia.

47 *The Constitution of the Federated States of Micronesia*, Article IX, Section 1.

48 *The Constitution of the Federated States of Micronesia*, Article VIII, Section 1.

49 My personal opinion as no literature exists on this particular topic. Many leaders rigidly follow the constitutional process and the law to solve their differences. Unfortunately, apparently no one has bothered to consider negotiation outside the constitutional process to settle this difference and find a solution based on FSM traditional principles of fairness and equity.

striking a balance based on mutual interests to strengthen national unity.[50] Traditional leaders may therefore have a role to play in the undefined legal areas.

Political and Economic Challenges

Since colonisation, economic goals for Micronesia have always been set by outsiders and designed to benefit outsiders. For example, during the Japanese period, economic development in Micronesia was seen as very successful, although such success did not benefit Micronesians. The US, under the trusteeship agreement, was tasked with developing the islands but failed to carry out its mandate. After Micronesians' pushed for a new political status, the US poured millions of dollars into Micronesia to compensate for years of neglect.[51] This sudden injection of money resulted in the creation of the classic model of economic dependency. This model characterises Micronesians as being incapable of fending for themselves due to a lack of economic infrastructure, a social system that hinders capitalism and an unfriendly legal system that discourages foreign investment necessary to stimulate economic activities to promote the trickle-down effect.[52] The problem with this analysis is that it applies a neoclassical economic model, which is better suited to big economies, not Micronesia. It is therefore not surprising that the trickle-down effect has not been very effective in Micronesia. The Micronesian social system, which is the backbone of Micronesian survivability, continues to be misunderstood by outside economists. It should be remembered that the implantation of any economic philosophy that requires the dismantling of the central pillar of indigenous life—communal and kinship support— is doomed to fail. The nature of the Micronesian economic system as inherently opposed to wholesale capitalism should be subject to further studies to ensure the development of a suitable economic model to sustain continuity.

---

50 My personal opinion.

51 Yet, oddly, the predominate literature has portrayed the US as neglecting the FSM since the end of WWII. See Hanlon, *Remaking Micronesia*, pp. 90–91.

52 The FSM has been characterised by many reports by outsiders as lacking infrastructure and having unfriendly laws for foreign investment. See e.g. Asian Development Bank, *Federated States of Micronesia Development Framework 2012. Looking to the Future: A Foundation for Discussion at the FSM Development Partners Forum*, 2012, www.adb.org/sites/default/files/linked-documents/cobp-fsm-2014-2016-oth-01.pdf.

In his State of the Nation address in 2012, President Mori expressed the need for Micronesians to change their mindset:

> our governments need to prioritize and align development efforts with its development plan. Our governments must always ensure that the allocation of our financial resources adheres to our development plans. Our governments must formulate sound policies and regulations that are business and development friendly in order to attract more foreign investments and improve related ratings by the World Bank. We must also facilitate the privatization of our government-owned enterprises. These steps are essential to promote economic growth.[53]

While this speech articulated sound goals for developing the FSM's economy, there was no roadmap provided for how this would be achieved. Decades of development rhetoric has not translated into anything concrete to benefit the people. Development theories are illusive concepts that have been routinely fed to the public for political purposes rather than economic benefits.[54] By and large, they have never filtered down to capture the public's attention and support.

From this author's perspective, development means devising and implementing processes that allow a country to utilise knowledge, skills and attitudes that sustain a desired lifestyle. It means sustaining self-sufficiency and adapting the modes of production in conjunction with global forces to suit local context. A wholesale import of economic models designed to overwhelm Micronesia's unique circumstances are not conducive to the FSM's development.[55] Micronesians have tried to grapple with what development entails ever since the traditional social system came into contact with the colonial economic system. Theories of economic development are far removed from the realities of day-to-day

---

53 Emmanuel Mori, *State of the Nation Address*, 18 May 2012, p. 9.

54 Political rhetoric on economic development has been fed to the public since the beginning of the Compact in 1986. However, in reality, nothing much came from successive economic plans. See Giff Johnson, 'Ad Hoc Decisions Don't Make It in an Increasingly Complex World', *Pacific Institute of Public Policy*, 9 October 2013.

55 Since the ideas of development have entered Micronesia, they seem to suggest that the Micronesian lifestyle has problems. Micronesians have seemingly believed this suggestion and want to imitate the capitalist way of life. The question remains, why? For some explanations, see Francis X. Hezel, 'Reflection of Micronesia's Economy', *Micronitor*, Majuro, 29 April 1973, www.micsem.org/pubs/articles/economic/frames/reflectfr.htm.

life for most Micronesians.[56] What they know is that their subsistence lifestyle provides sustenance and keeps the extended family together. By comparison, Western economic development seems abstract and unrelated to the life they have been accustomed to since their ancestors made the islands their home. Those that do not move into the wage economy and remit money are often on the margins of this system and still rely, in part, on *ainang* for support.

The Western mode of economic production based on mass commercial consumerism is not suitable for the FSM's circumstances due to a lack of appropriate technology, lack of infrastructure, the small size of the islands and the social structure.[57] To Micronesians, development is about protecting and sustaining their subsistence way of life and safeguarding their traditional practices with small-scale technology that may complement their lifestyle. For example, a small outboard engine for fishing, solar energy to provide lighting and operate electrical household appliances, new models of cooperative stores for bartering goods and handicrafts, and small retail outlets that will provide necessary manufactured items and jobs. To this end, 'development' may then be defined as the capacity to accommodate changes while maintaining the health of the environment and sustaining the extended family system, particularly in the low-lying islands.[58] The low-lying islanders' ideas could be applied to the economies of the volcanic islands, utilising their different capacity for integrating traditional and modern economic practices, so long as development does not negatively affect the fragile environment. Again, appropriate technology and infrastructure to cater for both domestic and international consumerism may be possible, but within the Micronesian brand of development and under local control.[59]

---

56   My encounters with many people at the grassroots level during my field study (in Pohnpei, January 2011, and Chuuk, June 2013) suggest that the language of development, such as 'statistics', 'evidence' and 'gross national product', are foreign concepts that are not yet fully understood by many Micronesians (despite even my attempts to explain these concepts in the simplest form possible). Planting taros, gardening and fishing dominated our discourses.

57   The geographical conditions and cultural system of the FSM are incompatible with the ideas of capitalism, something that consultants have often misunderstood. Capitalism does not seem to be a viable way for the future development of the FSM.

58   J. Dobbin and Francis X. Hezel, 'Sustainable Human Development in Micronesia: Origin and Meaning of the Term', *Micronesian Counselor*, No. 21, March 1998, www.micsem.org/pubs/counselor/frames/sushumdevfr.htm.

59   Dobbin and Hezel, 'Sustainable Human Development in Micronesia'.

Revisiting the Traditional System

Traditional economic practices are premised on a network system, patterned along socio-cultural lines in terms of labour relations; resource management; and the interconnection between families, clans, villages, islands and regions. This system remains central to Micronesia's economic sustainability and is intrinsically linked to Micronesians' identity, which is deeply rooted in the nation's history. It is about assisting each other when the need arises, for example, in agricultural and fishing activities, construction of houses and canoe building, and the maintenance of local knowledge and the clanship system.[60] For example, the *sawei* system in Yap and clanship connections in Pohnpei, Chuuk and Kosrae maintain the flow of ideas and goods and help redress inequality throughout Micronesia today.

The Micronesian labour system has been modified to adapt to the new economic circumstances introduced under colonialism and maintained through globalisation. Today, labour relations have two major aspects, voluntary and paid work.[61] For example, in the low-lying islands, many people continue to volunteer their labour in exchange for a particular item as payment, or they may be obliged to assist due to familial ties. The volunteer, in return, expects the recipient of such labour to reciprocate when the need for future work arises, thus triggering the obligation and response cycle.[62] The interconnection and voluntary model underscores the foundation of the economic mode of production in traditional Micronesian societies. It also protects members of the community from exploitation. This practice has continued through successive colonial periods until today. In some instances, labour can be paid for with items like cigarettes, alcohol and other Western items that are considered temporary but a luxury.[63]

---

60   Gonzaga Puas, *Labour Standards in the FSM*, FSM Department of Justice, Palikir, Pohnpei, 12 April 2005, pp. 2–5.
61   Puas, *Labour Standards*, pp. 2–5.
62   Puas, *Labour Standards*, pp. 2–5.
63   Puas, *Labour Standards*, pp. 2–5.

Figure 18: People of Rewow village, in 2014, on Lekinioch work to replace pandanus sheets on foeng, the *ainang faal* of Sopunpi, demonstrative of the principle of *alilis fengen*.
Source: Photograph taken by Amanson Ansin in 2014.

Observers and historians, such as Hezel, have noted that the rise of the cash economy is weakening the very foundation of the Micronesian family structure.[64] It has ruptured the family connection, and many wage or salary earners are forming what sociologists refer to as 'nuclear families'. Nuclear families, by and large, manage their own family affairs and depend on money they earn as self-contained and self-supporting economic units. They can afford luxuries in life and buy many things they want without sharing with their extended family.[65] Hezel's observation may be true in a few cases; however, Micronesians prefer to remain within the extended family system as it provides security, certainty and social acceptance. One can argue that the cash economy is not threatening traditional Micronesian socio-cultural foundations but, rather, has reinforced its structure. The strength of the traditional system rests with how Micronesians rearticulate the forces of the cash system to suit their contemporary lifestyle. Some examples can be illustrated by the way money has been absorbed and distributed like a commodity itself within the extended family structure.

---

64   Hezel, *The New Shape of Old Island Cultures*, pp. 1–10.
65   In the Trust Territory period, nuclear families formed when people were new to a place and had no relatives nearby (e.g. when working on assignment for the government). It was not due to a deliberate move to be separated from the rest of the extended family. Today, the 'nuclear family' does not exist in the FSM.

Money is not new to Micronesians; it first appeared during the colonial period. It has been used by Micronesians to buy Western commodities to supplement one's lifestyle. For example, when food items are bought, they are distributed to close relatives who live nearby. In return, traditional foods are shared with the members who earned the cash.[66] Further, when a member of the extended family needs money to satisfy a community obligation, other members of the extended family will pool their money together to assist the member who sought assistance. Those who cannot assist can volunteer their services to perform the tasks required. Funerals and family meetings naturally oblige extended family members to contribute. Family members who have an earning capacity cannot operate outside the extended family system, as to do so would bring social stress upon themselves. As my grandfather once said, 'people do not eat money, but food'. This is in reference to WWII, where money was worthless. It is also about the fact that a person may have money, but what could that person do if people refuse to sell their food to them? Or, to put it simply, what can money earners do when faced with sudden unemployment or illness? Would they eat the money they earned? Who would provide care in lieu of the members of the extended family? Even those families now living in the heartland of the cash economy, the US, continue to maintain connections with each other, especially when important social events arise that require the pooling of financial resources.

Conclusion

Micronesians face many challenges today, ranging from economic development and constitutional issues to education, health and the development of a new generation of leaders. Maintaining the fluidity of the traditional system is the foundation for Micronesians' future survival. It is an evolving system that has been at the heart of Micronesian history. It has adapted, transformed and rearticulated itself, even under the stresses caused by ongoing engagement with the outside world and the current tides of globalisation. Successive waves of colonial regimes attempted to undermine the traditional system by inserting their own brands of development and different regimes of governance, all of which

---

66   My personal experience. On weekends, the extended family worships together and share, and exchanges food while visiting each other. Money is also circulated at this time through food shopping and by request from relatives.

were largely unsuccessful. Micronesian countermeasures were adopted through the process of adaptation, which arrested alien practices that could not be assimilated into its indigenous cultural practices. That is, Micronesians only accepted the essential elements of colonialism that ensured indigenous continuity. The current, relatively new, Micronesian Government has the task of ensuring that its modern legal, political, social, health and economic institutions perpetuate relevant traditional historical doctrines that define how Micronesia's future should be shaped.

Bibliography

Reports

Asian Development Bank, *Federated States of Micronesia Development Framework 2012. Looking to the Future: A Foundation for Discussion at the FSM Development Partners Forum*, 2012, available at www.adb.org/sites/default/files/linked-documents/cobp-fsm-2014-2016-oth-01.pdf.

Asian Development Bank, *Federated States of Micronesia: Strengthening: Infrastructure Planning and Implementation* (Financed by the Japan Fund for Poverty Reduction) (ADB Technical Assistance Report, Project Number: 44471), November 2011.

Australian Aid, *Food Security: Securing Food Resources in the Federated States of Micronesia* (Pacific Adaptation Strategy Assistance Program (PASAP)), Commonwealth of Australia, 2013, available at terranova.org.au/repository/paccsap-collection/securing-food-resources-in-the-federated-states-of-micronesia.

Charter of the United Nations and Statutes of the International Court of Justice, available at www.un.org/en/about-us/un-charter/full-text.

Chuuk State Constitution, available at fsmlaw.org/chuuk/constitution/entire.htm.

Compact of Free Association between the Federated States of Micronesia and the United States of America, Compilation of Documents as Amended, Palikir, Pohnpei, FSM, 2003.

Country Operations Business Plan October 2014, Federated States of Micronesia, 2015–2017, available at www.adb.org/sites/default/files/institutional-document/110928/cobp-fsm-2015-2017.pdf.

Federated States of Micronesia Constitution, available at fsmsupremecourt.org/WebSite/fsm/constitution/index.htm.

FSM Climate Change Policy, Palikir, Pohnpei, 2011.

FSM Code Title 42, available at fsmlaw.org/fsm/code/index.htm.

FSM Information Services, *Pohnpei, Federated States of Micronesia, Pacific Islands Report, Pacific Islands Development Program*, East-West Center, With Support From Center for Pacific Islands Studies, University of Hawai'i, 22 April 2014.

FSM Press Release #1402-09, *Moscow-Russia, the New Market Place for the National Aquarium Center (NAC)*, Palikir, Pohnpei, FSM Information Services, 20 February 2014.

Gootnick, David, *Micronesia Faces Challenges to Achieving Compact Goals: Testimony before the Insular Affairs Subcommittee, House Resources Committee, U.S. House of Representatives: Attachment III: Estimated FSM Per Capita Compact Grant Assistance, Fiscal Years 1987–2023*, United States Government Accountability Office, Washington, DC, 10 June 2008.

Henry, Rosita, Jeffery, William and Pam, Christine, *Heritage and Climate Change in Micronesia: A Report on a Pilot Study Conducted on Moch Island, Mortlock Islands, Chuuk, Federated States of Micronesia*, James Cook University, Townsville, Queensland, Australia, January 2008.

Hezel, Francis X., 'Micronesians on the Move: Eastward and Upward Bound', *Pacific Islands Policy*, No. 9, East-West Center, Hawai'i, 2013, available at www.eastwestcenter.org/publications/micronesians-the-move-eastward-and-upward-bound.

International Monetary Fund, *Federated States of Micronesia (FSM): 2012 Article IV Consultation Concluding Statement of the IMF November 19, 2012*, available at www.imf.org/en/News/Articles/2015/09/28/04/52/mcs111912.

International Monetary Fund, *IMF Executive Board Concludes 2012 Article IV Consultation with Federated States of Micronesia Asia and Pacific Department*, 17 January 2013.

Island Community Food Community of Pohnpei, *Let's Go Local: Culture, Health, Environment, Economy and Food Security*, Koloia, Pohnpei, 2013, available at www.Islandfood.org/index.html.

Kosrae State Constitution, available at fsmlaw.org/kosrae/constitution/entire.htm.

Lekinioch Municipality Constitution, Lukunor Island, 1989.

Nationwide Climate Change Policy 2009: The Federated States of Micronesia, 14 December 2009.

Nimea, Fabian, *Federated States of Micronesia: National Assessment Report. Support for the Formulation of National Sustainable Development Strategies in the Pacific Small Island Developing States*, Palikir, Pohnpei, 2006.

Office of Statistics, Budget and Economic Management, Overseas Development Assistance and Compact Management, *Millennium Development Goals and Status Report 2010: The Federated States of Micronesia*, Palikir, Pohnpei, 15 December 2010.

Office of the National Public Auditor, Federated States of Micronesia, *CFSM Public Projects and Social Programs: 1.6 Million Approved without Clear Criteria. Audit Report Number 2015-04*, 2014, available at www.fsmopa.fm/files/onpa/2014/Audit%20Report%202015-04.pdf.

Pohnpei State Constitution, available at fsmlaw.org/pohnpei/index.htm.

Raatior, Vid, 'Audit Confirms That FSM Congress Misuse of 1.6 Million of Public Funds', Chuuk Reform Coalition, 10 February 2015. available at www.chuukstate.org/audit-confirms-that-fsm-congress-misuse-1-6-million-of-public-funds/.

Report of the First Quarterly Meeting of the Chuuk Advisory Group on Education Reform, Weno, Chuuk, 20 February 2013.

Report to Congress on the Compact of Free Association with the Federated States of Micronesia (FSM) and the Republic of the Marshall Islands (RMI) for Fiscal Year 2006, Washington, DC, 2006.

Solomon, A. N., *Report by the US Government Survey Mission to the Trust Territory of the Pacific Islands*, Washington, DC, 1963.

Summary of the Political Status Talks of the Joint Committee on Future Status, Congress of Micronesia, Saipan, 1973.

Susumu, Gibson and Kostka, Mark, *Federated States of Micronesia Food Security Assessment Report* (Final Draft), Palikir, Pohnpei, March 2011.

Susumu, Gibson and Kostka, Mark, *Food Security Vulnerability Assessment Report*, Palikir, Pohnpei, 2012.

Susumu, Gibson, Wichep, John and Silbanuz, Marlyter, *Preliminary Damage Assessment (PDA) Report Federated States of Micronesia: Agricultural Damage Report*, December 2009.

'The Federated States of Micronesia Strategic Development 2003–2023: The Next 20 Years Achieving Economic Growth and Self Reliance', Vol I: *Policies and Strategies for Development*, The Federated States of Micronesia's Presidential Election System and Proposed Constitutional Analysis, Palikir, Pohnpei, 2004.

WikiLeaks Documents, available at cablegatesearch.wikileaks.org/search.php?qo=86528.

World Health Organization, 'Micronesia, Federated States of', in *Western Pacific Country Health Information Profiles*, 2011, pp. 218–233. iris.wpro.who.int/handle/10665.1/10522.

Yap Constitution, available at fsmlaw.org/yap/constitution/index.htm.

Articles, Chapters, Papers and Theses

Ahlgern, Ingrid, Yamada, Seiji and Wong, Allen, 'Rising Oceans, Climate Change, Food Aid, and Human Rights in the Marshall Islands', *Health and Human Rights Journal*, Vol. 16, No. 1, 2014, pp. 1–12.

Alkire, William, 'Cultural Ecology and Ecological Anthropology in Micronesia', in *American Anthropology: An Assessment*, edited by Robert C. Kiste and Mac Marshall, University of Hawai'i Press, 1999, pp. 81–106.

Alkire, William, 'Land, Sea, Gender, and Ghosts on Woleai-Lamotrek', *American Anthropological Association*. Reprinted from Special Publication, No. 25, 1989, pp. 79–94.

Alkire, William, 'Technical Knowledge and the Evolution of Political Systems in the Central and Western Caroline Islands of Micronesia', *Canadian Journal of Anthropology*, Vol. 2, No. 2, Winter, 1980, pp. 229–237.

Alkire, William, 'Traditional Exchange Systems and Modern Political Developments in the Yap District of Micronesia', in *Persistence and Exchange: Papers from a Symposium on Ecological Problems of the Traditional Societies of the Pacific Region*, edited by Ronald W. Force and Brenda Bishop, August–September 1979.

Anckar, Dag, 'Archipelagos and Political Engineering: The Impact of Non-Contiguity on Devolution in Small States', *Island Studies Journal*, Canada, Vol. 2, No. 2, 2007, pp. 193–208.

Australia Radio (Melbourne), 'Fish Losing Survival Instinct Due to Climate Change: Study Research on PNG Reefs Says Fish Behavior Becoming Riskier', *Pacific Islands Report*, 15 April 2014.

Bautista, Lola Q., 'Building Sense Out of Households: Migrants from Chuuk (Re)create Local Settlements in Guam', *City and Society*, Vol. 23, No. 1, June 2011, pp. 66–90.

Berg, M. L., 'Yapese Politics, Yapese Money, and the Sawei Tribute Network Before World War I', *Journal of Pacific History*, Vol. 27, No. 2, December 1992, pp. 150–164.

Bertram, Geoff, 'Introduction: The MIRAB Model in the Twenty-First Century', *Asia Pacific Viewpoint*, Vol. 47, No. 1, April 2006, pp. 1–13.

Blas, Phillip H., 'Traditional Chuukese Sailing Canoe Reaches Guam. Crew Navigated 500 Miles without Using Modern Technology', *Pacific Islands Report*, Guam, 19 June 2013, available at www.pireport.org/articles/2013/06/19/traditional-chuukese-sailing-canoe-reaches-guam.

Boughton, James M., 'Globalisation and the Silent Revolution in the 1980s', *Finance and Development*, Vol. 39, No. 1, March 2002, available at www.imf.org/external/pubs/ft/fandd/2002/03/bought.htm.

Brandt, Philippa, 'The Geopolitics of Chinese Aid', Lowy Institute, Sydney, 4 March 2015, available at www.lowyinstitute.org/publications/geopolitics-chinese-aid.

Brown, Terry, 'Small Island States and Global Warming', *Anglican Communion News Service*, Niagra, Canada, 5 June 2014.

Bruton, Larry, 'Successful Renewable Energy Projects in the FSM', Paper presented at the 26th Pacific Islands Environment Conference, 22–25 June 2009, Saipan, CNMI.

Cain, Tess N., 'Convergence, or Clash? The Recognition of Customary Law and Practice in Sentencing Decisions of the Courts of the Pacific Islands Region', *Melbourne Journal of International Law*, Vol. 2, 2001, available at www.austlii.edu.au/au/journals/MelbJIL/2001/2.html.

Carreon, Benadette H., 'Pacific Leaders Launch Green Initiative', *Marianas Variety*, 11 August 2010.

Chapman-Smith, Ben, 'Income from Sea Bed Mining in Cooks could Eclipse Tourism and Cook Islands has "World Class Resource" Worth 'a Vast Sum'', *Cook Island News*, 15 May 2014.

Chappell, David A., 'The Post-Contact Period', in *The Pacific Islands: Environment and Society* (revised edition), Moshe Rapaport, University of Hawai'i Press, 2013, pp. 134–143.

Christian, Peter, 'Patriot Games: Island Voices in a Sea of Contest', *Pacific Institute of Public Policy*, Discussion Paper No. 21, June 2012, pp. 1–5.

Christian, Peter, *Speech to the 17th Congress of the Federated States of Micronesia*, Palikir, 2012.

Connell, John and Roy, Peter, 'The Greenhouse Effect: The Impact of Sea Level Rise on Low Coral Islands in the South Pacific', *Implications of Expected Climate Changes in the South Pacific Region: An Overview*, UNEP Regional Seas Reports and Studies No. 128, UNEP, 1990.

Cook, William, 'U.S. Department of State Diplomacy in Action Executive Summary', Washington, DC, June 2014.

Corfield, Penelope J., 'All People are Living Histories—Which is Why History Matters', *Making History*, School of Advanced Study, University of London, 2008, available at www.history.ac.uk/makinghistory/resources/articles/why_history_matters.html.

D'Arcy, Paul, 'American Administration of Micronesia: 1946–1958', University of Hawai'i, 1986. (Unpublished paper).

D'Arcy, Paul, 'Connected by the Sea: Towards Regional History of the Western Caroline Islands', *Journal of Pacific History*, Vol. 36, No. 2, 2001, pp. 163–170.

D'Arcy, Paul, 'Cultural Divisions and Island Environments since the Time of Dumont d'Urville', *Journal of Pacific History*, Vol. 38, No. 2, 2003, pp. 217–236.

D'Arcy, Paul, 'Introduction', in *The Pacific World: Lands, Peoples and History of the Pacific, 1500–1900. Vol. 3, Peoples of the Pacific: The History of Oceania to 1870*, edited by Paul D'Arcy, Ashgate Variorum, Burlington, VT, USA, 2008, pp. ix–xiv.

D'Arcy, Paul, 'The Lawless Ocean? Voluntary Compliance Regimes and Offshore Resource Exploitation in the Pacific', *Asia and the Pacific Policy Studies*, Vol. 1, No. 2, 2014, pp. 297–311.

D'Arcy, Paul, 'Leading by Example: Micronesians and the Sea as World's Best Practice', paper delivered at the Micronesian-Australian Friends Association (MAFA) Symposium, The Australian National University, 28 April 2014.

D'Arcy, Paul, 'The Nourishing Sea: Partner Guardianship of Fishery and Seabed Mineral Resources for the Economic Viability of Small Pacific Island Nations', *Sustainability*, Vol. 5, No. 8, pp. 3346–3367.

D'Arcy, Paul, *The Pacific World: Lands, Peoples and History of the Pacific, 1500–1900. Vol. 3, Peoples of the Pacific: The History of Oceania to 1870*, edited by Paul D'Arcy, Ashgate Variorum, Burlington, VT, USA, 2008.

D'Arcy, Paul, 'The Role of the Tuna Fishery in the Economy of the Federated States of Micronesia', *Pacific Economic Bulletin*, Vol. 21, No. 3, 2006, pp. 75–87.

D'Arcy, Paul, 'The Role that Myths and Oral Traditions Should Play in the Study of Micronesian History', University of Hawai'i, 1986. (Unpublished paper).

D'Arcy, Paul, 'Spanish and German Colonial Rule: With Reference to Spanish and German Colonial Rule in the Caroline Islands Identify the Various Parties Influencing the History of this Era? What Perceptions and Objectives Were They Motivated By?', University of Hawai'i, 1986. (Unpublished paper).

D'Arcy, Paul, 'The Teaching of Pacific History: Introduction Diverse Approaches for Diverse Audience', *Journal of Pacific History* (Forum), Vol. 46, No. 2, September 2011, pp. 197–206.

D'Arcy, Paul, 'What was the Impact of Japanese Rule on the Indigenous Population of Japan's South Seas Mandate?', University of Hawai'i, 1986. (Unpublished paper).

Descantes, Christophe, 'Integrating Archaeology and Ethnohistory: The Development of Exchange between Yap and Ulithi, Western Caroline Islands (Micronesia)', PhD thesis, UMI Dissertation Services, Ann Arbor, Michigan, 1998.

Dobbin, J. and Hezel, Francis X., 'Sustainable Human Development in Micronesia: Origin and Meaning of the Term', *Micronesian Counselor*, No. 21, March 1998, available at www.micsem.org/pubs/counselor/frames/sushumdevfr.htm.

Doty, Tammy, 'Interior Releases Report on FSM Economy', *Micronesia Forum*, 16 November 2011, www.micronesiaforum.org/index.php?p=/discussions.

'Dumont d'Urville's Divisions of Oceania: Fundamental Precincts or Arbitrary Constructs?', *Journal of Pacific History* [Special Issue], Vol. 38, No. 2, September 2003, pp. 155–288.

Ehrlich, Paul, '"The Clothes of Men": Ponape Island and German Colonial Rule, 1899–1914', PhD thesis, State University of New York at Stony Brook, Stony Brook, New York, 1973.

Einstein, Albert, 'Why Socialism?', *Monthly Review: An Independent Socialist Magazine*, Vol. 61, No. 1, May 2009, available at monthlyreview.org/2009/05/01/why-socialism/.

Fairlamb, John, *Office of Compact Negotiations, U.S. Department of State Compact of Free Association Negotiations: Fulfilling the Promise*, A Paper Originally Presented to Island State Security Conference Asia-Pacific Center for Security Studies, Honolulu, Hawai'i, June 2001.

Falanruw, Margie V. Cushing, 'Food Production and Ecosystem Management in Yap', *ISLA: A Journal of Micronesian Studies*, Vol. 2, No. 1, Rainy Season 1994, pp. 2–22.

Falgout, Suzan, Poyer, Lin and Carucci, Laurence, 'The Greatest Hardship: Micronesian Memories of War', *ISLA: A Journal of Micronesian Studies*, Vol. 3, No. 2, Dry Season 1995, pp. 203–221.

Field, Christopher B., Barros, Vicente, Mohamed, A. K. Abdrabo, et al., *IPCC: Intergovernmental Panel on Climate Change. WGII AR5 Phase I Report Launch. Climate Change 2014: Impacts, Adaptation, and Vulnerability Summary for Policymakers*, 31 March 2014.

Firth, Stewart, 'Sovereignty and Independence in the Contemporary Pacific', *The Contemporary Pacific*, Vol. 1, No. 1 & 2, Spring & Fall 1989, pp. 75–76.

Force, Roland and Force, Maryann, 'Political Change in Micronesia', in *Induced Political Change in the Pacific: A Symposium*, edited by Roland W. Force, Honolulu, Hawai'i, 1961.

FSM Updates, 'President Mori Declares "State of Emergency" as Ping Da 7 Post Greater Threat Sitting on Nan Kepkepin Param Reef in Pohnpei', 23 January 2014, available at myfsm.blogspot.com.au/2014/01/president-mori-declares-state-of.html.

Gavin, Daws, 'Comment: Texts and Contexts: A First Person Note', *Journal of Pacific History*, Vol. 41, No. 2, September 2006, pp. 249–260.

Gaynor, Daleno, 'High Seas Flood Tiny Lekinioch, Chuuk', *Pacific Daily News*, Guam, 3 May 2007.

Goodenough, Ward, 'Skyworld and This World: The Place of Kachaw in Micronesian Cosmology', *American Anthropology*, Vol. 88, No. 3, 1986, pp. 551–568.

Gootnick, David, *Compact of Free Association: Implementation Activities have Progressed, but the Marshall Islands Faces Challenges to Achieving Long-term Compact Goals, Testimony Before the Insular Affairs Subcommittee*, House Resources Committee, US House of Representatives, 24 July 2007, available at www.gao.gov/assets/a117460.html.

Gray, Kirk, 'Modernization in Micronesia: Acculturation, Colonialism and Cultural Change', PhD thesis, Western Michigan University, Kalamazoo, Michigan, 1974.

Grieco, Elizabeth, *The Federated States of Micronesia: The 'Push' to Migrate*, Migration Policy Institute, 1 July 2003, available at www.migrationpolicy.org/article/federated-states-micronesia-push-migrate.

Haglelgam, John, 'Federalism and Multiculturalism: Federalism in the Federated States of Micronesia', Asian Resource Centre for Decentralisation, 2006, available at localgov.up.edu.ph/federalism-and-multiculturalism-haglelgam-federalism-in-the-federated-states-of-micronesia.html.

Haglelgam, John, 'Problems of National Unity and Economic Development in the Federated States of Micronesia', *ISLA: A Journal of Micronesian Studies*, Vol. 1, No. 1, Rainy Season 1992, pp. 5–12.

Hal, Friedman M., 'The Limitations of Collective Security: The United States and the Micronesian Trusteeship, 1945-147', *ISLA: A Journal of Micronesian Studies*, Vol. 3, No. 2, Dry Season 1995, pp. 339–370.

Hanlon, David, 'Another Side of Henry Nanpei', *Journal of Pacific History*, Vol. 23, No. 1, April 1988, pp. 36–51.

Hanlon, David, 'Magellan's Chroniclers? American Anthropology's History in Micronesia', in *American Anthropology in Micronesia: An Assessment*, edited by Robert C. Kiste and Mac Marshall, University of Hawai'i Press, 1999, pp. 53–80.

Hanlon, David, 'Micronesia: Writing and Rewriting the Histories of a Nonentity', *Pacific Studies*, Vol. 12, No. 2, March 1989, pp. 1–21.

Hanlon, David, 'On Hezel's *The First Taint of Civilization*', in *Texts and Contexts: Reflection in Pacific Islands Historiography*, edited by Doug Munro and Brij Lal, University of Hawai'i Press, 2006, pp. 202–212. doi.org/10.1515/9780824842918-018.

Hanlon, David, 'Patterns of Colonial Rule in Micronesia', in *Tides of History: The Pacific Islands in the Twentieth Century*, edited by K. R. Howe, Robert C. Kiste and Brij V. Lal, University of Hawai'i Press, 1987, pp. 93–118.

Hanlon, David, 'Sorcery, "Savage Memories" and the Edge of Commensurability for History in the Pacific', in *Pacific Islands History: Journeys and Transformation*, edited by Brij V. Lal, 1993, Journal of Pacific History, pp. 107–128, available at openresearch-repository.anu.edu.au/handle/1885/132633.

Hanlon, David, 'Tosiwo Nakayama', Paper Presented in Tokyo, Japan, 2011.

Hanlon, David, 'You Did What, Mr. President!? Trying to Write a Biography of Tosiwo', in *Telling Pacific Lives: Prisms of Process Nakayama* edited by Brij V. Lal and Vicki Luker, ANU E Press, Canberra, 2008, available at doi. org/10.22459/TPL.06.2008.

Hanlon, David and Eperiam, William, 'The Federated States of Micronesia: Unifying the Remnants', *Politics in Micronesia, Vol. 3*, edited by Ron Crocombe and Ahmed Ali, *Politics in the Pacific Islands* (series), Suva, 1983, pp. 81–99.

Hanson, Ferguson, 'Don't Ignore the Big New Player in Fiji', *The Sydney Morning Herald*, 9 May 2008, pp. 1–2, available at www.smh.com.au/articles/2008/05/08/1210131163040.html.

Hau'ofa, Epeli, 'Our Sea of Islands', in *We are the Ocean: Selected Works*, University of Hawai'i Press, 2008, pp. 27–40.

Hay, Peter, 'A Phenomenology of Islands', *Island Studies Journal*, Vol. 1, No. 1, 2006, pp. 19–42.

Hayward-Jones, Jenny, 'China No Rival in the Battle for Island Influence', Lowy Institute, 17 May 2013, available at www.lowyinstitute.org/publications/china-no-rival-battle-island-influence.

Hempenstall, Peter, 'Imperial Manoeuvers', in *Tides of History: The Pacific Islands in the Twentieth Century*, edited by K. R. Howe, Robert C. Kiste and Brij V. Lal, University of Hawai'i Press, 1987, pp. 29–39.

Hezel, Francis X., 'A Brief Economy of Micronesia', *Past Achievements and Future Possibilities*, Majuro: Micronesian Seminar, 1984, pp. 11–62, available at micsem.org/pubs/articles/economic/frames/ecohistfr.htm.

Hezel, Francis X., 'Book Review: *Double Ghosts: Oceanian Voyages on Euroamerican Ships*', *Journal of World History*, Vol. 10, No. 2, 1999, pp. 479–481.

Hezel, Francis X., 'The Catholic Church in Yap: A Foothold in the Carolines', *Micronesian Seminar*, 2003, available at www.micsem.org/pubs/books/catholic/yap/index.htm.

Hezel, Francis X., 'Chuuk Independence: Why and How?', *Pacific Institute of Public Policy*, 2 March 2015, available at pacificpolicy.org/2015/03/chuuk-independence-why-and-how/.

Hezel, Francis X., 'The Chuuk Problem: At the Foot of the Political Pyramid', *Micronesian Counselor*, No. 50, April 2004, available at www.micsem.org/pubs/counselor/frames/chuukprobfr.htm.

Hezel, Francis X., 'Congries of Spirit: The Meaning of Religion', *Micronesian Seminar*, Pohnpei, 1995, available at www.micsem.org/pubs/articles/religion/frames/congspiritsfr.htm.

Hezel, Francis X., 'Cultural Patterns in Trukese Suicide', *Ethnology*, Vol. 23, July 1984, pp. 193–206, available at www.micsem.org/pubs/articles/suicide/frames/cultpatfr.htm.

Hezel, Francis X., 'High Water in the Low Atolls', *Micronesian Counselor*, No. 76, 2009.

Hezel, Francis X., 'How Much is Enough? US Aid and Free Association', *Marianas Variety*, Saipan, 22 March 1985, available at www.micsem.org/pubs/articles/economic/frames/howmuchfr.htm.

Hezel, Francis X., 'Is that the Best You Can Do? A Tale of Two Micronesian Economies: The Plea to Grow Economy', East-West Centre, Hawai'i, 2006, available at www.micsem.org/pubs/articles/economic/frames/taleoftwofr.htm.

Hezel, Francis X., 'Is the Congress of the FSM Becoming too Powerful?', *MicSem Monthly Discussion*, No. 2, 13 October 1993.

Hezel, Francis X., 'Micronesian Governments: A View From Outside', *Micronesian Counselor*, No. 55, April 2005.

Hezel, Francis X., 'Possession and Trance in Chuuk', *ISLA: A Journal of Micronesian Studies*, Vol. 2, No. 1, 1995, available at www.micsem.org/pubs/articles/socprobs/frames/posstranfr.htm.

Hezel, Francis X., 'Reflection of Micronesia's Economy', *Micronitor*, Majuro, 29 April 1973, available at www.micsem.org/pubs/articles/economic/frames/reflectfr.htm.

Hezel, Francis X., 'Rough Seas Ahead: The FSM Economy During Compact II', *Micronesian Counselor*, No. 44, January 2003, available at www.micsem.org/pubs/counselor.htm.

Hezel, Francis X., 'Spirit Possession in Chuuk: A Socio-Cultural Interpretation', *Micronesian Seminar*, Pohnpei, 1991, available at www.micsem.org/pubs/articles/socprobs/frames/spiritposschkfr.htm.

Hezel, Francis X., Petteys, Edwin Q. P. and Chang, Deborah L., 'Sustainable Human Development in the FSM. Chapter 2: The People and Their Cultures', *Micronesian Seminar*, 1997, available at micsem.org/pubs/articles/economic/shd/frames/chapter02fr.htm.

Hezel, Francis X., Petteys, Edwin Q. P., and Chang, Deborah L., 'Sustainable Human Development in the FSM. Chapter 3: History and the Development of Government Systems', *Micronesian Seminar*, 1997, available at micsem.org/pubs/articles/economic/shd/frames/chapter03fr.htm.

Hiroa, Te Rangi (P. H. Buck), 'Social and Political Evolution: The Value of Traditions in Polynesian Research', in *The Pacific World: Lands, Peoples and History of the Pacific, 1500-1900. Vol. 3, Peoples of the Pacific: The History of Oceania to 1870*, edited by Paul D'Arcy, Ashgate Variorum, Burlington, VT, USA, 2008.

Hofschneider, Freddy E., 'US Coast Guard Completes Western Pacific Maritime Patrol 40 Day Mission Monitors FSM, RMI, and Palau's EEZs', *Marianas Variety*, Saipan, CNMI, 12 May 2014.

Howe, Kerry R., *Nature, Culture and History: The 'Knowing' of Oceania*, University of Hawai'i Press, Hawai'i, 2000.

Hunter-Anderson, Rosalind and Zan, Yigal (Go'opsan), 'Demystifying the Sawei, A Traditional Interisland Exchange', *ISLA: A Journal of Micronesian Studies*, Vol. 4, No. 1/Rainy Season 1996, pp. 1–45.

Jarvis, Heather, 'Voices of Young Women Need to Be Heard, Says Micronesian Youth Leader, Interview with Lucille Sain', *ABC Radio Australia*, 11 March 2014, available at www.radioaustralia.net.au/international/2014-03-07/voices-of-young-women-need-to-be-heard-says-micronesian-youth-leader/1265114.

Jaynes, Bill, 'Cabinet Member to Stand Trial on FSM Criminal Charges', *Kaselehlie Press*, 13–26 April 2015, p. 3.

Jaynes, Bill, 'FSM Congress Pushes for Exclusive Fishing Rights: Single Foreign Country Would Have Access to Grounds', *Kaselehlie Press*, 26 July 2010.

Jaynes, Bill, 'GAO Official Says Compact Impact Reporting is Not Reliable or Consistent', *Kaselehlie Press*, 29 July 2013.

Jaynes, Bill, 'Senate Appropriations Committee Takes Concrete Steps to Begin Barring Some FAS Citizens from Entry to the United States', *Kaselehlie Press*, 19 September 2011.

Jaynes, Bill, 'Special Seats For Women', *Kaselehlie Press*, 25 September 2012.

Johnson, Giff, 'Ad Hoc Decisions Don't Make It in an Increasingly Complex World', *Pacific Institute of Public Policy*, 9 October 2013.

Johnson, Giff, 'No More Compact for the RMI', *Pacific Islands Report*, 5 November 2010, available at pidp.eastwestcenter.org/pireport/.

Johnson, Giff, 'US Lawmakers Seek Limit on Micronesian Migrants: Marshall Protests, Cite Compact Terms', *Marianas Variety*, 23 May 2011.

Johnson, Giff and Carreon, Bernadette, 'Micronesia's Access to U.S. under Review', *Marianas Business Journal*, 18 July 2011, available at kshiro.wordpress.com/2011/07/21/micronesia's-free-access-to-u-s-under-review/.

Jones, Jenny H., 'Big Enough for All of Us: Geo-strategic Competition in the Pacific Islands', Lowy Institute, 16 May 2013, available at www.lowyinstitute.org/publications/big-enough-all-us-geo-strategic-competition-pacific-islands.

Käser, Lothar, 'Light in the South Seas. Wilhelm Friedrich & Elisabeth Kärcher: The Life and Work of a Liebenzell Missionary Couple', Verlag Der Liebenzeller Mission (Unpublished).

Keim, Mark E., *Sea Level Rise Disaster in Micronesia: Sentinel Event for Climate Change*, Cambridge University Press, 8 April 2013.

Kellam, Henry H., *Social Sector: Education, Part I: Education: Background Analysis: Understanding the Educational System in the FSM*, September 2001.

Ken-ichi-Sudo, 'Rank, Hierarchy and Routes of Migration: Chieftainship in the Central Caroline Islands of Micronesia', in *Origins, Ancestry and Alliance: Explorations in Austronesian Ethnography*, edited by James Fox and Clifford Sather, ANU E Press, Canberra, 2006, available at doi.org/10.22459/OAA.10.2006.

King, Edward C., 'Custom and Constitutionalism in the Federated States of Micronesia', *Asian-Pacific Law & Policy Journal*, Vol. 3, No. 2, July 2002, pp. 249–281.

Kiste, Robert, 'A Half Century in Restrospect', in *American Anthropology in Micronesia: An Assessment*, edited by Robert Kiste and Mac Marshall, University of Hawai'i Press, 1999, pp. 443–467.

Kiste, Robert, 'Overview of US Policy', in *The Ninth Annual Pacific Islands Studies Conference Proceedings: History of the US Trust Territory of the Pacific Islands*, edited by Karen Knudsen, University of Hawai'i, 1985.

Kiste, Robert, 'Termination of the US Trusteeship in Micronesia', *Journal Pacific History*, Vol. 21, No. 3, July 1986, pp. 127–138.

Knudson, Kenneth E., 'Resource Fluctuation, Productivity, and Social Organization on Micronesian Coral Islands', PhD thesis, University of Oregon, Eugene, Oregon, 1970.

Komai, Yoko, 'The Failure to Objectify Culture: A Lack of Nationalism in the FSM', *People and Culture in Oceania*, Vol. 19, No. 41, 2005, pp. 19–41.

Kupferman, David W., 'On Location at a Nonentity: Reading Hollywood's "Micronesia"', *Contemporary Pacific*, Vol. 23, No. 1, 2011, pp. 141–168.

Landman, Jane and Ballard, Chris, 'An Ocean of Images: Film and History in the Pacific', *Journal of Pacific History*, Vol. 45, No. 1, June 2010, pp. 1–20.

Latukefu, Sione, 'Oral Traditions: An Appraisal of Their Value in Historical Research in Tonga', *Journal of Pacific History*, Vol. 3, No. 1, 1968, pp. 135–143.

Lessa, William, 'The Social Effects of Typhoon Ophelia on Ulithi', *Micronesia*, Vol. 1, 1964, pp. 1–47.

Lessa, William, 'The Social Effects of Typhoon Ophelia (1960) on Ulithi', in *Peoples and Cultures of the Pacific: An Anthropological Reader*, edited by Andrew P. Vayda, The Natural History Press, New York, 1968.

Lessa, William, 'Ulithi and the Outer Native World', *American Anthropologists*, Vol. 52, 1950, pp. 27–52.

Levy, Josh, 'Micronesian Nationalism Revisited: Reclaiming Nationalism for the Federated States of Micronesia', Paper delivered at Native American and Indigenous Studies Association, Uncasville, Connecticut, 5 June 2012.

Lianyuen, Zhang, '25 Years' Run toward Amity and Prosperity. Commemorating the 25th Anniversary of Diplomatic Relationship between China and FSM', *Kaselehlie Press*, 6 April 2014.

Lieber, Michael, *Using Custom in a Court of Law*, Association of Social Anthropologists in Oceania (ASAO) Conference, San Antonio, Texas, 5–7 February 2012, pp. 1–12.

MacIver, Robert and Page, Charles, 'Custom', *Sociology Guide*, available at www.sociologyguide.com/basic-concepts/Custom.php.

Māhina, Okusitino, 'The Poetics of Tongan Traditional History, Tala-e-fanua: An Ecology Centred Concept of Culture and History', *Journal of Pacific History*, Vol. 28, No. 1, June 1993, pp. 109–120.

Marck, Jeffrey C., 'Micronesian Dialects and the Overnight Voyage', *Journal of Polynesian Society*, Vol. 95, No. 2, June 1986, pp. 253–258.

Marshall, Keith, 'The Structure of Solidarity and Alliance on Namoluk Atoll', PhD thesis, University of Washington, Seattle, Washington, 1972.

Marshall, Mac, '"Partial Connections": Kinship and Social Organisations in Micronesia', in *American Anthropology in Micronesia: An Assessment*, edited by Robert C. Kiste and Mac Marshall, University of Hawai'i Press, 1999, pp. 107–143.

Mauricio, Rufino, 'Ideological Bases for Power and Leadership on Pohnpei, Micronesia: Perspectives from Archaeology and Oral History', PhD thesis, University of Michigan, Ann Arbor, 1993.

Morgan, Amanda, 'Mystery in the Eye of the Beholder: Cross Cultural Encounters on 19th Century Yap', *Journal of Pacific History*, Vol. 31, No. 1, June 1996, pp. 27–41.

Mori, Emmanuel, *State of the Nation Address*, Congress of the Federated States of Micronesia, Palikir, Pohnpei, 18 May 2012.

Mulalap, Clement, 'Islands in the Stream; Addressing Climate Change from a Small Island Developing State Perspective', in *Climate Change and Indigenous People: The Search for Legal Remedies*, edited by Randall Abate and Elizabeth Warner, Edward Elgar Publishing, Cheltenham, United Kingdom, 2013, pp. 377–408, available at www.elgaronline.com/view/9781781001790.00032.xml.

Munro, Doug and Lal, Brij, 'The Texts in Its Context', in *Texts and Contexts: Reflection in Pacific Islands Historiography*, edited by Doug Munro and Brij Lal, University of Hawai'i Press, 2006, pp. 1–11.

Nakayama, Masao, 'Statement before the Committee of Religious NGOs and the United Nations. The Last Push Before Copenhagen: Defining Positions Strategies and Goals on Climate Change', New York, 10 November 2009.

Nakayama, Masao and Ram, Fred, *Traditional Native Approaches to Ocean Governance*, United Nations University, 1974.

Ngemaes, Maria, Berdon, Johannes, et al., 'NOAA: Republic of Palau, The Federated States of Micronesia and Republic of the Marshall Islands', Paper presented in Noumea, 3–4 July 2013.

Pacific Islands Report, East-West Center, Hawai'i, 24 June 2010.

'Pacific Maritime Patrol 40 Day Mission Monitors FSM, RMI, and Palau's EEZs', *Marianas Variety*, Saipan, CNMI, 12 May 2014.

Panuelo, David, 'Where Did Our Real Friends Go?', *Honolulu Civil Beat*, 5 April 2012, available at www.civilbeat.com/2011/08/12669-where-did-our-real-friends-go/.

Perlo, Art, *Capitalism and Unemployment*, 17 October 2011, available at peoples world.org/capitalism-and-unemployment/.

Peter, Joakim, 'Chuukese Travellers and the Idea of Horizon', *Asia Pacific Viewpoint*, Vol. 41, No. 3, December 2000, pp. 253–267.

Peter, Joakim, 'Eram's Church (Bell): Local Appropriations of Catholicism on Ettal', *ISLA: Journal of Micronesian Studies*, Vol. 4, No. 2, Dry Season 1996, pp. 267–287.

Petersen, Glenn, 'Dancing Defiance: The Politics of Pohnpeian Dance Performances', *Pacific Studies*, Vol. 15. No. 4, December 1992, pp. 13–27.

Petersen, Glenn, 'Differences, Connections, and the Colonial Carousel in Micronesian History', *Pacific Asia Inquiry*, Vol. 2, No. 1, Fall 2011, pp. 9–20.

Petersen, Glenn, *Federated States of Micronesia in Pacific Ways: Government and Politics in the Pacific Islands*, edited by Stephen Levine, Victoria University Press, 2009.

Petersen, Glenn, 'Kanaegamah and Pohnpei's Politics of Concealment', *American Anthropologist Association*, Vol. 95, No. 2, 1993, pp. 334–352.

Petersen, Glenn, 'Lessons Learned: The Micronesian Quest for Independence in the Context of American Imperial History', *Journal of the Humanities and Social Sciences*, Vol. 3, No. 1–2, December 2004, pp. 45–63.

Petersen, Glenn, 'Regime Change and Regime Maintenance', *Discussion Papers Number 12, Ethnicity and Interests at the 1990 Federated States of Micronesia Constitutional Convention*, The Australian National University, 1993, pp. 1–75.

Petersen, Glenn, 'Routine Provocation and Denial from the Tonkin Gulf and Hainan to Kyoto and the Pacific Islands', in *Security Oceania in the 21st Century*, edited by Erie Shibuya and Jim Rolfe, Asia-Pacific Center for Security Studies, 2003, pp. 193–218.

Petersen, Glenn, 'Strategic Location and Sovereignty: Modern Micronesia in the Historical Context of American Expansionism', *Space and Polity*, Vol. 2, No. 2, 1998, pp. 200–210.

Pinsker, Eve C., 'Traditional Leaders Today in the Federated States of Micronesia', in *Chiefs Today: Traditional Pacific Leadership and the Postcolonial State*, edited by Geoffrey M. White and Lamont Lindstorm, Stanford University Press, California, 1997, pp. 150–174.

Poyer, Lin, 'The Ngatik Massacre: Documentary and Oral Traditional Account', *Journal of Pacific History*, Vol. 20, No. 1, 2003, pp. 4–22.

Poyer, Lin, 'Yapese Experiences of the Pacific War', *ISLA: A Journal of Micronesian Studies*, Vol. 3, No. 2, Dry Season 1995, pp. 223–255.

Price, Samuel T., 'The Transformation of Yap: Causes and Consequences of Socio-Economic Change in Micronesia', PhD thesis, Washington State University, Ann Arbor, Michigan, 1975.

Puas, Gonzaga, 'The Evolving Relationship between the Federated States of Micronesia and China', *Asia-Pacific Relationships in Resource Development*, edited by Paul D'Arcy, Patrick Matbob and Linda Crowl, Divine Word University Press, Madang, 2014, pp. 168–177.

Puas, Gonzaga, 'Federated States of Micronesia Still a Colony', *Pacific Daily News*, Guam, 15 January 2000.

Puas, Gonzaga, 'The FSM Legal System: Responses to US Influence', Paper presented during the Association for Social Anthropologist in Oceania, Portland Oregon, 6 February 2011.

Puas, Gonzaga, 'How Could the Agricultural Sector Become More Conducive towards Climate Change Mitigation and Adaptation?', Paper written for CliMates International Student Organisation, Paris, France, April 2012.

Puas, Gonzaga, 'Is China a Threat in the Pacific? The Case of the Federated States of Micronesia', Paper presented at the Pacific Islands Political Science Association (PIPSA), Apia, Samoa, 2012.

Puas, Gonzaga, *Labour Standards in the FSM*, FSM Department of Justice, Palikir, Pohnpei, 12 April 2005.

Puas, Gonzaga, 'Micronesia and the Rise of China: Realpolitik Meets the Reef', Paper presented at the Pacific History Association, Taiwan, December 2014.

Puas, Gonzaga, *Review of the Current Health Protection Practises in the FSM: Law, Regulation and Policy Regimes*, Palikir, Pohnpei, 30 July 2013.

Puas, Gonzaga and Puas, Anelita, 'How Can Development be Linked to Climate Change Adaptation Policies?', CliMates International Student Organisation, Paris, France, December 2012.

Rauchholz, Manuel, 'Notes on Clan Histories and Migration in Micronesia', *Pacific Asia Inquiry*, Vol. 2, No. 1, Fall 2011, pp. 53–68.

Raynor, Bill, 'Resource Management of Upland Forests of Pohnpei: Past Practices and Future Possibilities', *ISLA: A Journal of Micronesian Studies*, Vol. 2, No. 1, Rainy Season 1994, pp. 49–64.

Reeves, Rachel, 'China Not Threatened by U.S. Presence at Pacific Forum. Vice Foreign Minister: Clinton's Visit Not Attempt to Override Influence', *Pacific Scoop*, 2 September 2012.

Rich Harris, Rich and Provost, Clare, 'The Millennium Development Goals: Big Ideas, Broken Promises?', *The Guardian*, 24 September 2013.

Richard, Wartho, 'Conceptualization of Oceania in the New World Order', *Pacific Viewpoint*, Vol. 36, No. 2, 1995, pp. 211–226.

Ridgell, Reilly, Ikea, Manny and Uruo, Isaoch, 'The Persistence of Central Carolinian Navigation', *ISLA: A Journal of Micronesian Studies*, Vol. 2, No. 2, Dry Season 1994, pp. 181–206.

Rosen, Bob D., 'Oceania Memorandum to Speaker of the Congress of the Federated States of Micronesia', Issac Figir, 7 January 2011.

Rothenberg, Laurence E., *Globalization 101: The Three Tensions of Globalization*, Occasional papers from the American Forum for Global Education, No. 176, 2002–2003. webspace.ship.edu/hliu/347/14global/3-tensions.pdf.

Rubinstein, Donald, 'An Ethnography of Micronesian Childhood: Contexts of Socialisation on Fais Island', PhD thesis, Stanford University, Stanford, California, 1979.

Rubinstein, Donald and Mulalap, Y. Clement, 'A Proposed Chinese Mega-Resort in Yap: Vulnerabilities, Opportunities, and Pacific Geo-politics', Paper presented at Micronesian Symposium 'Micronesia in Focus', The Australian National University, Canberra, 28–29 April 2014.

Russell, Scott, 'Roots of the Falawasch', Mangilao, Guam, MARC Library, n.d. (Unpublished MS paper).

Samo, Marcus, *Health Progress Report: 2008–2011*, Palikir, Pohnpei, 1 January 2012.

Shareef, Riaz, *Small Islands Tourism Economies: A Snapshot of Country Risk Ratings*, Department of Economics, University of Western Australia, Perth, Australia, available at www.mssanz.org.au/MODSIM03/Volume_03/B05/04_Shareef_Snapshot.pdf.

Sharma, Ankush, 'Customary Law and Received Law in the Federated States of Micronesia', *Journal of South Pacific Law*, Vol. 10, Issue 1, 2006, available at www.paclii.org/journals/fJSPL/vol10/7.shtml.

Shinn, Rinn-Sup, 'Trust Territory of the Pacific Islands', in *Oceania, A Regional Study*, edited by Frederica M. Bunge and Melinda W. Cooke, Area Handbook Series, Foreign Area Studies, The American University, Washington, DC, 1984, pp. 295–348.

Sitan, Peter (Chairman), *Judiciary and Government Operation, Standing Committee Report No. 16-10*, January 2010.

Sitan, Peter, 'The Development of the Tuna Fisheries in the Federated States of Micronesia', Unpublished paper presented at the Micronesian Symposium, The Australian National University, 3–4 April 2014.

Smith, Graeme, 'Chinese Reaction to Anti-Asian Riots in the Pacific', *Journal of Pacific History*, Vol. 47, No. 1, March 2012, pp. 93–109.

Smith, Graeme and D'Arcy, Paul, 'Global Perspective of Chinese Investment', *Pacific Affairs*, Vol. 86, No. 2, June 2013, pp. 217–232.

Smith, Terrence W., 'China in Oceania: New Forces in Pacific Politics', *Pacific Islands Policy*, No. 2, East-West Center, Hawai'i, 2007, pp. 13–19.

Smith, Terrence W., 'Self-Determination in Oceania', *Race and Class, Institute of Race Relations*, Vol. 48, No. 3, 2007, pp. 29–46.

'Speaker Halbert Responds to Audit Report', *The Fourth Branch*, 16 February 2015, available at www.tfbmicronesia.com/articles/2015/2/16/speaker-halbert-respondstoaudit-report.

Taonui, Rawari, 'Polynesian Oral Traditions', in *Vaka Moana: Voyages of the Ancestors*, edited by K. R. Howe, University of Hawai'i Press, 2006.

United Nations Human Rights, *International Covenant on Economic, Social and Cultural Rights*, available at www.ohchr.org/EN/ProfessionalInterest/Pages/CESCR.aspx.

United States of America and the Federated States of Micronesia, Minutes of the Inaugural Meeting of the Joint Economic Management Committee (JEMCO), 11 August 2004, Pacific Guardian Center Honolulu, Hawai'i.

Warrick, R. and Oerlemans, J. 'Sea Level Rise', in *Climate Change: The IPCC Scientific Assessment*, edited by J. T. Houghton, G. J. Jenkins and J. J. Ephraums, Cambridge University Press, Cambridge, 1990, pp. 263–267, available at www.ipcc.ch/site/assets/uploads/2018/03/ipcc_far_wg_I_chapter_09.pdf.

Wilson, Peter, 'A Tuna Industry in Micronesia?', *Micronesian Counselor*, No. 66, April 2007, available at www.micsem.org/pubs/counselor.htm.

Winter, Stephen J., 'Water for an Island', The FH Foundation, Long Beach, California, 1995.

Wortel, Oliver, 'China Increasing Its Presence in FSM in Big and Small Ways', *Kaselehlie Press*, 7 February 2007, available at www.fm/news/kp/2007/feb07_3.htm.

Yamase, Dennis, *The Supreme Court of the Federated States of Micronesia: The First Twenty-five Years*, FSM Supreme Court, Palikir, Pohnpei, 12 July 2006, available at fsmsupremecourt.org/fsm/rules/FSMSupCt25YrsforPDF.pdf.

Younger, Stephen M., 'Violence and Warfare in the Pre-contact Caroline Islands', *The Journal of the Polynesian Society*, Vol. 118, No. 2, June 2009, pp. 135–164, available at www.jps.auckland.ac.nz/docs/Volume118/Volume%20118%20No%202/3%20Violence%20and%20warfare.pdf.

Yui, John, 'Border Security: Transnational Crime in Micronesia. Part 3: Micronesia and Its Law Enforcement Problems', *Asia-Pacific Defence Reporter*, Singapore, 6 March 2012.

Zhang, Yongjin, 'A Regional Power by Default', in *China in Oceania: Reshaping the Pacific?*, edited by Terence Wesley Smith and Edgar A. Porter, Berghahn Books, USA, 2010, pp. 60–61.

Zotomayor, Lexi V., 'Mega-Casino Resort Project Reportedly "Still on the Table". In Yap 10,000-room Chinese-backed Project "Continues to Divide Community"', *Marianas Variety*, Saipan, Commonwealth of the Northern Marianas Islands, 5 June 2014.

Books

Adam, Thomas, *Western Interests in the Pacific Realm*, New York University, Random House, New York, 1967.

Alkire, William, *An Introduction to the Peoples and Cultures of Micronesia* (2nd edition), University of Victoria, British Columbia, 1977.

Alkire, William, *Lamotrek Atoll and Inter-Island Socio-Economic Ties*, University of Illinois Press, 1965.

Bautista, Lola Q., *Steadfast Movement around Micronesia, Satowan Enlargements beyond Migration*, Lexington Books, Maryland, USA, 2010.

Blackshield, Tony and Williams, George, *Australian Constitutional Law and Theory: Commentary and Materials* (2nd edition), The Federation Press, Sydney, 1998.

Bodescu, Marina, Burgos, Stephanie, Puas, Gonzaga, et al., *Climate Change Refugees* (8th edition), International Forum for Sustainable Development, UNESCO, Paris, 2013.

Brownlie, Ian, *Principles of Public International Law* (5th edition), Oxford University Press, 2001.

Cambers, Gillian and Diamond, Paul, *Sandwatch: Adapting to Climate Change and Educating for Sustainable Development* (revised and expanded edition), United Nations, Educational, Scientific and Cultural Organization, France, 2011.

Crocombe, Ron, *Asia in the Pacific Islands: Replacing the West*, University of the Pacific, Suva, 2007.

D'Arcy, Paul, *The People of the Sea: Environment, Identity, and History of Oceania*, University of Hawai'i Press, 2008.

Damas, David, *Bountiful Island: A Study of Land Tenure on a Micronesian Atoll*, Wilfrid Laurier University Press, Canada, 1994.

Debuce, Andrew L., *Cultural Change in Horticultural Practices on the High Island of Kosrae - Micronesia*, University of Oregon, 1996.

Diaz, Vincente, *Repositioning the Missionary: Rewriting the Histories of Colonialism, Native Catholicism, and Indigeneity in Guam*, University of Hawai'i Press, Honolulu, 2010.

Douglas, Bronwen and Ballard, Chris (eds), *Foreign Bodies: Oceania and the Science of Race 1750–1940*, ANU E Press, Canberra, 2008. doi.org/10.22459/FB.11.2008.

Duane, Nason J., *Clan and Copra: Modernization of Etal, Eastern Caroline Islands*, University of Michigan, University Microfilms International, Ann Arbor, Michigan, 1971.

Fisher, John and Fisher, Ann, *The Eastern Caroline Islands: Human Relations Area*, Files Press, Connecticut, 1970.

Fletcher, Charles H. and Richmond, Bruce M., *Climate Management and Adaptive Strategies*, University of Hawai'i Sea Grant College Program, 2010.

Flinn, Juliana, *Diplomats and Thatch Houses: Asserting Tradition in a Changing Micronesia*, University of Michigan Press, Ann Arbor, 1992.

Gale, Roger, *The Americanization of Micronesia: A Study of the Consolidation of U.S. Rule in the Pacific*, Washington, DC, 1979.

Gladwin, Thomas, *East is a Big Bird: Navigation and Logic on Puluwat Atoll*, Harvard University Press, Cambridge, Massachusetts, 1970.

Goodenough, Ward, *Property, Kin and Community on Truk* (2nd edition), Archon Books, Connecticut, 1978.

Goodenough, Ward, *Under the Heaven's Brow: Pre-Christian Religious Tradition in Chuuk*, American Philosophical Society, Philadelphia, 2002.

Hanks, Peter, Cass, Deborah and Clarke, Jennifer, *Australian Constitutional Law: Materials and Commentary* (6th edition), Buttersworth, Sydney, 1999.

Hanlon, David, *Making Micronesia: A Political Biography of Tosiwo Nakayama*, University of Hawai'i Press, 2014.

Hanlon, David, *Remaking Micronesia: Discourses Over Development in a Pacific Territory, 1944–1982*, University of Hawai'i Press, 1988.

Hanlon, David, *Upon a Stone Altar: A History of the Island of Pohnpei to 1890*, University of Hawai'i Press, Honolulu, 1988.

Hau'ofa, Epeli, *The Ocean in Us*, University of Hawai'i Press, 1998.

Hau'ofa, Epeli, *We Are the Ocean: Selected Works*, University of Hawai'i Press, 2008.

Hempenstall, Peter and Rutherford, Noel, *Protest and Dissent in the Colonial Pacific*, University of the South Pacific, Fiji, 1984.

Hezel, Francis X., *Strangers in Their Own Land: A Century of Colonial Rule in the Caroline and Marshall Islands*, University of Hawai'i Press, 1995.

Hezel, Francis X., *The First Taint of Civilization; A History of the Caroline and the Marshall Islands in Pre-Colonial Days, 1521–1885*, University of Hawai'i Press, Honolulu, 1983.

Hezel, Francis X., *The New Shape of Old Island Cultures: A Half Century of Social Change in Micronesia*, University of Hawai'i, 2001.

Higuchi, Wakko, *Pre-war Japanese Fisheries in Micronesia-Focusing on Bonito and Tuna Fishing in the Northern Marianas*, University of Guam, 2003.

Howe, Kerry R., *Nature, Culture and History: The 'Knowing' of Oceania*, University of Hawai'i Press, Honolulu, 2000.

Jeffery, Bill, *War in Paradise WWII: Sites in Truk Lagoon, Chuuk, Federated States of Micronesia*, Chuuk Historical Preservation Office, 2003.

Kim, Myjoylnn, *Into the Deep: Launching Culture and Policy in the Federated States of Micronesia*, Secretariat of the Pacific Community (SPC) and Federated States of Micronesia Office of National Archives, Culture and Historic Preservation, Pohnpei, Federated States of Micronesia, 2011.

Labby, David, *The Demystification of Yap: Dialectics of Culture on a Micronesian Island*, University of Chicago Press, 1976.

Lamour, Peter, *Foreign Flowers: Institutional Transfer and Good Governance in the Pacific Islands*, University of Hawai'i Press, 2005.

Lessa, William, *Ulithi: A Micronesian Design for Living*, University of California, Los Angeles, Holt Rhinehart and Winston, Inc., 1966.

Lieber, Michael, *More Than a Living: Fishing and Social Order on a Polynesian Atoll*, Westview Press, Boulder, 1994.

Lingenfelter, Sherwood, *Yap: Political Leadership and Culture Change in an Island Society*, University of Hawai'i Press, 1975.

Lobban, Christopher S. and Schefter, Maria, *Tropical Pacific Island Environments*, University of Guam Press, USA, 1997.

Marshall, Mac, *Namoluk beyond the Reef: The Transformation of a Micronesian Community*, Westview Press, USA, 2008.

Marshall, Mac, *The Weekend Warrior: Alcohol in a Micronesian Culture*, Mayfield Publishing Company, Palo Alto, California, 1979.

Meller, Norman, *Constitutionalism in Micronesia*, The Institute for Polynesian Studies, Brigham Young University, Hawai'i, 1985.

Moore, Alan, *The Fatal Impact: An Account of the Invasion of the South Pacific, 1767–1840* (revised edition), Harper and Row, USA, 1987.

Munro, Doug and Lal, Brij, *Texts and Contexts: Reflections in Pacific Islands Historiography*, University of Hawai'i Press, 2006.

Naich, James, *Sustaining the Spirit of the Compact Partnership: Comments on the US Report on the First Five Years of the Amended Compact of Free Association*, Embassy of the Federated States of Micronesia, Washington, DC, 1 October 2010.

Nakano, Ann, *Broken Canoe: Conversations and Observations in Micronesia*, University of Queensland Press, St Lucia, 1983.

Petersen, Glenn, *Traditional Micronesian Societies: Adaptation, Integration and Political Organisation*, University of Hawai'i Press, Hawai'i, 2009.

Poyer, Lin, *The Ngatik Massacre: A History and Identity on a Micronesian Atoll*, Smithsonian Institution Press, London, 1993.

Rainbird, Paul, *The Archaeology of Micronesia*, Cambridge University Press, 2004.

Ryan, Daniel P., *Essential Principles of Contract and Sales in the Northern Pacific: Federated States of Micronesia, the Republics of Palau and the Marshall Islands and US Territories*, iUniverse, USA, 2009.

Segal, Harvey, *Kosrae: The Sleeping Lady Awakens*, Kosrae Tourist Division, Department of Conservation and Development, Kosrae State Government, Federated States of Micronesia, 1989.

Smith, Linda T., *Decolonising Methodologies*, London, Zed Books Ltd, 2001.

Spennemann, Dirk H. R., *Melimel: The Good Friday Typhoon of 1907 and its Aftermath in the Mortlocks, Caroline Islands*, Albury, NSW, 2007.

Tamanaha, Brian, *Understanding Law in Micronesia: An Interpretive Approach to Transplanted Law*, Studies in Humanities (series), Center of Non-Western Societies, Leiden University, The Netherlands, 1993.

Uman, Oha, Saladier Ferdun and Chipen, Anter, *Uruon Chuuk: A Resource of Oral Legends, Traditions, and History of Truk*, Vol. 1, ESEA Title IV Omibus Program for Social Studies, Cultural Heritage Trust Territory of the Pacific Islands, Moen, Truk, July 1979.

Wallerstein, Immanuel M., *World Systems Analysis: An Introduction* (2nd edition), Duke University Press, USA, 2005.

Walter, Ansito, *Desirability, Problems, and Methods of Achieving National Independence: Opinions of Citizens and Senators of the Federated States of Micronesia*, Ann Harbour, Michigan, USA, 1985.

Wederveen, Pieterse, *Development Theory: Deconstructions/Reconstructions* (2nd edition), Sage Publications, London, January 2010.

Zines, Leslie, *The High Court and the Constitution*, Butterworths, Sydney, 1981.

Court Cases

Alaphanso v FSM, 1 FSM Intrm. 209 (App. 1982), available at fsmlaw.org/fsm/decisions/index.htm.

Chuuk v Secretary of Finance, 8 FSM Intrm. 353 (Pon. 1998).

Etpison v Perman, 1 FSM Intrm. 405 (Pon. 1984), available at fsmlaw.org/fsm/decisions/index.htm.

FSM v Alaphonso (Truk 1982), available at fsmlaw.org/fsm/decisions/index.htm.

FSM v Mudong, 1 FSM Intrm. 135 (Pon. 1982), available at fsmlaw.org/fsm/decisions/index.htm.

FSM v Tammed, 5 FSM Intrm. 426 (Yap 1990), available at fsmlaw.org/fsm/decisions/index.htm.

In re Sproat, 2 FSM Intrm. 1 (Pon. 1985), available at fsmlaw.org/fsm/decisions/index.htm.

Mailo v Atonesia, 7 FSM Intrm. 294 (Chk. S. Ct. Tr. 1995) CA no. 73-92, available at fsmlaw.org/fsm/decisions/index.htm.

Semens v Continental, 2 FSM Intrm. 200 (Pon. 1986), available at fsmlaw.org/fsm/decisions/index.htm.

Field Interviews

Berdon, Johannes (director of Chuuk Weather Station), Interview, Weno Island, 4 April 2015.

Chol, Paulis (local fisherman), Interview, Sokehs, Pohnpei, June 2012.

Dereas, Mariena (associate professor), Interview, College of Micronesia, National Campus, Palikir, Pohnpei, 20 January 2011.

Ehmes, Delina (associate professor), Interview, College of Micronesia National Campus, Palikir, Pohnpei, 20 January 2011.

Elders and officers of Lukunor Municipality, Interview, Pohnpei, 26 January 2014.

Haglelgam, John (professor), Interview, College of Micronesia, National Campus, Palikir, Pohnpei, 11 January 2011.

Halbert, Dohsis (senator, FSM Congress), Interview, Sokehs, Pohnpei, 2010.

Henry, Bethwel (first speaker of the former Congress of Micronesia), Interview, Kolonia, Pohnpei, 28 June 2012.

Henry, Marion (secretary of Resources and Development), Interview, Kolonia, Pohnpei, 18 July 2013.

Ilon, Epel (special advisor for SBOC), Interview, Palikir, Pohnpei, 13 January 2011.

Jackson, Joanes (local historian from Chuuk), Interview, Kolonia, Pohnpei, 2015.

James, Sirel (police officer, Maritime Surveillance), Interview, Nett, Pohnpei, 2014.

Jaynes, Bill (journalist and chief editor of *Kaselehlie Press*), Interview, Kolonia, Pohnpei, 7 January 2011.

Kandy, Kauten (local fisherman), Interview, Likie, Pohnpei, 28 June 2013.

Lianyuen, Zhang (Chinese ambassador to the FSM), Interview, Palikir, Pohnpei, July 2013.

Likichimus, Kamilo (master canoe builder and oral historian from Lukunor Island), Interview, Weno, Chuuk, 20 June 2013.

Lippwe, Jeem (deputy ambassador, FSM Permanent Mission to the UN), Interview, 1 May 2014.

Lippwe, Kippier (national coordinator for Non-Communicable Disease and Chuukese historian), Interview, Kolonia, Pohnpei, July 2012.

Lohn, Peter (*Wasai* of Sokehs and speaker of the Pohnpei Legislature), Interview, Nett, Pohnpei, June 2013.

Lucas, Aser (police officer, Maritime Surveillance), Interview, Nett, Pohnpei, 3 April 2011.

Maluweirang, Robert (Retired Commander, Maritime Surveillance Wing), Interview, Nett, Pohnpei, 12 January 2011.

Marar, David (Wing Commander, Maritime Surveillance), Interview, Nett, Pohnpei, 13 January 2011.

Naich, James (deputy ambassador, FSM Embassy), Interview (online), Washington, DC, 21 December 2014.

Nimea, Fabian (director of SBOC), Interview, Palikir, Pohnpei, 21 January 2011.

Pretrick, Samson (deputy secretary of Foreign Affairs), Interview, Kolonia, Pohnpei, 17 January 2011.

Rayphand, Abrham (mayor and Chuukese historian), Interview, Weno, Chuuk, 10 July 2012.

Reim, Takasy (chief of police, FSM National Police Force), Interview, 11 January 2011.

Robert, Lorin (secretary of Foreign Affairs), Interview, Palikir, Pohnpei, 7 January 2011.

Robert, Wilfred (Chuukese historian), Interview, Weno, Chuuk, 11 June 2011.

Samo, Marcus (deputy secretary of FSM Social and Health Affairs and Chuukese historian), Interview, Nett, Pohnpei, 21 January 2011; Palikir, Pohnpei, 21 June 2013; Kolonia, Pohnpei, 9 July 2013.

Setik, Lipus (fishing vessels observer), Interview, Palikir, Pohnpei, July 2013.

Sitan, Peter (FSM congressmen and Chuukese historian), Interview, Kolonia, Pohnpei, 27 January 2011.

Sitan, Peter (president of the FSM National Fisheries Corporation), Interview, Micronesian Symposium, The Australian National University, 28 April 2014.

Siten, Pius (teacher), Interview, Sokehs, Pohnpei, 20 January 2011.

Sivas, Vincent (assistant deputy officer FSM Embassy in China), Interview, Nett, Pohnpei, 13 July 2013.

Solomon, Nickolson (CEO, National Fishing Corporation), Interview, Kolonia, Pohnpei, 17 January 2011.

Soram, Jackson (deputy assistant secretary, Foreign Affairs, International Division), Interview, Nett, Pohnpei, 10 October 2012.

Soram, Jackson (head of Climate Change Advisory Body to the FSM Government), Interview, 21 January 2011.

Soryz, Brymer (police officer), Interview, Maritime Surveillance, Palikir, Pohnpei, 11 January 2011.

Walter, Inos (Chuuk State legislator and Chuukese historian), Interview, Guam, 16 July 2012.

Walter, Inos (mayor of Lukunor), Interview, February 2011.

Weidong, Zhang (Chinese ambassador to the FSM), Interview, Palikir, Pohnpei, 19 January 2011.

Weitto, Simion (captain, FSS *Micronesia* (FSM surveillance ship)), Interview, FSM Maritime Surveillance Wing, Nett, Pohnpei, 11 January 2011.

Yangitesmal, Paulino (FSM police officer), Interview, Nett, Pohnpei, 10 January 2011.

Zhang, Yongjin (Chinese ambassador to the FSM), Interview, Palikir, Pohnpei, 13 July 2013.

.